CW01080463

THE DARFUR SULTANATE

To my English, Irish, Norwegian, and Sudanese family.
To my grandchildren, Eirinn and Bushra;
my sons Marcus, Ciaran, and Dominic, and my
daughter-in-law, Majduline El Hagg El Tahir,
and the memory of Lene Voldsund,
Eirinn's mother and Ciaran's wife.

R. S. O'FAHEY

The Darfur Sultanate
A History

HURST & COMPANY, LONDON

First published in the United Kingdom by
HURST Publishers Ltd,
41 Great Russell Street, London, WC1B 3PL
© R. S. O'Fahey, 2008
All rights reserved
Printed in India

The right of R. S. O'Fahey to be identified as
the author of this volume has been asserted by
him in accordance with the Copyright, Designs
and Patents Act, 1988.

A catalogue data record for this volume is available
from the British Library.

ISBN 978-1-85065-853-5

www.hurstpub.co.uk

CONTENTS

PART TWO: STATE AND SOCIETY

CONTENTS

MAPS

DIAGRAMS

[Unless otherwise indicated the diagrams come from R. S. O'Fahey, *State and Society in Dar Fur*, 1980]

PREFACE

There is a degree of opportunism behind the present volume. Sadly I do not need to explain why I am writing a history of Darfur. The present book builds upon my *State and Society in Dar Fur*, published in 1980 (London: Hurst & Co.); here I have tried to incorporate subsequent research and have in some matters expanded or modified my earlier interpretations. I decided not to go beyond 1916, the final demise of the sultanate, for several reasons. First, 1916 marks the end of Darfur's centuries of existence as an independent state. Secondly, I am sceptical that much can very usefully be said on the British interlude (1916-56), not least because of the destruction of the 600 or so files kept in al-Fashir (they are described my (1980), 186-7; see further *Sources and Bibliography*) in the late 1970s; I am the only professional historian to have used them while they were still intact. They were marvellously rich, but my interest when I went through them in 1970 was in what they had to say about the days before the British.[1] Finally, a flood of books and articles are appearing on Darfur, of uneven value; for me, it is too soon to say much of more than journalistic value about the present crisis.

Since I am in some way part of the story, I need to explain how I came to be involved. I spent part of my childhood in Kenya and had always wanted to be a historian, in those days of Rome. At school in London aged about seventeen, I received a letter from a friend in Mombasa, saying that her parents had had as a dinner-guest a

---

1 There is a small but important point here; the National Records Office in Khartoum has numerous files on Darfur, but what it lacks are the crucial 66, tribal files series. These were lost in Darfur, but they were crucial to how the British interacted at the local level.

professor of African History. This was the first time "Africa" and "history" had come together in my life, and it was enough to decide me as to my future career. I sought out the professor mentioned in the letter, Roland Oliver at the School of Oriental and African Studies, and took my BA in African and Middle Eastern History there. I won a doctoral scholarship to write a history of the Darfur Sultanate; I cannot in all honesty really remember why I chose Darfur, but I was much influenced by and indebted to my first teacher in all things Sudanese, Professor P.M. Holt (who sadly has recently passed away). By this time I was married and my wife was expecting our first child and I needed a real salary (in those days doctoral scholarships presupposed celibacy). Through Holt I got a job at the University of Khartoum as lecturer in African History, registering as an external doctoral student of the University of London.

Between 1966 and 1980 (by which time we were in Bergen) my research focused on Darfur, with visits of about two to three months at a time in 1969, 1970, 1974, 1976 and 1977, usually accompanied by one or more Darfurian or other Sudanese students. By 1983 I had published various articles and two and a half books on Darfur's pre-colonial history. Thereafter, I moved on to write on Sufism and later in the 90s, with my friend John Hunwick, to embark on our series of volumes, *The Arabic Literature of Africa* (Leiden: Brill, 1994–). But I never lost my interest in Darfur, either its past or its present, and continued to write articles on aspects of its history or to publish documents that I had photographed on my fieldtrips.

In late 2004, when Darfur was very much in the news, I was abruptly re-connected through an invitation to take part in a conference in Khartoum organised by the UN University for Peace on the crisis in Darfur; this led to a three-month consultancy with the UN Mission to the Sudan (UNMIS) in 2005, during which I revisited Darfur for the first time since my last visit in 1993, and in 2006 to a three-week stint at the Abuja peace talks, working as a resource person for the African Union. More recently, I have written reports on such topics as tribal rule and land tenure in Darfur as a consultant to the World Bank and such work seems likely to continue. I have thus been brought back to Darfur very sharply, immediately and intensely, but to a very different Darfur from the one I had known before—to a world of the UN and its family of organisations, the World Bank, the innumerable INGOs, the human rights communities, the international media and the Darfurian movements. By no means do I speak their language, and I am probably too old to learn it. Thus, do I have anything much to contribute other than which I have already published? I think so; talking to Darfur chiefs in Khartoum recently about the present and the future has given me new insights into the past, while I have begun to appreciate that their own understanding of the past has changed in the light of the present.

In a very moving article, Ghassan Salamé, a senior Lebanese UN official, talks of the need of UN officials to respect and understand the "Collective Historical Memory" of the communities they were dealing with.[2] I began to understand, especially in Abuja and in Khartoum, that I, in a way, represented for the younger Darfurians a version of their "Collective Historical Memory", that I was a link to their fathers and grandfathers, and, ironically, to the British, despite coming from a London Irish nationalist background. But the "Collective Historical Memory" moves on; I have been recently been told that the *haddadin*, a caste of ironworkers traditionally outcastes in Darfur, are renaming themselvs *ustawat*, "skilled craftsmen".

I wrote my main work on Darfur, *State and Society in Dar Fur* in the mid-1970s. It was a work of its time; a piece, I suppose, within the jigsaw puzzle that my mentors, Oliver, Holt and others, saw as a necessary stage towards the systematic creation of Africa's history. Darfur was to prove complicated within that puzzle, because Darfur was not simply Africa, but also had an Arab dimension. The present work is written with a keen awareness of what is going on in Darfur as I write; however, I have sought to avoid Herbert Butterfield's critique of a certain interpretation of English history (Whig) namely, "the study of the past with direct and perpetual reference to the present".[3] The purpose of the book is not teleological; it will serve only in part to explain the present.

---

2   Salamé (2005), 81-98.

3   *The Whig Interpretation of History*, London 1931, 11.

PREFACE

My involvement in Darfur was a two-way process. In 1966, the
Darfur Development Front (DDF) was established, a loose coalition
of Darfurian students in Khartoum and some of the more progressive traditional leaders. I first went to Darfur in 1969 and spent a
period in al-Fashir in 1970 followed by several other visits. Many
years later, in 1993, I was officially invited to Darfur by the province
administration to be honoured by the Darfur Heritage Centre at the
University of al-Fashir for my work on Darfur's history. There was an
official reception at the People's Assembly hosted by the then Governor, al-Tayyib Muhammad "Sikha", at which none of my Darfur
friends put in an appearance; he was not appreciated by them, given
his involvement in the death of a Darfur hero, Da'ud Bulad. As I was
leaving to go back to the resthouse, I was intercepted and taken to
the *zawiya* or religious centre of the Sufi Nyasiyya Tijaniyya brotherhood then led by a dynamic young shaykh, the late Ibrahim Sidi (d.
1999), who wrote commentaries on the great mystical philosopher,
Ibn al-'Arabi, and with whom I conversed in French (he had studied
at Kaolack in Senegal). There were all my Darfur friends and I was
greeted by a choir of boys singing the *ahzab* or praise-hymns of the
Tijaniyya—it was a very moving moment for me. In the course of
the evening, *malik* Rihaymat Allah al-Dadinqawi, as *abbo daadinga*
the hereditary ruler of al-Fashir, explained to me that the DDF had
decided in 1970 to help me; they wanted their story told. They, of
course, did not tell me at the time, perhaps it was better that way.

If I contrast Darfur then with now, the difference is profound.
Today, under one aspect, Darfur lives on the internet and within the
diaspora; while at Abuja, at the peace talks in 2006, the Darfurians
there told me not to publish on paper, but to put what I wrote on
the web, which I am dutifully doing, a task made the more laborious
because all my Darfur research was pre-computer. One consequence
of the present crisis is the staggering abundance of "information"
on Darfur on the web; even the most assiduous researcher can not
keep track of several million hits (as of 20 May 2006, there were just
under 50 million hits for Darfur). Here, on more recent matters, I
have been aided by an informal network, Ali Dinar (grandson of his
namesake), Renaud Detalle, Julie Flint, Insaf Idris, Kjell Hødnebø,

Abdelbagi Jibril, Jemera Rone, Endre Stiansen, Jérôme Tubiana and his mother and father Marie-José and Joseph (who sadly died recently), and others, who have helped me not to miss that which I should not have missed. Even so, I have probably missed much. I wish to pay tribute to an older and largely departed generation who influenced me greatly; Roland Oliver and the late P.M. Holt, the late Richard Hill and my especial Sudanese mentor, the late Muhammad Ibrahim Abu Salim, and far from least my friend John O. Hunwick, with whom my friendship goes back to 1964 and who published my first article on Darfur in 1969. Another of an older generation now gone from us, to whom I want to pay tribute, is the Rev. Dr A.J. Arkell, whom I went to see in Buckinghamshire where he was a retired vicar in 1966; when I explained that I wanted to write on Darfur, he took me up to his attic and bade me borrow his notes on Darfur (some 2,500 pages; now in the library of the School of Oriental and African Studies, London; see *Sources and Bibliography*). Looking back, I realise that Arkell was my link with the British colonial presence in Darfur; he constantly admonished me not to compare the Sudan with my childhood experiences in Kenya.

I should like to pay a heartfelt tribute to someone whom I much admired and who influenced my career (as that of so many others) by his willingness to publish our books, Christopher Hurst, who has just died. Hurst will always be linked to the world of Darfur and Chad by his courageous determination to see into print Gustav Nachtigal's monumental *Sahara and Sudan*, as translated by my teacher, Humphrey Fisher and his father, A.G.B. Fisher.

I most willingly thank Justin Willis of Durham University, who critically read an earlier draft and confirmed me in my decision not to go much beyond 1916.

Of my Norwegian colleagues, I owe an abiding debt to Alf Kaartvedt, who was my mentor in establishing African Islamic history in Bergen, to Knut S. Vikør for much scholarly and practical help, and to Anne K. Bang for keeping me intellectually young and alert and for reading the present draft with an historian's and a novelist's eye.

In recent years, I have also been greatly aided by lively discussions with my son, Dominic M. O'Fahey, especially on legal matters, and with my daughter-in-law, Majduline El Hajj El Tahir, herself from Kordofan, especially on ecological aspects (her research field), but also in bringing the Sudan into my family—we have all been enriched at many levels. I can now *really* sympathise with the sultans; I now know what it means to be part of a large Sudanese family.

One existential question upon which my daughter-in-law and I disagree is the implicit assumption on my part, throughout the present work, that Darfur is not "naturally" a part of the Sudan. For Majduline Darfur is that, like her native Kordofan; for much of Kordofan I willingly concede to Majduline. For Darfur, my argument is twofold; for most Northern Sudanese intellectuals the core of the modern Sudan are the lands of the Funj Sultanate (c. 1504 to 1821), that is the Nile Valley south of Aswan and the Gezira between the Blue and White Niles; even the Beja lands of the Eastern Sudan, like those of eastern Kordofan, have interacted intimately and over centuries with the Nile Valley. The modern Sudan's core identity, and its current ruling elite, have grown from Funj times, through Turco-Egyptian colonial rule (1821-82), the brief triumphalism of the Mahdist state (1882-98) and the bureaucratic administration of the Anglo-Egyptian Condominium (1898-1956). By contrast, Darfur's contact with the Nile Valley has been intermittent and sporadic, an exception being the relatively short period (c. 1785-1821) of Darfur's hegemony in Kordofan. Majduline's counter-argument builds upon her experience at school in Khartoum and at the University of Khartoum, where her encounter wth Darfurians of a similar background, in terms of language and religion, would support her view. The truth lies somewhere between, but the fact that as late as 1898 'Ali Dinar could successfully re-establish the sultanate suggests that the core idea of separateness was still then operative. Here I would also raise the question of whether states fare better independently than as dependencies; Darfur was undoubtedly richer (I make no judgment about that wealth's internal distribution) and better and more sensitively run under the sultans of the nineteenth century than under the stagnation and marginalisation of the British and Northern Sudanese—even the British records admit this. But these are arguments that Sudanese intellectuals need to tackle in the future; Majduline and I will undoubtedly continue to argue about these issues within the family. But on the issue of Darfur's separateness I still reserve judgment.

The focus of the present book is Darfur, its sultanate and institutions; outside forces are discussed only as they impinged upon the former. If my emphasis in the present book is on the ruling institutions, on the sultans, the royal women, the holy men, the traders and others, this is at this stage in our knowledge unavoidable; here I am simply constrained by my sources. Social history, gender and ecological studies, local historical studies must be the agenda for the future; a start is being made here at the three universities of Darfur (al-Fashir, Nyala and Zalingei). My underlying purpose is to write a record of the history and cultures of Darfur in all their variety, complexity and richness. Darfur is changing, as I write, very rapidly; if the future of Darfur in the short term seems to be grim, who knows what may be its future. Darfur does not have to be a failed land, but that is for the Darfurians to determine. In short, *The Darfur Sultanate. A History* attempts to sum up my encounter with Darfur over forty years. I hope my Darfurian readers especially will accept it for what it is, a gift given in friendship at a difficult time.

On practical matters, I have kept transliteration simple, using only ' to mark the presence of the consonant *ain* and the medial *hamza*. For Arabic-speakers this should not cause any problems; for Fur and other Darfur languages, I have used the simplest of forms, but the combination "*ng*" in Fur is pronounced as in "si*ng*ing". Fur is a complex tonal language; to represent it accurately is far beyond my competence. References to "dollars" are to Maria Theresa thalers or similar silver coins.

I hope, *In Sha'Allah*, in the years to come to follow the present book with two further volumes, one on Darfur and the British, a sourcebook with an introductory essay; the second will be an interpretative essay on the state in Sudanese history. Finally I hope to place upon the Web—http://www.smi.uib.no/darfur/— as much of my material as I can, both English and Arabic, in the years to come. Here I have already made a start.

So, for whom do I write the present book? First for young Sudanese especially from Darfur, for academics, for the probably mythical "general" reader, for the aid and international specialists, and for the curious. I have not eschewed an academic apparatus, because it needs to be in place (and I need it to give me legitimacy), but I hope what I have written is readable. Above all, I hope I can convey something of the "thisness" of Darfur, that these are real people with a past and an identity, in fact many, and that hopefully they will indeed have a worthwhile future.

Bergen, September 2007   R. S. O'Fahey

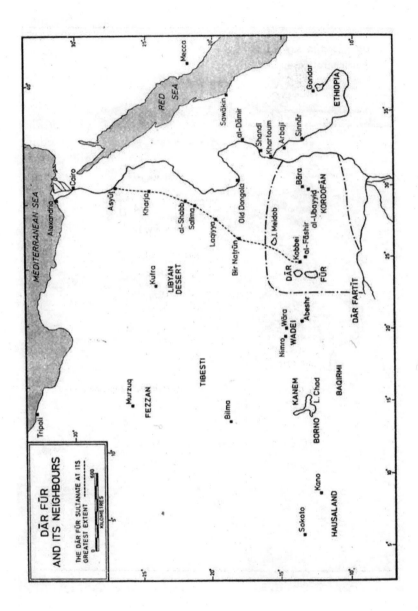

DĀR FŪR
AND ITS NEIGHBOURS

THE DĀR FŪR SULTANATE AT ITS
GREATEST EXTENT

0   500
KILOMETRES

MEDITERRANEAN SEA

RED SEA

Mecca

Gondar

ETHIOPIA

Sawākin

al-Dāmir

Shandi
Khartoum

Arbaji

Sinnār

Cairo

Alexandria

Tripoli

Asyūt

Kharja

al-Shabb
Salīma

Laqiyya

Bir Natrūn

Old Dongola

J. Meidob

Kobbei

al-Fāshir

Bāra

al-Ubayyid

KORDOFĀN

DĀR
FŪR

DĀR FARTĪT

Nimro
Wāra

WADEI

Abeshr

Kufra

LIBYAN
DESERT

TIBESTI

FEZZAN

Murzuq

Bilma

KANEM

L. Chad

BORNO

BAQIRMI

Sokoto

Kano

HAUSALAND

xvii

THE DĀR FŪR SULTANATE:
Administrative divisions

DAR AL-TAKANAWI..... PROVINCES
INGA.....SHARTAYAS OR OTHER
ADMINISTRATIVE DIVISIONS

0   KILOMETRES   150

W. Howar

C A M E L   N O M A D S

Teiga
Plateau

Meidob
Hills

KOBE   GALLA TUER   ARTAG

KABJA   Karnoi
             Wells

QIMR   SUWAYNĪ   BEIRI

        DĀR   AL-TAKANĀWĪ

        SURAYF   FURUNG

MADE   Kutum

                      INGA   HAMRA   Mellit

FIA   Kabkābiyya   Kobbei   Umm
                            Khiribān   Jadīd al-Sayl   Kiddāda
                    Umm   Al-Tawīla   ⊡Al-Fāshir   SIMIYĀT
                    Haraz   Qōz Bayna
                           TURRA   Kerio   DĀR DAALI
KERNE   KONYIR   Hākūrat
                           al-sultān
Murnei   J.Kedingir
        TEBELLA ARIBO   Jadīd Rās al-Fīl
    ZAMI BAYA   DĀR   Manawāshī
                 DIIMA   Kās   DĀR UMŌ
    KULLI   Garsila   Rīl
        KOBARA
    ZAMI TOYA   Umm Haraz
                                          Dāra
            SURRO
                            SOUTHERN   MAQDUMATE

    HĀKŪRAT AL-SULTĀN

FONGORO

    C A T T L E   N O M A D S
                                              Shaqqā

                            Bahr al-ʿArab

xviii

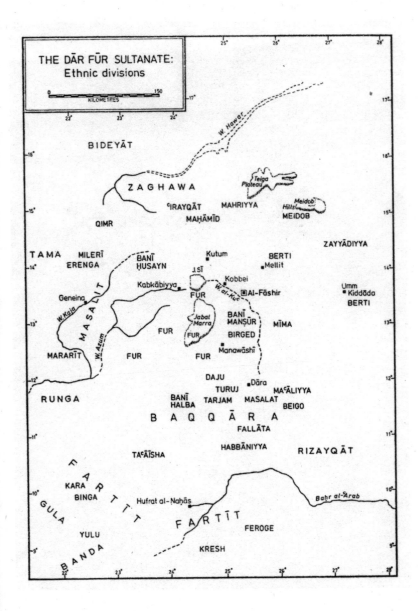

THE DĀR FŪR SULTANATE:
Ethnic divisions

0 ——————————— 150
KILOMETRES

BIDEYĀT

ZAGHAWA

Teiga
Plateau

ʿIRAYQĀT   MAHRIYYA

Meidob
Hills

QIMR   MAḤĀMĪD   MEIDOB

ZAYYĀDIYYA

TAMA   MILERĪ   BERTI
         ERENGA   BANĪ   Mellit
                    ḤUSAYN   Kutum

                    J.SĪ
                         Kobbei   Umm
         Kabkābiyya   W.al-Kuʿ   ⊡Al-Fāshir   Kiddōda
Geneina   FUR   BERTI

W.Kaja   Jabal   BANĪ
        Ma   Marra   MANṢŪR   MĪMA
        S
        A   FUR   FUR   BIRGED
W.Azum L
        I   FUR
        T
MARARĪT   FUR   FUR   Manawāshī

                    DAJU   Dāra
RUNGA   TURUJ   MAʿĀLIYYA
         BANĪ   TARJAM   MASALAT   BEIGO
         ḤALBA
              B A Q Q Ā R A
                    FALLĀTA

                    HABBĀNIYYA   RIZAYQĀT
         TAʿĀĪSHA

    F
    A
    R   KARA
G   T   BINGA   Hufrat al-Naḥās   Bahr al-ʿArab
U   Ī
L   T
A   YULU   F A R T Ī T   FEROGE
    B
    A   KRESH
    N
    D
    A

xix

PART I
THE FIRST KEIRA SULTANATE

1
GEOGRAPHY, ECOLOGY
AND ETHNOGRAPHY

Geography

Darfur is a remote and still relatively sparsely peopled land. Forming today the three westernmost states (*wilaya*) of the Republic of the Sudan,[1] it is a land of great geographical and ethnic variety, covering an area of some 114,000 square miles (approximately 295,259 square kilometres), roughly the size of France, with an estimated population (2006) of 6-6.5 million. It is difficult to give any reliable estimates for population density, given the present situation in the region.[2]

---

1 The three states are Southern Darfur (capital, Nyala), Western Darfur (capital, al-Jinayna) and Northern Darfur (capital, al-Fashir). These divisions were introduced in 1994; before that, in the early 1990s, Darfur Province was divided into Northern Darfur (capital, al-Fashir) and Southern Darfur (capital, Nyala). The Darfur Province of the British period (1916-56) and the early years of independence corresponded approximately to the Sultanate of the nineteenth century. Darfurians today often refer to the sultanate/province as Dar Fur *kabira* (or *kubra*), "Greater Darfur", and the question of reunifying the states has been an issue in the recent peace talks.

2 This chapter is written in a kind of unreal "historic present". What I am descrbing is in part a Darfur of the 1950s and 60s, not of the brutal realities of 2007.

Although now part of a country dominated by the Nile, Darfur is a Sudanic land, a part of the vast transitional belt that runs across Africa south of the Sahara. In the north the Libyan Desert increasingly presses southwards into the *sahil* or "coastal" zone between the true desert (*sahra* pl. *sahara*) and savanna. Central Darfur is dominated by Jabal Marra, an extinct volcanic range rising to about 10,000 feet at the southern end around the two Deriba lakes and some 70 miles long, fertile along its western foothills, rocky and less hospitable along its eastern flank. The open savanna country around the mountains shades off southwards imperceptibly through wooded and marshy land into the Bahr al-Ghazal. Fundamental to the human geography of Darfur are the great distances between concentrations of fertile land and people, the difficulties of movement, the harshness and precariousness of the environment,[3] and the fluctuations in rainfall.

A geographical profile of Darfur describes many of the fundamental traits of its history. The central savannas suitable, but variably, for rainfed hoe agriculture, were defined by pasture lands to the north and south. Historically, the northern zone led only to the desert which in turn became Darfur's main highway to the outside world,[4] while the south opened onto populated regions that were to provide the sultanate with slaves. Eastwards Darfur and Kordofan form a natural geographical unity that found political expression when the former ruled the latter between 1785 and 1821. This vast area (340,000 square miles) is divided by K.M. Barbour into four sub-regions, Western Darfur, the Semi-Desert, the *Qoz* or stabilised sand-dune country and the Nuba Mountains.[5]

---

3 The *Sudan Almanac* for 1965-66 showed the mean maximum temperature in al-Fashir as going from 88°F (31°C) in January to a high of 113°F (45°C) in May of the same year; the same figures appear in the 1967 *Sudan Almanac*. Darfur is a hot region; what global warming will mean in the future in the region is hard to say, but nothing good, I imagine.

4 The role of the desert and where it leads to has fluctuated; the famous "Forty Days Road", *darb al-arba'in*, to Upper Egypt will be discussed later, but in 1974, I was in Mellit, just north of al-Fashir. In the market there one could buy all manner of electrical goods brought in from Libya. There was an abundance that Khartoum could not match; the Libyan oil fields were the cause.

5 Barbour (1961), 151.

Historically, the heart of the sultanate was western Darfur; its northern lands are dry and support a pastoral economy with goats, sheep and some cattle herded mainly by Fur, Zaghawa, Meidob, and Bani Husayn. During the rainy season (October to January/February), the *jizzu* grazing land in the deserts of the far north along the Wadi Hawar come to life, attracting the herds of the Kababish from Kordofan, the Zaghawa and Meidob from Darfur and the Bideyat and Gura'an from Chad. This pattern has been seriously disrupted in recent years. The main settlement on the northern margins of the savanna is Kutum, where date-palms, unknown further south, give the town a Northern Sudanese appearance.

The Fur heartland in the southwest is the most fertile part of Darfur, particularly along the Wadi Azum, where Fur villages vary in size from around fifty huts or some 150-200 people to 200 huts or more.[6] The Fur grow *dukhn* (bullrush millet), *dhurra* (common millet), groundnuts, maize, sesame and onions, sowing in June/July and harvesting in November/December, and practise a variety of crafts—the spinning and weaving of cotton, grown locally, iron-working, salt-extraction and pottery. The Wadi Azum is a frontier zone, ethnically and ecologically; to the markets of the region the Arab cattle nomads of the south come to buy grain in exchange for milk and butter.[7]

The Marra Mountains (Jabal Marra) are the geographical and historical kernel of Darfur; they not only mark the effective limit of Arabisation from the East, they were both the base and refuge of the sultans in historical times and Fur resistance movements more recently. As regards flora the mountains are a Mediterranean island in the midst of Africa.[8] Parts, especially on the western side around Guldo, Nyertete and Kalokitting, are very beautiful. The mountain slopes are covered by a complex system of stone terracing, which give the impression that the mountains supported a larger population in

---

6   Barbour (1954), 172-82.
7   Haaland (1969), 58-73.
8   Wickens (1976).

the past than they do today.[9] The impression may not be misleading, since historically the Fur people do appear to have moved south and southwestwards away from the mountains, a movement accelerated under Condominium rule (1916-56) both because of greater security on the plains and for British administrative convenience.[10] The mountain Fur are "Highlanders" (Fur, *fuugokwa*, from *fuugo* "mountain") and speak a distinctive dialect of the common language.

Stretching away east of the mountains across eastern Darfur and Kordofan to the White Nile, the *Qoz* sub-region takes its name from the *qoz* patches or ridges, basically sand-dunes of poor light soil but, before the coming of mechanised farming, more easily cultivated than the heavy clay soils. Open wooded country occupied by scattered communities, whose most valuable export is gum arabic, the *Qoz* is dominated by loose conglomerations of Arabic-speaking peoples, Birged, Hamar, Jawami'a, Dar Hamid and Bidayriyya. Across the *Qoz*, approximately on the 14th parallel, lie the only towns of the region, al-Jinayna in Dar Masalit, al-Fashir and Kobbei (deserted in the late nineteenth century), Umm Kiddada, al-Ubayyid and Bara, the latter two in Kordofan (Sinnar on the Blue Nile, capital of the Funj Sultanate, is also on the same parallel). Nyala, further south and now the largest urban area in Darfur, is a colonial foundation. The southern part of the *Qoz* is the home of the Baqqara or Arabic-speaking cattle nomads, who occupy a belt of territory stretching across southern Kordofan and Darfur westwards to Wadai and Bagirmi in the modern Chad Republic.

In the north the *Qoz* merges into Barbour's third sub-region, the Semi-Desert, the home of the Kababish and Kawahla in Kordofan and the Zayyadiyya and Zaghawa in Darfur. Extensive ruins at Malha near Jabal Meidob, a mountain enclave in the heart of the *sahil* inhabited by the Meidob, may suggest an ancient and extensive "desert-edge" economy based upon the salt trade.

---

9   Hale (1964), 17-23 and idem (1966, thesis).

10 PA (al-Fashir), *Western Darfur District Handbook*. Cf. Roden (1972), 79-99. On the earlier expansion of the Fur into the southwest, see my (1982) and below.

A much more extensive mountain enclave, or series of enclaves, the Nuba Mountains in southeastern Kordofan, make up Barbour's fourth sub-region. A bewildering complex, both geographically and ethnically, the Nuba Mountains were never directly controlled by Darfur, but for both the Darfur and Funj Sultanates the Nuba people were an important and continuing source of manpower.

Ecology and demography

Darfur is a harsh environment, hot, dry and dusty away from the mountains. The rains frequently fail and water is always and everywhere a scarce commodity.[11] Famine or its threat has always been integral part of Darfur's history. According to the environmentalists, Darfur has since the early 1980s been going through an environmental crisis. Before considering this, the question of population growth needs to be examined.

The demographic history of Darfur is something of an unresolved and perhaps unresolvable mystery. The German traveller Gustav Nachtigal, who was in Darfur from January to July 1874, estimated the total population of Darfur at 3.5 million.[12] Nachtigal was one of the greatest of the travelling scholars of the nineteenth century, in the same company in Africa as Heinrich Barth and John Lewis Burckhardt; a medical doctor by training, he was a very careful and experienced observer and explains in detail how he arrived at his estimate,

To get an estimate of population I have noted down and added together as many villages as I could get information about in every administrative district and in every province. For the twelve districts [i.e. *shartaya*s] in the

---

11 In a recent meeting (September 2006) with a number of senior chiefs from Southern Darfur, at the conclusion of our meeting I asked what was their single most important problem; they as one voice and spontaneously said water.

12 Nachtigal (1971-87), iv, 358. Earlier in a letter published in *Petermanns Mitteilungen*, 21, 1875, 19-23 he had suggested a figure of 4-5 million. The latter figure is also suggested by Perron in an appendix to al-Tunisı (1845), 393. Perron, like Nachtigal a medical doctor, never went to Darfur, but in his years in Cairo he collected much information from visitors from Darfur.

northern province, I got 5,900 hamlets, which, at ten houses to a hamlet, and five inhabitants to a house, would give a total population of approximately 300,000.

Similarly for the eastern province I get about 200,000 inhabitants, for the fairly populated southern province 500,000, for the most densely populated southwest province about 600,000 [essentially Dar Diima, by far the most fertile part of Darfur] and for the three separate regions of the west [probably meaning Dars Fia, Madi and Kerne stretching from west of Jabal Marra across to include what is now Dar Masalit] together 500,000, while in the Jebel Marra, directly administered by the King [i.e. *hakurat al-sultan*], there might be about 100,000. Thus, taking into account only the districts and hamlets which I have actually listed, the total sedentary population would be 2,500,000. But since it has to be borne in mind that all of them could not be listed, and probably a third to a quarter of the existing districts were left out, the total sedentary population of Darfur can be put at something more than 3 million. If in addition the nomads, who in the northeast, east and south of the country are camel- or cattle-herdsmen, are estimated at half a million, we reach a total population of at least 31/2 million.

Nachtigal emphasises that this is just an estimate, but it does not seem to be entirely unreasonable.

In 1916, Sir Reginald Wingate, Governor-General of the Anglo-Egyptian Sudan, who masterminded the conquest and annexation of Darfur in 1916, estimated the sultanate's population in the year of the conquest at under one million.[13] This estimate of a seemingly drastic decline in population receives indirect support from the administrative correspondence of Darfur's last Sultan, 'Ali Dinar (r. 1898-1916), where he constantly exhorts his chiefs to repopulate the land and to rebuild villages (see Chapter Thirteen). The background to 'Ali Dinar's exhortations and Wingate's estimate of 1916 is that between the first conquest of the sultanate in 1874 and its restoration in 1898, Darfur went through a series of catastrophic famines and population displacements, from both natural and man-made causes, comparable to the situation today, the so-called *Umm Kwakiyya*, "the time of troubles" (see Chapter Thirteen). Between 1916 and 1956,

---

13 R. Wingate, Second Supplement to the *London Gazette*, 25 October 1916; this is a published version of Wingate's official report of the Darfur Campaign.

the years of British rule, the population of Darfur appears to have grown very slowly. In the most detailed census ever undertaken in the Sudan, that of 1955-56, the population of Darfur was given as just under 1.5 million, more precisely 1,328,765, of whom 375,100 are described as Arabs.[14] By the time of the census of 1983, nowhere as detailed as the 1955-56 census, the population of Darfur appears to have nearly doubled, to about 2.8 million.[15] Subsequent estimates have plotted a rate of growth of about 4.15%, well above the natural rate of increase of 2.8-3%; the growth is explained in part by immigration by nomads from Chad.[16] In 2006 the United Nations and other international bodies were working with a figure of 6-6.5 million.[17] So we have a population history over some 130 years that goes from 3.5 million in 1874 via 1 million in 1916, a census figure for 1955-56, and a second census figure from 1983 of 2.8 million to the present estimates of 6.25-6.5 million. It is hard to make sense of these figures. Working backwards, the 4.15% growth rate requires a very high rate of fertility and/or a very low rate of mortality, for

---

14 Department of Statistics, *First Population Census of Sudan 1955/56. Final Report*, 4 vols., Khartoum 1962, iii, table 6.1. A second census seems never to have been made acessible.

15 I have not had access to the Second or Third Censuses, which appear never to have been fully published, but base myself here on Davies (1983), 23-35. One factor that Davies emphasises is the rapidity of urbanisation, a crucial factor in the current changes in the demography of Darfur.

16 USAID, *Steps towards the Stabilization of Governance and Livelihoods in Darfur, Sudan*, March 2005. The highest rate elsewhere in Africa is Niger at 3.5%. I owe much in this discussion to my colleague, Ståle Dyrvik, who gives the following analysis, "I assume that the figure for 1955-56, 1.33m, seems reasonable. After that we have 2.8m in 1983 and 6.25m in 2006. This gives an annual growth rate of 2.69% from 1955 to 1983 and 3.55% from 1983 to 2006, or 3.08% for the whole period 1955 to 2006. Under the conditions in the Sudan Darfur should have a birthrate of around 40 per 100 and a mortality rate of around 10. This will give an annual growth of about 3% (2003). The mortality rate must have been higher earlier, with a growth rate of under 3%. The figure 2.69% can be right (see above), but 3.55% over the last ten years seems very high, indeed unlikely. Therefore, I am very sceptical to the figure of 6.25m today."

17 It is hard to establish how this figure has been arrived at, but it is accepted and used by the UN and the UN family of organisations.

both of which there is no evidence, while the immigration thesis has little hard evidence behind it. Much of the movement across the Sudan, Chad and Central African frontiers is seasonal and linked to nomadic migratory patterns. Perhaps the figures in the two censuses are too low, but the 1955-56 census breaks its figures down to tribal, local and sub-chiefly levels which can be cross-checked; however, it may still be too low, while I suspect the 1983 census almost certainly is. The latter suggestion is only a guess on my part, but the immediate post-independence period in the Sudan (excluding the south), at least until the early 1980s, was a period of relative growth; there were functioning hospitals and dispensaries in Darfur in the late 1960s and 70s, the health budget nearly doubled between 1956 and 1965.[18]

But whatever the real demographic history of Darfur is, dramatic population growth in the twentieth century does seem to have been a major factor in the processes of desertification and environmental degradation.

The problem with contemporary or near-contemporary studies on such themes as desertification, loss of soil fertility, the impact of population growth and the huge increase in livestock population is that they lack any historical dimension. In fact, very little basic research has been done in recent years, for obvious reasons; most of the studies we have were carried out in the eighties. Famine due to the failure of the rains seems always to have been a factor in Darfur; a major drought in 1913 is well documented, others appear to have occurred in the 1830s, 1860s and 1889-90. It is, however, difficult to link these to particular historical developments; as Morton puts it, "The first and overriding difficulty in interpreting environmental

---

18 Bayoumi (1979), 106; LS 2,662,204 in 1955-56 and LS 4,917,543 in 1965-66 fiscal year. The only other *khwaja*s or "Europeans" in al-Fashir when I lived there in 1970 were Russian doctors at al-Fashir General Hospital, built on the site of the "Old Palace", *bayt al-qadim*. We nodded to each other in the market but never spoke; the Cold War played out in the middle of Africa. A factor in the impulse towards urbanisation in Darfur today and a cause of the leakage of IDPs from the camps into the towns is the building of hospitals in the towns (where it is safe) by the aid agencies; the magnificent German-financed (Knights of St. John) hospital in Nyala is a true magnet, as I saw in 2005.

change is to distinguish any affect of human activity from the immensely powerful effects of climate." He continues by cataloguing the depth of our ignorance of the climatic history of the region.[19]

Given that Darfur was and is an unforgiving and unpredictable land and drought a constant factor, it is not surprising that local communities have developed complex and appropriate survival strategies.[20] A knowledge of wild edible plants, effective storage techniques and the like was part of each community's lore. As we shall see, much of the sultanate's bureaucracy was concerned with the storage and distribution of food and control over natural resources. Sadly Darfur's foreign rulers, British or other, have been far less understanding. "Donkeys" (so-called because of their silhouette) or water-pumps emptying non-renewable aquifers or mechanised agriculture producing wheat rather than millet (the former much more water-intensive) were not necessarily the ways to go.

Ethnography

Ethnographically, Darfur is a complex region; what follows is a very utilitarian guide to the peoples who make up or neighbour Darfur. But the use of terms like "people" or "tribe" does not indicate ethnicity; at best they indicate locality and self-identity.

Ethnicity is a very moveable and slippery concept, and nowhere more so than in Darfur. What follows is a catalogue of labels; what the content of this or that label is or was at any given time or place it is impossible to say definitely. Ethnic labels have several different levels. Some are generic, that is, used by outsiders or distant neighbours to describe those "over there". Zaghawa is one such generic label, used by the medieval Arab geographers to describe a people located between Kanem/Borno (Western Chad) and Darfur, who were allegedly one-time rulers of what became the state of Kanem

---

19 Morton (1994), 153 and 96-100. La Rue (thesis,1989) makes an effort to link periods of drought to specific historical processes, but the evidence is very uncertain.

20 The pioneering study is Tubiana & Tubiana (1977), but see also Holy (1980) and (1983), and De Waal (2005).

as it coalesced around western Lake Chad in about 1,000 CE. The label became localised in the eighteenth and nineteenth centuries, to describe peoples living in Chad and Darfur, speaking a language called *Beri-a*, with a complex relationship with the states of which they were intermittently a part, Wadai and Darfur.[21] Then there is another kind of generic label, used largely and pejoratively of enslaveable peoples, *hajaray*, "people living on tops of rocks", *jabalawiyyin*, "mountain dwellers", *fartit*, non-Muslim peoples living below Darfur who could be hunted for slaves. But in some inarticulate way, the Fartit were kin of the Fur, a memory of kinship lingered across the religious divide.

But even seemingly solid ethnic labels dissolve on closer inspection. The Fur expansion southwestwards was marked by the incorporation of non-Fur groups; the term Fartit came to be used of those who were not yet assimilated or who had escaped assimilation by migration southwards.[22] This can be demonstrated by the antiquity of the rulers of the region, the *aba diimang* (the present *aba diimang* is the eighteenth of that name), with the relative shallowness of the lineages of their subordinate chiefs, the *shartays*.

The Fur, the largest ethnic group in Darfur (constituting about a third of the total population, whose rulers are the main subject of this book), are relatively isolated linguistically and their origins are beyond speculation. They speak a language classified by the linguists as belonging to the Nilo-Saharan language group, to which most of the languages of the Wadai/Darfur region belong.[23] They divide themselves into three great sections, the Tamuurkwa west of Jabal Marra and the Kunjaara and Karakiriit in and east of the mountains. Below these geographical divisions the Fur are divided into a number of named groups or *orrenga*. MacMichael considered them to be local and totemistic, while Arkell thought they were either functional

---

21 Tubiana (1964), 17-19; to the references there may be added Wansbrough (1970), 98-99 and Lange (1977), 120-29. We now have the important study of 'Uthman (2006), which greatly enriches our understanding of Zaghawa history.

22 O'Fahey (1982), 75-87 describes the process in detail.

23 Doornbos (1983), 43-79.

groups, such as the *sambalanga* "people of the throwing knife (*sam-bal*)", or followers of particular chiefs like the *baasinga*/"the people of a prince".[24] Clarity has been brought to this question by the research of Jørg Adelberger, who defines *orrenga* thus,

> ...the *orrenga* are bilateral but weakly structured descent-groups, which are corporate to varying degrees. They are based on the principle of patrilineal descent and the name is usually taken from the father. Each person, however, claims relationship to the descent groups of both mother and father. Bridewealth and inheritance heritage [sic] are distributed bilaterally, and spiritual powers can be inherited from either one's father or one's mother. The *orrenga* are marked by a high degree of endogamy. This not only leads to the superimposing of genealogical ties but also a concentration of relatives within a given area.[25]

Adelberger makes the illuminating comment, "Historically, the Fur appear to have been composed of a small number of descent groups, from which the Keira emerged as the dominant one", and they expanded by incorporating groups known generically as Fartit.[26]

The most complex kind of slipperiness or moveability comes with the African/Arab divide. The sultans recognised two main identities within their state, Arab and *'Ajam*. In a charter of Muhammad Tayrab (r. 1752/3—1785/6), the phrase *sultan al-'Arab wa'l-'Ajam*/"Sultan of the Arabs and non-Arabs", appears, while a letter to a holy man on the Nile accompanying sumptuous presents from Sultan Muhammad al-Fadl (r. 1803-38) opens abruptly, *min sultan Fur*/"From the Sultan of [the] Fur.[27] What *'Ajam* meant to Tayrab is impossible

---

24 Al-Tunisi (1965), 143-44 (134 & 218-19); Nachtigal (1971-87), iv, 348 gives some fifteen names and says he noted forty in all. See further MacMichael (1922), i, 94 and Arkell (1951a), 61.

25 Adelberger (1990), 138 [English summary of German original]. On pp. 141-85 he lists all the known *orrenga*—over a hundred. The strength of Adelberger's work is that he combines detailed fieldwork (1986) with a thorough examination of all the material I had collected over fifteen years before (sadly, much of which had already disappeared) and to which Adelberger had complete access.

26 Ibid., and see my (1982), 75-87.

27 DF173.18/33, undated and O'Fahey and Spaulding (1981), 38-43, where the text and translation of the letter is given.

to know, perhaps something between someone whose first language was not Arabic and "barbarian".

The question of Arab identity is slippery to the point where it almost defies analysis. Speaking Arabic does not necessarily mean one is Arab; the Berti and Birged have lost their languages within the last century or so, but seemingly do not yet regard themselves as Arab.[28] They may soon do so. Thirty years ago the Mileri of Jabal Mun in northern Dar Masalit asserted a sort of Arab identity; now they are officially called Misiriyya/Mileri or Jabal Misiriyya.[29] Ultimately, Arabs are those who identify themselves as Arab and have or have constructed genealogies to prove it. The whole question is now highly politicised.

Leaving to one side the question of how many Arabs actually entered what is now the Sudan, Spaulding argues that the processes of Arabisation/Arabicisation/Islamisation—and the interaction between the three processes—are the product of the seventeenth and eighteenth centuries, dominated by urban centres along or near the Nile, Khandaq, Dongola, Shendi, Arbaji, al-Masallamiyya and al-Ubayyid, where a combination of itinerant trader (*jallaba*) and holy man (*faqih*, with the anomalous plural *fuqara*) laid the foundations of northern Sudanese culture and a very specific Sudanese Arab identity. He calls these centres "Enclaves" where Islamic norms, law, language and seclusion of women prevailed.[30]

Under the British, the processes of Arabisation and Arabicisation were speeded up, not least because the British simply assumed the superiority of the Arabs.[31] Indeed, one British official, H.A. (Sir

---

28 Berti was virtually extinct by the time of the British occupation; a British officer, H.H. Spence, collected a wordlist, now a ms. in the University of Khartoum; see Petracek (1975), 107-18 and (1978), 155-80. When I visited Ghor Abeshei, capital of Birged Kajjar, the *shartay*, Adam Adam Ya'qub, told me that there some old women who remembered some Birged. The Sudanese linguist, Ushari Ahmad, went and collected some material.

29 Hasan and O'Fahey (1970), 152-61, and personal observation, Khartoum 2005.

30 Spaulding (1985), 150-58.

31 British racism, its assumption of racial hierarchies, and its impact on the Sudan is an understudied topic, but given the Indian and Egyptian

Harold) MacMichael, codified the genealogies in a monumental work entitled *A History of the Arabs in the Sudan* (2 vols., London 1922).[32] This British prejudice fed into the emerging *'uruba* or "Arabism" movement of the 1920s and 30s associated with the literary journals *al-Fajr* and *al-Nahda*.[33] But "Arabism" was the concern of a small group of Northern Sudanese writers and intellectuals clustered around Gordon Memorial College and was hardly relevant to Darfur until very much later.

The ethnographical and genealogical mapping of MacMichael and others provides an uncertain guide to Darfur. Beyond entrapping the reader in the mire of Arab pedigrees, the genealogical approach has small utility; more useful are the non-ethnic occupational or "culture area" approaches of Theobald and Horowitz.[34] The scanty linguistic data and scattered oral traditions can uncover at least some of the main groupings. Although migration is used too easily in ethnographic mapping, Darfur's very position makes immigration a likely and constant factor, especially from east and west where there were few natural obstacles to movement. Thus, working crudely backwards in time, there is the constant factor of migration from West Africa and the Nile Valley; the Zaghawa and Bideyat infiltration into the northwest; the emergence of the Baqqara Belt as a distinct entity, and the more exiguous movements of Arab camel nomads into and within the *sahil*. Very much earlier, according to the linguistic evidence, are the Nubian connection of the Meidob and Birged peoples, the possible movement from the northwest of the Berti as remote precursors of the Zaghawa, and the apparent westward drift of the

---

background of the first generation of British administrators, it needs to be taken seriously.

32 Note the "in" in the title; MacMichael makes no secret of his prejudices; writing of the Bani Halba, he says, "The Beni Helba of Darfur are a particularly low type of Arab, poor in spirit and physique, incurably lazy and with none of the finer qualities that distinguish the nomad Arabs of Kordofan" (1922), i, 295. On the chronicle and genealogical literature, see O'Fahey (1994), 41-52. For a critique of the genealogical approach, see Cunnison (1971), 186-96.

33 See Sharkey (2003).

34 Theobald (1965), 5-16 and Horowitz (1967), 381-400.

13

Daju. All this leaves much unaccounted for, not least the position of the largest and most cohesive non-Arabic-speaking people, the Fur, and that of the "founding fathers" of state formation in the Darfur and Wadai region, the Tunjur.

The migration of West Africans (i.e. peoples from west of the Chad/Sudan frontier) has been unobtrusive and continuous. For at least the last two or three hundred years small groups of pilgrims, learned *fuqara* and *'ulama*, traders and slaves, and semi-pagan Fulbe (Fulani) cattle nomads have drifted into and settled in Darfur. There is a very pervasive Fulbe presence among the Baqqara; the Khalifa 'Abdullahi's grandfather appears to have been Fulani, while the first to swear allegiance to him upon the death of the Mahdi in June 1885 was another Fulani, the aged Muhammad al-Dadari, who had served in the *jihad* of Usman dan Fodio nearly eighty years before.[35]

From the absence of earlier references, the overland route from West Africa through Darfur to the Nile and the holy places in Arabia was probably not much used before the seventeenth century, in other words not much before the rise of Muslim states in Wadai and Darfur. Thereafter, it has been increasingly used, although richer pilgrims have always preferred the shorter desert crossing to North Africa (now replaced by the aeroplane). Some would-be pilgrims never moved on, some were kidnapped and stayed as slaves, others settled on their way back from the holy cities, now with the status of *al-hajj*.[36] Along with the poorer migrants and pilgrims, the prey of all along their way, came the holy men and scholars, some of whom were tempted to settle by offers of land and position from the sultans; a number of Fulani and Kanembu settlements at Kerio, Khiriban, Fata Barnu and Manawashi arose in this manner.[37] Another strand of western immigration was and is the cyclical drift of the Fulbe nomads; this is evidently a very old movement, judging from the continuum of assimilation and difference represented by the various

---

35 Abu-Manga, Hunwick, Kanya-Forstner, Lovejoy and O'Fahey (1998), 85-108.

36 Al-Naqar (1972), Birks (1978) and Yamba (1995).

37 On Kerio, see O'Fahey (1977b), 147-66.

communities now in Darfur. Around Umm Tullus in southern Darfur the Fallata have been established as a Baqqara tribe (*qabila*) for at least 200 years, but into the early twentieth century their assimilation was uneven, one section speaking Arabic, the other Fulfulde.[38] These slow and undramatic movements from the west have deposited throughout Darfur communities of Hausa, Fulbe, Kanuri, Kanembu, Kotoko and Maba peoples, all in varying stages of assimilation to the now dominant Arabic/Muslim culture.[39]

Immigration from the Nile Valley was responsible for the secondary Islamisation of Darfur and for the spread of the Arabic language. Darfur appears but, as it were, somewhat off-stage in the great biographical compendium of the early nineteenth century Nilotic Sudan, the *Tabaqat* of Muhammad b. Dayf Allah.[40] In the earlier period, relatively few seem to have immigrated from the Nile, although a branch of the Awlad Jabir holy family seem to have settled among the Zayyadiyya in the late seventeenth century.[41] Scarcity of land in the northern Sudan, a tradition of migration both to the north and south and periods of political instability on the Nile, particularly in the eighteenth century, led to an intermittent diaspora of Ja'aliyyin, Danaqla and others away from the river. They came as *fuqara* or holy men, as *jallaba* or travelling merchants; their commercial skills, experience of urban life and religious prestige led them to open up trade and trade routes and to establish towns west of the Nile.[42]

Immigration from west and east in historical times is reasonably well documented, but more speculative is the origin of the Arab nomads now in Darfur. The key text—and indeed the only one—is a

---

38 PA (al-Fashir), *Nyala District Handbook*; MacMichael (1922), i, 83-84.

39 Our understanding of these processes has been profoundly deepened by Braukämper (1992). On the Fallata in the Sudan but especially in Darfur, see Bidayn (n.d. [1995]).

40 Dayf Allah (1971).

41 'Abd al-Jalil (1955), 252. Documents DF141.18/1 to DF198.18/58, which I photographed in Mellit in 1974, record the affairs of the Awlad Jabir over a period of over two hundred years, the largest and oldest such archive found in Darfur. On the Awlad Jabir, see Holt (1973), 88-103.

42 El-Sayed El-Bushra (1971), 63-70.

letter written by the ruler of Borno, Abu 'Amr 'Uthman b. Idris, in 794/1391 to Sultan al-Zahir Barquq of Egypt, complaining that the Judham Arabs and others were attacking and enslaving his people and requesting the return of those enslaved from Egypt. As Yusuf Fadl Hasan points out, the letter shows that, "firstly, the Judham had strong ties with Egypt, and probably some of them were still living in Upper Egypt; secondly, the Arabs had by the eighth/fourteenth century penetrated beyond Kordofan and Darfur in sufficiently large numbers to alarm the Muslim rulers of the central *bilad al-Sudan*".[43]

The present occupational division of the Arabs of Chad, Darfur and Kordofan into Baqqara or cattle nomads living along the tenth parallel north from Lake Chad to the White Nile and the less numerous camel nomads (*abbala*, *jammala*) of the northern *sahil* probably does reflect different migratory patterns, although there has undoubtedly been much movement between the two zones. Braukämper concludes convincingly that the Baqqara way of life coalesced in Wadai in the seventeenth century. But given the fluidity of Baqqara social structure, its tendency towards fission, the incorporation of local groups, and the heavy West African ethnic and linguistic influences upon them, it is unlikely that any of the present-day tribes are very old, as Braukämper shows.[44]

Genealogies offer some clues to the early history of the camel nomads in that they regard many of the modern tribes as originating in a great Fazara federation.[45] Hasan concludes that the Fazara were an amalgam of various Arab groups—probably located earlier in Upper Egypt—who "migrated from Egypt via a route to the west of the Nile, and not those to the east of it", whence they spread out into the

---

43 Hasan (1967), 163; the letter is to be found in al-Qalqashandi (1913-19), i, 306 and vii, 116-18. On its Borno context, see Ajayi and Crowder (1971), i, 180.

44 Braukämper (1992), 82-116.

45 Some of the main references: Browne (1806), 325; al-Tunisi (1965), 139, and in the French transl., al-Tunisi (1845), 129 (where "Farârah" is a misprint; hereafter the French pagination will be given in parentheses after the Arabic followed by the English transl., 214); Nachtigal (1971-87), iv, 350, and MacMichael (1922), 255.

Bayuda lands north of Kordofan.[46] Among trade documents from sixteenth-century Egypt, one refers to merchants travelling to *barr al-Sudan Fazara*, "The land of the Fazara blacks" (?), in about 1530; the context makes it reasonable to assume that the merchants were travelling to Kordofan and Darfur.[47]

These vague indications point to a slow movement by Arab nomads into and across northern and southern Darfur between the fifteenth and seventeenth centuries and their gradual coalescence into the modern tribal groupings. Thus, out of the Fazara the Zayyadiyya had emerged by the early eighteenth century as the largest camel-owning tribe in the north, where there also roamed various smaller groups, Nu'ayba, Mahamid, 'Irayqat and Mahriyya, later known collectively as the "Northern Rizayqat" because of their alleged kinship with the southern Rizayqat.[48] Also by the eighteenth century the main cattle-owning tribes were beginning to be defined, namely the Ta'aisha, Bani Halba, Fallata, Habbaniyya and Rizayqat, going from west to east across southern Darfur.[49]

Linguistic relationships suggest another movement (over what timespan it is impossible to say), namely the infiltration from the northwest into northern and central Darfur of peoples speaking Nilo-Saharan languages: the Berti, Zaghawa and Bideyat.[50] Within Darfur the earliest Berti homeland appears to have been in and around the Tagabo Hills in the northeast where, probably by the late seventeenth century, a line of Berti kings ruled. By the late eighteenth century other Berti groups had moved east into the Umm Kiddada/al-Tuwaysha region.[51] The localisation of the generic name "Zaghawa" to

---

46 Hasan (1967), 167.

47 Walz (1978), 7-8.

48 MacMichael (1922), i, 262-63 and 298-300.

49 *Ibid*, i, 271-301 and Braukämper (1992), 107-16. On both the northern and southern Rizayqat, see also Abu Salim (1979), 35-140. On Ta'aisha traditions, see Muhammad (1982).

50 Greenberg (1966), 131-33; Petrácek, 1975, 107-18 and *idem* (1978), 155-73.

51 Holy (1974), ix.

peoples living in an arc in northern Wadai and Darfur seems to have been a phenomenon of the seventeenth century and before.

Another wider linkage may seemingly be discerned between the Meidob and Birged in that they speak or spoke languages of the Nubian language group—the former strongly and the latter more faintly—and maintain traditions of migration from the Nile Valley.[52] Here the linguistic evidence, which suggests an ancient cleavage, and the oral traditions are at variance, but in the present state of historical and linguistic research on the problem of Nubian origins little more can be said. Also related to the question of Nubian origins and linkages west of the Nile are the wider linguistic affiliations of the Daju of southeastern Darfur, the region's first "historical" rulers, and the Beigo further south with peoples in both Kordofan, the Western Bahr al-Ghazal and Chad. Robin Thelwall's research points to Kordofan as the original point of dispersal.[53]

This catalogue of ethnographic facts and possible relationships might be greatly prolonged, but data so arid lead rapidly to speculation. Reverting to an ecological perspective, Darfur may be divided into three zones, corresponding to rainfall boundaries which tend to encompass three ways of life: camel nomadism, rainfed hoe agriculture and cattle nomadism. This tripartite division should not be taken too rigidly; the Berti and the Zayyadiyya are neighbours and occupy similar land, but the former are more sedentarised, the latter more nomadic. Environmental determinism needs to be balanced against cultural norms and preferences. Within this approximate ecological framework, ethnic identity and cohesion appear as a complex function of descent, mechanisms of incorporation, language in some cases, and the notion of a common tribal homeland (*dar* or now, *hakura*), reinforced by the experience of external and internal political domination.

---

52 On the Nubian language group, Tucker and Bryan (1956), 75-77, and on the traditions of migration, MacMichael (1922), i, 58-64, and *shartay* Muhammad Adam Ya'qub (Ghor Abeshei, 26.6.1969).

53 Tucker and Bryan (1956), 59-61 and Thelwell (1981 thesis).

The tribal/occupational frontiers are both stable and permeable. Haaland in the 1960s described both facets as they operated along the Fur/Bani Halba frontier on the Wadi Azum. Successful Fur farmers invested in cattle until a point was reached when the value of their cattle outweighed that of their fields; to protect their investment in livestock they were constrained to cross the ethnic frontier, leaving their own way of life and eventually their language to adopt that of the Baqqara as being the appropriate idiom for cattle nomadism.[54] A similar process occurred on the Fur/Zaghawa frontier in the north, i.e. on a sedentary/camel nomad frontier; here the pressures on the Fur to conform to Zaghawa values were particularly intense.[55] Conversely, when herds were lost through drought, sickness or war, the nomads were forced to become farmers, but even when they remained sedentarised a nostalgia for nomadism and the use of agricultural slave labour survived.[56]

Such trans-ethnic and occupational mobility suggests that tribal or ethnic labels have only a limited content or stability, and that mainly political mechanisms accounted for the preservation of territorially defined groups in an area of open frontiers. Changes in political allegiance were later legitimised by changes in one's ancestors. The mobility becomes apparent from an examination of tribal and clan (*khashm al-bayt*) names, since these generally reveal a high proportion of stranger ancestors.

This survey of Darfur's geography and demography has been written in a kind of "historic present" *anno* 1970; it does not describe the realities on the ground at the time of this writing (2006). The ethnic, ecological and demographic realities are changing rapidly. The conflicts and environmental changes of the last thirty years have led to vast population movements; some 4 million people are displaced, living either in IDP (internally displaced persons) camps or on the

---

54 Haaland (1969), 58-73.
55 Haaland (1972), 149-72.
56 Compare Hill (1968), 58-70 describing the Habbabin of Kordofan.

margins of pre-existing urban centres.[57] Most will probably not go back where they came from. The nomads, whether cattle-keepers or camel-herders, want to settle, to obtain access to schools, medical services and cash-paying jobs, to provide for their children; nostalgia for the nomadic way of life has markedly diminished. Ethnicity is constantly evolving and is increasingly being redefined on the Web; outcaste ironworkers are now skilled professionals. In the end, we define ourselves.

---

57 Nyala has grown from 300,000 in 1999 to about 1.5 million in 2005. It is now the second largest city in the Sudan. It is also now a boom town, not least as the capital of the livestock trade.

2

STATES AND STATE FORMATION
DAJU, TUNJUR AND KEIRA[1]

Introduction

The development of states in the Darfur region operated in counter-point to its geography and ethnography; if the savanna lands provided the *Lebensraum*, the mountains provided the base, and if Arab immigration modified the region's ethnic configuration, state formation seemingly owed little directly to the immigrants. The complex traditions which describe the origins of the successive kingdoms of the Daju, Tunjur and Fur are paradigms of how the past was and is understood in relation to the peoples and the power structure of the present; of a piece with such paradigms is the commonly-heard interpretation of the Tunjur Sultan's black turban as a symbol of the Tunjur's lost greatness.[2]

States and state formation in the region were based on identifiable, but not necessarily stable or homogeneous, ethnic groups, whose expansion beyond the group's borders was a function of military

---

1   For a reinterpretation of the "pre-history" of Darfur, we now have McGregor (2001). This is essentially a re-evaluation of the material to be found in the Arkell Papers (see Sources and Bibliography) complemented by a thorough and careful use of my own writings. If McCregor has not significantly thrown new light on any topics discussed in this chapter, he has clarified the issues admirably and in effect pointed out where the archaeologists need to go.

2   Al-Tunisi (1965) 138 (128 & 213); Nachtigal (1971-87), 347-8 calls it a veil.

strength aided in later times by the ideology of religion, in this case Islam. Legitimising legends such as those of the "Wise Stranger" served to explain the transfer of power from one group to another, with the variables of Islam and the "Wandering Arab" thrown into the mix. In most cases the mythopoeic complexities are beyond reasonable analysis and I have not attempted to do so here.

Because of this complexity, any simplistic assumption that the influx of Arabic-speaking groups into the region at the same time signalled the arrival of Islam, that Arabs brought Islam to the region, is doubtful. As Braukämper has convincingly demonstrated,[3] the genesis or formation of Arabic-speaking cattle-herding groups, the *Baqqara*, within the central Sudanic belt (i.e. the modern Chad region) was so intermingled with Fulani elements, already Islamised within West Africa, that their Arab/African/Islamic identities are almost impossible to disentangle. What I am suggesting here is that Islam arrived as states emerged, creating conditions that for reasons discussed below were favourable for the reception of a new religion. The notion that Arabs immigrated into the region bringing Islam with them does not fit the complexities of the traditions we have.[4]

In what follows I have tried to match the oral record to external contemporary references; here I am not making a judgment about the relative value of the evidence; if oral tradition is perhaps distorted over time, contemporary, mainly Arab geographical sources may well be distorted over distance and time, as one geographer repeats something from the twelfth century as evidence for the fourteenth

---

3 Braukämper (1992), 82-102 *et passim*.

4 If I can make a parallel with the nineteenth century in Africa; the arrival of Europeans in Africa did not on its own facilitate the spread of Christianity. The Portuguese in sixteenth century Kongo used Christianity as an instrument of state policy, but it was a fragile implantation that did not long survive. With the coming of European colonial structures in the late nineteenth century, Christian missionaries, who sometimes acted as as instruments of the colonial state, successfully proselytised under the state's umbrella. There is a parallel between the success of the Christian missionaries in late nineteenth-century colonial Africa and the success of the Muslim holy families in sixteenth-century Darfur.

century. What I write here is essentially tentative, but important in showing the depth of Darfur's identity.

Oral traditions

To match the oral traditions, we have a rich store of material remains associated with the various layers of the oral tradition. In a reductionist mode, each site tends to be identified with an ethnicity, a "Daju site", a "Tunjur site" etc.; how real these identifications are remains to be tested.

Likewise there is very little internal consistency in the traditional accounts of state formation of the Daju, Tunjur and Keira. What Nachtigal learned in al-Fashir differs considerably from what I learned in the same city almost exactly a century later. The differences do not in themselves invalidate either version; Nachtigal was a century closer in time and was functioning in a still self-confident society, albeit one under threat, while by my time perspectives, not least in terms of power relations, had changed. In what follows, I have attempted to be non-judgmental, i.e. not attempting to decide between different versions of the traditions, and have consciously sought to take the easy way out, i.e. looking for an external contemporary source. In the latter case, we do have some useful signposts that at the very least give us a reasonably reliable chronological framework. What we can perhaps deduce is that Darfur experienced state formation of some kind from about the twelfth century onwards, associated with three different ethnic groups, the Daju, Tunjur and the Fur. Here we can only review the evidence as we have it, but without being too confident as to its reliability.

My intention here is not to present an exhaustive analysis of the traditions on the Daju, Tunjur and early Keira state, but rather to highlight those elements that illustrate continuity and the chronological depth of the state-forming impulse in the region. Many of the institutions of Darfur have roots going back long before the Darfur Sultanate: *shartay*, the title of middle-ranking chiefs comes from the Daju, *chorte*; some of the great Keira title-holders like the Konyunga had their roots in Tunjur times, terms such as *mayram* for

23

royal women and *fashir* for court have been used throughout central Sudanic Africa for centuries. In addition, if we accept the description of Darfur in D'Anania in about 1583, the state was already a multi-ethnic structure, not that much younger than many European states and older than most.[5]

Daju and Tunjur [6]

The Daju are a widespread people living in eastern Chad,[7] the Western Bahr al-Ghazal, Darfur and Kordofan; their main divisions are Mongo, Sila, Nyala, Beigo [Ar. Bayqu], Nyalgulgule, Lagawa, Shatt and Liguri.

The traditions about the Daju can be briefly summarised. A long time ago the Daju rulers, who appear to have come from the east, lived in the southeast region around Jabal Marra, but their sway was limited since the chiefs of the Fur and other tribes simply paid them tribute. Their first king, Gitar or Kosbur, was a pagan and so probably were his successors; another was 'Umar Kassifuroge, whose nickname implies that he warred against the Fur or Feroge, the latter now a group in the Western Bahr al-Ghazal. The Daju were superseded by the Tunjur:

The intellectual superiority of the immigrant Tunjur, and their more refined customs (their hospitality was especially celebrated), wrested power from the Daju without any fighting, or violence.[8]

---

5   In the discussion that follows I have not discussed the period the archaeologists identify as the Tora Stone Culture on the basis of a distinctive stone-building technique; this is because it cannot be linked to any body of oral tradition, but see McGregor (2001), 16-21. Nevertheless, there seem to be some similarities between Tora building techniques and later Fur/Keira building styles.

6   What follows is partly based on my (1980b), 47-60 but also on recently discovered contemporary sources on the Tunjur. I have not discussed the material remains associated with the two groups which are the main topic of McGregor (2001).

7   Thelwall (1981 thesis) 1.

8   Nachtigal (1971-87), iv, 274.

The last Daju king, called in some versions Ahmad al-Daj, was
so oppressive a tyrant that his subjects persuaded him to mount a
teital antelope which galloped away with him to Dar Sila in present-
day Chad, where a Daju state which survived until recent times was
established.[9]
There are some seemingly contemporary references to the Daju in
the form of notices in the Arab geographical literature of the Middle Ages of a people called Tajuwiyyin living approximately between
Sudanese Nubia and Kanem in modern Chad. The first and most
substantial reference to the town (*madina*) of Tajuwa and to the
Tajuwiyyin comes in the geographical *magnum opus* of the Sicilian
geographer al-Idrisi (d. 1166), writing in 1154.[10] Thereafter, we have
a number of intermittant references, most of which are seemingly
dependent upon Ibn Sa'id, writing in about 1240, whose work is
known mainly through later quotations.[11] Arkell argues that these
notices should be taken as references to the Daju.[12] Little can be
added here, except that the repetition of Ibn Sa'id's notice by later
writers without any additional information may be a clue to the limited duration of "Daju hegemony", perhaps in the 12th and 13th
centuries, in the region. What is significant is that by contrast to
the marrying of tradition and contemporary sources in the equation
Tajuwiyyin=Daju, we have no contemporary references to the Tunjur as such before about 1550.
The Tunjur lie tantalisingly just beyond our ken. We know from
contemporary references that there was a Tunjur state in Darfur and
Wadai in the sixteenth century. I set out the evidence here, but can
add very little in exegesis. We have one or two contemporary references which intermesh in a way with the oral record; what follows is
complex, but it is a necessary part of the tale of Darfur's emergence as

9   Daju traditions are recorded in Cadalvène and Breuvery (1841), ii, 198-
    9; Nachtigal (1971-87), iv, 272-4; MacMichael (1922), i, 71-6; Hillelson
    (1925), 49-71; Arkell (1952a), 62-70 and Balfour-Paul (1955), 9-10.
10 See Mus'ad (1972), 125-6 and Vantini (1975), 266-7; Vantini's translations
    must be used with caution.
11 Ibid., 399-404.
12 Arkell (1951a), 62-5.

a defined entity within Africa. The Tunjur, I suspect, are the crucial state-forming actors just off-stage.

The traditions on the Tunjur can be reduced to four themes, two on origins and two on their downfall. On origins, the more pervasive set of traditions identifies them as Bani Hilal Arabs, links them to the folk-hero Abu Zayd al-Hilali and brings them to the Sudan across the Sahara from Tunis. A Tunjur song from Kanem nostagically recalls their home in Tunis "the Green" (*Tunis al-khadra*),

> *Emmenez-nous dans le pays de Tunis la verte,*
> *Si nous manquons de mil, l'eau de Tu-*
> *nis suffira à nous faire vivre.*
> *Emmenez-nous dans le pays qui n'a pas de taons,*
> *Tunis la verte est un paradis hors de ce pays-ci.* [13]

In what is the fullest compilation of Tunjur traditions we have, Gros gives an account of Abu Zayd al-Hilali and the Bani Hilal in North Africa.[14] After their adventures in North Africa, the Bani Hilal are said to have penetrated the area between the Ennedi Mountains (northern Chad) and Dar Kababish (northern Kordofan) under the leadership of 'Abd al-Majid. Because of attacks by the people of the Ennedi in which two Bani Hilal/Tunjur rulers were killed, they moved south under Sultan Sa'd and conquered Dar Qimr on the present Chad/Sudan border. There Sa'd quarrelled with his sons, 'Ali and Ahmad, who were driven out and established themselves near Jabal Marra at the expense of the Daju.

Ahmad, Sa'd's son, is otherwise Ahmad al-Ma'qur. In Slatin's version of the story, Ahmad and his brother 'Ali were Arabs wandering in the desert, where they fell out over 'Ali's wife.[15] 'Ali was hamstringed by his brother, hence the nickname *al-ma'qur*, and

---

13 Carbou (1913), 147-9 for the complete song; see also Idem (1912), 73-4, and Nachtigal (1971-87), iv, 347-8.

14 Gros (1951).

15 Slatin (1896), 38-41. Shuqayr's version (1903), ii, 111-13 is probably based on Slatin.

abandoned in the desert, but Ahmad then in remorse sent two slaves, Zayid and Birged (forefathers of the Zayyadiyya and Birged peoples), to help him. Ahmad made his way to the court of Kor, king of the Daju, whose favour and daughter he won by inroducing new and more civilised ways; thus by introducing regular mealtimes he did away with quarrels that arose because of the old "first come, first served" system. In other versions, the innovation was the saying of the *basmala*, "In the name of God, the Compassionate, the Merciful", before eating, thus introducing an Islamic element.[16]

There are a number of variants of the Ahmad al-Ma'qur story, all containing ingredients from the "Wise Stranger" paradigm as noted by Holt.[17] The most significant variation is that in some later versions Ahmad comes to the court of the last Tunjur king, Shaw Dorshid. In this variant, Ahmad, the *jadd* or "ancestor" of the Keira, thus mediates the transition from Tunjur to Keira rule, not Daju to Tunjur.

An alternative version of Tunjur origins is that they are Arabs from the east; thus Heinrich Barth,

[The Tunjur] are said to have come from Dongola, where they separated from the Batálesa, the well-known Egyptian tribe originally settled in Bénesé [al-Bahnasa in Upper Egypt]. Adancing from Dongola, the Tynjur are said to have vanquished first the Dájó ...[18]

Linked to this eastern version are the legends that bring Abu Zayd al-Hilali and Ahmad al-Ma'qur to the Sudan from the east or up the Nile.[19] Thus the earliest written record of Ahmad al-Ma'qur, in a French travel source around 1820, describes him as an 'Abbasid, a descendant of the uncle of the Prophet, who at the head of some Arab nomad tribes conquered Kordofan and Darfur and introduced Islam. This source's confusion is shown by its description of "Tunjur" as one of the last Daju rulers.[20]

---

16 AP¹, 4/13, 47 and Muhammad Ibrahim (Zalingei, 25.5.1969). The latter version is given my thesis (1972), 70-1, where other versions are also given.

17 Holt (1973), 76-8.

18 Barth (1857-59), ii, 546-7.

19 For different versions, see MacMichael (1912), 231-4.

20 Cadalvène and Breuvery (1841), ii, 198-9; see O'Fahey (1973b), 34.

The claim to 'Abbasid descent is widespread in the riverain Sudan, but is particularly linked to the Ja'aliyyin, living north of Khartoum along the Nile. In a late version from Darfur, ascribed to the ubiquitous and probably fictitious genealogist Mahmud al-Samarqandi, after the Banu'l-'Abbas had conquered Nubia, Abu Zayd, together with Ahmad al-'Abbasi, crossed the White Nile to attack the Nuba of Kordofan. The Nuba were defeated but Ahmad was wounded (hence his nickname) and lost; he was later found but stayed on among the Nuba where he fathered the Abu'l-Sakaring, the old kings of Jabal Taqali. He later moved to Darfur where he married Shaw Dorshid's daughter.[21]

This division of the traditions on Tunjur origins into western versus eastern is probably too simple. What we seem to have is a continuum of stories whose variations are as much ideational as geographical; North African Hilali versus Nile Valley 'Abbasids.

Common to most versions is that in its heyday Tunjur hegemony is said to have stretched from Darfur across Wadai to the borders of Bagirmi (central Chad). The traditions are unclear as to whether this vast area was ever ruled as one state, but primacy in terms of time and overlordship belonged to the Darfur Tunjur. A central point in the traditions is that the Tunjur in Darfur were overthrown before their kin in Wadai.

The downfall of the Darfur Tunjur is obscure. Gros' version says that Ahmad al-Ma'qur had two sons, Ahmad Kanjar and Musa Tanjar; the first succeeded his father in Darfur and, although Gros does not say so, presumably became the eponymous founder of the Kunjaara Fur dynasty (Kunjaara being the section of the Fur from which the Keira lineage came). Musa went west and in alliance with the Mahamid Arabs began the subjection of Wadai to Tunjur rule.[22] This bifurcation of Tunjur and Kunjaara is paralleled linguistically by the t or d/k singular/plural form in Fur (for example, sing. *duo*

---

21 AP [1], 4/16, 6-7, a brief genealogy in Arabic of the Darfur rulers. On al-Samarqandi, see MacMichael (1922), ii, 6-8 and Holt (1973), 83-4.

22 Gros (1951) 13-14.

pl. *kwa* "husband") and in a number of neighbouring but unrelated languages.[23]

Although Barth straightforwardly says the Tunjur in Darfur were overthrown by Kúro (Kuuruu of the kinglists), the third predecessor of Sulayman Solongdungo, and is unaware of any closer relationship,[24] most versions stress a kin connection between the Tunjur and Keira. The last Tunjur ruler in Darfur was the mysterious and tyrannical Shaw Dorshid—an apparently historical figure (see below)—whose name meant "The master over us".[25] He treated his subjects with great harshness, forcing them to undertake numerous campaigns and to level the peak of a mountain, *mailo fugo jurto* (Fur, "Mailo, the dug-up mountain"), so that he could build upon its summit. Finally, his notables became so exasperated that they asked his half-brother, Daali or Dalil Bahr, to seize power. Daali did so, and Shaw Dorshid fled the Marra Mountains on a white horse, or in other versions on a *teital* antelope (shades of Ahmad al-Daj!) and disappeared. The traditions are reasonably consistent that there were several rulers between Daali and Sulayman in the mid-seventeenth century.

Although virtually all versions stress a kin connection between the Tunjur and Kunjaara, one variant recorded by Arkell at Uri, one of the most famous sites in Darfur, says that Daali was a eunuch of Shaw Dorshid who administered Uri after his master's departure.[26] Yet other variants of the Ahmad al-Ma'qur story make the hero come to Shaw's court, thus transferring him from the role of the Tunjur "founding father" to that of the Kunjaara/Keira.

By contrast to Darfur, the numerous traditional accounts of the overthrow of the Tunjur in Wadai and their replacement by the Maba dynasty (c. 1630 to 1912) are relatively straightforward and have a "historical ring", varying mainly as to details.[27] Gros alone

---

23 Bryan (1959), 1-21.
24 Barth (1857-59), ii, 546-7.
25 Nachtigal (1971-87) iv, 276, but this is not Fur.
26 Arkell (1946a), 185-202; on Uri, see McGregor (2001), 60-4.
27 The traditional accounts, except for Gros, are given in Tubiana, Khayar and Deville (1978).

gives the names of the three sultans said to have succeeded Musa Tanjar, 'Ali, 'Umar and Da'ud al-Mirayn, who had their capital at Kadama. Da'ud was to be overthrown by the son of an immigrant from the Nile Valley: the immigrant was Yame (or Jami') or Salih, a Ja'ali Arab from Shendi on the Nile who had settled in Wadai. 'Abd al-Karim, his son, studied with some Fulani holy men at Bidderi in Bagirmi; returning to Kadama he became involved in a liaison with Sultan Da'ud's daughter, the *mayram* or princess A'isha, or in other versions married her. Da'ud became increasingly suspicious of 'Abd al-Karim, which led the latter to make the classic move of the Muslim reformer (as he is described)—*hijra* or withdrawal from the capital. Rallying the support of various Maba and Arab tribes, the latter including the Mahamid, Mahriyya, Nu'ayba, 'Irayqat and Bani Halba, he declared a *jihad* and overthrew Da'ud and the Tunjur.

The overthrow of the Tunjur in Wadai is much less ambiguously remembered than in Darfur and is couched in a familiar Sudanic idiom. A Muslim holy man succeeds in arousing the more Muslim (or more discontented) sections of the population against their semi-pagan or nominally Muslim kings. The revolution carried through successfully, a new and consciously Muslim dynasty takes power and consigns its predecessors to near-oblivion.

The contemporary record

Can we marry this complex, often detachable, body of stories and legends to any contemporary reports, in the absence of any archaeo-logical research? As we have seen, we have some contemporary or near contemporary references in the Arab geographers to the Tajuwi-yyin, reasonably if not certainly identified with the Daju. By the late thirteenth century, some Arab sources give placenames away from the Nile, west and east. But these are difficult to interpret, although Uri may be one of them.[28]

But by the sixteenth centuries, Darfur begins to emerge from the mists. In 1582 Lorenzo d'Anania published in Venice *L'Universale Fabrica*, a kind of guide to trading possibilities around the known

---

28 My (1980b) deals with these in some philological detail.

world, a literary construct to accompany Venice's trading potentialities in neighbouring lands. He gives a description of Uri which places it firmly within a Darfur world,

Uri, a very important city, whose prince is called Nina, or emperor, and who is obeyed by neighbouring countries, namely the kingdom of Aule, Zurla (which we have mentioned above [Alas, he did not]), Sagava (or Sagaua), Memmi, Musulat, Morga, Saccae and Dagio. This prince, who is allied to the Turks [who had conquered Egypt in 1517], is very powerful and is supplied with arms by merchants from Cairo.

D'Anania notes further that the ruler had some sort of trade agent at Barca on the Libyan coast.[29] The tributaries can be variously identified, but "Sagava" must equal Zaghawa, "Memmi" Mima, "Musulat" Masalit, "Morge" possibly Birged, "Saccae" Berti and "Dagio" Daju.[30]

A newly-discovered piece of information further complicates the puzzle; this is a document of authentication issued in Medina, dated 24 Shawwal 983/25 January 1576, of an endowment (*waqf*) of various houses, palm trees and gardens in Medina for the benefit of a group of holy men, made originally in Cairo. This endowment is linked in an unspecified way to one previously made by the Sultan Shaw b. al-Sultan Rufa'a and his brother, Diyab.[31] The endowment is made by one Fakhr al-Din b. Nur al-Din 'Ali al-Maghribi who seems to have been a relative of the Sultan, and is witnessed by two figures who have the ethnic labels, al-Hawwari al-Dikayrani. Now the Dikayrab Hawwara, of remotely Berber origin, are an

---

29 Lange and Berthoud (1972), 342-5.

30 These and other disputable identifcations are discussed in my (1980b) and re-analysed in McGregor (2001), 63-4; there is no great disagreement between our interpretations.

31 The document is printed in Ibrahim (1996), 322-4. This is a study of the traditions and legends of the migrations of the Banu Hilal Arabs from Arabia to North and Central Africa. The author says that the document was given him by the renowned Sudanese folklorist al-Tayyib Muhammad al-Tayyib. I looked through my own collection of al-Tayyib's books, but have found no further reference, although Dr al-Tayyib has certainly carried out research in Arabia. Rufa'a is the commonest name given as the father of Shaw in the Tunjur regnal lists. I hope to publish the text and translation of the document.

old-established trading community living near al-Ubayyid in Kordofan.[32] This Tunjur endowment seems to have existed for well over a hundred years; in a local Medinan chronicle there is a notice of one 'Abd al-Rahman b. 'Abd Allah al-Fawwal al-Tunjuri who settled in 1100/1688-89 in Medina, where—as his name, al-Fawwal, confirms—he set up shop as a seller of *ful* or beans. He and his descendants became the administrators (*mutawalli*) of the Tunjur endowments of houses and date-palms (*awqaf al-Tanajara min buyut wa-nakhil*) in the city.[33] These references suggest that the Tunjur rulers, or at least their agents abroad, were asserting an Islamic identity, while in the traditions they are ambiguously described as pagan.

Some thirty to forty years after D'Anania's notice, slaves are being sold in the Cairo markets who bear the ethnic label "Tunjur" (whether these refer to the slave or the trader is impossible to determine).[34] We have two further sources: a marginal comment dated 1068/1657-58 on a manuscript of an Egyptian Encyclopedia by al-Nuwayri describes Tunjur merchants coming to Cairo from Darfur and the newly-converted kingdom of Dar Salih, i.e. Wadai;[35] and the Dominican Vansleb's (or Wansleben) description in 1663 of Darfur seemingly makes the first reference to the Fur:

To the west of Cairo lies the land of Fur (Fohr), to which caravans repair frequently in order to purchase slaves. Its sultan resides in Ogra. The present sultan is called Urimellis.[36] When the *kafila* (caravan) goes there from Cairo, it comes by of Kab Dago and Issueine to Fur in one and a half months. From that country it brings as goods, ostrich feathers,

32 MacMichael (1912), 220.
33 O'Fahey (1997), 342 (334-51). Other central Sudanic rulers made similar endowments in Medina; see ibid. I am grateful to Stefan Reichmuth for finding one of these texts and helping me decipher the other.
34 O'Fahey (1980b).
35 O'Fahey, Hunwick and Lange (1978), 16-24.
36 On my misreading of this name see Adelberger (1991), 177-8.

tamarind, elephant tusks, pitch-black male and female slaves, and even little children.[37]

Vansleb also describes the sale of slaves, who were tattooed (probably facial scars or *shullukh*),[38] in Cairo; to entice would-be buyers, the women were paraded naked, although for potential European buyers it was a case of *noli me tangere* ("You must not touch me"; Vansleb's profession explains the Latin). The one and a half month's route fits the later name for the desert route from Upper Egypt to Darfur, the *darb al-arba'in*, "The Forty Days Road".[39] That the trade route was in regular use by the end of the seventeenth century is confirmed by the account of some Franciscan missionaries on their way to Sinnar; in September 1689 they were at the Kharja Oasis, the first main stage on the desert route from Egypt, where they saw merchants preparing to go to Dongola, Sinnar and Ethiopia, while others were preparing to set off to the kingdom of Fur (*regno di Fur*).[40]

These references are inconclusive, but may be interpreted to suggest that at some time in the mid-seventeenth century a Tunjur state based in northern Darfur gave way to, or was superseded in some way by, a Fur state based in northern Jabal Marra. Nor do the references deny the possibility of some dynastic connection between Tunjur and Keira as the traditions imply, but we may never know unless by chance new documents come to light like those concerning the Tunjur endowments in Medina.

Jabal Marra: the cradle of the Keira

In the northern part of Jabal Marra around Turra are a series of ruins associated by local tradition with a line of Keira rulers, principally

---

37 Wansleben in Paulus (1792-98), iii, 45-6. "Kab" is probably al-Kab on the Nile near Isna, "Dago" may be Daju or the Kharja Oasis and "Issueine" probably Suwayni in Northern Darfur, in Dar Zaghawa. I owe these suggested identifications to the Rev. Dr A.J. Arkell.

38 On which see Hasan (1976). There is an informative review of Hasan's work by Peter Clark, *Times Literary Supplement*, 13 January 1978.

39 Shaw (1929).

40 D'Albano (1961), 47.

Daali, Kuuruu, Tunsam, Sulayman, his son Musa, and Musa's son, Ahmad Bukr.[41] Turra was the cradle of the Keira state, where most of the sultans were buried, and where annual sacrifices were made (see Chapter Five).[42]

If Shaw Dorshid flourished about the mid-sixteenth century and Sulayman Solongdungo a century later, then it is reasonable to assume that the Tunjur/Keira transition occurred within that timespan. At what point hegemony over Darfur passed from the Tunjur in the north to the Keira described below is as yet unknown. Of the rulers listed above, Daali appears to be a semi-historical figure who established some of the most fundamental Keira institutions. From the sacred tree, *numang fadda*, at Turra he divided the kingdom into the provinces of *Dar daali* (east, later to be extended east of the mountains), *Dar aba uumo* (southeast of the mountains), *Dar aba diima* (southwest), *Dar al-gharb* (west) and *Dar al-Takanyawi* (north). From its Arabic name, *Dar al-gharb* sounds like a later innovation; possibly it arose from the campaigns of Ahmad Bukr and his sons in the west (see Chapter Three). If so, and if *Dar al-gharb* never had much administrative reality, the four remaining provinces recall the quadrant provincial organisation of Kanem/Borno, as Arkell has pointed out;[43] but they may have been simply an inheritance from the Tunjur. These provinces remained the essential territorial units of Keira administration until they were overshadowed by the Maqdumate system in the nineteenth century.

Daali is also credited with the codification of the laws and customs of the Keira kingdom in the so-called *kitab* or *qanun daali* (there is a linguistic play here; *daali*, pl. *kalinta* means "tongue" in Fur). Sultanic law (a better description than customary law) evolved over time, but punishment was largely by fine, except in cases of death or injury, where forms of blood-compensation or *diyya* evolved.

41 See Arkell (1937), 91-105 and Wickens (1960), 147-51. These sites have been resurveyed and reevaluated in McGregor (2001), 91-7 whose account supersedes anything that I and others have written.

42 MacMichael (1926), 75-7.

43 Arkell (1952a), 131-5, but see Brenner (1973), 18-19.

Nachtigal explains the fines system as, "An effort to secure power and an income for the ruler and to bind the two more closely together".[44] In much of Darfur, fines were paid in livestock or rolls of cloth, *takkiyya*, the latter being in many parts of Darfur the main unit of payment throughout the life of the sultanate. Arkell collected several manuscripts purporting to be the *kitab daali* and concluded that Daali's code was an attempt to reconcile sultanic law with the Sharia according to the Maliki School, one of the four dominant Sunni schools that came to prevail, as it still does, in Darfur.[45]

Among the complex of ruins at Turra, *tong daali*, "Daali's house or palace" at Jabal Foga is a large, roughly circular structure, containing blocks of circular stone-built rooms. Nearby is *tong kuuri*, "the house of power or authority", the palace of Kuuruu, a successor of Dali usually described as the father of Sulayman, a large compound over a hundred yards in diameter with particularly massive walls. At Jabal Naami, the most conspicuous peak at Turra, is another, seemingly more complex compound associated with Sulayman and his son Musa. Arkell, who first described the Turra ruins, discerned a decline in the quality of building from the well-constructed *tong daali* to the clumsier but more massive *tong kuuri* and *tong kiilo*, the palace of Sulayman. He speculates that *tong daali* was the work of foreigners and the decline was due to civil war and upheaval in the time of Kuuruu and Sulayman.[46]

Whether this was the case or not, the traditions, as recorded by Nachtigal, say that there was after Daali a long period of conflict; ten kings are said to have followed him in rapid succession. Nachtigal interpreted what he was told to mean that Kuuruu did not actually rule at Turra, but whether he did or not, it was in his reign that a major split occurred among the Keira. Kuuruu quarrelled with his

---

44 Nachtigal (1971-87), iv, 277 & 369-70; he looked for but never found a copy of the *kitab daali*; a hundred years later in the same town, I did likewise but equally to no avail; see further Chapter Nine.

45 Arkell (1952a), 145-6; the manuscripts are in AP[1], 17; they seem to be garbled versions of the Maliki law compendium, the *Mukhtasar* of Khalil b. Ishaq. See further O'Fahey and Abu Salim (1983), 8-11.

46 Arkell (1937), 91-105; McGregor (2001), 91-6 is non-committal.

brother Tunsam over some land in Dar Fia, west of the mountains, and was forced to flee with his son, Sulayman, to Dar Masalit in the west. There Sulayman grew up among his mother's people, the Serbung section of the Masalit, until he was strong enough to wrest back Jabal Marra from his uncle. Tunsam and his followers fled east, to the border country between Darfur and Kordofan, emerging as a distinct ethnicity known to others as the Musabba'at in popular etymology, "the people of the east" (from *sabah*, "morning, east"), and to themselves as Basna or Baasanga (Fur "royal"). The Musabba'at never forgot their claim to Darfur and over the next hundred years or so were to be a constant thorn in the Keira's side (see Chapter Four).

Sulayman's predecessors, Daali, Kuuruu and others whose names appear in the regnal lists, and indeed Sulayman himself remain shadowy figures remembered in traditions first recorded some 200 years later. Nor can we disentangle them from the Tunjur; indeed, the civil war between Kuuruu and Tunsam may be linked to the collapse of the Tunjur empire. Until the palaces at Turra are excavated, we can only note that the traditions credit Daali with the establishment of the Keira state and are unanimous in regarding Sulayman, several generations later, as the second founder of that state.

Founding Fathers: Sulayman and Musa

Many of the seals of the Darfur sultans stamped upon their documents give a pedigree back to Sulayman; none go beyond him, Daali, Kuuruu etc. are consigned to oblivion. Sulayman Solungdungo, meaning "the Arab" or of "reddish complexion",[47] so-called either because of his complexion or because of his alleged descent from Ahmad al-Ma'qur, reigned probably between 1660 and 1680.[48]

---

47 Nachtigal (1971-87), iv, 277-9. In Fur in the 1970s, *solong* was used of the then piastre/*qirsh* coin, more bronze coloured than red.

48 We have no contemporary references. Browne (1806), 280 implies a date of roughly 1645-65; Cadalvène and Breuvery (1841), ii, 198 give 1100-13/1688-89—1701-2 (see O'Fahey (1973b), 35); Nachtigal (1971-87), iv, 274, 1596-1637; Shuqayr (1903), ii, 113-14 gives dates for two Sulaymans, 848-80/1444-45—1475-76, which seems too early on genealogical grounds, and 1106-26/1694-95—1714-15, which seems too late.

Although Fur tradition remembers little about Sulayman's deeds beyond vague generalities, it is clear that he and his two immediate successors, Musa and Ahmad Bukr, were responsible for the transformation of their Fur tribal kingdom into a multi-ethnic empire in succession to the Tunjur.

Sulayman is remembered as a warrior and conqueror; in one version he is said to have led thirty-three campaigns, conquering the Masalit, Orra or Qimr and Mararit to the west, the Zaghawa to the north and the Birged, Beigo and Tunjur to the south and east. The frontiers of his kingdom are said to have stretched as far north as the deserts where the Bideyat nomads lived and as far east as the Atbara River.[49] This is too sweeping to be likely and has no support from the Nile valley records. But the Fur do seem to have been raiding into Kordofan; a raiding party was captured by the Bani Jarrar Arabs there and taken to the *faqih* Hammad b. Umm Maryum (1055-1142/1646 —1729/30), who lived near the confluence of the two Niles. They were converted to Islam and sent back to their country, "probably to act as missionaries".[50]

The motive for Sulayman's conquests and raids was probably to increase his catchment area for the trade items, pre-eminently slaves, which he could barter with the merchants from Egypt and the riverain Sudan for arms and armour, war-horses from Dongola (much bigger than the local breeds) and fine cloth, with which to reward, arm and encourage his followers and chiefs. Evidence for this come from the notices of Vansleb and D'Albano described above.

The Keira kings of Jabal Marra were essentially divine kings on the common African model, as were the rulers of Sinnar and probably of Nubia before them. What is not known is whether the Keira took over any of the ritual and customs of divine kingship from the Tunjur or whether these rituals (described in Chapter Five) were part of their Fur heritage. The survival of such titles as *shartay* (Daju) and *takanyawi* (Fur, *togoing*, but almost certainly Tunjur in origin) suggest a pre-Keira layer. Divine kingship can be quickly learnt; the

---

49 Nachtigal (1971-87), iv, 279-80 and Shuqayr (1903), ii, 113-14.
50 Dayf Allah (1971), 180 and Hasan (1971), 82.

37

Feroge of the Western Bahr al-Ghazal, below Darfur, created in the nineteenth century a Keira-like state in imitation of the slave raiders from the north.[51] The Keira sultans never lost their divine aura, although it became transformed under the impact of Islam.

The traditions credit Sulayman with the introduction of Islam as the state cult, building mosques for his subjects—a practice that virtually all the later sultans continued—and encouraging Islamic practices. The traditional accounts are ambiguous on the religious affiliations of the Tunjur and the early Keira kings—they may have been pagan, although the Medinan document referring to Shaw Dorshid suggests otherwise—and some versions stress Sulayman's religious zeal:

He preached Islam in Jabal Marra and after several conversions, also converted *malik* Dukkume, chief of the Tomourki (Tumura or Tumurkwa; one of the three main Fur sections), whom he circumcised with a razor that he had brought from Cairo and which had to do for several thousand people.[52]

But the Islamisation of the Keira state was a slow process; pre-Islamic beliefs co-existed at the court with Islam and continued to be expressed in the state rituals throughout the history of the state, although some were discontinued as older beliefs came to be frowned upon. There was a gender divide as women maintained the old rituals (Ar. *awa'id*, Fur, *aadinga*) well into the twentieth century. As throughout the Sudanic Belt, the slow spread of Islam was the work of itinerant holy men. The relationship between holy man and ruler, as we shall see (Chapter Ten), was to be enshrined later in legal formulas, the granting of land, rights and tax immunities, and the building of mosques, but in the earlier period it was probably more informal.

Several holy families have traditions that their ancestors settled in the sultanate in Sulayman's time. One such is the Jawami'a *fuqara* family of Azagarfa, just north of al-Fashir, whose ancestor came from the east and was invited to settle in Darfur by Sulayman. Later they moved to Azagarfa where Sultan Muhammad al-Fadl (1215-

---

51 Santandrea (1957), 115-90; O'Fahey (1973a), 34 and O'Fahey (1982), 85.
52 Lauture (1855-56), 79.

45/1801-38) built them a mosque that still stands.[53] Near Azagarfa at Arari is another Jawam'ia family which traces its origins through twelve generations to one Ahmad, who was given land at Arari by Shaw Dorshid, the grant later being confirmed by Sulayman.[54] Another Jawami'a family whose ancestor came in the time of Sulayman or his son, Musa, were the *imam*s of Turra. Their ancestor, Idris, who came from Kordofan, was granted land at Turra as *imam* of the mosque with responsibility for the royal tombs there, and the position and land have been in the family ever since.[55]

Sulayman's position as the "founding father" of the Keira state is stressed not only in the oral traditions but on the seals of the later sultans, who invariably trace their descent back to him and no further; on one he is called "the pious and bountiful lord" (*sahib al-birr wa'l-ihsan*).[56] His son and successor, Musa (probable regnal dates c. 1680-1700), is a more shadowy figure. The confusion of the regnal lists at this point probably reflects a confused reign, while the paucity of traditions about Musa suggests a short one. Nachtigal records Musa fighting the Qimr in the west with little success and the Musabba'at under their chief, Janqal, with greater success, the latter being defeated at Tina and Kolge, the sites of his *fashir*s.[57] Like his father, Musa was buried at Turra.

---

53 PA. DP 66. B. 28, note by Keen, 17 November 1930.

54 PA DP. 66. k. 1/31, Arari Dinligia, note by Aglen, 22 June 1948. There are extensive ruins at Arari; on the area, see O'Fahey and Abu Salim (1983), 38.

55 MacMichael (1922), i, 198; ibid. (1926), 75-7 and McGregor (2001), 96, from the Arkell Papers.

56 On the seal of Sultan Ibrahim Qarad, reproduced in Shuqayr (1903), ii, 148.

57 Nachtigal (1971-87), iv, 280. Nachtigal appears to locate Tina south of Jabal Marra, but there is a Tina east of Jabal Marra near al-Tawila.

Diagram 1. THE KEIRA SULTANS

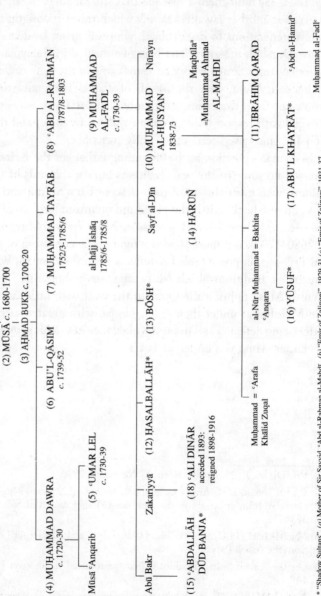

* "Shadow Sultans". (a) Mother of Sir Sayyid ʿAbd al-Raḥmān al-Mahdi. (b) "Emir of Zalingei", 1929-31 (c) "Emir of Zalingei", 1931-37

3
DOWN FROM THE MOUNTAINS: THE EXPANSION OF THE KEIRA STATE

The state as warband: the wars with Wadai

For a hundred years, from Sulayman's time to that of Tayrab, roughly 1680 to 1780, Darfur was a vigorous expansionist state, threatening its neighbours east and west. It was a dynastic state, whose dynasts fought as fiercely among themselves as they did against their neighbours. It was a state of warbands and warlords, increasingly bands of heavily armoured horsemen (*fursan*) backed by Fur tribal levies (*jurenga*) wielding the ferocious iron throwing-knife (*sambal*). What comes forth from our sources are dynasts of great vitality willing to war among themselves while pursuing war against the west and later the east.

The Wadai/Chad factor is as relevant to Darfur today as it was in the seventeenth and eighteenth centuries. Darfur looks westwards and eastwards simultaneously; however much influenced by the Nilotic Sudan, it has never really been part of the northern Sudan; it has a western dimension that was and is decisive. When the Keira state first moved away from the Marra Mountains, they moved westward; the history of the state between about 1700 and 1780 was of wars between Darfur and Wadai intermeshed with complex conflicts among the Keira themselves. When the Keira finally turned east-

41

ward, into Kordofan, it was in essence because Wadai was too strong to overcome.[1]

Al-Tunisi describes the title-holding structure of the state as a warband (see Chapter Six) and the sultans of the eighteenth century were essentially warlords.

Musa was succeeded by the youngest of his eight sons, Ahmad Bukr. It was intended that the eldest, Giggeri, should succeed, but on the day of his accession he had an epileptic seizure and since it was impossible for one "possessed by the devil" to accede, he was replaced by Bukr. In the latter's old age, Giggeri tried to regain the throne and Bukr was forced to seek refuge in Dar Kulli in the southwest, where he armed his slaves and returned to Turra to drive out and kill his brother.[2]

Bukr's reign marked a further stage in the growth of Islamic influence and a further wave of immigrant holy men from both east and west. From the east came Abzayd al-Shaykh 'Abd al-Qadir, a pupil of al-Zayn b. al-shaykh Sughayrun of the Awlad Jabir (d. 1086/1675-76), one of the most famous holy families of the Nilotic Sudan. Abzayd travelled in both Wadai and Darfur and died in the latter. From the west came 'Ali b. Yusuf al-Futawi from Futa Toro in Senegal, who passed through Darfur on the pilgrimage. He was induced to return by the promise of land, establishing a prolific and prominent holy lineage whose fortunes were to be closely intertwined with those of the sultans.[3] It was presumably one of these itinerant holy men who taught the Sultan to read, the first of his line to do so.

The kingdom's centre was still Jabal Marra and the lands to the west and southwest of the mountains. Bukr had *fashir*s at Gurri in

---

1   We lack a decent history of Wadai, which is a pity. There are sources in abundance, not least al-Tunisi and Nachtigal and much solid ethnography since. A well-constructed monograph is a desideratum. I was told in the 1970s that 'Ali Silek, then Sultan of Wadai, had a collection of Arabic materials.

2   Nachtigal (1971-87), iv, 281-82. Again, we have no certain dates. Cadalvène and Breuvery (1841), ii, 198 give 1128-41/1715-16–1728-29; Nachtigal, op.cit., 1682-1722 and Shuqayr (1903), ii, 115 1138-58/1725-26–1745-46.

3   On Abzayd, Dayf Allah (1971), 73 & 106; on the Awlad Jabir, Holt (1973), 88-103, and on al-Futawi and his family, my (1977b), 147-66.

Dar Kerne immediately west of the mountains, at Murra in Dar Fia, further to the north (Kerne and Fia are among the oldest of the present-day *shartaya*s or chieftaincies in Darfur), and at Abu 'Asal in the mountains, where a rectangular red-brick construction survives, the earliest example of the use of brick in Keira times.[4]

Both Darfur and Wadai had a common origin in a Tunjur past, a fact allegedly acknowledged by the latter paying tribute to the former.[5] But conflict over control over the borderlands soon came, when the third Wadai Sultan, Ya'qub 'Arus b. Kharut, refused to pay the tribute and invaded Darfur in Musa's time, reaching as far as Gurli (or Gerli), west of the mountains and just south of the Wadi Barei; dissension broke out in Ya'qub's army and the Wadaians retreated. In Bukr's time, Ya'qub tried again, reaching as far as Kabkabiyya at the entrance of the main pass through the mountains, giving out that he was going on the pilgrimage and demanding a Keira princess to comfort him on the journey. Bukr retreated to Abu 'Asal, imported firearms including a cannon from Egypt, and eventually crushed the Wadaians at Kabkabiyya, whose name in Fur—*kebi kebbia*, "they threw away their shields"—commemorates the defeat.[6] A species of peace followed during the reign of Bukr's son and successor, Muhammad Dawra.

But Darfur's weakness was always Wadai's opportunity, and opportunity came again in the reign of Dawra's son and successor in defiance of Awlad Bukr, 'Umar Lel "the donkey". The then Wadai Sultan offered to support Lel's uncles, the sons of Bukr, in an attempt to oust Lel; this misfired and Lel decided to invade Wadai in retaliation. 'Umar sent two armies ahead into Wadai, one under the title-holders the *aba diimang* and *aba uumang*, the other under the *aba konyunga*; one was successful, the other was defeated. The two sultans joined their armies and in the final battle Lel was deserted by his army and captured. He is said to have spent his captivity at Abu

---

4   Nachtigal (1971-87), iv, 280 and McGregor (2001), 95.
5   Nachtigal (1971-87), iv, 281 and Carbou (1912), ii, 112.
6   Nachtigal (1971-87), 209 & 281 and Barth (1857-59), ii, 644.

Kundi in the Jumbo district, "where he spent his days in reading the Quran and now lies buried there."[7]

War with Wadai became a backdrop to the internal conflicts among the Keira and the continual machinations of the Musabba'at. The "donkey's" successor was his uncle, Abu'l-Qasim, remembered as a strong ruler who sought to curb the Keira by recruiting slaves into the army and appointing non-Fur such as the Zaghawi Bahr as Wazir, which simply provoked the Keira and Fur. Again war with Wadai followed, with the Sultan levying a war-tax of one head of cattle per household, but in the crucial battle Abu'l-Qasim further insulted the Fur by putting them in the second rank behind his slave troops and the Wazir Bahr's men. Yet again, the Fur deserted their ruler, shouting,

Children of Fur, take to flight, for only flight can save us. Let the cows which he has taken from us and the Zaghawi, Bahr, fight for him.[8]

The Sultan was wounded and left for dead, the Fur only returning to the fight when they saw the sacred drum, *al-mansura*, in danger of being carried off by the Wadaians.

With Abu'l-Qasim removed from the scene, the Keira and the Fur lords chose his brother, Muhammad Tayrab, as Sultan. But Abu'l-Qasim was not dead, having been nursed back to life by an Arab from the Mahamid, who migrated as nomads between Darfur and Wadai (as they still do). When Abu'l-Qasim reappeared, Tayrab wanted to abdicate, but the title-holders opposed this and put the unwanted ruler to death. Abu'l-Qasim's death signalled an agreement between Tayrab and Sultan Jawda (r. 1747-95) of Wadai which consolidated the border between the two states for over a century, and turned Tayrab's attention to the east.

Wadai, with its ethnic Maba core, had proved too strong; the east, i.e. Kordofan, offered both easier pickings and an ongoing challenge in the form of the would-be dynasts, the Musabba'at.

---

7   Nachtigal (1971-87), iv, 210; Cadalvène and Breuvery (1841), ii, 206-7; Slatin (1896), 42; Carbou (912), ii, 112, but al-Tunisi (1965), 75 (55 & 73-4) and ibid., 83-4 says he was killed in the battle.

8   Nachtigal (1971-87), iv, 211-12 & 285-6 and Slatin (1896), 42.

The sons of Bukr and the oath

The wars with Wadai, in which one Sultan lost his life and another his liberty, were fought out against a background of bitter internal conflict within the Keira lineage; the result of the internal struggles and the wars abroad was the emergence, in the persons of Bukr and later his son Tayrab, of the sultan as the strongest institution within the state.[9] During these conflicts, roughly for the first sixty years of the eighteenth century, the old order of powerful Fur chiefs, strongly based on local loyalties, serving a sultan who was but *primus inter pares*, gave way to new institutions, a supratribal bureaucracy, maintained by grants of land and tax-rights, slave troops and increasing Islamisation, all centred on the sultan.

Bukr was the second father of the state; not only did the administrative structure begin to coalesce in his reign, all his successors descended from him. He had many sons and from them, the Sons of Bukr, came all the later branches of the Keira. A distinction developed, how and why is unclear, between the *baasinga*, who were elegible to succeed and those, the *tellanga*, who were not.[10] The reigns of the four successors of Bukr, Muhammad Dawra, 'Umar Lel, Abu'l-Qasim and Tayrab were all marked by conflicts among the sons of Bukr—in essence a struggle between those attempting to consolidate the Bukr lineage and regularise the succession brother-to-brother and those who, having acquired power as sultans, sought to turn against the Bukr lineage and consolidate power in their own line.

On his deathbed Bukr is said to have assembled the title-holders to swear that the succession would pass to each of his sons in turn, that no son of a son would succeed while an uncle still lived.[11] An echo

---

9 By sultan I mean the ruler and his immediate entourage, but here I do not discount the role of personality; it is clear that Bukr and Tayrab were very strong personalities. Here, if I can use analogy, my informants in the 1960s and 70s, in speaking of 'Ali Dinar, constantly emphasised his forcefulness, but in a very positive way.

10 SAD, P.J. Sandison's Papers.

11 Al-Tunisi (1965), 73 (55 & 112).

of this oath appears in an undated, but probably from about 1785, charter of Sultan 'Abd al-Rahman, issued shortly after the end of the civil war with Ishaq, in which the Sultan addresses "all the notables who will take charge of this kingdom after me from the offspring of my father the late Sultan Ahmad Bukr".[12] Over sixty years after his death, Bukr's wishes still resonated among the ruling elite.

Dawra (Fur, "iron-hearted") or Harut was co-opted as ruler or *khalifa* in his father's lifetime; we have two charters issued by Harut but stamped with Bukr's seal; they are the two earliest documents we have from Darfur and must date between 1700 and 1720. Dawra is remembered as a ruthless ruler who killed off many of the sons of Bukr. In violation of the oath to Bukr, Dawra named his son Musa 'Anqarib (Ar. "bed", why he was so called is not remembered) as his successor. Musa revolted when his father favoured another son, 'Umar Lel (Fur "the donkey", allegedly because of his patience); in the civil war that followed Musa defeated his father just north of al-Fashir. A mediation attempt by various holy men led the father to beat his son to death.[13]

Dawra had palaces at Mojalla (or Majalla) in Ro Kuuri in western Jabal Marra and at Komora at Terjil; he is said to have died at Mojalla of leprosy.[14]

Despite the oath to Bukr, 'Umar Lel did succeed his father, but the tension between the nephew and his uncles ensured that the former had a very fraught reign, a tension aggravated by the sultan's determination to rule as a good Muslim. Shuqayr provides a vivid fragment of tradition that highlights the Islamic dilemma:[15]

Three days after his accession, 'Umar went to his council of state and announced that he wished to abdicate in favour of one of his Bukr uncles. The council refused and he went into seclusion for a week; when he emerged he

---

12 O'Fahey (1992), 68-9.

13 Nachtigal (1971-87), iv, 282-3.

14 McGregor (2001), 95.

15 Lel is dated 1732-39 by Nachtigal (1971-87), iv, 283, and 1170-77/1756-57—1763-64 by Shuqayr (1903), ii, 115. Cadalvène and Breuvery (1841), ii, 199 give 1159-67/1746-47—1753-54 which seem the most probable. All the sources agree on a reign of about seven years.

carried horns, made of wood, resembling those of goats and cows. 'Umar told his followers that he wished peace and justice to prevail so that the goats of the weakest of the women among his subjects would be safe and their horns grow to the size of those he carried. Soon after he received complaints of oppression (Ar. *zulm*) against thirty leading chiefs; he had fifteen executed by the men's gate and fifteen by the women's gate of the *fashir*.

'Umar's position continued to be precarious as he faced challenges from the Musabba'at from Kordofan (see below 53); these he overcame, at least temporarily, but then he embarked on his disastrous invasion of Wadai.[16]

The Fur had come down from the mountains under a line of warrior sultans. In the course of expansion, the lineage chiefs, ritual experts and war leaders (Fur, *ornang*) had grown into a class of hereditary title-holders and the stakes for which they contended became much greater than before as land, men and women and booty fell into their hands. But as the state grew, the interests of the sultans and their tribal supporters and their chiefs began to diverge. To reap the profits of an expanding state, even to keep it together, the sultan needed to concentrate more and more power in his own hands, a process that could not fail to bring clashes with other interested parties. There were various ways in which the sultan could strengthen his position *vis-à-vis* the title-holders; he could recruit slave troops and officials, who would be free of clan or tribal loyalties, dependent upon the sultan alone for advancement; he could exercise a tight control over the trade of the state and he could seek to supplant tribal institutions and values by Islamic ones.

Alienation between between ruler and title-holders was not peculiar to Darfur; similar expedients were adopted by rulers throughout the central and eastern Sudanic region. The famous *mai* or ruler of sixteeenth-century Borno (Western Chad), Idris Alawma (1580-1617), attempted by appointing *qadi*s to wrest control of the administration of justice from the tribal leaders; indeed much of Borno's history is concerned with attempts of the *mai*s to centralise their state

---

16 McGregor (2001), 95 describes Lel's palace at Gogorma near the Wadi Jeldama west of the mountains.

at the expense of the title-holders.[17] In Darfur's imperial neighbour
to the east, Sinnar, the eighteenth-century ruler, Badi IV Abu Shu-
lukh (1136/1724–1175/1762), is described in the Funj Chronicle as
seizing the lands of the old title-holders and of making use of Nuba
slave troops and mercenaries such as the Musabba'at followers of
Khamis b. Janqal, a son of the second Musabba'awi ruler in Kordofan. Badi's innovations, in the context of a much weaker centre than
in Darfur, eventually led to a conservative reaction by the title-holders under Muhammad Abu Likaylik and the establishment of the
Hamaj Regency.[18]

This process of centralisation and the conflicts it engendered are
remembered in traditions recorded in the nineteenth century or later,
at a time when the state was an established institution with a capital
away from the mountains. Episodes like the story of 'Umar Lel above
and the death of Abu'l-Qasim below are fragmentarily reported and
are not contextualised. However, before the long, successful and thus
stabilising reign of Muhammad Tayrab, under 'Umar Lel and especially Abu'l-Qasim, the power struggles of the Sons of Bukr seem to
have weakened relations between the title-holders and the sultans,
forcing the latter to seek new bases for support, slaves and non-Fur
elements among them.

Between Lel and Abu'l-Qasim, the nature of the conflict changed
from a struggle within the Keira clan to a more general conflict
between the sultan and his title-holders. Abu'l-Qasim's attempt to
create a new power base led to his death. Nachtigal's account of the
strangling of the Sultan by 'Abd al-Qadir Wir with a cloth hints
at ritual regicide.[19] Abu'l-Qasim's sister, the *iiya baasi* (title of the

---

17 Cf. Urvoy (1949), 80-8; the process is well described in Cohen (1966), 87-
105.

18 Makhtuta (1961), 20-1.

19 This hint is reinforced by a remark in the diary of the Scottish explorer James
Bruice, writing in Sinnar, 1 August 1772, "It is at Darfour they put he king
to death, with two razors, in a seshe, or handkerchief. At Sennar he is killed
with a sword, by one of his own relations, the Gindi, or common executioner
of the town," Murray (1808), 425. Bruce's note suggests that news of the
killing of Abu'l Qasim had reached Sinnar and had been interpreted in line

senior royal sister) Zamzam Sendi Suttera, was also executed and her title was given to Korongo, the sister of the new Sultan, Muhammad Tayrab. The executioner, 'Abd al-Qadir Wir from Dar Tama, was given the office of *abbo daadinga* (Ar. *al-dadinjawi* or *al-dadinqawi*), which among other duties included responsibility for public executions; his descendants formed a line of notable generals and administrators until the end of the sultanate and beyond.[20]

Tayrab,[21] *Kordofan and the Musabba'at*

The reign of Muhammad Tayrab (c. 1758 to 1785) was arguably the most decisive in the sultanate's history, if only because the Sultan irrevocably realigned the state eastwards and, ultimately, into the orbit of the Nilotic Sudan. From about the middle of his reign, all the capitals of the sultanate were east of the Marra Mountains, open to the savannas of eastern Darfur and western Kordofan. By contrast to the western frontier lands between Darfur and Wadai—defined, if often disputed, by hills and riverbeds—the eastern savannas, interrupted only by the Nuba Mountains, stretched as far as the White Nile. Tayrab confronted the logic of this lack of a natural eastern frontier in his decision to invade Kordofan towards the end of his reign. Although the realignment eastwards may have been motivated to deal from the immediate threat of the Musabba'at from Kordofan, there were longer-term causes and consequences.

---

with Funj practice; there is no other evidence for ritual regicide in Darfur, see Hasan (1970), 32-47.

20 Nachtigal (1971-87), iv, 289.

21 From Tayrab's reign chronology becomes more certain; DF 166.18/26, a charter from Tayrab, has the seal-date 1172/1758-59 (the reading is uncertain; it may be 1173/1759-60). There is no certainty, taking into account other seals, that this is Tayrab's accession date, and Nachtigal's dates (iv, 287) of 1752-85 may well be correct since it seems almost certain that he died in 1200/1785-86. The accession date given by Cadalvène and Breuvery (1841), 199 1176/1762-63 is thus too late, and both dates given by Shuqayr (ii, 116), 1181-1202/1767-68—1787-88 appear to be wrong. Support for Nachtigal's dates comes from al-Tunisi (1967), 74 (56 & 113) who says that he reigned for 33 lunar years.

One cause was negative, the growing strength of Wadai which under its greatest Sultan, Muhammad Sabun (1804-15), captured much of the central Sudanic trade through the Fezzan to Tripoli. Relations between the two sultanates remained important throughout the nineteenth century, but the eastward realignment was not to be reversed, although Darfur always faced two ways, just as it does today. The eastward realignment had another long-term consequence, whose effect is still crucial: an internal bifurcation between Arabic and non-Arabic speakers east and west, in which the mountains marked a symbolic and real divide. The openness of eastern Darfur eastwards opened it to cultural and religious influences from the Nile Valley, a process speeded by Tayrab's incorporation of Kordofan into the sultanate.

The choice of Tayrab as Sultan presents something of a puzzle. One objection to Abu'l-Qasim had been his reliance on Bahr and the Zaghawa; Tayrab was half-Zaghawi, his mother, Kaltuma, coming from the ruling Angu clan of Zaghawa Kobe,[22] and he made even greater use of the Kobe Zaghawa. He made his maternal uncle, Kharut b. Hilan, Sultan of Kobe and gave him the *nahas* or copper drum as symbol of his authority. Two of Kharut's sons were given office; 'Umar was made *orrendulung*, majordomo of the *fashir* and the main intermediary between the sultan and his subjects, and Hasib *abbo irlingo*, whose honorary task was to place the turban on the sultan during the accession ceremonies, but who also ruled the Tunjur and Mima peoples of eastern Darfur.[23] The Zaghawa/Keira connection continued into the next generation and was to be a factor in the civil war between Tayrab's son and brother.

In the early years of his reign, Tayrab had his main *fashir* at Shoba near Kabkabiyya and Gurli (where Abu'l-Qasim had a palace) at the western end of the pass between Jabals Si and Marra; here he

22 SAD, P.J. Sandison's Papers. Kaltuma is buried at Sawla Jami' near Gorgor in Dar Kerne, where her descendants were living in the 1930s. 'Uthman (2006), 199 implies that Kaltuma was the mother of both Abu'l-Qasim and Tayrab, but gives no source.

23 Nachtigal (1971-87), iv, 287, "In all nineteen dignatories are said to have belonged to the Zoghawa tribe".

had built a magnificent redbrick palace complex and mosque and settled various Fur groups. But in his middle years, probably in the late 1760s, Tayrab moved east of the mountains and embarked on a series of campaigns that consolidated Keira control in the region.

The Birged, living in southeastern Darfur and nominally under the rule of the *abbo uumo*, are said to have rebelled because they thought Tayrab was selling as slaves the girls they sent him each year as concubines or servants. The Birged probably did not object to sending some of their daughters as such, since one could well become the mother of the next sultan to the advantage of her family and people, as was to be the case of Umm Buza, the Beigo and Sultan Muhammad al-Fadl. To suppress the revolt Tayrab moved his *fashir* to Ril in Dar Birged.[24]

The Birged had been organised into a series of petty chiefdoms, Musku, Adawa, Doleaba and Muhajiriyya, but these Tayrab began to suppress in favour of larger units under his own nominees at the expense of the original chiefly families. He is said to have given large tracts of Dar Birged as *hawakir* to a Kinani Arab from the Blue Nile, Sulayman b. Ahmad Jaffal, who won the Sultan's favour by his skill in the treatment of horses. I give here at length traditions about Sulayman and Tayrab and the construction of a new Dar Birged Kajjar (i.e. the southern Birged region) from two of Sulayman's descendants, which vividly illustrate the dynamism of Keira expansion in the east and the complexities of land and chieftaincy,[25]

Sulayman b. Ahmad Jaffal was a Kinani Arab who came from Sinja in the Blue Nile Province. He came to Darfur in the time of Muhammad Tayrab. He went to Shoba and was given the area around Marshing between Mana-washi and Jabal Marra as an *hakura*. On one occasion he was summoned by

---

24 Nachtigal (1971-87), iv, 289.

25 Namely *shartay* Muhammad Adam Ya'qub at Ghor Abeshei (26 June 1969) and his brother, a one-time Education Officer, Darfur Province, Sabil Adam Ya'qub (al-Fashir, 4.6.1970 and many other interviews). Sabil, in the 1960s and 70s, was without doubt the best informed local scholar on Darfur historical traditions, to whom I owe an immense debt and many pages of notes. His sons published recently some of his material posthumously as *al-Qaba'il fi Darfur* (Khartoum, 2005). Unfortunately I failed to obtain a copy, despite the resources of the UN mission to the Sudan.

Tayrab to treat some sick horses, since Sulayman was skilled in the treatment of horses. Tayrab was so pleased that he said, "I add to your *hakura* at
Marshing a place called Torba". Torba was just north of Malumm. When
Tayrab was preparing to attack Hashim al-Musabba'awi, he gave Sulayman
another part of Dar Birged; in order to do so, he dismissed the previous
Birged *shartay* of Shawnga, between Torba and Marshing. Sulayman fought
well in the campaign in Kordofan. Later after he returned from Kordofan, in
the time of Sultan 'Abd al-Rahman, other parts of Dar Birged were given to
him—Jabal Adawa and Kudmal and his southern boundary was said to have
stretched as far south as the Bahr al-'Arab.

From that time on all the *shartay*s of Dar Birged Kajjar have come from the
family of Sulayman b. Ahmad.

Tayrab brought two other peoples, the Beigo in the southeast and
the Berti around Mellit in the northeast, more firmly into the Keira
orbit.[26] The Berti have a long tradition of chieftainship and kingship
associated with the *Basanga* clan, going back to their "culture hero",
al-hajj Muhammad Yambar. But this early tradition of chieftainship
seems to have declined with the migration of successive Berti groups
away from the Tagabo Hills southeastwards to the area around Umm
Kiddada. In the north the line of Muhammad Yambar continued to
rule as they do to this day.[27]

In eastern Darfur various Berti *shartaya*s emerged, some descended
from two brothers, Muhammad Tamr and Hammad from Bagirmi,
who settled among the Berti on their way back from the pilgrimage. A son of Hammad, Musa Warak, was appointed *qadi* at Ril by
Tayrab, beginning a line of *qadi*s throughout the sultanate, while
other descendants became *shartay*s.[28]

From Ril Tayrab set out to bring the Rizayqat cattle nomads of
the far southeast to heel in a series of campaigns, but as the Sultan's
forces moved south, the nomads simply withdrew ever further south

---

26 Nachtigal (1971-87), iv, 287.

27 Holy (1974), 116-18.

28 AP1, 4, 16, 24-31, informant shartay Mahdi Sabil Abu Kuduk.

into the land of the Dinka. Tayrab had little success and such campaigns were probably more costly than they were worth.[29]

The consolidation of Keira rule east of the mountains and the
fact that there is no natural frontier between Kordofan and Darfur
seem in the early 1780s to have turned Tayrab towards the idea of
conquering Kordofan. He probably had two sets of motivations in
pursuing the idea, one linked to the perennial intra-Keira succession
conflict, the Sons of Bukr versus the desire of the ruling Sultan to
ensure the succession of his son, in this case his appointed successor, the *khalifa al-hajj* Ishaq, who was already ruling northern and
western Darfur on his father's behalf.[30] The outcome of this conflict
is discussed below (…). A second motivation was a determination
to deal with once and for all with a Keira bugbear since the early
eighteenth century, the Musabba'at.

The Musabba'at were in origin Keira adventurers who had been
cast out or had fled from the sultanate, and who based themselves
in the borderlands between Darfur and Kordofan.[31] Kordofan was
an ideal base since it was a no man's land which for most of the
eighteenth century was controlled by no one power, although Sinnar
had a varying suzerainty over the eastern area through its clients, the
Ghudiyat.[32] The inner core of the Musabba'at was formed by the
Basna clan; the name, probably from the same root as *baasi* in Fur,
meaning "royal", but came to be used loosely to describe their ad-
herents, Arab nomads, Nuba slave troops and traders from the Nile
Valley, and eventually the Musabba'at "became" a tribal designation

---

29 Nachtigal (1971-87), iv, 288 and Slatin (1896), 46.

30 Two documents illuminate this; DF 154.18/14, a confirmatory charter from
    alsultan al-khalifa al-hajj Ishaq (seal-date 1193/1779-80) for the Awlad Jabir
    faqihs of the Zayyadiyya. The second is a court hearing from Khiriban just
    north of al-Fashir (DF 100.12.8 (undated [O'Fahey & Abu Salim (1983,
    54-56]) that refers to an earlier judgment given by Ishaq.

31 On whom see my (1973b), 32-42; O'Fahey and Abu Shouk (1999), 49-64,
    and O'Fahey and Spaulding (1972), 316-33.

32 On the geopolitical and economic place of Kordofan within eastern Sudanic
    Africa, see Stiansen and Kevane (1998), 1-45.

for a group of communities stretching from Darfur to Kassala in the eastern Sudan.

The Musabba'at sultans had two strategies that they pursued for nearly two hundred years through three generations, grandfather Janqal, father 'Isawi and son Hashim. The first was engagement in Keira dynastic politics in Darfur; the details need not concern us here but they ended in about 1753 when Abu'l-Qasim crushed decisively an attempt by 'Isawi to intervene in Darfur's dynastic politics. It was 'Isawi's son Hashim who, through a career that lasted from 1770 to 1800, attempted a second strategy, namely to create a state in central and eastern Kordofan that would rival or possibly supplant Darfur and Sinnar. The fascination of Hashim's career is that we have in effect a series of snapshots of a savanna knight (Ar. *faris*) using a motley crew of condottieri tirelessly over thirty years to attempt to create his state: state formation not shrouded in myth and legend, but in nearly full daylight.[33]

Hashim seems to have had an advantage over his father and grandfather; he had spent his youth in Darfur and may well have been a cousin of Tayrab.[34] He began his remarkable career by securing a base in the Kaja/Katul mountains at the northern end of the putative Darfur/Kordofan frontier and at the southern end of the Wadi al-Malik leading to the Nile above Dongola, where he secured his position by sinking wells (Ar. *saniya*) through the rock. Hashim

---

33 O'Fahey & Spaulding (1972), 316-33 explores Hashim's career in detail. A vivid contemporary account of a battle between Hashim and the Funj survives in which the writer gives the casualties, giving thanks that so many of the horses had survived; see O'Fahey and Spaulding (1980), 42-6.

34 'Awad Hamid Jabr al-Dar, son of the last titular Sultan of the Musabba'at in Kordofan (Khartoum North, 30.8.1969) noted that Hashim and Tayrab were cousins since their mothers were sisters, daughters of the Sultan of the Mima, a small non-Arab tribe living around Wada'a south of al-Fashir on the road to Nyala. This contradicts other sources saying that Tayrab's mother was a Zaghawa lady, Kaltuma, from Kobe. The tradition would make better sense, in that chronologically Tayrab seems to belong to an older generation than Hashim, if one of Tayrab's wives was a daughter of the Mima Sultan, the sister of Hashim's mother. The Keira link, kinship and residence in Darfur, undoubtedly gave Hashim an insider's understanding of the politics of the sultanate.

was soon well placed to exploit the weakness of the Funj and the tension between Tayrab and the Sons of Bukr. But first Hashim looked eastwards; in 1772, possibly with help from Tayrab, he occupied al-Ubayyid, driving out the Funj who were too weak to resist.[35] For the next eight years Hashim controlled central Kordofan, but in 1780 the Funj under the Wazir Rajab b. Muhammad drove him out and he again sought refuge in Kaja/Katul.[36]

Hashim now turned his attention westwards, sending his followers raiding into eastern Darfur and reaching on one occasion as far west as Ril itself. His followers included Danaqla (sing. Dunqulawi, from Dongola), Shaiqiyya (from the Nile Valley), Kababish (nomads from northern Kordofan) and Rizayqat. It was a war of raid and counter-raid where the advantage lay largely with the Musabba'at, who were more mobile.[37]

Tayrab, who was elderly, had had enough; he could best solve the internal problem of the Sons of Bukr and the securing of his son's succession and the external problem of Hashim by simply invading Kordofan, so he assembled the warband, taking care to take with him the Sons of Bukr, the leading title-holders, and the royal women. Hashim made no attempt to resist, but fled to his Shaiqiyya allies on the Nile.

Two succession crises and two wars

Tayrab is said to have reached the Nile near Shendi and Kordofan was firmly incorporated into the sultanate, which was to rule the region for nearly forty years.[38] Darfur plus Kordofan, an area larger

---

35 Murray (1808), 425 from Bruce's diary for 1 August 1772. Bruce mentions neither Hashim nor the Musabba'at but says the army advanced from Ril; see also Cadalvène and Breuvery (1841), ii, 209.

36 Makhtuta, 31.

37 Al-Tunisi (1965), 84 (97 & 128-9); Nachtigal (1971-87), iv, 288 and 'Awad Hamid Jabr al-Dar (30.8.1969).

38 Shuqayr (1903), ii, 120 says that Tayrab fought allies of the Funj near Omdurman; Slatin (1896), 46. See also Spaulding in Stiansen and Kevane (1998), 46-59.

than modern Nigeria, thus became the largest pre-modern state created within what is now the Sudan.

But like Alexander the Great's men Tayrab's soldiers were tired of
conquest and wanted to go home. The host withdrew to Bara, north
of al-Ubayyid, where Tayrab died, leaving the great ones of the states
to confront a succession crisis far from home.

Apparently, Tayrab on reaching Bara knew he was dying; realising
this he wrote to his son, *al-hajj* Ishaq, telling him to come immediately to Kordofan, leaving his son, Khalil b. Ishaq, in charge of
Darfur.[39]

But the news that Tayrab was dying began to be known in the
camp and factions were fast forming. Muhammad Kurra, a eunuch
and thus able to visit the *harim*, discussed the situation with the *iiya
baasi* Kinana. Kinana wanted her son, Habib b. Tayrab, as sultan,
but Kurra pointed out the problem of the Awlad Ahmad Bukr and
seems to have implied that 'Abd al-Rahman b. Ahmad Bukr was a
more viable candidate.[40]

Besides being a son of the great Sultan, 'Abd al-Rahman had other
qualifications; nicknamed *al-yatim* "the orphan", he was poor, lived in
obscurity and had no children.[41] For the elite of the day, these were attractive qualities to have in a new sultan since he would be in a weaker
position to establish new lineages to compete with the old. Kurra thus
approached 'Abd al-Rahman with a plan. In exchange for Kurra and
Kinana's support, 'Abd al-Rahman agreed to give the eunuch the title
abbo shaykh daali, the most powerful slave title in the hierarchy.

Meanwhile Tayrab, who was slowly sinking, called together the
leading title-holders, among them 'Ali b. Jami', Kurra's owner or patron, Hasab Allah Jiran, a military leader, Ibrahim b. Ramad, head of
the Fur Konyunga clan,[42] the *abbo shaykh daali* 'Abd Allah Juta, and

---

39 Al-Tunisi (1965), 93 (76 & 142) and Nachtigal (1971-87), iv, 377-8.
40 Al-Tunisi (1965), 94, *li'annahu huwa sahib al-dawla ba'd al-sultan Tayrab*,
translated by Perron as "Car à lui reviendra l'empire après le Sultan
Tayrab".
41 Al-Tunisi (1965), 94 (77 & 144).
42 On which see Adelberger (1990), 163-4.

an unnamed *amin*. To each, the sultan gave a task; to 'Ali b. Jami', to take the army back to Darfur and hand it over to Ishaq; to Hasab Allah to take charge of the camels and livestock; to the *abbo shaykh daali* to take charge of the royal family, especially the women, while the unnamed *amin* was entrusted with the weapons and clothes. The assembled title-holders, all of whom except 'Abd Allah Juta were sons-in-law of the Sultan, swore to obey Tayrab's wishes and wept to see him dying. Tayrab, perhaps the greatest of the Keira sultans, then died.[43]

Kinana gave Kurra the dead Sultan's rosary, handkerchief, seal and amulet to take to 'Abd al-Rahman as proof of Tayrab's death. The Sultan's body was then embalmed in preparation for its journey back to Darfur to be buried in the royal cemetery at Turra in Jabal Marra. But 'Abd al-Rahman was still unsure of his position and took the Sultan's possessions to his elder brother, Riz, who appears to have been the head of the Awlad Bukr. When the Sultan's death was announced, they went, with their brothers Rifa and Tahir, to the royal encampment.[44]

Once the death was made public, the dynamics of the crisis changed. The title-holders seem to have doubted that they could carry out Tayrab's wishes in the face of opposition from the Awlad Bukr. But 'Ali b. Jami' was determined to try and ordered Kurra to tell the former's son, Muhammad Dokkumi b. 'Ali, to assemble the army before the royal encampment. But Kurra subverted his master's plans by telling the son that his father wanted the soldiers assembled outside the encampment of the Awlad Bukr. He then returned to the father and told him that this was what his son had done. To the father this was the final betrayal and he is said to have committed suicide by taking poison in disgust. With the death of 'Ali b. Jami', the other title-holders gave up, each returning to his own command.

The crisis had now evolved into a new phase and within the camp all was tense. There were three factions. First, there were the rank and file who simply wanted to get back to Darfur as speedily as pos-

---

43 Al-Tunisi (1965), 95 (79 & 145).
44 Al-Tunisi (1965), 96 (83 & 146).

sible; this faction probably included many of the title-holders, whose positions were in some sense in suspense until a new sultan emerged. There were two factions among the Keira, the Awlad Bukr, and their nephews, the other "sons of the sultans", namely the sons of Tayrab, 'Umar Lel, Muhammad Dawra and Abu'l-Qasim. And back in Darfur was Ishaq, also of the generation after Ahmad Bukr.

There now followed an intervention by the *fuqara* and *'ulama* in their characteristic role as mediators. Some of the title-holders, to solve the deadlock, asked them to go to the Awlad Bukr and ask them to choose one of their number as the next sultan.[45] The Awlad Bukr nominated Riz, as apparently being the eldest, but for reasons not given by al-Tunisi both the "sons of the sultans" and the army rejected him.

The next nominee, Tahir, was rejected because he had too many children.[46] In the end "the orphan", 'Abd al-Rahman, was accepted by the title-holders and the army as the next sultan. But he had still win Darfur from *al-hajj* Ishaq.

The crisis in Bara had ended in a reaffirmation of the primacy of the Awlad Bukr; the civil war that followed was in effect between two generations, that of Ahmad Bukr and that of Tayrab.[47]

The civil war that followed was fought through Kordofan and Darfur and lasted some three years. In some respects it was a war between Fur and Zaghawa. Bukr had married a daughter of Hilan, the fourth ruler of Dar Kobe from the Angu clan; her son, Tayrab, in turn married a daughter of Kharut, a son of Hilan and ninth ruler of Kobe. *Al-hajj* Ishaq was a result of the last union; in other words he was three-quarters Zaghawi.[48]

---

45 Here I follow al-Tunisi (1965) 98 (84 & 144). There is a variant version in Shuqayr (1903), iii, 452-3, but it does not differ much in substance.

46 Nachtigal (1971-87), iv, 289 emphasises this argument from his informant, a grandson of Tahir b. Bukr.

47 On the civil war, see al-Tunisi (1965), 101-11 (89-100 & 156-72); Nachtigal (1971-87), iv, 290-2; Shuqayr (1903), iii, 453 and 'Uthman (2006), 201-11.

48 Tubiana (1965), 27.

Upon his accession, 'Abd al-Rahman received the allegiance of the title-holders and gave away much of the treasury and many of the women of his dead brother.[49] Once he had secured his position in Bara, the new Sultan started back to Darfur, pausing only at al-Ubayyid, where he left a governor for the newly-acquired province, and near the Nuba Mountains where he forcibly recruited Nuba into his army. He then passed, travelling in a southwesterly direction, through the territory of the Misiriyya and Rizayqat. Their shaykhs agreed to supply men to fight against Ishaq in exchange for any booty they could seize.

'Abd al-Rahman attempted to avoid war by writing to his nephew offering to recognise him as *khalifa* in exchange for his allegiance. Ishaq rejected the proposal. The war that followed was fought in eastern Darfur from south to north. The first battle was at Tabaldi-yya, northeast of Nyala, between 'Abd al-Rahman's forces and those of Ishaq under the command of *al-hajj* Muftah; the latter was defeated.[50] Ishaq collected another army and met the Sultan at Taldawa, near Tayrab's old *fashir* at Ril. During the battle, Ishaq's main commander, the *abbo jabbay* Bahr, deserted to 'Abd al-Rahman and Ishaq's men broke and fled. Ishaq retreated northwards, defeating on the Wadi Bowa, just north of Kutum, an army sent against him under the *takanawi* Tumsah. In a final battle fought near Jarku (possibly Jarkul near Mellit), Ishaq was defeated, dying of his wounds a few days later. 'Abd a-Rahman was now undisputed Sultan.

There was no precise or automatic rule of succession.[51] All sons of previous sultans were more or less eligible, depending on their age, resources and what support they could muster. As we have seen

---

49 On the latter practice, see my (1992), 57-93.

50 Al-Tunisi (1965), 104-6 (92-3 & 157-62) says that the battle was won by the skilful use of the *safarog*, the wooden throwing stick, by 'Abd al-Rahman's men. Although widely used, the *safarog* is above all the weapon of the Fur.

51 This is true of most Sudanic, indeed of most African states; thus in Borno, "The basic criterion for succession was (and is) the kingly status of one's own father. In practice, the status of the mother's family and her personal character also helped, but the good opinion of the court was absolutely necessary", Cohen (1966), 97.

a reigning sultan could try and perpetuate the rule within his own lineage by pre-mortem appointment of one of his sons as *khalifa*, but from 'Abd al-Rahman's reign on until the end of the first sultanate in 1874, power was so concentrated in al-Fashir that father to son succession became the norm; however, the transition was never automatic or uncontested, as the succession from 'Abd al-Rahman to his son Muhammad al-Fadl shows.

Towards the end of his life 'Abd al-Rahman began to plan the transfer of power to Muhammad al-Fadl, with Kurra as the instrument of his will.[52] Indeed, to help Kurra carry out his wishes the Sultan is said to have had the *abbo shaykh daali*'s mortal enemy, the Wazir Muhammad Dokkumi b. 'Ali, imprisoned in Jabal Marra. Upon the death of the Sultan, Kurra went to Muhammad al-Fadl, who as a boy of about fourteen was still living in the *harim*, and gave him the dead Sultan's regalia. The young Sultan was then brought out and shown to the title-holders within the grounds of the *fashir*, all swore allegiance, although the aged *malik al-nahas*, Ibrahim b. Ramad, disapproved of the choice. This showing of the new Sultan was carefully stage-managed by Kurra, who lavished bribes of estates, dollars and war horses and armour on the waverers.

But the "sons of the sultans" were unappeased and retired to their estates to plot and plan. After some delay they came together and led their forces to al-Fashir. Kurra sent an army under the Keira warlord, Muhammad Daldang w. Binayya, who easily crushed them. Sixty of the princes were publicly executed in a field just outside al-Fashir called thereafter *qoz al-sittin*, "the field of the sixty". This blood-letting marked the end of the old-style opposition of *awlad al-salatin*; the accession of Muhammad al-Fadl was secured and Kurra's position seemed unassailable.

Shuqayr records a tradition of the new Sultan that illustrates the advantages of marrying into the Keira; one of the first acts of Mu-

---

52 The main sources are al-Tunisi (1965) 129-31 & 324 (122-5, 350, 200-4 & 461-3) (al-Tunisi arrived, as a young teenager, in Darfur only four years later); Nachtigal (1971-87) iv, 298-300; Slatin (1896), 44-5 and Shuqayr (1903), iii, 455. No reason is given for the choice of Muhammad al-Fadl, but the influence of his mother, Umm Buza, may have played a part.

hammad al-Fadl was to free his mother's tribe, the Beigo, from all obligation to provide slaves and indeed forbade anyone to enslave them. He also gave his maternal uncle, Fazari, extensive estates.[53]

The next four years (1215/1800-1 to 1219/1804-5) saw the complete ascendancy of Kurra. The Sultan was too young to resist, while the opposition were cowed. But gradually an opposition group began to coalesce around the Sultan, who increasingly resented his slave's power. Meanwhile Kurra continued to rule Darfur autocratically, allegedly taking stern action to suppress corruption—what is meant is unstated; Nachtigal records that he was called *jabir al-dar*, "tyrant of the land", and was honoured as if he were the sultan,

The people fell back at a distance from his path, and squatted on one side, brushing the ground with the palm of their hands.[54]

Matters came to a head in about Rajab 1219/October-November 1804, when the breach between the young Sultan and Kurra came out into the open. Shuqayr records an anecdote on what triggered it; at a banquet Kurra became very drunk and invited the Sultan with a pun on the ruler's name, *al-fadl ma'ana* "Please [stay] with us", that is to eat with him, a drastic breach of the etiquette surrounding a Keira sultan who never ate in public.[55] The battle lines were now clearly drawn.

Both factions were now located on different sides of *rahad* Tandalti in the centre of al-Fashir, with Kurra's men on the northern side. Al-Tunisi reports that at this point Kurra was considering replacing the Sultan with Kurra's brother, 'Awad Allah.[56] If this report is true, Kurra was proposing a dynastic change for the first and only time in the sultanate's history.

---

53 Shuqayr (1903), iii, 455.

54 Nachtigal (1971-87), iv, 299.

55 Shuqayr (1903), iii, 455. Nachtigal (1971-87), iv, 300 has another version of the split; 'Abd al-Rahman had left a letter with one of his wives to be given to his son after three years, warning him to get rid of Kurra. The letter fell into Kurra's hands, but he nevertheless passed it on to the Sultan.

56 Al-Tunisi (1965), 69 (81 & 106). Although al-Tunisi was in Darfur at the time, he may have misunderstood or misremembered the episode. See the next fn.

To force a decision, the Sultan ordered his supporters to prevent Kurra's men from drawing water from the *rahad*. For three days Kurra drew his water from Jadid al-Sayl, just northeast of al-Fashir, but he was finally forced to withdraw to Jadid al-Sayl, only to find his way blocked by a contingent of the Sultan's men under Muhammad Daldang. In the ensuing battle Daldang was killed, and in a second battle the Sultan's forces were again defeated. Alarmed, Muhammad al-Fadl fled to Jadid al-Sayl.

But Kurra's brother, 'Awad Allah, had been killed in the fighting and his position was precarious. To rally support, Kurra proclaimed *baasi* Tahir b. Bukr as Sultan.[57] Despite this attempt to rally the partisans of the Awlad Bukr to his side, during the night many of Kurra's supporters slipped away, aided by a miraculous beating of the sacred drum, *al-mansura*. The following day, in a desperate battle, Kurra and his adopted son, Shaylfut, were defeated and killed, the victorious commander being the Baqirmawi, Ahmad Jurab al-Fil.[58] Kurra's death came in Rajab 1219-October/November 1804.

Muhammad al-Fadl was now firmly on the throne and an era of two long reigns began.

---

57 Cadalvène and Breuvery (1841), ii, 214 (O'Fahey (1973b), 41-2). It is thus probable that al-Tunisi misunderstood 'Awad Allah's role; he may have been Kurra's commander with *baasi* Tahir as the sultanic candidate from the beginning.

58 Al-Tunisi (1965), 71 (53 & 108-10); Nachtigal (1971-87), iv, 300; Slatin (1896), 45 and Shuqayr (1903), iii, 457-8.

4

STABILITY AND STAGNATION: NINETEENTH-CENTURY DARFUR

The founding of al-Fashir

Despite his victory over Ishaq, 'Abd al-Rahman's position in the early years of his reign appears to have been fragile. He had been chosen as sultan for largely negative reasons and did not command a party of his own. This he set out to remedy. His close friend, the Fulani, Maliki al-Futawi, was made Wazir, made guardian over the nomadic Fulani, and granted extensive estates around al-Fashir, particularly to the south at Kerio.[1] Muhammad Dokkumi, son of Tayrab's Wazir, the faithful 'Ali b. Jami', was also made Wazir. The head of the tax collectors, the *abu'l-jabbayyin* Bahr, despite his services in the civil war, was executed and replaced by the Musabba'awi, Ahmad Tumbukei, who received both the title and the area southwest of al-Fashir between al-Tawila and Tarni as an estate. Both the lineages of Maliki and of Tumbukei still owned the estates in the 1970s.[2]

The new Sultan, about fifty or sixty when he became ruler, had spent most of his life as a *faqih*. Not surprisingly his reign was marked

---

1   On the history of Maliki and his lineage, the Awlad 'Ali, see my (1977b), 147-66.

2   Nachtigal (1971-87), iv, 294; PA majlis DP.FD. 66..K.1.5 Fasher District, Tawila Omodia, G.E. Moore, note 13 February 1933, and shartay Hasab Allah Abu'l-Bashar (Tarni, 9.4.1974). Some documents concerning the Tarni estate are published in my (1990 & 1991), 71-83 & 79-112.

by definite impetus towards the Islamisation of the state. No longer was the coexistence of Fur and Islamic custom and law so easily accepted. While still in Kordofan he abolished, on the grounds that it had no sanction in Islam, the week's seclusion that inaugurated the accession rituals (see Chapter Five). Less successful was his attempt in 1793 to prohibit the drinking of *marisa* or millet beer, which was and is widely drunk in Darfur. *Marisa* continued to be drunk, even, it was said, in the Sultan's *harim*.[3]

Just as the earlier wars of Sulayman and Bukr had taken them and their *fashir*s down to the lower western slopes of Jabal Marra, so the campaigns of 'Umar Lel against the Musabba'at, but especially those of Tayrab in eastern Darfur and Kordofan, had moved the centre of gravity of the state east of the mountains. This move took the sultans away from the Fur heartlands, and if it did not directly weaken their links with the Fur, it made the former more open to new impulses, to traders and holy men from the Nile Valley and to the first European visitors and contacts. It led to a strengthening of the Islamic elements within the state and remotely involved Darfur in the culture of the northern riverain Sudan. This change should not be exaggerated; the links between the court and the Fur lie outside the historical record, if only because they were conducted in Fur. The Keira sultans remained Fur and Fur-speaking until 'Ali Dinar's death in 1916, but the move to the east does mark a definite reorientation in the cultural and economic life of the sultanate. The older elements re-emerged when the sultans took refuge in the mountains with the Fur there, the people least affected by Islamisation and Arabicisation within the state, after the invasion of al-Zubayr in 1874.

This reorientation was consolidated when 'Abd al-Rahman moved his *fashir* to Rahad Tandalti, east of Jabal Marra, on the margins of the savanna and semi-desert, in about 1206/1791-92.[4]

The Tandalti region was well chosen; it lay near the main west-east route as it came out of the Kawra pass through the mountains,

---

3   Browne (1806), 291; al-Tunisi (1965), 115 (103 & 176); Felkin (1884-85), 218, and Shuqayr (1903), ii, 138-9.

4   Al-Tunisi (1965), 114 (103 & 176).

just as Kabkabiyya and Shoba lay near the western end of the pass. The *rahad*, still the heart of the town—its causeway is still today a favourite place for an evening's promenade—provided water. It was a day away to the southeast from Kobbei (Ar. Kubayh), the growing trade entrepot at the Darfur end of the Forty Days Road; yet it was not too far north for the court to be supplied from the rainfed agriculture of the area or from the sultan's estates in Jabal Marra and Dar Fongoro.

Before 'Abd al-Rahman moved there, Tandalti had been the capital of the northern province, *Dar al-rih*, and its ruler, the *takanawi*. With the move of the Sultan to Tandalti, which became known as al-Fashir, "the *fashir*", the *takanawi* moved northwards to near Kutum.[5]

After the defeat of Ishaq, 'Abd al-Rahman at first stayed at Gurli (Gerli) southwest of Kabkabiyya, before the move to Tandalti. Al-Fashir was destined to be the capital under the sultans, the British and the independent Sudan until 1994, when Darfur was divided, and it has continued as the capital of North Darfur State. Although 'Abd al-Rahman moved around, as the century wore on, the sultans became much more sedentary.[6]

Kordofan

Whether Tayrab's invasion of Kordofan was intended by the Sultan as an extended raid or a permanent conquest, 'Abd al-Rahman was determined on the latter and left behind a garrison and a governor before marching west to fight Ishaq. Predictably, Hashim returned, driving out the garrison and setting himself once more as ruler of central Kordofan. 'Abd al-Rahman was determined to retain Kordofan and sent Kurra to expel Hashim.

Kurra (Fur, "Tall") was from about 1200/1785-86 until his death in 1804 the most powerful man in Darfur after the sultan, as we

---

5   AP1, 3, 13, 47 informant, Ahmad Adam al-Kinani and PA majlis DP.FD.66. K.15 Azagarfa Omodia, note Bredin 22 February 1931.

6   Browne (1806), 239 says that during his stay (1793-96) he saw the Sultan first at al-Hajlij, then at Tina and then at Tandalti, but all are near or in al-Fashir.

have seen (above Chapter Three). His origins are disputed; he is variously described as slave or freeman.[7] In Tayrab's time he entered the *korkwa* or palace guards; from the *korkwa* he moved to the *soming dogala*, "children of the palace", probably as an official rather than a simple page. Kurra was accused of interfering with one of the Sultan's concubines and to avert his master's wrath castrated himself. Despite this drastic demonstration of innocence, the Sultan gave him to the Wazir 'Ali b. Jami', who later made him head of his household's *soming dogala*. Sometime after he was given the high rank of *malik al-korayat*, "master of the royal grooms".[8] As such he accompanied his master to Kordofan, where, as we have seen, he was instrumental in securing the sultanate for 'Abd al-Rahman even at the cost of his master's death. With the defeat of Ishaq, 'Abd al-Rahman appointed Kurra as *ab shaykh daali*, head of the slave hierarchy and ruler of *Dar Daali*, now a much expanded eastern Darfur because of Tayrab's campaigns. Kurra established himself at Abu'l-Judul (Umm Judul on the maps), southeast of al-Fashir.

The sultanate's innate conservatism shows itself in how 'Abd al-Rahman dealt with his new acquisition. It was not constituted separately but was rather treated as an extension of the northern, *Dar al-rih*, and eastern, *Dar Daali*, provinces, which were now regarded as stretching as far as the Nile.[9]

In about 1206/1791-92 Kurra marched east with two hundred heavy cavalry, the tanks of Sudanic warfare, and met and defeated Hashim at Umm Jinayhat near Bara. Once more Hashim fled northwards to his Shaiqiyya allies on the Nile.[10] Kurra was joined by Ib-

---

7 Al-Tunisi (1965), 63 (45 & 96) denies the story that Kurra was born of a palace slave and says he was born free; al-Tunisi, as a teenager, had met Kurra just before his death. Nachtigal (1971-87), iv, 294 says he was from the Tunjur; Abu Adam 'Abdallahi (Nyala, 29.6.1969) called him a Tarjawi (pl. Turuj) from a Nuba slave group settled in eastern Darfur by Tayrab.

8 Al-Tunisi (1965), 80-3 (63-6 & 122-7).

9 PA majlis DP.FD. 66.K.15 Azagarfa Omodia, note Bredin 22 February 1931, and majlis DP.FD. 66.K.I.12 Turra Dimligia, note, Lomax 13 January 1934.

10 Al-Tunisi (1965), 128 (120 & 199) and Cadalvène and Breuvery (1841), ii, 211.

rahim b. Ramad and the two attacked the Bani Jarrar nomads, who were among Hashim's staunchest supporters. Ibrahim—"the son of ashes", an allusion to his illegitimacy—was a powerful figure; he was *abbo Konyunga*, head of the Konyunga clan, and *malik al-nahas,* "master of the drums".[11] Ibrahim was probably sent to keep an eye on Kurra.

Kurra and Ibrahim, and later Musallim, governed Kordofan wisely, reconciling the interests of the Danaqla and Ja'aliyyin traders of Bara, al-Ubayyid and elsewhere with those of the Keira state. Estates were granted or confirmed; the Awlad Najm, a section of the Shuwayhat in northeastern Kordofan, had their rights to land they had "opened up " (*ihya al-mawat*) confirmed—interestingly, the charters note that the land had been used for hunting before being settled—while some Kinana Arabs living near Jabal Taqali had their privileged status (*jah*) first granted them by the rulers of Taqali confirmed by Musallim.[12] The rule of Darfur in Kordofan was to be favourably remembered and contrasted with the harshness of the Turco-Egyptians some thirty years later.[13]

Hashim had not given up; in the summer of 1794 Browne saw five provincial officials executed for being in treasonable correspondence with Hashim. The following year, the English traveller watched a parade of troops to be sent as reinforcements to Kordofan, where over half the garrison had died from smallpox. During the parade spoils, including slaves and livestock taken from Hashim, were displayed.[14]

Ibrahim was recalled and replaced by Musallim (*recte* Musallam, but Musallim in Darfur sources), a slave eunuch like Kurra. Yet again Hashim made an appearance; yet again he was driven out. Some

---

11 Browne (1806), 203-4; Nachtigal (1971-87), iv, 299-300, and Sabil Adam Ya'qub (al-Fashir, 4.6.1970).

12 On the Awlad Najm, see my (1986), 43-63 and on the Kinana my (1997), 347, n. 52. The latter charter was photographed in Taqali by Dr Janet Ewald; we disagree on its authenticity. She considers it to be a twentieth-century forgery; I, on internal evidence, do not. Some of the Kinana charters are published in Dawra (1994), 106-8.

13 Cuny (1863), 177; Pallme (1844), 14 and Lejean (1862), 854-82.

14 Browne (1806), 223 and 228.

time after 1796, a rift developed between Kurra and his master; Muhammad Dokkumi, a bitter enemy of Kurra whom he blamed for his father's suicide, was sent to bring the eunuch back. Kurra cleared his name, but never returned to Kordofan, which was jointly ruled by Muhammad Dokkumi and Musallim.[15]

In the tense period surrounding the accession of Muhammad al-Fadl and the killing of Kurra, the indefatigable Hashim, now growing old, sent his youngest and presumably most expendable son to Musallim to petition the sultan to allow him to end his days in peace in Kordofan. He was rebuffed, and is said to have made a last desperate appeal to the supporters of the Musabba'at cause to rally to him; 12,000 did so, but in 1801 he was routed by the Darfur garrison. It was the definitive end to a doomed imperial enterprise.[16] Darfur rule in Kordofan was to be undisturbed for twenty years.

Darfur and the outside world: the French connection

Under Tayrab and 'Abd al-Rahman Darfur became known to the outside world as a remote but rich member of the Muslim *umma*. Tayrab ordered a copy for a thousand gold coins from the great Indian lexicographer and scholar, Muhammad Murtada al-Zabidi (d. 1791), of his *magnum opus*, the *Taj al-'Arus 'ala sharh al-Qamus*, still the definitive dictionary of the Arabic language.[17] 'Abd al-Rahman wrote to the Ottoman Sultan, sending presents of ivory and ostrich feathers. The Ottoman Sultan replied thanking him for his gifts and

---

15 The intrigues are reported in detail in our sources: al-Tunisi (1965), 128 (120-1 & 199-200); Cadalvène and Breuvery (1841), ii, 212-13 and Nachtigal (1971-87), iv, 294-6.

16 Cadalvène and Breuvery (1841), ii, 213 say that Hashim appropriately met his death in this final battle; more prosaically, Burckhardt (1819), 257, reports that he was killed sometime before 1814 in a conspiracy against the ruler of Shendi.

17 Reichmuth (1999), 96. In his introduction, al-Zabidi calls the Darfur ruler sultan, but refers to the Ottoman sultan merely as *malik*. As an Indian with a widespread network of contacts in Muslim Africa, as Reichmuth documents, he seems to have had a different perception of the dimensions of the Muslim world of his day. In this he prefigures Ahmad b. Idris and other "neo-Sufis" of the next generation (see Chapter Ten).

bestowing upon 'Abd al-Rahman the honorific *al-rashid/*"the just", which duly appeared on the Sultan's seals.[18] Darfur became known to the outside world via Egypt and the "Forty Days Road", not only a crucial trade link to Egypt and a source of Darfur's riches but also a highway for the transmission of learning with books, students and scholars travelling both ways.[19] Egypt was Darfur's door to the wider world and the source of consumer goods for the elite; it was also to be, through its imperial ambitions, Darfur's nemesis.

The learned world in Europe began to hear of Darfur; in 1788 the African Association, newly established in Britain to further exploration in Africa, sent the American John Ledyard to Cairo, whence he was to explore the Sahara. Ledyard died in Cairo after a few weeks, but not before he met Rosetti, the Venetian Consul there, who had trading connections with Darfur, and saw Darfur slaves for sale in the Cairo market.[20]

An Englishman, W.G. Browne, was the first European to visit and return to write a description of Darfur.[21] Although Browne stayed in Darfur for nearly three years, in the guise of a North African merchant which seems to have fooled few, and was clearly a sharp and educated (Oxford University) observer, his account is disappointing compared to the magisterial Nachtigal, who never concealed his Christian identity, or the Muslim insider, al-Tunisi. When writing of what he saw, particularly on the sultanate's commercial life, he is invaluable, but the xenophobia he encountered and the disputes, especially over a slave girl, that he got himself into make his account somewhat disappointing.

Browne left Egypt in April 1793 on the Forty Days Road, arriving in Darfur in July. He himself confesses that he would have preferred to follow Bruce's footsteps in Ethiopia; Darfur was a poor

---

18 Browne (1806), 214 and Shuqayr (1903), ii, 121.

19 Reichmuth brings this out in his account of al-Zabidi's Darfur contacts; Reichmuth (2004), 143-4.

20 Hallet (1965), 200-3; ibid. (1964) 58-9 and Ledyard (1817), i, 190. The latter two quote from Ledyard's letters.

21 Hallet (1965), 276-86 and Hill (1967), 88.

second choice. After three frustrating years, he left Kobbei in March 1796. Most of his time was spent in Kobbei, hardly a typical Darfur town (see Chapter Eleven), or al-Fashir; in the latter he had several encounters with 'Abd al-Rahman. He describes one encounter:

I contrived to gain admittance to the interior court by a bribe. The sultan was hearing a cause of private nature, the proceedings on which were only in the Furian language. He was seated on a kind of chair which was covered with a Turkey carpet, and wore a red silk turban; his face was then uncovered: The imperial sword was placed across his knees, and his hands were engaged with a chaplet of red coral [presumably a *misbah* or rosary].[22]

The caravan that took Browne back to Cairo brought on its return in November 1796 another European visitor to Darfur, Ahmad Agha.[23] He was in origin one Giovanni Gaeta, one of three Greek brothers from the island of Xanthos, who had migrated to Egypt to seek their fortune and, becoming Muslim, had entered the service of Murad Bey, one of the rulers of Egypt, as Mamluks. Ahmad Agha won favour with his master through his skill in the casting of cannon.[24]

Ahmad Agha was approached by Carlo Rosetti, the Venetian Consul; the latter traded with merchants from Darfur and Sinnar and in the first instance seems merely interested to increase his business, although he apparently thought Darfur could be easily conquered. Back in Darfur, the merchants told the Sultan that Rosetti was offering to supply him with cannon. The Sultan was interested and in September 1796 the merchants reported to Rosetti that the Darfur ruler wanted a specialist in cannonry sent as well as a physician. At Rosetti's prompting, Murad Bey agreed to send Ahmad Agha by the next caravan. Auriant suggests that Murad wanted Ahmad to spy out the land for a possible invasion attempt.[25]

---

22 Browne (1806), 232.

23 The main source for what follows is Auriant (1926: the name is apparently a pseudonym), 181-234. Auriant appears to have made use of unpublished letters of Rosetti, but is far from precise about his sources. See also my (1972), 202-3 and Walz (1978), 225.

24 Browne (1806) 92 & 166-8.

25 Murad Bey al-Qazdughli and Ibrahim Bey ruled Egypt more or less continuously from 1784 until Bonaparte's invasion in 1798; Holt (1966),

In November Ahmad left for Darfur, where he was well received by the Sultan. But he was effectively put under house arrest for the next two years; 'Abd al-Rahman evidently did not trust him. Whether he built cannon is not known.[26] Finally in 1798 Ahmad was able to persuade the suspicious Sultan to let him send letters by the doctor, Sulayman, to Egypt. But Sulayman found a drastically different Egypt awaiting him; in July 1798 Napoleon Bonaparte had landed there. Rosetti took Sulayman to describe Darfur to the French authorities. In the meantime an exceptionally large caravan was about to reach Egypt, carrying 12,000 slaves as well as ivory and gum, led by the *khabir al-hajj* Muhammad b. Musa. The *khabir* wrote to General Desaix, who was chasing fugitive Mamluks in Upper Egypt, for permission to enter the country; this was readily granted.[27]

Another caravan was approaching Egypt led by the *khabir* Yusuf al-Jallabi, this time carrying a letter from 'Abd al-Rahman addressed (in translation) *"au glorieux sultan des armées françaises"*, that is Bonaparte. In it the Sultan congratulates Bonaparte on his victory over the Mamluks—probably sincerely, given the outrageous duties levied on the Darfur imports—and requested safe passage for the caravan, and mentioning Ahmad Agha, who seems to have told the Sultan that the French would undoubtedly win. Bonaparte replied in the following year with two friendly letters (12 and 24 Messidor an viii/30 June and 12 July 1799), explaining that he had been away in Syria and in the second asking the Sultan to send 2,000 able-bodied male slaves; the French had a manpower problem and the few black slaves they had bought in the market and employed as auxiliaries had performed well.[28] The slaves were seemingly not sent, but French/Darfur rela-

---

99-100.

26 The sultans did acquire cannon; two inscribed with the words "liberté" and "égalité" were found on the battlefield at Bara in 1821 by the Turco-Egyptian forces; Douin (1944), i, 205.

27 Courrier de l'Egypte [the newspaper put out by the French], xxii, 2 nivôse an viii [from the revolution]/22 December 1798, "On rapporte que celle caravane amméne douze mille esclaves, elle est le plus nombreuse qui soit venue depuis long-temps".

28 Translations of the letters are given in *Pièces Diverses*, 187 & 216.

tions continued amicably until the end of the occupation of Egypt in 1801.[29]

The French continued to be interested in Darfur and Rosetti continued to peddle the notion of invading Darfur and recruited Poussielgue, *Intendant Général des Finances*, thus a very senior French official, into his schemes. Poussielgue wrote to Bonaparte in Syria emphasising Darfur's riches, among them control of the alluvial gold of Jabal Shaybun and Taqali in Kordofan: "Once established, the European detachment could, from the interior of Africa, hold out its hands to the expeditionary force [in Egypt] and increase its resources a hundred-fold."[30] Bonaparte seems to have been sceptical, but Darfur has the dubious distinction of being the first part of the modern Sudan Republic to be the object of Western imperialist machinations.

Otherwise, French interest was more innocent; further information on Darfur was collected by the *savants* or scholars that Bonaparte took with him to Egypt and published in the great *Description de l'Égypte* (in its second edition, Paris, 1821-29, 26 vols. of text, plus 26 vols. of plates)—perhaps one of the most extraordinary records of the encounter between the West and the Muslim world ever made and certainly one of the most beautifull visually. Vivant Denon, artist and scholar, who accompanied the French forces to Upper Egypt, met at Jirja a Keira prince, apparently a brother of 'Abd al-Rahman, who was returning from India and who was going to join another brother accompanying a caravan of 800 slaves from Sinnar to Cairo. The prince told Denon that there was trade between Darfur and Timbuktu.[31]

---

29 'Abd al-Rahman wrote at least two further letters to the French authorities on behalf of inbound caravans. The originals and other relevant correspondence are in the archives of the French army: Ministère de la Défense, État-Major de l'Armée de Terre, Service Historique, Vincennes, B6 54, 13.10.1800. Some, but not all, are reproduced in Auriant (1926).

30 Walz (1978), 226 and Auriant (1926), 205 & 216-17.

31 Denon (1809), i, 166-7.

Meanwhile Ahmad Agha in Darfur seems to have become enmeshed in a conspiracy against the Sultan. The plot was betrayed and
the hapless Greek executed.[32]

There is a final footnote to the French connection and the first
echo of Darfur in the New World in the career of Félix Darfour, a
Haitian patriot.[33] He was apparently a slave from Darfur, who as a
young man was purchased by a general of the French army of occupation who is said to have been of Caribbean origin, who named him
Félix Darfour after his country of origin. When the French evacu-
ated Egypt in 1801 Félix accompanied his master to France where
he seems to have been well educated and imbued with the ideals
of the Revolution. We know very little, but in 1818 he emigrated
to Haiti, the first black Republic, where he founded two newspa-
pers, *L'Eclaireur Haitien ou le Parfait Patriote*, a political journal, and
L'Avertisseur Haitien, which seems to have been a trade journal. He
became embroiled in the bitter politics of Haiti which pitched the
mulatto elite against the black masses. He submitted a memoran-
dum to the National Assembly denouncing the government's policies towards the blacks, was tried for treason, and was executed in
September 1822.

Darfur and Wadai

The conquest of Kordofan, Darfur's increasing engagement with
Egypt both commercially and culturally, and the religious and cultural impulses coming from the Nile Valley need to be seen against
the reality that Darfur was and is a part of central Sudanic Africa.[34]

---

32 Auriant (1926), 221-6 identifies Ahmad with Zawana Kashif in al-Tunisi
(1965), 118-21 (113-18 & 183-8). Al-Tunisi describes Zawana (possibly a
corruption of Giovanni) as a Mamluk of Murad or another Mamluk leader,
who had fled to Darfur after the French invasion. In Darfur he became
involved in a plot with al-Tayyib b. Mustafa, who had married a daughter of
Sultan Muhammad Tayrab.

33 Abbakr (1992), 176-9 and Kurita (unpublished paper, 2000).

34 Which I would define as being from western Kordofan to modern Niger.
It is this failure to understand where Darfur is that bedevils so much of the
modern crisis.

Since Tayrab's time relations with Wadai had been peaceful, but Muhammad al-Fadl was twice involved in conflict with Wadai, once over a border dispute and towards the end of his reign in a Wadai succession dispute. Both episodes were to underscore Darfur's relative fragility, a failure of will compared with the eighteenth century sultans and their warbands.

The border dispute concerned Dar Tama, a border kingdom subject to Darfur. Wadai was now ruled by an energetic Sultan, Muhammad Sabun, who came to power in Rajab 1219/May-June 1804.[35] Early in Sabun's reign the Tama began to raid into Wadai.[36] Since Dar Tama was a tributary of Darfur, Sabun wrote to Muhammad al-Fadl to complain of the behaviour of the Tama *malik*, Ahmad. A conciliatory reply was sent from al-Fashir, but soon afterwards some Masalit subjects of Wadai came to Abeche, the Wadai capital, to complain of further Tama raids. Sabun sent a second letter of complaint, but also an army to Wadai's northeastern border under Jab Allah, governor or *'aqid al-sabah* of eastern Wadai. Muhammad al-Fadl responded that he was sending Ahmad Jurab al-Fil, the Bagirmi warrior who had finished off Kurra, to warn off *malik* Ahmad.[37]

However, the Tama continued raiding and Sabun decided on invasion. He was joined on the expedition by 'Umar al-Tunisi, father of the traveller, who brought with him twenty-two musketeers recruited from the Fezzan, Tripoli and Benghazi. These were able to give covering fire when the Wadaians stormed the mountain, probably Nyeri, where Ahmad had his stronghold, but the latter had already fled to Darfur. Muhammad al-Fadl's response was to support a Wadaian pretender, one Asil, who however was soon disposed of by Sabun. Sabun sent a second expedition to Dar Tama; again Ahmad appealed for help, but al-Fashir merely sent food. By now it seems that Sabun had decided to annex Dar Tama to Wadai and

---

35 Al-Tunisi (1851), 73; Barth (1857-59), iii, 530 gives 1805.

36 Al-Tunisi (1851), 188; al-Tunisi's father, 'Umar, was a close adviser of the Wadai Sultan and much involved in the events that followed.

37 Ibid., 192.

sent a third force. Ahmad submitted on terms providing for annual payment of a hundred horses and a thousand slaves.[38]

Ahmad later asked Sabun to reduce the number of slaves, since the Tama could no longer so easily hunt for them in Dar Fartit because of Fur opposition. The tribute was reduced to a hundred. Ahmad also wrote to Muhammad al-Fadl to explain that he had only submitted to avoid further devastation. But the whole episode is symptomatic of the Keira sultanate's military weakness in relation to its neighbours.

This military weakness became more and more evident during the nineteenth century. 'Abd al-Rahman had fought Ishaq in person, but neither Muhammad al-Fadl nor Muhammad al-Husayn, who between them ruled for seventy years, went on campaign as sultans. The court seems to have been more interested in trade than war.

The sultanate could still mobilise an army. After Sabun's death in 1230/1815-16, Wadai fell prey to a series of succession disputes; when 'Abd al-'Aziz died in about 1836, he was succeeded, amidst growing chaos, by his infant son, Adam. A younger brother of Sabun, Muhammad Sharif, was living in Darfur, having apparently married a Fulani woman from the sultanate.[39] Sharif had supporters in Wadai and Muhammad al-Fadl is said to have used the pretext of Sharif's claims to try and seize Wadai for his son, Muhammad al-Husayn.[40] In 1837 an expedition was sent under the combined leadership of the Wazir 'Abd al-Sid, the *malik al-korayat* 'Abd al-Fattah and the *aba diimang* 'Abd al-Rahman Kalbas, accompanied by Sharif and Muhammad al-Husayn.[41] Adam's partisans were routed and Sharif installed as sultan, promising to pay annual tribute of "a hundred

---

38 Ibid., 110 & 199-206.

39 Lauture (1855-56), 78.

40 Nachtigal (1971-87), iv, 218-21 (Wadai version) & 304 (Darfur version).

41 Cairo, Abdin Archives, box 262, dossier Sudan (unnumbered), Yusuf Ziya to Maiya Saniya, 25 Safar 1253/31 May 1837 [a reference I owe to Richard Hill who simply gave me his Cairo notes on Darfur]; Fresnel (1848), 247 dates it to 1251/1835-36; Barth (1857-59), iii, 533 to al-tom al-awwal 1250/August-September 1834. See also AP2, 10, 48, 108 and al-Tunisi (1851), 235.

slaves, a hundred loads of ivory" and other items by the hundred. But after the first payment, the *'ulama* of Wadai sanctioned Sharif's repudiation of the agreement. The Darfurians returned home; 'Abd al-Sid, fearful of failure, allegedly committed suicide.[42] Ironically, Muhammad Sharif proved to be one of Wadai's strongest rulers and Dar Tama remained disputed territory.

The expedition, the last of its sort mounted by the Keira state, had its repercussions elsewhere; a fracas broke out between the Darfur and Wadai students at al-Azhar in Cairo, forcing the latter to de-camp to the mosque of Sayyidna Yahya in Damascus.[43] Presents were occasionally exchanged between the two states; Nachtigal in 1873 took a horse as a present from the Wadai Sultan 'Ali (r.1858-74), and advice to the new Darfur Sultan on how to deal with the loom-ing threat of the slave trader al-Zubayr.[44]

The loss of Kordofan

Halfway through Muhammad al-Fadl's long reign, a new force appeared in the Nilotic and eastern Sudan that was eventually to bring about the destruction of the first sultanate. The ruler of Egypt, Muhammad 'Ali Pasha (1811-49), prepared to invade the Sudan. In 1821 his armies entered Sinnar, capital of the virtually defunct Funj state, without resistance.[45]

On 20 April 1821, a second expeditionary force left Egypt under the Pasha's son-in-law, the *daftardar* Muhammad Bey Khusraw; its goal was the conquest of Kordofan and Darfur.[46] Khusraw's route was up the Nile to the Dongola Reach, leaving the river at al-Dabba and crossing the Bayuda Desert to Jabal Haraza and then to Kajmar and finally to Bara and al-Ubayyid. Khusraw left al-Dabba in July 1821 to begin his march across the desert. Darfur's governor in Kordofan

---

42 Fresnel (1849 50), xi, 73-4 and Nachtigal (1971-87), iv, 304-5.

43 Lauture (1855-56), 93.

44 Nachtigal (1971-87), iv, 229 & 371-2.

45 Holt and Daly (1988), 49-53 and Hill (1959), 8-18.

46 Al-Jabarti (1879), iv, 318 makes it clear that Darfur was to be conquered, not just Kordofan.

was still Musallim, who although he had been warned by merchants from Lower Nubia in Sha'ban 1236/May-June 1821 of the impending invasion seems not to have appreciated the danger he was in.[47] He made few preparations to meet the invasion beyond informing the Sultan and ignored the suggestion of the shaykh of Jabal Haraza, a Nubian outpost well north of al-Ubayyid, that they should attempt to stop the invaders at Jabal Haraza as they came out the desert still weak from crossing the Bayuda: a suggestion that could have anticipated the Mahdi's great victory at Shaykan sixty-two years later.[48]

If Musallim seems not to have taken the threat seriously, neither did the Sultan, and indeed there may have been some coolness between the two. Burckhardt had been told some years before that Musallim would have liked to make himself independent.[49]

Thus, while Khusraw with an army of some 3,000 men and a battery of thirteen cannon advanced into Kordofan, Musallim sat waiting in al-Ubayyid. On 18 August, Musallim moved from al-Ubayyid to Bara with an army of about 8,000 infantry and 1,200 horsemen, including two hundred mailed cavalry. The next day, in a desperately fought battle, the Darfur army was crushed by cannon and musket fire; Musallim was killed and his heavy cavalry destroyed. The battle marked an end to the traditional predominance of mailed cavalry in the Sudanic region.[50]

Apart from Musallim, nearly thirty Darfur notables, including the *abbo daadinga* Ibrahim b. 'Abd al-Qadir Wir, were killed as well 700 of the rank and file, for the loss of a hundred and fifty.[51]

---

47 Cadalvène and Breuvery (1841), ii, 214.

48 Lauture (1855-56), 80; Lejean (1865), 300-13 and Beltrame (1879), i, 137.

49 Burckhardt (1822), 482; Nachtigal (1971-87), iv, 301 says that Musallim was intriguing with the Sultan's brother, Muhammad Bukhari, and Shuqayr (1903), ii, 462.

50 As Hill (1959), 12-13 notes, there are no eye witness accounts of Bara, but Douin (1944), i, 205 makes use of Egyptian archival sources, while Driault (1927), 231 quotes from a letter from the French Consul, Bernadino Drovetti, quoting from a dispatch from Khusraw, dated Muharram 1236/ October-November 1821.

51 Ibid.; Holroyd (1839), 163-91 mentions one "Ibrahim Idwir" killed at Bara; interview, malik Rihaymat Allah al-Dadinqawi, al-Fashir 19.5.1970, on the

The loss of Kordofan was, of course, was a blow to the sultanate, mainly for commercial reasons. But Khusraw was forced to abandon any plans to invade Darfur because of belated but fierce resistance by the riverain Sudanese; he returned to the Nile taking with him some of Musallim's men whom he had recruited.[52]

Muhammad al-Fadl did make what seems to have been a half-hearted attempt to recover the province, sending a force under his nephew, the Wazir Ahmad, but the expedition was hurriedly recalled following some plotting against the Sultan. In another version, the force under under one Abu'l-Likaylik (otherwise unknown and an unlikely name from Darfur) was defeated by the Turco-Egyptians near Sodiri.[53]

Darfur had not simply lost a province, it had acquired an all too powerful neighbour. In 1245/1829-30, possibly in response to the plotting around a pretender, Muhammad Abu Madyan, to the throne of Darfur, Muhammad al-Fadl had his children's tutor, Muhammad b. 'Ammari al-Azhari, write a stout letter refuting Muhammad 'Ali's claims to Darfur and asserting his state's independence.[54] He is also said to have sent presents from time to time to the Ottoman court in order to bolster his position vis-à-vis Egypt.[55] Understandably no

---

death of his ancestor.

52 Brocchi (1841-43), v, 207.

53 Cadalvène and Breuvery (1841), ii, 231 for the first version and Shuqayr (1903), ii, 130 for the second. The defeat in western Kordofan seems confirmed by a letter from Shaykh Muhammad al-Amin al-Kanemi of Borno to Major D. Denham, dated Rajab 1240/May 1825, reporting the defeat of a Darfur army at Kaja (just north of Sodiri); Bovill (1966), iv, 741.

54 The text is given in Shuqayr (1903), ii, 132-3; another version is given in Muhammad 'Abd al-Rahim, al-Durr al-Manthur fi-ta'rikh bilad al-'Arab wa'l-Fur (ms. NRO, Khartoum, f.115), which was taken to Egypt by a prominent merchant, Abbakr al-Khandaqawi, on whom see Bjørkelo (1989), 125. On Turco-Egyptian/Darfur relations, see Kropacek (1970), 73-86. On Abu Madyan, see al-Tunisi (1965), 343-64 (370-94 [not given in the English transl.]); Nachtigal (1971-87), iv, 303 and Mengin (1839), 495.

55 Vaudey, trader and vice-consul of Sardinia in Khartoum, quoted by D'Abbadie (1852), 387.

Darfur ruler would acknowledge another's rule in his land, although a Bagirmi eunuch of Muhammad al-Husayn, Muhammad Dayfan, told Arkell that he had heard the Sultan say, "the only true sultans were those of Bornu and Constantinople, and that the sultan of Darfur was only their wazir."[56] 'Ali Dinar paid irregular tribute to the British to keep them off his back, but took care never to meet them, not even Rudolph von Slatin, his old acquaintance from their days as prisoners of the Khalifa in Omdurman (see Chapter Thirteen).

After Bara, Muhammad al-Fadl retaliated by forbidding Egyptian merchants to return home. A sort of trade war followed between Sultan and Viceroy, with the former closing the Forty Days Road and the latter making the export of weapons to Darfur a capital offence.[57] Thus, by 1837, the Russian Consul-General in Egypt was reporting that caravans from Darfur had almost stopped coming, preferring to go to North African ports.[58] Darfur acquired, almost certainly undeservedly, a reputation as an inaccessible and inhospitable land, in part because of false reports of the alleged killing of two European travellers there.[59] With Egypt relations improved in the 1850s and 60s, not least because of a trade boom, but Egypt never totally abandoned its predatory designs.

The wars against the nomads: North and South

The sultanate's expansion in the eighteenth century across Darfur's central savanna lands brought it up against the *sahil* or "coastal" lands to the north contiguous with the Sahara and the well-watered lands in the south, into contact therefore with nomads, both north and south. As the sultanate evolved from tribal kingdom to multi-ethnic state, so the nature of its relations with the nomads changed. The Zaghawa had early on become integrated, often contentiously, into

---

56 AP1, 5, 13, 54-5.

57 Douin (1944), i, 301 and Hill (1959), 30.

58 Cattani (1931), ii, 388 and Hill (1959), 30.

59 These were Eduard Vogel (1829-56) who was killed in Wadai and Charles Cuny (1811-58), who died of dysentery soon after arriving in al-Fashir; see Nachtigal (1971-87), iv, 130 fn and Hill (1967), 106.

the state. The problem for the sultans was that their state was nourished by what lay beyond the nomads, both north and south. To the north was the Forty Days Road and the routes northwest to the Fezzan and the Libyan coast; from the south, in and beyond the Baqqara or cattle nomad belt, came many of Darfur's most lucrative exports, copper ore from Hufrat al-Nahas, south of the Ta'aisha nomads, ivory,[60] ebony (a much prized export), tamarind, ostrich feathers, animal skins and slaves (see Chapter Eleven). Of Darfur's major exports, only gum arabic came from the central zone, from eastern Darfur.

Along all boundaries between nomads and farmers frictions occur; disputes over water and grazing rights, livestock migration routes (Ar. *marahil*), the tendency of farmers to enclose and nomads to roam, all can or will lead to tensions. But two factors generally mitigate these potential frictions. One is interdependence, the exchange of the produce of the soil for those of livestock, the value of manure upon the fields, investment and partnership possibilities, and intermarriage, often leading to changes in ethnicity. The potential for conflict is surely there, but it is in no way inevitable. The other factor was and is the customary laws (Ar. *'urf* or *'ada*) that provide for dispute resolution; the livestock routes are a good example. These were and are demarcated; nomads moving livestock along these routes employed "guarantors" (Ar. *damin*) whose task was to broker compensation to farmers for crops damaged by animals. In other words, an assumption of deep-seated hostility on occupational or racial grounds is historically ungrounded.

From Tayrab's time the nomads became increasingly a *political* factor. Tayrab had campaigned inconclusively against the Rizayqat, while 'Abd al-Rahman had Misiriyya allies in his war against Ishaq. Browne reports that the Baqqara were supposed to pay a tenth of the herds in tribute, which if paid would amount to 4,000 head of cattle

---

60 The history of Darfur's fauna is as yet not fully known; I was told that lion were still to be found in Jabal Marra in the early Condominium and I certainly saw baboon there in the late 60s, and the deer, mainly Thompson's Gazelles, and snakes reminded me of Kenya. See Wilson (1979), 323-38 and (1980), 85-101. I have no idea what the situation is now.

(seemingly a small figure). But they had not paid for two years and so an expedition was sent against them that netted 12,000 head.[61]

The nomads as a political factor grew in counterpoint to the growth of Darfur's external trade, above all with Egypt. Here, ironically, in contrast to today when the camel nomads have been a greater threat than the cattle nomads to the settled peoples, the failure of the sultans to impose their will on the cattle nomads was to prove a danger when outside forces appeared on the scene south of Darfur. The expansion of trade with Egypt created a demand in Darfur for slaves and other exportable products that led to intensified exploitation within the Baqqara territories and beyond. By the 1840s and 50s, with the opening up of the Bahr al-Ghazal region, the direction of the *salatiyya* or *ghazwa* raiding parties seems to have changed from the southwest to directly south, and they seem to have been accompanied by large number of *jallaba* or petty traders.[62]

In the early nineteenth century the main Arab groupings in the north were the Mahamid and Mahriyya in the northwest, the 'Irayqat, 'Itayfat and Umm Jallul in the centre and the Zayyadiyya in the east, bordering on Kordofan. The Fazara confederation of the sixteenth century had long since drifted apart and new tribal units such as the Zayyadiyya and the Kababish in northern Kordofan had emerged.[63] The Zayyadiyya seem always to have enjoyed good relations with the sultans,[64] and it was the 'Irayqat and to a lesser extent the Mahamid who bore the brunt of the Keira raids. The Mahamid were at least able to seek refuge with the main body of their tribe in Wadai, where they had a privileged position within the sultanate.[65]

---

61 Browne (1806), 344-5.

62 Gray (1961) and my (1973a), 29-43.

63 Al-Tunisi (1965), 139 (129 & 213-14) and Burckhardt (1822), 481. Some of the northern nomads have traditions that their original grazing grounds were around the Wadi Sharangol, some hundred miles due north of Kutum, an area now completely waterless; PA DP.66.B.3 Northern Rizaygat, note C.G. Dupuis, 26 June 1925.

64 Hakim (1976), 10-20.

65 PA DP.66.B.3 Northern Rizaygat, notes Dupuis 26 June 1925 and Charles 1948, and Rouvreur (1962), 344-50.

Small bands of mailed cavalry were effective in keeping the camel nomads down—their big imported horses almost literally rode the nomads' ponies down. During Browne's visit (1793-96), the Mahriyya and Mahamid quarrelled. To quell them, 'Abd al-Rahman sent a *malik* with about sixty horsemen who seized half the camels they found and "where they found five took three, as the fifth could not be divided".[66] The 'Irayqat resisted more sternly, deriding the rule of Muhammad al-Fadl because of his youth. A force was sent north under the *baasi* 'Umar, who seized every fifth camel from the tribe. But the trouble continued and seven years later a large expedition went north, which met with disaster. Finally the Wazir 'Abd al-Sid went north and crushed the 'Irayqat, seven of whose chiefs were executed before the Sultan. It was the end of the 'Irayqat as a tribal entity for several generations.[67] The camel nomads were more vulnerable to Keira reprisals than their cousins in the south since they had nowhere to go except the desert.

Turning to the south, the Bani Halba were the particular objects of Muhammad al-Fadl's wrath. Of all the cattle-keepers they had the most intimate relationship with the Fur along the Wadi Azum, where the Bani Halba spend most of the year (September to February) before going south to the Bahr al-'Arab.[68] It was their wealth in livestock and the independence of the Bani Halba that the Sultan resented, but the Fur were also pushing southwards from the Wadi Azum into Dar Fongoro at this period. The Arabs paid a terrible price in the "bloodbath of the Bani Halba" which laid the tribe low for at least a generation.[69]

---

66 Browne (1806), 345.

67 Nachtigal (1971-87), iv, 302 and Slatin (1896), 45-6, whose remark that the Sultan ordered the Mahriyya, Mahamid and Nu'ayba to move north into the 'Irayqat lands seems based on a misunderstanding; there are Mahamid, Mahriyya and Nu'ayba among both the cattle and camel nomads.

68 Haaland (1969), 58-73. There are smaller Arab groups like the Hotiyya and Tarjam, as well as Fulani Bororoje who live virtually permanently among the Fur, with whom they have close relations.

69 Nachtigal (1971-87), iv, 301-2 and Slatin (1896), 45. The Bani Halba proved as much of a problem to the Mahdists and to 'Ali Dinar; Holt (1970), 165 and Theobald (1965), 136-7.

Southeast of the Bani Halba lay the lands of the Rizayqat and their allies, the Habbaniyya and Ma'aliyya. The Rizayqat *dar* is vast, poorly-watered and difficult of access;[70] their nomadic cycle gave them strategic advantage. In the dry season, from March to June, they take their herds to the Bahr al-'Arab in the far south and then in June, when the rains begin, make their way as far north as Dar Birged and just south of al-Fashir, where they stay from about September to January, when they move south again.[71]

The Rizayqat and the sultans undoubtedly shared a mutual interest in slave-raiding, but the latter never really succeeded in incorporating them into their state—and perhaps never really tried. In any event, the Rizayqat needed the sultanate as an outlet for their slaves and other trade goods, so there was a mutual interest in good relations.[72] This seems to have begun to change late in Muhammad al-Fadl's reign; he sent the *soming dogala* Sa'id b. Muhammad south as *maqdum*. Sa'id had some success and is said to have captured by trickery several Rizayqat chiefs.[73]

All this was to change drastically by the mid-nineteenth century; Muhammad al-Husayn during his long reign organised eighteen campaigns against the nomads, and these campaigns were the harbingers of the end of the first sultanate.[74] The cause was the growing trading empires based on armed encampments or *zaribas* and trading companies (Ar. *kubaniyya*) in the Western Bahr al-Ghazal; the centre of gravity within Darfur and the sultanate's trading networks had shifted southwards. Instead of being relatively marginal, the Baqqara

---

70 And now seemingly rich in oil, as block 6, assigned to the National China Petroleum Corporation, stretches across it from western Kordofan.

71 PA Nyala District Handbook, notes by G.D. Lampen, describing the cycle in the 1920s and 30s.

72 My (1973), 31-2.

73 Sa'id was of Berti origin; his father, Muhammad b. Hanafi, had married into the Rizayqat; Abu Adam 'Abd Allah, a descendant of Sa'id, Nyala 29.6.1969; Nachtigal (1971-87), iv, 302. One of the chiefs captured was 'Ali, the grandfather of Musa Madibbu, the famous Rizayqat chief of Mahdist times. The present (2006) *nazir 'umum* of the Rizayqat is Sa'id Mahmud Musa Madibbu, whose mother was the sister of the Sultan of Dar Masalit.

74 Nachtigal (1971-87), iv, 308.

belt through which the slaves and ivory passed, the latter crucial to
the new European obsession with the pianoforte and the making of
billiard balls, became central to the economic life of the state.[75] The
Baqqara lacked any central leadership; they seemed to split on any
major issue before them—a tendency that appears clearly at the time
of al-Zubayr's invasion. If one group was not willing to co-operate
with the traders, another was.

The *abbo soming dogala* 'Abd al-'Aziz began a series of raids on
his own initiative; his progress, or lack of it, illustrated the difficulties of fighting the Baqqara. At first the Darfurians were able seize
considerable numbers of cattle, but they were ambushed returning
northwards and all the leaders save 'Abd al-'Aziz were killed. The
sultan was furious and 'Abd al-'Aziz was disgraced and condemned
to death, but save himself by a judicious bribe to the sultan, who
indeed made him *maqdum* of the south.[76]

For three years 'Abd al-'Aziz ruled the south in peace from Dara,
now emerging as the province capital. Then he began to put pressure on the Habbaniyya whose territory was more accessible than
that of the Rizayqat; the Habbaniyya were successfully coerced, but
the Rizayqat slipped away to the Bahr al-'Arab. But the *maqdum*'s
dilatory campaigning irritated the Sultan, who ordered him to make
one supreme effort—sending him a letter of commission with a red
seal instead of the customary black one and a black *burnus* or turban
instead of the usual red, both bad omens. 'Abd al-'Aziz moved south
in the autumn, but in a three-day running battle the Keira forces
were broken up and 'Abd al-'Aziz was killed by Rizayqat slaves.

---

75 Barth (1853), 120-2 for Fur accounts of these routes.
76 Nachtigal (1971-87), iv, 308-10. Nachtigal was in al-Fashir some thirty
    years after these events and talked to many involved. A report to Muhammad
    'Ali from Khalid Khusraw, governor of the Egyptian Sudan, dated 29 Safar
    1262/26 February 1846, reporting 'Abd al-'Aziz's preparations to attack the
    Rizayqat, gives an approximate date; Cairo, Abdin Archives, carton 19, no.
    17 [from Richard Hill].

He was replaced as *maqdum* by Khalil b. 'Abd al-Sid, a son of the Wazir who had led the expedition to Wadai.[77] Forces were concentrated; Hasan Siqiri, *maqdum* of the north, and *abbo shaykh daali* Rahma, governor of the east, joined Khalil. But all was in vain, the Rizayqat simply melted away, ambushing any stray soldiers. Khalil was dismissed and the Wazir Adam Bosh promised the Sultan that he would deal with the nomads.

From his base at Tabaldiyya in the south, the Wazir was at first somewhat more successful than his predecessors, until he, like them, was tempted into venturing southwards into the marshy lands just north of the Bahr al-'Arab. His soldiers became hopelessly entangled in the marshes and while attempting to draw back to Shakka, on the northern border of Dar Rizayqat, he and his men were slaughtered by the nomads, probably in 1856.[78]

After Adam Bosh's death there was a peace of exhaustion. A son of 'Abd al-'Aziz, Ahmad Shatta, was appointed *maqdum* in the south with his base at Dara, northeast of Nyala, and later replaced Khalil as Wazir. He spent the next fifteen years building up a force of slave troops armed with rifles. But it was too late; although he had some success against the nomads, Shatta and his Sultan had left the re-equipping of the Keira forces too late. Al-Zubayr in the Bahr al-Ghazal had a twenty-year head start.

---

77 Nachtigal (1971-87), iv, 310-11. Barth (1857-59), ii, 675 gives an itinerary of about 1854 that refers to a village of the *maqdum* Khalil, just south of Nyala.

78 Nachtigal (1971-87), iv, 311; Slatin (1896), 50 & 188 (Slatin's account of fighting the Rizayqat underlines the difficulties); and Cuny (1858), 11-12 who reports Bosh's death by that year. The latest document we have from Bosh is DF 63.8/1, dated 25 Rajab 1267/5 June 1851. The campaigns are briefly described in Brun-Rollet (1855), 45 & 129.

PART TWO
STATE AND SOCIETY

5
SULTAN AND FASHIR

Introduction

The apex of the ritual and political order within the state was the sultan and the heart of the state was the *fashir* or palace complex.[1] Both institutions, sultan and palace, were animated by two parallel, complementary and contradictory ideologies, which may simplistically be termed Fur and Islamic. But it would be misleading to analyse the evolution of the state in terms of a simple diachronic process whereby an African kingdom with its own institutions and culture, its own complex of relations between ruler and subject, was exposed to and changed over time by Islamic influences coming in as a result of external contacts, the immigration of *fuqara*, or the growth of trade, particularly with Egypt. Change there was, and occasionally ideological confrontation, but the pristine Fur state "uncontami-

---

1 The palace's role long survived the sultans, for until 1977 'Ali Dinar's exquisite two-storied gem, complete with a minstrels' gallery, designed by architects from Tunisia, was the official residence of the provincial governors of the Condominium and independent Sudan, a sense of continuity reinforced by the placing of 'Ali Dinar's throne directly behind the governor's desk. The palace is now an attractively maintained museum.

nated" by the outside world, which alone would have provided a yardstick to measure change, either never existed as such or is beyond recovery. The Fur and Islamic, indigenous and external dimensions were seemingly present from the outset, sometimes competing, sometimes complementing each other. The vitality and the duality of the two dimensions can be seen in the use of language; Fur was the spoken language of the court until the reign of 'Ali Dinar, whereas Arabic was always the language of chancery.[2] Neither usurped the other's position; indeed it was this two-dimensionality that was behind the hybridity of many of the titles mentioned here, as they were compounds formed from both languages. Although in time the traditional Fur religion was driven underground (or, literally, to the hilltops where its cult centres were located) or into the hands of women (although some of the divine kingship rituals became unacceptable and were purged), Fur culture retained its identity, though within an increasingly Islamic frame of reference.

The sultan

To the Fur their ruler was the *aba kuuri*, "father of obeisance". An older or variant title was *ari* or *eri*, meaning "exalted", as in the phrase *forang eri*, "exalted of the Fur". The older title was preserved in the *abbo ari*, a ritual official who in certain ceremonies such as the procession to the mosque for the Friday prayers took the sultan's place under the royal umbrella (Ar. *dallal*).[3]

The sultan had his praise-names:

See the buffaloe, the offspring of a buffaloe, a bull of bulls, the elephant of superior strength, the powerful Sultan abd-el-rachman-el-rashîd—May

---

2 By "chancery" I mean an organised secretariat to deal with sultanic correspondence. This certainly existed under 'Ali Dinar and it is clear that from the pre-1874 charters and other documents that certain scribes had responsibility for particular kinds of documents—this can be deduced from their handwriting; see further, O'Fahey and Abu Salim (1983).

3 Nachtigal (1971-87) iv, 335-36; *eri* is the usual term for the sultan in the Fur texts recorded in the 1840s by the Tutschek brothers, see under Tutschek (1921-30) and (1941-42).

God prolong the life!—O Master—May God assist thee and render thee victorious.[4]

The written counterparts to these praise-names, the common heritage of African kings, are to be found in the Islamically inspired Arabic titles and honorifics used in sultanic documents. These are already elaborate in the earliest documents we have, namely charters issued by Muhammad Dawra (r. *c.* 1720-30) and Muhammad Tayrab (r. 1752/53-1785/86), which include such phrases as *sultan al-'Arab wa'l-'Ajam* and *khalifa rabb al-'alamin,* "Caliph of the Lord of the Universe".[5] The sovereign title "sultan" was never confined solely to the Keira ruler, although *sayyidna,* "our master", does seem to have been exclusively his. By Sultan 'Abd al-Rahman's time the titles and honorifics had become very elaborate. To give but one example,

From the presence of the most noble, the lord, who is most generous to the generous among his servants, the lord, Sultan of the Muslims and Caliph of the Prophet of the Lord of the Universe, he who trusts in the Creator, the One, the Benefactor, our beneficent Sultan 'Abd al-Rahman, may God render him victorious, Amen, son of the late Sultan Ahmad Bukr ...[6]

There was little consistency in the sultans' diplomatic practice; Muhammad al-Fadl is abruptly styled *sultan Fur* in a letter accompanying sumptuous presents to a *faqih* near Old Dongola, but *amir al-mu'minin,* "Commander of the Faithful", among a galaxy of titles in his charters.[7] It is tempting to see these honorifics as an Islamic echo of African praise-names, as an example of the duality discussed above. As a nod in the other direction, the fiction of descent from the 'Abbasids occasionally appears in 'Ali Dinar's decrees, in one of which he calls himself *al-Hashimi al-'Abbasi.*[8]

---

4   Browne (1806), 236; Hartmann (1863), 68 and anhange, 16.
5   These titles come from DF142.18/2: 160.18/20: 166.18/26 & 173.18/33 (seal-date 1172/1758-59).
6   DF 145.18/5 (seal-date 1214/1799-1800).
7   O'Fahey and Spaulding (1981), 38-43.
8   32.7/5 (25 Dhu'l-hijja 1318/11 April 1901).

Sultanic succession was patrilineal; all "sons of the sultans", *aw-lad al-salatin* (Fur, *baasinga*) were in theory elegible to succeed.[9] In the eighteenth century, when ethnic loyalties seem to have been stronger, the mother's status and kin were important. The maternal links of *al-hajj* Ishaq with the Zaghawa of Kobe helped swing the Fur notables behind 'Abd al-Rahman in the war of succession that followed Tayrab's death in Kordofan. In the following century they became less important; Umm Buza, Muhammad al-Fadl's mother, was a concubine from a slave-status group, the Beigo, and as al-Tunisi scornfully remarks, would not have fetched ten dollars in the market.[10] Muhammad al-Husayn, whose mother was an Ethiopian slave, succeeded in preference to his elder brother, Abu Bakr, the son of a freeborn Fur woman.[11]

But there were always many royal sons; Ahmad Bukr is reputed to have had over a hundred, Tayrab more than thirty, Muhammad al-Fadl left forty-six sons over sixteen years old at his death, and 'Ali Dinar sired 120 sons and innumerable daughters.[12] Out of this mass, who became a serious contender for the succession depended on personality, favour, mother's kin and intangible factors of time and place. As a distinct group within the state, "the sons of the sultans" were provided with estates and revenues, as were their sisters, but rarely with commands or administrative responsibilities.[13] Their exactions often made them unpopular; thus al-Tunisi suggests that Tayrab marched on Kordofan partly to divert his own sons from plundering their own people and to smooth the accession of his

9   'Ali Dinar was the grandson of a sultan, but felt it expedient to call his father, Zakariyya, "sultan" retroactively in his documents.

10 Al-Tunisi (1965), 192 (184 & 282).

11 Cuny (1854), 90.

12 Shuqayr (1903) ii, 115; al-Tunisi (1965), 79 (62 & 121), and SAD, P.J. Sandison's Papers.

13 My (1992), 57-93 provides a vivid depiction of the growth of an estate given to a son of Sultan Ahmad Bukr in the Berti country northeast of Mellit and the pain it caused the prince's neighbours. The failure of the British to implant a Keira Emirate in Zalingei between 1929 and 1935 suggests the wisdom of the sultans' policy.

favourite *al-hajj* Ishaq.[14] Occasionally the royal sons acted together in defence of their interests, as when they combined to oppose the engineering of Muhammad al-Fadl's accession (see Chapter Three). Moreover, lack of administrative duties and downward social mobility inhibited the emergence of an exclusive royal caste; sons granted estates often ended up as simple farmers; 'Aqrab, a son of Tayrab, apparently himself sowed the land at Khiriban allegedly granted to him by his brother, 'Abd al-Rahman; and if the court records we have are representative, "the sons of the sultans" did not enjoy any especial favour before the judges.[15]

As Brenner has noted of Borno, "Succession to the throne was the ultimate political contest";[16] unfortunately we usually know too little of the internal politics of the succession crises to generalise usefully. In a sense, each crisis was unique. In the eighteenth century no sultan could survive prolonged opposition from the Fur lords, which was the principal cause of the deaths of 'Umar Lel and Abu'l-Qasim. The succession provoked a continuing conflict between the reigning sultan and the Keira clan. From the perspective of the Keira as a whole and of the Fur lords, brother-to-brother succession was probably both desirable and sanctioned by custom. In the warlike eighteenth century, in a world of marcher lords and territorial nobles, inexperienced younger sons had little chance. Mature men were needed to preserve and extend the state, and only mature men were able to take over. But here there was a conflict within the system; strong sultans wanted to perpetuate their own line, using pre-mortem nomination of their chosen sons as *khalifa*, "successor", but this collided with the Keira preference for brother-to-brother succession—the mature man principle. However, pre-mortem nomination was rarely effective; Muhammad Dawra was nominated *khalifa* and did follow his father Ahmad Bukr. Dawra or Harut, indeed, may well have acted as co-

---

14 Al-Tunisi (1965) 86 (68 & 130).

15 On 'Aqrab and his disputes with his neighbours, see DF69.8/7, 5 Jumada I 1230/15 April 1815, and O'Fahey and Abu Salim (1983), 6163. As a nuisance to his neighbours, 'Aqrab lived up to his name, "Scorpion".

16 Brenner (1973), 91.

sultan, since the earliest documents found in Darfur, possibly dated between 1700 and 1720, are two charters issued by Dawra but bearing his father's seal.[17] Thereafter, nomination as *khalifa* was almost a guarantee of failure; Dawra nominated his eldest son Musa 'Anqarib, but then began to favour another son, 'Umar Lel, apparently at the instigation of 'Umar's mother. Musa took to arms in defence of his rights, but despite an attempt by some *fuqara* to mediate, he was caught by treachery and killed.[18] Although 'Umar did become sultan, he faced continual opposition from the chiefs and died a prisoner in Wadai, having been deserted by his men in battle (on the politics of succession, see Chapters Four and Six).[19]

The ritual cycle

Who became sultan was a political decision, but once chosen he entered an office profoundly circumscribed by rituals and taboos that had their roots in Fur religious beliefs and practices. Here, as in law (see Chapter Nine), the divide between the Fur and Islamic dimensions presents itself vividly.[20]

The sultan's death was kept a secret within the *fashir* for as long as possible while the political manuoevring went on; the leaking of Tayrab's death in the army's camp directly affected the outcome of the succession crisis there (see above Chapter Three). During the interregnum the palace complex was in the care of the *abbo shaykh daali*, the chief slave eunuch.[21] The accession ceremonies were preceded by a change in the tempo of the drums used to convey news throughout the palace and the surrounding settlements; the slow

---

17 See my (1979b), 13-17. The translations are very speculative given the incoherence of the Arabic originals. The late Dr Abu Salim suggested to me that the peculiar syntax of the two charters is a result of their being dictated in one language and taken down imperfectly in Arabic by a scribe who did not fully understand Fur.

18 Nachtigal (1971-87), iv, 282-3; Cadalvène and Breuvery (1841), ii, 198, for which see O'Fahey (1973b), 34-5.

19 Nachtigal (1971-87), iv, 284-5.

20 I say Fur, but most of these rituals are common thoughout Sudanic Africa.

21 Nachtigal (1971—87), iv, 328.

beat which announced the sultan's death was speeded up to proclaim his successor,

All Fashir was feasting and rejoicing [at a prominent wedding]. Suddenly the *nahas* [copper drums] sounded, and it got around that Sultan Husayn was dead.[22]

The new sultan's name was proclaimed to the people by the *moge*, the court jesters and criers.[23]

The accession rituals began when the new sultan went into seclusion for seven days in the huts within the innermost court of the palace, during which he transacted no public business.[24] On the eighth day the *habbobat*/"grandmothers" came under their *malika*/"queen" to the sultan; they, some slave, some freeborn Keira, were ritual experts in the *aadinga* (Ar. *'awa'id*)/"the customs" or traditional religion.[25] Each carried two throwing knives (Fur, *sambal*) which they clashed together, and one carried a brush which had been blanched and a jar containing a liquid, the composition of which was unknown to al-Tunisi's informants.[26] At intervals she sprinkled the sultan while all cried out certain ritual phrases; they then took him in procession together with the *korkwa* or royal guards to the drum-house (Ar. *bayt al-nahas*), located in an outer court by the *orre de* or "male" gate.

Since only the sultan and the *habbobat* entered the drum-house, al-Tunisi's informants could tell him little more, although given the importance of the drums this was probably the high point of the accession ceremonies and the enthronement that followed may have had less significance. The women apparently ranged themselves around the most sacred of the drums, the female *al-mansura*/"the

---

22 AP 1, 3/13, 54-5, informant Muhammad Dayfan; al-Tunisi (1965), 102 (89 & 158).

23 AP1, 3/13, 38-43.

24 Al-Tunisi (1965), 167 (160 & 250). The following account of the royal rituals is far from exhaustive; I have rather sought to underline their non-Islamic character.

25 Nachtigal (1971-87), iv, 326.

26 Arkell (1939), 251-68. The liquid may have been *balila*, corn soaked in water then boiled before eating, according to one of Arkell's informants, AP1, 3/13, 52-3.

victorious", repeating their cries and clashing their throwing knives. They then accompanied the sultan to where the *kukur* or throne was waiting.[27]

The sultan was then enthroned upon the *kukur* for the first and only time in his reign. While he sat there, one of his chiefs, the *abbo irlingo*, placed a *taqiyya* (cap) on his head, another chief his *'imma* (a long piece of cloth wound around the *taqiyya*), another his shawl until he was fully dressed. An oath of allegiance was then sworn by the assembled chiefs and it was announced that the sultan had been enthroned. The *kukur* was returned to drum-house and public life was resumed when "The new sultan opened his *diwan*".[28]

The sultan's public life was governed by taboos, protocols, rituals and festivals. Of the latter the most important public festival was the *jalud al-nahas/*"the covering of the drums", the great national festival. Around "the covering of the drums" clustered a series of rituals, feasts and parades during which the ruler's links to his people were cemented, tribute and taxes were brought in and counted, and punishments were awarded, all to the greater glory of the Keira.

The "covering of the drums" was held in about February or March, in the dry season, and lasted eight to ten days.[29] The festival proper was preceded by the reading of the Quran and the offering of sacrifices (*sadaqa*) at the tombs of the past sultans at Turra in Jabal Marra. Similar sacrifices were made at the tombs of the pagan kings, although here the Quran readings were omitted. All the members of the Keira clan, the title-holders, provincial governors and district chiefs were required to be present at the festival, which opened by the ceremony of the "first sowing". The sultan, wearing a simple white garment and

---

27 Al-Tunisi (1965), 98 (85 & 152).

28 Ibid. and AP1, 3/13, 52-3.

29 Nachtigal (1971-87), iv, 338 says the festival was held in the spring "notwithstanding the Muslim calendar", and was followed by the *kundanga* feast in Rajab (in the year of his visit, Rajab 1291=February/March 1874). This appears to be confirmed by Browne (1806), 344, that the festival was held on 27 Rabi' I each year [which date has no particular religious significance], which would mean approximately February/March for the years of his stay in Darfur.

sandals (both royal heirlooms) was escorted to a nearby field which had been cleared save for one tree. This he felled with an axe given him by the *sultan al-haddadin* (Fur, *mirong sagal*)/"the chief of the blacksmiths". He then sowed some *dukhn* in the seven holes he had made, which were afterwards covered by the *habbobas*.[30]

During the return to the *fashir*, a hunt was held in which it was made certain that some hares and gazelles were captured. At about the time of the evening prayer the sultan chose two white cows and a steer to be used in the ceremonies of the following day. The next day he killed the animals and the skin of one of them was cleaned by a group of title-holders; in the afternoon it was affixed to the drums by the "chief of the blacksmiths". The sultan then smashed a rib from the chosen cow over the *mansura* drum; "It would have been a very bad omen for the country if he had not succeeded in doing this; by proper preparation beforehand, care was therefore taken here too so that there should be no mishap".[31]

The next day a wether, "which had to be light-coloured and black around the eyes" was slaughtered. Its flesh was then distributed in a pre-determined order among the chiefs; "It was characteristic that, as much as possible, established connections were taken into consideration in this distribution. The chief of the Jellaba (i.e. the head of the merchant community), for example, had the right to the animal's feet and the lower part of the leg, since these merchants were continually travelling."[32]

Three days later the *kundanga* feast was held.[33] If the "covering of the drums" was a public affirmation of royal power in its eminent

---

30 Nachtigal (1971-87), iv, 338-9; Browne (1806), 323. Felkin (1884-85) 225-7 describes the festival as celebrated by a local chief after the downfall of the first sultanate.

31 Nachtigal (1971-87), iv, 339-40 and al-Tunisi (1965), 173-4 (165-6 & 257-8), the basmala which must be said in order that the flesh be lawful to Muslims was not said when the animals were killed. Compare Brun-Rollet (1855), 280-1 for a similar ceremony at al-Qallabat.

32 Nachtigal (1971-87), iv, 340.

33 Ibid., and *shartay* Hasab Allah Abu'l-Bashar (Tarni, 9.4.1974) and Beaton (1941), 186-7.

symbol, the drums, the *kundanga* feast was a direct and fearsome affirmation by the Keira clan of loyalty to the ruler, a kind of trial by ordeal. The entrails of the wether had been allowed to putrefy, and mixed with pepper and butter kept inside the drums from the previous year's festival; the princes and princesses were then obliged to eat some of the mixture, while behind them stood slaves ready to kill any who displayed the slightest hesitation, since it was believed that anyone contemplating treachery would be unable to eat.[34]

The feast may have at one time included a human victim, but on this the evidence is contradictory and inconclusive. Browne makes no mention of human sacrifice. Al-Tunisi reports that he was told that a young boy and girl, whose names had to be Muhammad and Fatima, were sacrificed and their flesh eaten: "If this be true, these people are infidels, barbarians outraging God and His Prophet."[35] Nachtigal was given a similar account but assured that it had been discontinued in Sultan Sulayman's time,[36] and indeed it is hard to reconcile the custom with, for example, the piety of Muhammad al-Husayn. The latter is said to have refrained from reprisal when his turbulent brother Abu Bakr coughed audibly at the *kundanga* as a deliberate affront to his brother.[37]

The feast was followed by a series of fantasias (Ar. *'arda*) during which the sultan reviewed his horsemen, the chiefs bringing with

---

34 Nachtigal (1971-87), iv, 340 includes only the royal family; al-Tunisi (1965), 174 (166 & 258) and Cuny (1858), 19-20 include the title-holders.

35 Al-Tunisi (1965), 174 (166 & 258); there was knowledge of the sacrifice outside Darfur. There is a highly-coloured version in Combes (1846), ii, 128-40, and a more sober version in Cuny (1858), 19.

36 Nachtigal (1971-87), iv, 340-1; the account was repeated to me by *shartay* Hasab Allah Abu'l-Bashar, who had assuredly not read Nachtigal (Tarni, 9.4.1974).

37 Cuny (1858), 19 says al-Husayn abolished human sacrifice, but I find it had to believe that it survived so late; on the Abu Bakr episode, see Nachtigal (1971-87), iv, 341. H.A. MacMichael, *Notes on Darfur* 1916 (typescript, University of Khartoum), 69-70 reports that the sacrifice was performed in 1898 by Husayn Abu Kawda, a Bideyati adventurer who briefly proclaimed himself Sultan before 'Ali Dinar's return. See also Tubiana (1964), 179-81. The issue of human sacrifice is inconclusively discussed in McGregor (2001), 78.

them their retainers, "Every man who has or can procure a horse shews him at the public meeting."[38] Nachtigal arrived in al-Fashir in time to see the sixth of the seven parades held on 13 March 1874,

No very imposing impression was to be expected, for many of the dignatories who were not absolutely obliged to take part had withdrawn to their *hawakir* because of the high corn prices.[39]

The great men were expected to give a present to the sultan at this time; Browne noted that the head of the merchants gave presents "worth sixty head of slaves".[40] Those holding estates from the sultan were particularly expected to provide presents in lieu of the taxes from which they were exempted. Provincial chiefs brought in not only taxes but also criminals, charged with murder or adultery; those found guilty were often beaten to death or, under 'Ali Dinar, hanged on the parade ground.[41]

"The great sultan appears almost as a divinity towards his subjects";[42] the sacrality of African kingship found throughout Sudanic Africa and beyond, reinforced by Islamic protocol, was expressed in a number of taboos and observances. When the sultan spat, his spittle was covered, when he sneezed all around him made a clicking noise; he wore a veil, as did all the Keira; he ate alone and of only certain kinds of food, and spoke through an intermediary, usually an official called *khashm al-kalam/*"the mouth of the speech".[43] Those coming into the royal presence had to bare themselves to the waist

---

38 Browne (1806), 344.
39 Nachtigal (1971-87), iv, 341. The *'arda* continued (not only in Darfur) under the British, who shared with their Sudanese subjects a love of horses and an interest in horse-breeding, and developed them into horseshows and gymkhanas.
40 Browne (1806), 245.
41 PA (al-Fashir), *Western Darfur District Handbook*.
42 Messadaglia (1888), 41-61.
43 On spitting and sneezing, al-Tunisi (1965), 198-9 (191 & 289-91); on eating taboos, Shuqayr (1903), ii, 124; MacMichael (1922), i, 116 and Pallme (1846), 354. Abu Madyan, a son of Sultan 'Abd al-Rahman, would not eat bread, the food "of servants and slaves" (al-Tunisi, op. cit.); on the khashm al-kalam, AP1 3/13, 38-43.

and squat upon their haunches, although here the rules varied with the rank of the chief. *Fuqara* were not required to squat, but instead raised their hands in a gesture of prayer for the ruler.[44] Naturally, the sultan's person was sacred, a taboo that embraced all the Keira. An Egyptian musketeer whose killing of the *khalifa* Ishaq ended the civil war was lavishly rewarded by 'Abd al-Rahman and then executed, while an oral account of the murder of Abu'l-Khayrat, one of the "shadow sultans", in 1891 emphasised that all his assassins met a violent death.[45]

The sultan's death mirrored the state's death; it placed all power and legitimacy in limbo, hence the necessity for secrecy until his successor had been chosen. Until Ahmad Bukr's time the sultan's death was also the signal for the death of the *kamni*, a title-holder of great prestige but little power. He functioned as a species of "shadow sultan" or *alter ego*, being metaphorically described as the "sultan's neck", and was expected to die in the same manner as had his master.[46]

Upon the sultan's death the sacred fire within the palace was allowed to go out, only to be relit upon the new sultan's accession.[47] The dead ruler's body was prepared for its journey to Turra where all the sultans except 'Umar Lel and Ibrahim Qarad were buried. Turra was sacred to the Keira; Tayrab's embalmed body was brought back from Kordofan to be buried there, while 'Abd al-Rahman had Ishaq buried there. The body was taken by camel along a traditional route by fixed stages, the cortège first stopping at the boundary of Dar Turra, then at Kamala Keirei "the camels can go no further", then at Difang Kowla and at Hajang Keingwo "the pilgrims have returned", where it was met by the *imam* of Turra who escorted the cortège to the burial ground. The tombs and the nearby mosque were under the

---

44 Nachtigal (1971-87), iv, 326-67 and AP1 4/16, 24-31.
45 Al-Tunisi (1965), 348-9 (376-7; not given in the English transl.) and SAD, P.J. Sandison's Papers.
46 Nachtigal (1971-87), iv, 326-7 & MacMichael (1922), i, 95-6.
47 Nachtigal (1971-87), iv, 328.

care of a Jawami'a *fuqara* clan who had settled at Turra in the late seventeenth century.[48]

This description of the ritual cycle is incomplete; its purpose here is less ethnographic and more to highlight the vitality of Fur tradition and the complexity of its response to Islam. There are hints of an increasing sense of "stage management" as one moves from al-Tunisi's to Nachtigal's description; whether this is a result of the vitality diminishing or of the travellers' different cultural backgrounds is hard to say. In form the ritual cycle was essentially the magnification by the state of local ritual life: the accession ceremonies paralleled those of the provincial and local chiefs, drums were everywhere the symbol of political unity and authority, old women were ritual guardians and seers at local shrines devoted mainly to snake and tree cults throughout the Fur lands, and the pervasive influences of religious norms and sanctions far older than Islam informed all aspects of the popular and political culture.

The Fashir

The [Kotoko] city became an intellectualised image of the universe in which each element as well as itself was a reflection of this universe.[49]

The cosmological dimension of the Keira *fashir*[50] is virtually lost to us, but its location, form and function can be traced over time. In Jabal Marra are palace sites within the Turra region associated with Sulayman Solongdungo, Musa (Tong Kilo at Jabal Nami) and Ahmad Bukr.[51] From about 1680, when the Keira moved down

---

48 AP2, 10/48, 235; informant imam 'Abd al-Latif of Turra. For a description of Turra, which was rebuilt by 'Ali Dinar in 1910, see McGregor (2001), 95-7.

49 Lebeuf (1969), 93.

50 *Fashir*, a word of unknown origin, was strictly the open area in front of the royal camp; it was used in Kanem/Borno, Palmer (1928), i, 36; in Bagirmi, Nachtigal (1971-87), iii, 314 and 316; in Wadai, Barth (1857-59) ii, 657, and in Sinnar, *Makhtuta* (1961), 51.

51 The various sites are described with a detailed map in McGregor (2001), 91-5.

Diagram 2

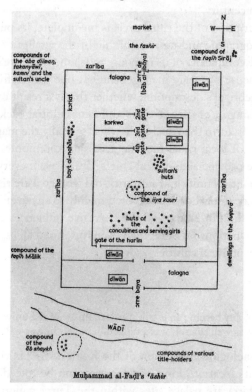

Muḥammad al-Faḍl's *ʿāshir*

on to the plains west of Jabal Marra, each sultan had one or more *fashirs*, their location reflecting the military and political priorities of the moment.[52] The last great *fashir* west of the mountains was Tayrab's magnificent palace at Shoba near modern Kabkabiyya, but it was Tayrab who shifted the epicentre of the sultanate east of the Marra Mountains. These royal camps were built of stone, brick or millet stalks (or a combination) according to available materials. The final phase was the emergence of a permanent capital at al-Fashir in approximately 1206/1791-92 around the *rahad* Tandalti, where two

---

52 Ibid., 95 for the sites of the fashirs of Muhammad Dawra, Abu'l-Qasim and Tayrab.

palaces *bayt al-qadim*/"the old house", seemingly south of the *rahad*, and *tong baasi*/"the royal house", north of the *rahad* (in the area now called *tombasi*), were built during the nineteenth century.[53] On his return 'Ali Dinar had a new two-storey square-shaped palace built on a ridge east of the *rahad*, which is one of the finest indigenous buildings in the Sudan.

Throughout these stages the basic structure of the *fashir* changed. All kept the traditional round "African palace" form of a series of enclosures encircled by a large outer or girdle wall. This is approximately the form of the palace complexes of the Turra/Ro Kuuri region. With the move to the plains, the central palace structure within the encircling walls began to take on a square form culminating in Tayrab's great palace at Shoba, a most potent symbol of Keira power in his reign.

Tayrab had a complex of buildings erected at Shoba including his own palace, a palace for his *iiya baasi* or royal sister, and a mosque, all built of burnt brick. Tayrab's palace is a square construction, a series of rooms around a central courtyard embedded in a maze of stone walls. The Sultan imported various Fur and slave groups to Shoba—the Buuranga, Kuuringa ("people of the ruler" a slave group) and Baasanga or Baasinga ("royal people")—partly to help in the building and partly to serve the *fashir*; they settled around the palace complex, taking the boundaries of their land from the four gates of the mosque compound. Near the palace were the "rock-gongs"—one small and two large boulders, which were pounded to summon the people.[54]

The *fashir* was the Fur household writ large; the male and female entrances, the layout of the huts, the *diwan*s or places of audience, the messes (Fur *daranga*) where men ate communally—all were features common to royal palace and prosperous households alike. The gender division, or better the divide between the public and the

---

53 Al-Tunisi (1965), 114 (103 & 176).

54 A plan of the palace is given in Balfour-Paul (1955), 25; on the rock-gongs, see Davidson (1959), 85. I am grateful to a former student of mine, Mustafa al-Hajj, for a collection of oral traditions from Shoba; see further Adelberger (1990), 145-6 and 148.

private domains, was fundamental; the *fashir*, usually aligned north/ south, was divided into a northern male sphere and a southern female sphere, entered by the *orre de*/"the men's gate" and the *orre baya*/"the narrow gate" (because the women's entrance was much smaller) respectively.[55] The *orre de* thus led to the public domain which housed the officials, servants and slaves of the sultan, the *orre baya* to the quarters of the royal women, concubines and some of the eunuchs.[56]

"The men's gate" led into a series of great enclosures; the first immediately to the right of the entrance, housed the royal horses and their grooms/*koriat* (Arabicised to *korayat*) and the royal heralds or messengers/*folgony* (Ar. *falqanawi*, pl. *falaqna*). Within the next enclosure were the huts of the *korkwa*/"spearmen", the sultan's body-guard, and within the final enclosure before that of the sultan were the *lofenga* or royal eunuchs. Intimacy of service was thus measured by proximity to the ruler.

This graduated intimacy also determined the functions of the *di-wan*s, rectangular earthern platforms covered with fine sand, upon which was a smaller platform covered with carpets where the sultan sat. There were three of these *diwan*s within the public domains, used for increasingly private purposes the nearer they were to the sultan's quarters.

Al-Tunisi places the huts of the *iiya kuuri* or premier wife in the centre of the sultan's quarters and his own huts in the northeast of the compound. Nearby were the store-houses built of earth as a protection against fire, in which the sultan's clothes and treasures were kept secure.

Al-Tunisi—not unreasonably from his own perspective—equates the female side of the palace with the *harim* of the palaces and houses of the Islamic heartlands. But this misses the significance of

---

55 Both Browne (1806), 579-80 and plan opposite p. 326, and al-Tunisi (1965) 203-7 (197-201 & 298-303) provide diagrams; the following is based upon them unless otherwise indicated.

56 In Darfur the sultan's intimates entered by the "men's gate", whereas in Wadai, where the palace had a similar layout, it was a mark of royal favour to be allowed to enter by the "narrow gate"; al-Tunisi (1965), 197-99 (189-91 & 288-90) and Nachtigal (1971-87), iv, 332.

SULTAN AND FASHIR

Diagram 3

THE HIERARCHY AS A WARBAND

órrengdulung
("the sultans's face",
rules 4 kings in Dār
Birged)

fórang aba
("father of the Fur",
rules 4 kings in east-
ern Dār Fūr)

kamni
("the sultan's neck,
rules 4 kings)

takanawi
("left hand", rules
12 *shartays* in the
north)

SULTAN

aba diimang
("right hand" rules
12 *shartays* in the
south-west)

āb shaykh dālī
("the sultan's backside",
rules 4 kings in eastern
Dār Fūr)

abbo umó
("the sultan's backbone",
rules 4 kings in the
south-east)

OFFICIALS OF THE FASHIR

malik warabāya
("king of the narrow
gate")

malik waradāya
("king of the male
gate")

TAX OFFICIALS

malik al-abīdiyya
("king of the (royal) slaves)

malik al-qawwārīn
("king of the tolls")

4 *amīns*

4 *mulūk al-kōrāyāt*
("kings of the grooms")

malik al-jabbāyyin
("king of the revenue")

soming dogala
("masters of the (palace) cadets")

malik al-haddādīn
("king of the ironsmiths")

103

Diagram 4

THE ROYAL AND STATE HIERARCHY

(according to Nachtigal,iv, 325-32)

(For definitions of the titles, see glossary)

SULTAN

OFFICIALS OF STATE AND KEIRA TITLES
in order of precedence

1.   *abó (habbóba)*
2.   *kamni (abbo fóre)*
3.   *āb shaykh dāli*
4.   *iiya baasi*
5.   *iiya kuuri (umm "kittir koa")*
6.   *umm soming dogala*
7.   *órrengdulung*
8.   *fórang aba*
9.   the *abónga (ḥabbōbāt)*, of whom there were several
10, 11.   *abbo irlingo and abbo iringa,* equal in rank
12, 13.   *abbo dugunga* and *abbo kunjara*
14, 15.   *miróng sagal (malik al-haddādīn)* and *abu'l-jabbayyin;* these four are of equal rank
16, 17.   the *baasinga,* equal in rank

PROVINCIAL GOVERNORS
who ranked after the officials of state and the Keira family
1.   *takanāwī* (north)
2.   *aba diimang* (south-west)
3.   *abbo umó* (south-east)

"AD HOC" APPOINTMENTS
1.   *maqdūm*
2.   *khabīr*
3.   *sulṭān al-ghazwa*

the "narrow gate"; Fur women, whether royal or commoners, had immeasurably greater social freedom than the women of al-Tunisi's homeland. Within the enclosure leading from the *orre baya* were the huts of the slave women and concubines engaged in the unending task of grinding millet and preparing food; here there were also two other *diwan*s, "where the sultan spends his evenings with his intimate friends and those he invites to be with him".[57]

"The house of tribute"

The *fashir* was the kernel of the state; it served as political arena, hub of the administration, training ground for generals and administrators, centre for the redistribution of goods and services, final court of justice, backdrop for the national festivals, audiences and parades held on the open ground before the palace compound which was the *fashir* proper. To the palace came a stream of petitioners seeking justice or favour, *fuqara*, adventurers, successful slavers from the south, and on one occasion a company of rope-dancers from Iran "on tour" in Darfur.[58] Only the long-distance merchants kept their distance at Kobbei (Ar. Kubbayh), a day's march northwest of al-Fashir. This followed a common Sudanic pattern whereby the political and commercial centres were kept apart: Sinnar and Arbaji in the Funj Sultanate, al-Ubayyid and Bara in Kordofan, Nimro and Wara in Wadai are other examples.

A common synonym for *fashir*—*bayt al-jibaya*/"the house of tribute"—emphasises its role as a clearing-house for taxes and tribute. By no means all the revenues were physically brought to the capital, but records of the collection, storage and distribution were controlled by the sultan through a network of *jabbayyin* or tax collectors. A distinction was made between the revenues in grain, cloth or animals intended to provision the palace and revenues assigned to maintain the military and administrative machine throughout the state. The former were the revenues of the "narrow gate", the latter those of the "men's gate".

Throughout the sultanate there were royal domains or estates whose revenues were assigned exclusively to the *fashir*. The largest was Jabal Marra itself, *ro kuuri* (Ar. *hakurat al-sultan*) or "the ruler's estate", but others included Dar Fongoro in the southwest and ap-

---

57 Al-Tunisi (1965), 207 (200 & 293) and Cuny (1854), 91-2.
58 Browne (1806), 260-1.

parently all the sites of the former *fashirs*.[59] These estates lay outside the provincial administration, and some, like Dar Fongoro—an area only lately colonised by the Fur—were administered by stewards of the sultan called *fore* ("beard").[60] The royal estates were constantly growing as the sultans planted slave settlements thoughout their domains. Lack of slaves was to force 'Ali Dinar to extract areas or communities from the jurisdiction of the local chiefs so that he could exploit them for the needs of the *fashir*. Two such communities, some of whose records survive, are those of Dar Simiyat, the Simiyat being a branch of the Berti, and the Jawami'a *fuqara* of Jadid al-Sayl, both communities lying northeast of al-Fashir. Both communities were constantly bombarded by demands from the *manzil al-'ali*/"the exalted house" or the *manzil al-jabai*/"the house of tribute" for money, 30 or 50 dollars at a time, quantities of grain, cloth or wood (see diagram 10).

Food was the main item brought from the royal estates,

During the days of Sultan |Dinar] all the Jebel Nas [the people of Jabal Marra] spent more than half the year carrying salt, corn, wheat, shatta [pepper], onion and honey from the Jebel Dars to Kalokitting where large dumps were collected by the head of the Jebel, Shartai Ali Abdel Galil, and then sent to El Fasher.[61]

Moreover Jabal Marra and Dar Fongoro supplied the sultan's table with delicacies, such as honey and wheat that were less common elsewhere. One sultan is said to have introduced bananas into Jabal Marra; 'Ali Dinar had them dug up and taken to al-Fashir, but they failed to thrive there.[62] Nearly as important was cloth brought to the palace, usually in pieces called *takkiyya* (pl. *takaki*), perhaps the commonest unit of exchange within the sultanate.

---

59 Ibid., 345-6; al-Tunisi (1965), 152 (138 & 226); Cadalvène and Breuvery (1841), ii, 206 note; Lauture (1855-56), 98, and Nachtigal (1971-87), iv, 326.

60 PA (al-Fashir), *Western Darfur District Handbook*; on Dar Fongoro, see O'Fahey (1982), 81-2.

61 PA (al-Fashir) *Western Darfur District Handbook*.

62 AP2, 10/48, 132 at Nuwo on the Wadi Deira.

All provisions for the palace were brought to the "narrow gate" which was under the control of the *malik al-warabaya*. Many of 'Ali Dinar's demands to the community at Jadid al-Sayl were made through Sitayba Khatir, *malik al-warabaya* and *amin al-takkiyya*, and in one document the community was said to "belong to the *takkiyya*".[63]

The palace community, numbering several thousand, was where aspirants for power and position sought the sultan's eye and favour at court. Provincial and district chiefs came mainly from local ruling lineages, but the central bureaucracy was recruited from within and around the palace. This recruitment was institutionalised in the *som* or palace school, for which Mamluk and Ottoman practice may have provided the model.[64] Located to the right of the second gate of the public domain, the *som* was "the assembly place where the people come together for conversation or a common meal".[65] Here the *soming dogala/*"the children of the school" congregated and were taught—how formally is not clear—by a group of officials of whom the head was the *abbo soming dogala*. This title was usually held concurrently with that of *malik al-nahas/*"king of the drums" by the chief of the powerful Konyunga clan. The domestic arrangements of the *som* were supervised by one of the sultan's wives, the *umm soming dogala*.[66]

The children or cadets of the *som* were probably taught to read and write. When 'Ali Dinar revived the school, the children of his chiefs were taught there by leading al-Fashir *fuqara*.[67] Both slaves

---

63 DF55.7/28 (22 Sha'ban 1317/26 December 1899), a demand for 50 dollars. On the malik al-warabaya, see al-Tunisi (1965), 183 (174 & 269-70).

64 In modern *Fur som* means Quranic school (Sudanese Ar. *khalwa* or *masid*), the meaning given in a word-list of 1812; see Seetzen (1816), 328.

65 Nachtigal (1971-87), iv, 335, recalling the *dara* or men's mess of Fur villages.

66 [66] Ibid., iv, 329.

67 The autobiography of al-hajj Muhammad Mahbub al-Bideyati, transcribed and translated by Issa Hasan Khayar, J. and M.-J. Tubiana (unpublished typescript), includes a description of the school, where he was educated. The whole autobiography gives a vivid picture of life at 'Ali Dinar's court.

and freemen attended the *som* whence they were recruited into the service of the *fashir*. The royal slaves came from the tithe paid to the sultan of the slaves captured in the south.[68] The drying-up of supplies was a problem for 'Ali Dinar and one expedient he adopted was to enslave the illegitimate children in Jabal Marra.[69] Another route to the *som* and royal service was the sanctuary offered by the palace to refugees from tribal feuds. Exile from the lineage, *muruj min al-ahl*, was a sanction used in cases of manslaughter within the lineage, which could not be dealt with so easily by blood-money settlement. A powerful chiefly family owed its origin to one Hanafi, a Berti who killed a fellow clansman and fled to al-Fashir where he took service under 'Abd al-Rahman.[70]

The palace was used to keep potential chiefs or lineage rivals in reserve as hopefuls or hostages. The Kiliba ruling clan of the Dar Galla Zaghawa achieved power through 'Abd al-Karim, one of two orphans taken to al-Fashir by their mother. He was taken up by Sultan Muhammad al-Fadl, and on reaching manhood was given command of some horsemen in an expedition against the 'Irayqat. 'Abd al-Karim drove the nomads from the Karnoi Wells in Dar Galla and was given command of the region by the grateful Sultan.[71] Chiefs could indeed be appointed from the *som*; Adam Sulayman was appointed Sultan of the Daju while still at the court school, his people being administered by a deputy or *wakil*.[72]

It is difficult to exaggerate both the *fashir*'s importance and the variety of the functions it fulfilled. It was the stage both for the sultan's

---

68 Browne (1806), 343 and al-Tunisi (1851), 474.

69 AP2, 10/48, 23, but the same practice is reported in the previous century; Henniker (1823), 174.

70 Abu Adam 'Abd Allah (Nyala, 29.6.1969); on exile, see Holy (1974), 120-51.

71 PA (al-Fashir) DP/66. B. 6; tribal affairs, General Zaghawa, vol. 11 and AP1, 5/21, 59-67.

72 PA (al-Fashir) DP/66. B. 31, Dago, note by G.D. Lampen (12.3.1932). Consciously or unconsciously, the British continued the system with the "Green Hats" school set up for chiefly sons by John Owen and Hugh Bousted in Zalingei in the 1930s; see Bousted (1971) 124 and 175-6.

public life[73] and for display and consumption by the elite whose control over land, herds and slaves enabled a conspicuous differentiation in rank and power to be displayed. Nevertheless the exploitative and economic functions of the palace, at least in the pre-1874 sultanate, were complemented by its ritual and cosmological roles. The spaciousness of the older *fashir*s contrasts sharply with the intimacy of 'Ali Dinar's palace, where a central inward-looking block, the sultan's residence, was surrounded by the *harim* (but still with its "narrow gate"), storerooms, guardhouses, stables and the like, the private and purposeful headquarters of a personal autocracy.

---

73 Browne (1806), 732-6 describes a public and several private audiences by the sultan; at the public ones he was mounted on a mule. Audiences were held in the mornings between 6 and 10 o'clock (225).

6
HIERARCHIES AND ELITES

Hierarchies

The *fashir* was the arena for a ruling elite whose composition and functions changed significantly over time. In tracing the evolution of this elite and of the institutions by which it maintained itself, our perspective is foreshortened because relatively little is known of its earliest phases; in compensation a rich and detailed picture of the elite in the nineteenth century can be drawn. The chapters that follow analyse the economic basis and political functions of this elite; here an analytical description is given of the main groups that were formally or informally part of the ruling establishment, and of those who were its challengers from within and without.

Both the written and oral sources present us with detailed accounts of the title-holding hierarchy that surrounded the sultan. Some clarity can be brought to this plethora of titles and offices by distinguishing between hierarchies and elites, between title and power. This distinction in fact describes the evolution of the ruling class, from the days of the warband in the late seventeenth and most of the eighteenth century when title and power went closely together. It was only with the establishment of a permanent capital, which gave birth to new political forms, that the gap between the ideal pattern of offices and titles and the actual wielders of power grew.

The ruling establishment was both more and less than the titled hierarchy—more in that the panorama of titles excluded a number of groups or "connections" (in the eighteenth century English meaning) that were very much part of the elite, and less in that the day-to-day exercise of political power was in the hands of a small informal circle of confidants around the sultan. This latter is the political elite which was recruited from and buttressed by the wider religious, military and commercial elites, by the *fuqara*, merchants, slaves, soldiers and courtiers. The hierarchy of titles statically presented by al-Tunisi and Nachtigal conceals the realities of all hierarchies: obsolescent offices, power without title, the political "joker in the pack", and the simple force of personality.

The creation of hierarchies was an ongoing process; the titled hierarchy was in fact a palimpsest of titles, each frozen at a point in time as the political and administrative realities moved on elsewhere. The provincial administration provides the clearest illustration of this progressive obsolescence; in the nineteenth century the sultans felt the need for roving commissioners to oversee and administer units larger than the pre-existing provinces or to carry out a specific task, hence the appointment of *maqdum*s. Some of these in turn became institutionalised and hereditary, so that after the restoration of the sultanate in 1898 'Ali Dinar felt impelled to superimpose commissioners or *mandub*s over the now static *maqdum*s (see Chapter Eight). The British in their turn experimented with the creation of an Emirate of Zalingei to which they appointed a son of Sultan Ibrahim Qarad; the experiment failed, as did an attempt by the present Sudanese Government in 1994 to restructure Dar Masalit to the detriment of the Masalit and the advantage of the Arabs.[1]

This process underlines both a major analytical difficulty for the historian and a real problem for the sultans. Appointment by the centre was sooner or later converted by the appointee or his descendants into locally-based power, as grants of land became hereditary and intermarriage linked the family to the local elites. Thus to situate a notable fully, one should know the lands he held and his kin connections, as well as his formal position in the hierarchy. Such information is rarely complete, and the resultant two-dimensional picture

---

1   Flint and De Waal (2005), 58-9.

produces a sharp dichotomy between rulers and ruled that ignores the localised and communal aspects of their relationship.[2] This diffusion of power throughout the state through a territorially-based nobility seems to have suited the pre-1874 sultans; 'Ali Dinar, by necessity or perhaps by temperament, was led to rule directly through his *mandub*s and generals. Ironically his unwillingness or inability to rely on the old ruling families forced him to deal with and strengthen the lower-level chiefs. When the British occupied Darfur in 1916 they found the tribal chiefs firmly entrenched and were never able effectively to restrain them, except in the Fur lands of the southwest where they were able to reinstall an element of the old Fur ruling elite, the *aba diimang*s, over the district and local chiefs.

The oldest stratum within the title-holding hierarchy was, unsurprisingly, from the Fur named groups or *orrenga* described in Chapter One. The Fur chiefs clustered around the Jabal Marra and early eighteenth century sultans were in origin lineage chiefs, warlords or ritual experts. It is from these core *orrenga* that the earliest title-holders came such as *abbo*[3] *dugunga, a. kunjaara, a. buldanga* and *a. konyunga,* the latter seemingly having a Tunjur connection. These appear genealogically to be among the most ancient titles. Equally ancient titles, which acquired a territorial dimension, were *aba* [here seemingly "lord"] *diimang,* the ruler of southwestern Darfur, and *ta-kanawi,*[4] governor of the north, also probably with a Tunjur origin. Ritual titles from the remote past included the *kamni* or "shadow sultan" and the *forang aba,* "father of the Fur", the guardian of Fur law and custom.

We possess two detailed descriptions of the title hierarchy, by al-Tunisi between 1800 and 1810 (but remembered over twenty years

---

2   My (1992), 57-93 comes close to this level of information, but there are still gaps.

3   *Abbo,* a Fur title of respect that often precedes other titles; it is rendered as *abu* or *ab*/"father" in the documents. I am tempted to equate them with Scottish and Irish clan titles such as "The O'Connor Don" or "The Great [*mor,* "great" in Gaelic] Campbell".

4   So written in the documents, but pronounced takanyawi; in Fur togoing. On the history of the title, see Tubiana (1985), 261-74.

later) and Nachtigal in 1873, an interval of approximately two generations. Their descriptions are given here in diagram 3. The main
impression that emerges from a comparison of the two is that al-
Tunisi is describing a functioning hierarchy and Nachtigal its shell.
Al-Tunisi's account is partial by comparison with Nachtigal's and
with oral sources,[5] but however frail his memory he does stress the
warmaking origins of the hierarchy, grouping the title-holders around
the sultan according to whether they commanded in the army on the
march; he was closer to the time of wars and expansion. Al-Tunisi
misunderstood much of what he was told, and thus his translations
of the titles are not literal but metaphorical interpretations of their
position within the warband.[6]

For al-Tunisi the central hierarchy of the warband consisted of
the four territorial lords, the *takanawi* (north), *aba diimang* (southwest), *abbo uumo* (south-east; *uumo* means fontanelle in Fur) and
ab shaykh daali (east); then followed the *kamni* (known to the Fur
as *abbo fore*), the *orrengdulung* (literally "the doorposts", the majordomo), and in his other guise as head of the slave hierarchy, the *ab*

---

5   Al-Tunisi fails to mention, for example, *maqdum* in his Darfur volume, only
     casually comparing it to the Wadai title *'aqid* in his Wadai work (1851), 144;
     I was in error earlier in saying that he failed to mention the title, O'Fahey
     and Spaulding (1974), 210, n. 69. Fortunately when Arkell, 'Abd al-Rahim
     and later myself were collecting oral traditions in Darfur, neither al-Tunisi
     (not printed in Arabic until 1965) nor Nachtigal (in German only until 1971)
     were available in Darfur. Some people knew Shuqayr; when I interviewed
     the then *maqdum* of Nyala, 'Abd al-Rahman Adam Rijal, in 1969, he had
     one of his *ajawid* or elders read Shuqayr for me almost ceremoniously; this
     was followed by another elder giving me a very different version. It was
     for this reason that I held out against having my own work translated into
     Arabic, but I was thwarted in the end by 'Abd al-Hafiz Sulayman 'Umar
     who elegantly translated *State and Society*.
6   Compare Shuqayr (1903), ii, 120; Tayrab's order of march for the Kordofan
     campaign is described anachronistically. "The governor of the capital",
     muhafiz al-'asima (for *orrengdulung*), leads the vanguard, the *maqdum al-
     sa'id* (for the *aba diimang*) is on the right flank, the *maqdum al-rih* (for the
     takanawi) on the left, and the *maqdum al-gharb* (for the *abbo uumo*) in the
     rear. Shuqayr's informant was interpreting the situation in the 1780s in the
     light of the 1870s; thus by 1870 the military functions of the *aba diimang*
     had been taken over by the *maqdum al-sa'id*.

114

shaykh again. Each title was firmly based upon a territorial command from which levies were drawn in time of war. Nachtigal's hierarchy is vastly more complex, and since it is unlikely that the number of venerable and ancient offices proliferated within two generations, al-Tunisi's account is assuredly abbreviated. Nachtigal, writing from within the perspective of al-Fashir, then the capital for nearly eighty years, divides the hierarchy into officials of the state, with whom he groups the royal or Keira titles, the provincial governors and *maqdum*s, and the officials, stewards and ritual experts attached to the two palaces in al-Fashir, *tong baasi* (now Tombasi) and *bayt al-qadim*, respectively north and south of the Rahad Tandalti. But Nachtigal describes a title-holding elite that had been in many ways emasculated, or swamped by new elites—or else, as Adelberger puts it, centralisation and land-grants, *hawakir*, seriously weakened the *orrenga*, which became less relevant, but not entirely.[7]

There was a Keira core, "today the kingdom"/*natu muluk keira*—Tayrab is said to have used this phrase to name the royal clan. The Keira clan was internally organised and disciplined, but played little corporate part in the day-to-day running of the sultanate. Membership was practically effective for only about two generations; third or fourth generation Keira, male and female, tended to disappear into the masses, a distinction expressed in those called *baasinga*/"royals" and *tellanga*/"distant", between those who had access to "sovereignty"/*mamlaka* and those who did not.[8] The male descendants of the sultans were supervised by several of their number, each responsible for the descendants of a particular sultan.[9] Sons and daughters were usually granted estates by their father, but apart from the nominated heir or others powerful for some particular reason, they played little part in the affairs of the state.

---

7   There is a further Gaelic comparison in the attempts of Elizabethan and Hanoverian rulers of England to tame the clans through titles and land; thus The O'Neil becomes the Earl of Tyrone, The Grahame the Marquis of Montrose and The Great Campbell the Duke of Argyle.

8   SAD, P.J. Sandison's Papers.

9   Nachtigal (1971-87), iv, 331-2.

The royal women were, by contrast, a more visible element, whether as *mayram* (pl. *mayarim*),[10] young and marriageable, or as a *habboba* (or in Fur, *abo*, both meaning "grandmother"), older and less shackled. Muslim visitors professed to be horrified or titillated by the freedom and power of the royal women in particular and women generally within the sultanate.[11] But the royal women were a segment of pre-Islamic Fur culture encapsulated in an increasingly Islamised court, and thus patterns of behaviour that would have gone unremarked in Fur villages were noticeable at court. Social freedom was matched by religious conservatism; just as in the countryside it was the women who preserved the traditional religion, so Browne heard that Sultan 'Abd al-Rahman's women still worshipped the old spirits within his *harim*.[12] Among the several royal female titles were *iiya kuuri*/"powerful mother", borne by the sultan's premier wife, *iiya baasi*/"royal mother", for the sultan's favourite sister, and *habboba* or Queen Mother.[13] Of the first two the *iiya baasi* was politically the most influential; an early royal sister, Zamzam, had been executed when her brother, Abu'l-Qasim, was put to death (see above Chapter Three). A later *iiya baasi*, Taja, used a women's power of shame to steel her brother, 'Ali Dinar, to resist the British, "If you don't fight, give me your trousers and take my *kanfus* [a type of skirt]. You are no man."[14]

Zamzam Umm al-Nasr, *iiya baasi* to Muhammad al-Husayn, dominated the later years of her brother's reign when circumstance and personality enabled her to become virtual ruler of the state. In 1856 her brother finally lost his sight and thereafter Zamzam

---

10 The title was used in Kanem/Borno, Wadai and Bagirmi as well as among the Zaghawa.

11 Al-Tunisi (1965), 93 (77 & 142-3).

12 Browne (1806), 350.

13 Al-Tunisi (1965), 93 (77 & 142-3) and Nachtigal (1971-87), 329.

14 SAD, P.J. Sandison's Papers.

Moved around the country at the head of her armed men, plundered the districts under her control, and easily got from the weak king those *hawakir* she particularly liked.[15]

Riding her horse like a man with her skirt hitched up, as the royal women customarily did, and issuing charters in her name, Zamzam was a formidable figure. Fearing his growing influence over her pious brother, she joined forces with the Wazir Ahmad Shatta to drive the *faqih* Muhammad al-Bulalawi (see Chapter Twelve) from Darfur despite the feeble protests of the Sultan. Yet when her brother died she starved herself to death and was succeeded as *iiya baasi* by 'Arofa, sister to Ibrahim Qarad, who was married to a prominent Kobbei merchant, Muhammad al-Imam.[16]

The royal clan, male and female; the clan or *orrenga* chiefs; the warlords and provincial rulers; the ritual experts and the guardians of the royal regalia and relics together present a bewildering complex of titles and offices. The investigation of each of these, even where their antecedents and holders are known, is unnecessary here since my purpose is to describe the evolution of hierarchy into elite rather than give a minute description of each component. What is signifi-cant is that the traditions of some of the oldest and most powerful and enduring chiefly lines suggest an origin as quasi-independent lords, that in other words the Jabal Marra kingdom expanded by incorporation which in turn led to formation of a hierarchy.[17] The geographical underlay can be faintly discerned; the *aba diimanga* of the southwest were probably as ancient a dynasty as the Keira, they were enthroned with much the same ritual and they ruled over the most populous part of the Fur heartlands. Although less is known of their history, the *abbo uumo* (the last died in 1965)—lords of the southeast—were probably of similar antiquity.

---

15 Nachtigal (1971-87), iv, 316.

16 Ibid, 106, 315-26, 329 and 365; Slatin (1896), 46-8 and O'Fahey (1977a), 123-4. DF291.39/4, undated is a charter issued by Zamzam in Dar Zayyadiyya, while DF190.18/50, 21 Ramadan 1289/22 November 1872, and DF198.18/56, 29 Ramadan 1270/16 June 1854, are court hearings by the *orrengdulung* Baraka acting on behalf (*bi-niyaba*) of Zamzam.

17 Adelberger (1990), 119-31.

The most powerful of the Fur clans after the Keira were the Kony-unga, whose claim to Tunjur origins indicates roots reaching beyond Keira times. Konyunga families held several titles, among them *takanawi*. According to one tradition the original *takanawi*s were chamberlains to the sultans at Turra. Ahmad Bukr's *takanawi* quar-relled with his master and tried to kill him; he was executed but the title descended to a son who, however, was sent away to govern the north. Another son was appointed *malik al-nahas* and yet another *abbo fore* or *kamni*.[18]

This tradition is evidently a late conflation to explain Konyunga claims to a range of titles, but the general outline is supported by oth-er sources. The original home of the Konyunga was in the Fata Barnu and Kurma regions west of Kutum, an area traditionally associated with the Tunjur; the *takanawi* and his people were based in this re-gion, particularly in Dar Inga whose chiefs also claim to be of Tunjur origin. Other Konyunga moved south to Birinjil and Muhajiriyya in Dar Birged; these were followers of the "master of the drums". Their most famous chief was Ibrahim w. Ramad; between 1790 and 1810 he was probably the second most powerful man in the sultanate, who played a crucial role in Kurra's downfall (see Chapter Three). He also campaigned frequently and profitably in Kordofan and the south, and Browne, who met him, describes him as "the most opulent man in the empire, except the Sultan".[19] Among Ibrahim's many sons was *malik al-hajj* 'Abd Allah, who appears as a judge in a number of land disputes, and Sa'd al-Din who succeeded his father as *malik al-nahas* and held the title *soming dogala*. Sa'd al-Din, a powerful figure in the latter years of Muhammad al-Husayn's reign, died fighting al-Zubayr at Dara; his son Tibn inherited his father's title under 'Ali Dinar, who gave him responsibility for al-Fashir market.[20]

18 AP1, 5, 21, 89.

19 Browne (1806), 224; AP1, 5.21,90 and AP2, 10/48, 232, and Sabil Adam Ya'qub, al-Fashir, 4.6.1970.

20 DF105.12/13 (seal-date 1255/1839-49 [O'Fahey & Abu Salim (1983), 58-61]) and DF174.18/34 are court hearings before 'Abd Allah. On Tibn, Hill (1967), 359; DF76.10/1, 21 Ramadan 1332/13 August 1914, is a

Elites

The evolution of an informal and diverse elite at court out of the older "Sudanic kingship" hierarchy was the result of the recruitment of new groups and connections into the ruling institution in response to new needs and situations. Royal marriage strategy increasingly integrated local or tribal elites into the centre, but could be perilous as the conflict between 'Abd al-Rahman, Ishaq and the Zaghawa illustrated (see Chapter Three); the needs of a literate bureaucracy called forth a class of scribes; military expansion and especially the needs of slave-raiding led to the supersession of tribal levies by professionals. One group whose membership of the elite was ambiguous were the long-distance merchants, since so much of their activity and capital lay outside the state's boundaries.

The establishment of al-Fashir speeded up the transition from hierarchy to elite, intensifying the emergence of factions and new groupings, or at least made them more visible. Marriage remained a vehicle of advancement as the formation of a Beigo "court party" demonstrated. The Beigo, speakers of a Daju dialect, were a despised semi-servile group living on the southeastern margins of the sultanate; their chance came when a Beigo woman, Umm Buza, became the favourite wife of 'Abd al-Rahman and mother of Muhammad al-Fadl. On the latter's accession the Beigo came into their own, as is symbolised by the story of Umm Busa's brother, Fazari. When a messenger came to tell Fazari of his nephew's accession he was watering his animals, and in a gesture he broke the mud walls around the well and let the water run into the ground. He thereupon rode off to al-Fashir where he was granted the taxes of the Majanin Arabs. The Beigo were freed from their semi-servile status, their chief entitled "sultan", and various Beigo achieved positions at court.[21] One,

---

confirmation from Tibn of the sale of a slave woman by public auction in al-Fashir.

21 On Fazari, see Shuqayr (1903), ii, 123-4, but see al-Tunisi (1965), 99-100 (88-9 & 158-60) where the Majanin are given to a Berti man by 'Abd al-Rahman, who marries Umm Busa en route to Kordofan; Nachtigal (1971-87), iv, 301 and 333 and Slatin (1896), 44-5. Muhammad al-Fadl's favour to the Beigo is echoed in two confirmatory charters (DF179.18/39 and 152.18/12),

119

Diagram 5. THE PALACE OFFICIALS *(according to Nachtigal, iv, 332-7)*
(Definitions of the titles where known are given in the Glossary)

"OLD PALACE" *(bayt al-qadīm*—north west of Rahad Tandalti)
"Those [officials] who belonged only to the royal household were
divided in accordance with the layout of the royal palace in two groups
completely separated from the others", Nachtigal.332.

"THE MALE GATE" *(órre de)*
abbo kotingo and *abbo daadinga,*
    were equal in rank
abbo soming dogala and 3
    mulūk-al-falāqna, were equal in rank;
    the former was "Master of the Male
    Gate"
6 chiefs of the *kórkwa*, of whom one was
    abbo kórkwa
    mulūk al-kōrāyāt, who included the
    following title-holders:
        abbo jinshiga and *abbo ari*
        malik al-mundanga and *malik karga*
        malik al-tunis and *qirqid al-kōrāyāt*
        abu'l-kōrāyāt and *malik al-zimām*
        malik al-sarj and *malik al-hizām*
        malik muruga and *malik al-hiṣān*, etc.

Other officials
included:
abbo dugo erre
malik kurringa
kham al-kalām

Among the officials of the "Male Gate"
were the "Guardians of the Royal
Regalia",*liakwa*, of whom there were 23,
among them:
    7 *kór dórming sagala*
    4 *sumókwa sagala*
    kukur sagala
    sambalanga sagal
    shiremang sagal
    bandaging sagal
    kere kasang sagal
    tadang morlengang sagal
and the keepers of the royal drums, of
whom one was the *malik al nahās*

"THE NARROW GATE" *(órre baya)*
abbo jóde, who had 14 subordinate
eunuch officials, among them the
    kitir koa
    kämmel koa
    gutto koa
    ᶜaqid
    malik saaringa
    mirriṇ kwa

"THE ROYAL HOUSE" *(tong baasi,*
or colloquially *tombaasi)*
(south-east of Rahad Tandalti)
The officials of the *tong baasi* were
mainly concerned with supervision
of various taxes in kind.
malik khamīs, a eunuch who had
under him:
    malik barr jues (*barr jues*, a royal
    domain west of al-Fāshir)
    malik "tom fal".
    malik "bitir"
    malik (or *amin*) *al-takkiyya.*

one from *amin* 'Abd al-Bari and dated Dhu'l-hijja 1231/December 1815-
January 1816, the other (undated) from his son, Muhammad al-Fadl
(named after the sultan?); both are addressed to the Awlad Jabir *fuqara* of
the Zayyadiyya.

'Abd al-Bari, became Wazir to the new Sultan but seems gradually to have lost power to Adam Bosh, a Meidobi slave who became more and more the Sultan's confidant. Towards the end of Muhammad al-Fadl's long reign, 'Abd al-Bari began to intrigue against the plans of the Sultan and Bosh to put Muhammad al-Husayn upon the throne. 'Abd al-Bari was outmanuoevred and committed suicide in chagrin.[22] The Beigo regained their position under 'Ali Dinar, one of whose confidants and fellow prisoners in Omdurman was Muhammad Kebkebe, who rode with the Sultan back to Darfur in 1898 and for whom 'Ali Dinar revived the title "sultan".

Darfur's power in the early nineteenth century, an empire stretching to the Nile, with great wealth from the trade with Egypt, attracted a variety of adventurers, among them mercenaries. Professional warriors embued with the knightly or *furusiyya* (from *faris*, "knight") ethos were common in eastern Sudanic Africa; the later history of Sinnar is full of the wars and skirmishes of such figures.[23] A famous example in Darfur was a mercenary from Bagirmi, Ahmad Jurab al-Fil al-Baqirmawi, who played a key role in Kurra's downfall. "A mature man renowned for chivalry (*furusiyya*) and courage", Ahmad was granted estates near Kobbei and married into the Fulani Awlad 'Ali lineage.[24] Another such figure was the slave-raider Muhammad Daldang w. Binayya. And although firearms seemingly had little place in knightly warfare, the sultans were interested in foreign experts in their use. The overseer of the royal muskets, the *bandaging sagal* (literally, "chief of the muskets [Ar. *bunduq*]") was said to be a descendant of a European, while the Baatinga, a Fur *orre* in the southwest, are said to trace their origins to a Syrian Mamluk captured by Tayrab in Kordofan. He was nicknamed *baati* from the leather bag (for musket balls?) which he constantly wore, and was

---

22 Nachtigal (1971-87), iv, 305-7.
23 'Abd al-Mahmud n.d. (1965), describes the poetry of this ethos.
24 Lauture (1855-56), 40; Shuqayr (1903), 125-6, and 'Ali Salih Bidayn, a descendant of Ahmad and a former student of mine who taught me much about the Fulani of Darfur, al-Fashir 30.3.1974.

much favoured by the Sultan who made him his *abbo ari*.[25] Another was the Greek who came to an unfortunate end, Ahmad Agha (see Chapter Four).

By the beginning of the nineteenth century the elite was beginning to be dominated by three elements, slaves, *fuqara* and merchants. The employment of slaves as a counterweight to a hereditary or territorial nobility was common in Muslim states and beyond. Darfur was no exception and career opportunities for slaves, albeit involuntary, were varied. Within the court complex they functioned as guards, administrators, concubines, domestics and attendants, organised in a complex hierarchy of groups and titles that paralleled and overlapped with the free hierarchy. The female area and the *harim* were administered by eunuchs most of whom came from Dar Runga, a province within Wadai's sphere influence to the southwest of Darfur. Al-Tunisi devotes a chapter to various anecdotes of the *harim* and of the power of the eunuchs, of whom there were more than 1,000.[26]

It was a eunuch who held the greatest office of state, that of *abbo shaykh daali*. Although the "Father Shaykh" had to be a eunuch in order to have access to all parts of the palace complex, not all who held the office were slaves, "whether they had been castrated as a punishment for some crime, or because of illness, or had done it themselves out of ambition".[27] Ambition undoubtedly motivated the greatest slave in Darfur's history, Muhammad Kurra. Kurra's revolt, especially if the story of his plan to supplant the Keira with his own family is true, which I doubt, has points of comparison with the successful *coup d'état* of Muhammad Abu Likaylik against the Sinnar Sultan in 1761-62, a *coup* that brought to power new forces in opposition to the old nobility.[28] But whereas the old Funj nobility appear to have lacked cohesion and an ethnic base, in Darfur the title-holders were too strong. Nevertheless the sense of two "parties"—old-es-

---

25 Nachtigal (1971-87), iv, 339 and AP2, 10/48, 105. "Baati" is described as being an artillery man. See Adelberger (1990), 144 & 146.

26 Al-Tunisi (1965), 249-67 (250-70 & 355-72).

27 Nachtigal (1971-87), iv, 329.

28 O'Fahey & Spaulding (1974), 93-5.

tablished territorial chiefs versus slave administrators and other "new men"—remained a constant until the end of the first sultanate. Kurra was the only slave in Darfur's history to achieve a quasi-independent position of power, but the brevity of his hold upon it demonstrated the inherent fragility of the slave's position. Free notables held and inherited by right and had kin connections to sustain them, but slaves were at the pleasure of their masters; once Muhammad al-Fadl was old enough to exercise the strength of his office Kurra was probably doomed. Neither benign treatment not great power altered legal or social status; slaves remained tools to be taken up or discarded at the will of their masters. Gifted individuals from the slave caste were raised up by the sultans precisely because they were more tractable than the hereditary nobility. And the Keira sultans had particular cause to be wary since two of their number, 'Umar Lel and Abu'l-Qasim, had met their deaths at the hands of the chiefs.

In a later generation another slave rose to power who was particularly representative of the "new men", namely Adam Bosh. A Meidobi, Adam was educated in the *soming dogala*; his nickname *tarbush*/"fez" (Bosh in the documents) was given him because on one occasion he had been presented to a merchant who had given Sultan Muhammad al-Fadl an especially fine *tarbush*. The overseer of the *soming dogala* bore Adam a grudge and sent him to be the Sultan's present; however, the Sultan ordered him to be brought back. He later served as *khabir* and royal merchant to Asyut and left a good reputation among the merchant community there.[29] Like Kurra, Adam got his chance through a succession crisis, and he came to power in 1838 with Muhammad al-Husayn, whose accession he had arranged at behest of the latter's father. For nearly twenty years he was the second man in the state despite the continuous hostility of various Keira led by Abu Bakr b. Muhammad al-Fadl; "[Adam] was indispensable to the king and could be maintained by the king in his position only by a great expenditure of tact and intelligence".[30] He met his end about 1856 at the hands of the Rizayqat (see Chapter

---

29 Nachtigal (1971-87), iv, 307-8 and Cuny (1858), 11-12.
30 Nachtigal (1971-87), iv, 314.

Four). Although Adam's position was emphasised by his title *al-wazir al-a'zam*/"Grand Wazir", reminiscent of Ottoman usage, he was no Kurra but rather an able and hardworking administrator.[31]

A similar role was played by Adam's son Bakhit, who soon began to advance as a chief in the *korkwa* or sultan's bodyguards. In the established tradition he played a crucial role in putting Ibrahim Qarad on the throne in Safar 1290/April 1873.[32] Like his father he was later rewarded with the title of wazir in a ceremony which Nachtigal witnessed and vividly describes.[33] He calls Bakhit a "half-slave" and this suggestion of a quasi-servile status may be implied by the phrase *tabi' li'l-sultan*/"servant to the sultan" which appears on the seals of several of the *ab shaykhs* but not on those of notables who, from other sources, were undoubtedly freeborn.[34]

While the slaves were an integral if distinct segment of the formal hierarchy, the *fuqara* and merchants were less formally linked to the court. Some *fuqara* were appointed as *qadis*.[35] Others operated at court with a variety of functions such as teaching the royal and chiefly children, acting as legal advisers, secretaries and mediators in political crises and, not least, interceding with the divine through magic.

There were always limits to the influence of the *fuqara*; Muhammad al-Husayn, a devout and apparently learned Muslim, surrounded himself with scholars and Sufis such as Muhammad b. al-Mukhtar al-Shinqiti (d. 1299/1881-82), a Mauritanian Sufi from Shinqit of the Tijaniyya *tariqa*, who initiated the Sultan into the order, thus introducing what has become the dominant order in Darfur ever since, and acted as his ambassador to Egypt. On another occasion he acted as the Sultan's envoy to the Sublime Porte.[36] Others included Ahmad

---

31 In DF63.8/1, dated 25 Rajab 1267/7 June 1851, his titles are given as *al-wazir al-a'zam al-ab al-maqdum*.

32 Nachtigal (1971-87), iv, 319-20 and Shuqayr (1903), ii, 133-4.

33 Nachtigal (1971-87), iv, 370-1.

34 A sequence of charters from the *ab shaykh daalis* appears in my (1991), 101-10.

35 See my (1977a),110-24.

36 See O'Fahey (1994), i, 287-8.

al-Dardiri from a Duwalib holy family, later also Tijanis, from Khorsi in Kordofan, and the unfortunate Muhammad al-Bulalawi.[37] But the Sultan's favour to such visitors aroused the contempt of the notables, not least his brother Abu Bakr, and he was not always strong enough to protect his favourites, as the fate of al-Bulalawi illustrates.

Already by the eighteenth century the *fuqara* were a visible element at court. Several married Keira women; Tahir Jamus, leader of the Borno community in Manawashi—in whose mosque the last Sultan of the first sultanate, Ibrahim Qarad, is buried—married Fatassa, a daughter of Tayrab; Nur al-Ansari of Kobbei married Hawwa bt. 'Abd al-Rahman, and there are other examples.[38] But they were a subordinate element at court, if only because they lacked the power of the notables and the wealth of the merchants. Here one may contrast the circumscribed position of the court *fuqara* with their rural counterparts whose influence, radiating out from their mosque settlements, derived not only from royal patronage but from the variety of services—spiritual, educational, magical and medical—that they could offer the communities around them.

Before the routinisation of their power within a static court, some holy men were able to play a quasi-political role as mediators, a part for which their religious prestige would superficially seem to have qualified them admirably. In fact they were rarely successful. The *faqih* 'Ali b. Yusuf al-Futawi and two others, one from Katsina (now in northern Nigeria), attempted to mediate between Muhammad Dawra and his son, Musa 'Anqarib. The three holy men sought to arrange a meeting between father and son. Fearing treachery by Dawra, they made the former swear on the Qur'an not to harm his son, but the religious sanction proved worthless, and at the meeting the father killed his son with his own hands.[39] The *fuqara* appear to have intervened more decisively in the Bara succession crisis, but a careful reading of al-Tunisi suggests that they were called in to sanction a

---

37 On Khorsi and the Dardiris, see Qasim (1996), ii, 850-1, MacMichael (1912), 93 and al-Tayyib (1991), 242-4.

38 Nachtigal (1971-87), iv, 293.

39 Ibid, 283 and Cadalvène and Breuvery (1841), ii, 200.

compromise already agreed upon by others. With a strong Sultan, the spiritual estate subsided even further; several holy men were the object of 'Abd al-Rahman's enmity. He tried to do away with Tahir Jamus of Manawashi, his brother-in-law and one of the most noted holy men of his day, because of his alleged preference for Tayrab's sons.[40] Even one of his closest confidants—Maliki al-Futawi, son of the unsuccessful mediator above—was deliberately excluded from the arrangements made by the Sultan and Kurra for Muhammad al-Fadl to accede. But when the other "sons of the sultans" moved on the capital to contest Kurra's *coup*, they were said to have been bewitched by Maliki.[41] The supernatural could still be useful.

Subordination of the religious to the political establishment is a norm in the Muslim world; only in times of stress or political upheaval is the religious leadership able to come into its own. Similarly subordinate were the merchants, but just as the *fuqara* were more independent than the *'ulama* of Cairo or Baghdad precisely because they were in a frontier environment and operated in a Sufi world, so the merchants were more visibly part of the elite because the structure of the trading networks made them more independent.

The merchants and their trade are discussed below (Chapter Eleven), but it is relevant to their place within the elite that the heyday of Darfur/Egyptian trade, 1750 to 1860, was a crucial factor in the emergence of a centralising sultanate. The sultans were concerned primarily to profit from the trade, but not necessarily to administer it in all its aspects. However, since the organisation of a large caravan often of several thousand camels to cross the desert required great resources, and the caravan's reception in Egypt was a quasi-diplomatic affair, trade and politics were intimately linked. And throughout the period of flourishing trade the sultans actively traded on their own behalf through royal merchants and servants. These royal merchants—whether primarily agents or relatives of the sultan, or merchants acting as his agents—used the profits on the

---

40 Nachtigal (1971-87), iv, 293.
41 Al-Tunisi (1965), 324-5 (350-1 & 462-3). The Fulani holy men in Darfur have a reputation as masters of magic.

goods sold in Egypt to trade on the sultan's account, operating with ambassadorial status (as the French clearly understood, see Chapter Four).[42]

A number of the *khabir*s or large-scale merchants became intimately connected with the court, a fact recognised in the customary way, by intermarriage with the Keira. The *khabir* Muhammad al-Imam from Dongola married a daughter of Muhammad al-Husayn, while an earlier Sultan, probably Tayrab, married Fatima bt. Idris Bakrawi of the Danaqla merchant community in Bara.[43] Nachtigal comments on the close friendship between his travelling companion on the road from Wadai, the merchant *al-hajj* Ahmad Tangatanga, and 'Abd al-Rahman, a son of Muhammad al-Husayn.[44] A representative figure was 'Ali Bey Ibrahim; when the German traveller Robert Hartmann met him in 1859 at Asyut, 'Ali described himself as *ser'asker* or general to Muhammad al-Husayn. In 1874 Nachtigal met him at Kobbei, where he maintained of the two mosques there. The *khabir* himself told Shuqayr a revealing little snippet,

I went one day to the sultan to greet him, taking with me a valuable present of Egyptian goods worth 9,000 piastres and he presented me with 200 of the finest camels.[45]

Several of the merchants were described as *khadim* or "servant" of the sultan; in 1902 Sultan Muhammad Salih of Wadai, better known

---

42 Browne (1806), 346 and Frank in Denon (1809), ccxxxvii.

43 Nachtigal (1971-87), iv, 329; on Muhammad and his brother, Hamza, Hill (1967), 150-1, and on Fatima, Muhammad 'Abd al-Rahim's Papers, NRO, box 8.

44 Nachtigal (1971-87), iv, 377, his numerous references to al-hajj Ahmad make a rounded and sympathetic portrait.

45 Hartmann (1863), 68; Nachtigal (1971-87), iv, 254 and Shuqayr (1903), ii, 146, 132 and 134 (a similar story involving Sultan Ibrahim Qarad). Shuqayr also gives a photograph of 'Ali Bey (opp. ii, 134). See O'Fahey and Abu Salim (1983), 113-18 for documents concerning an estate of 'Ali's at Kobbei. 'Ali, from the Tirayfiyya section of the Ja'aliyyin, was born in Kobbei in 1819 and studied with one of Tunjur *fuqara* of Khiriban, 'Abd al-Rahman Kakama (see ibid., 53-8). He returned to Darfur after the restoration of the sultanate and died in al-Fashir in 1912, an honoured associate of 'Ali Dinar; Qasim (1996), iv, 1602-3. See also LaRue (1984).

as Dud Murra (r. 1902-9), issued a safe-conduct for Muhammad Abu Takkiyya, "merchant and servant" of 'Ali Dinar, to return to Darfur.[46] Others were employed as ambassadors; it was the *khabir* al-Khandaqawi who took Muhammad al-Fadl's defiant assertion of Darfur's right to independence to Egypt (see Chapter Four) and *al-hajj* Hamza b. al-Imam who travelled to Egypt in 1873 in an attempt to stave off al-Zubayr's invasion.[47] More peacefully, when the *iiya baasi* Zamzam made the pilgrimage in 1830, she was accompanied by the *khabir* "Kunn", probably Muhammad Kannuna.[48]

However close their relations with the sultans, the merchants as a body kept their distance physically by staying at Kobbei. The difficulties inherent in the relationship come out in the story of the caravan *daldalat rihayma*/"a little mercy comes down", so called (caravans were commonly given nicknames, just as lorries are today) because Darfur was experiencing famine at the time (*c.* 1910). Led by *al-hajj* Badawi Zayn al-'Abdin, a leading merchant and *wakil* ("agent") to 'Ali Dinar, the caravan went to Wadai but was attacked on its way back by the Tama. Badawi appealed to the French for protection and compensation which he received, but meanwhile rumours reached the ever-suspicious Sultan that his *wakil* was intending to defraud him. When Badawi arrived he was ordered to camp by the tomb of the Sultan's father, Zakariyya (just west of the palace on the slope down to the Rahad Tandalti), pending an investigation; after an agonising delay Badawi was finally cleared and only then allowed to see his family and home.[49]

---

46 DF85.10/10, 12 Muharram 1320/21 April 1902; text and transl. in Kapteijns and Spaulding (1988), 161-63, where they refer to a copy in the Ministry of Culture in Khartoum, but I photographed the original in al-Fashir in 1974; how it ended up in the ministry I do not know.

47 Nachtigal (1971-87), iv, 375. See also the letter reproduced in Deny (1930), plate liii.

48 Cuny (1854), 111. On Kannuna, see O'Fahey and Abu Salim (1983), 106-13.

49 'Ali al-hajj Badawi Zayn al-'Abdin (al-Fashir, 13.8.1976); the son told the story very vividly.

The politics of the elite

The underlying movement within the elite was from a formally structured and titled hierarchy, of the type commonly found ruling Sudanic states, to a looser elite composed of interest groups operating within an increasingly bureaucratic framework (in the sense of a literate, less kin-based structure). As with so many other facets of the sultanate's history, the evolution was abruptly cut off in 1874, to be resumed in very different conditions in 1898. It was one symptom of a profound reorientation within the state which gathered pace through the nineteenth century, of which other aspects were the growth of the estate system, the appointment of *maqdum*s or commissioners to oversee the territorial chiefs, and an increasingly literate bureaucracy and judiciary. To call this evolution Islamic is to ignore the economic and political realities that underpinned it; Islam largely articulated the changes, but it did not precipitate them.

The only occasions when we can dimly watch the elite "playing politics" are the succession crises, when the court became an arena in which people fought and died for lineage and group interests. Death came to the losers not only at the hands of the victorious, because for a Muslim society suicide was surprisingly common among the elite: the Wazir 'Ali b. Jami', the *maqdum* 'Abd al-Sid, the Wazir 'Abd al-Bari and the *iiya baasi* Zamzam all took their own lives following political or military failure.

Each succession crisis was resolved when the new sultan and his supporters took power, the Zaghawa with Tayrab, Kurra—albeit briefly—and the Beigo with Muhammad al-Fadl, Adam Bosh with Muhammad al-Husayn, and Bakhit b. Adam Bosh with Ibrahim Qarad. If one considers those who acted in opposition—the *abbo konyunga* Ibrahim w. Ramad and Muhammad w. Daldang (a nephew of Tayrab) against Kurra, and an array of title-holders (the *abbo daadinga, orrengdulung* and the *abu'l-jabbayyin* among others) against Bosh and *malik saaringa* (among other titles) Ahmad Shatta against Bosh's son—it seems possible to discern two consistent poles of opposition; it would be going too far to call them parties, "connections" in its eighteenth-century English meaning would be more accurate.

129

The proponents and "insiders" were the slave and court confidants, and the opponents, and increasingly in terms of decision-making "outsiders", the territorial chiefs and heads of the great lineages.

The *dramatis personae* of the succession crisis of 1873 reveals the nature of the two "connections", while its dénouement reveals the reasons for the "insiders" success. Before he died in April 1873, Muhammad al-Husayn arranged with his confidants Bakhit b. Adam Bosh and Khayr Qarib—the latter a Fartit slave described as *amin al-khaziniyya* or "secretary to the Treasury"—that his younger son, Ibrahim Qarad, should succeed him. However, a faction led by the *faqih* al-Dardiri and Ahmad Shatta wanted as sultan the eldest son Abu'l-Bashar who was married to the Wazir's daughter. The slaves and merchants had dominated the state under Muhammad al-Husayn, and the Fur grandees led by Shatta were determined to assert their interests; thus was the crisis interpreted to Nachtigal while still in Wadai on his way to Darfur: "It was therefore very probable that there would be a conflict between the slaves and soldiers under Ibrahim, the claimant to the throne, and the free Fur under Hasib Allah [Hasab Allah, a brother of Abu'l-Bashar, and a possible candidate]".[50]

As the old Sultan lay dying, al-Dardiri summoned Ahmad Shatta back from Dara in the south where he was *maqdum*, while Abu'l-Bashar entered the capital with 1,000 riflemen. In the long drawn-out "stand-off" that preceded the Sultan's death, it was Bakhit who controlled the palace and the most armed men, and by the time Shatta arrived from Dara, al-Dardiri was in prison. Arkell, nearly fifty years later, recorded the actual day of the crisis from an eye-witness,

When Sultan Husayn died the *amins* having often heard Husayn's wishes at once appointed Ibrahim without informing anyone. That was the day of *mayram* Zahra's wedding to 'Abd al-Qadir Dinga. All Fashir was feasting and rejoicing. Suddenly the *nahas* [drums] sounded and it got around that Sultan Husayn was dead. The *amins* sent for the wazir [Shatta] and said, "Who shall we make sultan?" He said, "Abukr, the eldest son" [possibly an error for Abu'l-Bashar, but there was an Abukr involved]. They said, "Lift the curtain"; and

---

50 Nachtigal (1971-87), iv, 70-1, 88 and 319-20, and Shuqayr (1903), ii, 133-4. One is tempted to interpret the Fartit slave's name as "Good to have nearby"!

then he saw Ibrahim already on the throne. He then craved forgiveness. They sent for the *malik* Khamis al-Burqawi and the same then happened. The wazir and *malik* Khamis were then kept under restraint for 30 days.[51]

---

51 AP1, 3/14, 54-55, informant Muhammad Dayfan, a Bagirmi eunuch who had been given as a present to Muhammad al-Husayn by the Wadai Sultan.

7

LAND AND PRIVILEGE

"[The Sultan] speaks in public of the soil and its productions and of the people as little else than his slaves."[1]

Prelude

The present chapter is based on Chapter Four in my 1980 book and the various articles, including translations of land documents, that I and others have subsequently published. The corpus of some 350 documents photographed mainly by myself can be found on the Web (see *Sources and Bibliography*). The current importance of the topic explains this prelude.

My recent experience with the UN Mission to the Sudan, the African Union and the World Bank has caused me to rethink my earlier interpretations. This re-interpretation is based on a simple point, namely that the language in which these documents were formulated and recorded in the documents we have came from the lawbooks of the Maliki School of Law, principally the *Mukhtasar* of Khalil b. Ishaq (d. 776/1374). This language is both precise and ambiguous; precise because the formulae are used consistently throughout the *corpus* of documents that we have, ambiguous because they in effect conceal the underlying principles behind these grants, in particular one, namely that *all* grants were made at the sultan's pleasure and their renewal was dependent on that pleasure.

---

1   Browne (1806), 314.

Before going further with this discussion, there are issues of understanding that need clarifying. What did terms like "to grant", "estate", "ownership" etc. actually mean to the actors involved? This not just a historiographical or semantic issue, but a deadly living issue in today's Darfur. In the flood of literature produced by the international organisations—the World Bank, the UN, USAID and the like— *hakura* has taken on a life of its own, as meaning ownership-rights in some absolute sense.[2] *But* what did the following mean to those who wrote it and those who received and guarded the document?

They [the plaintiffs in a lawsuit] occupied it [*ha'izin*, i.e. land from the time of Sultan Musa] and had free disposal of it [*tasarruf al-mallak*] for cultivation and growing. From that time [it passed] from testator (*muwarrith*) to inheritor (*warith*) until Sultan Abu'l-Qasim's time?[3]

Traduttore traditore, "the translator betrays"; I am now much less confident about what the terminology used in these document means than I was thirty years ago; the translation from the very precise Arabic of the Maliki lawbooks as transmitted in documents from an Africa of the savannas to the sonorous but specialised English of Stubbs and Blackstone is a treacherous business. My feeling now is that the comment by Browne, that opens this chapter, is crucial; estates were indeed granted, passed from generation to generation, were objects of litigation in court, and indeed the charters were in some guise title-deeds. But that the documents gave away land as

---

2   For example, "the customary mode of absorbing immigrants is to provide them with pasture and farmland, provided they accept the customs and norms of the dominant group in the area (the 'owner' of the 'hakura' or land area)," USAID, *Steps Towards the Stabilization of Governance and Livelihoods in Darfur, Sudan*, 2006, 4. The rest of the report discusses the issue in detail, largely, I suspect, on the basis of my own writings, unacknowledged. This same formulation was repeated to me in September 2006 by the nazirs of the Rizayqat, Bani Halba, Fallaita (Fallata) and the *maqdum* of Nyala. When I suggested otherwise, I was greeted with a repetition of the same formulation. The Darfur Peace Agreement (DPA), paragraph 158, refers to *hawakir* as "tribal land ownership rights".

3   DF72.8/10, hearing before Sultan Muhammad al-Husayn, dated 126[0-9]/1844-54; the hearing revolved around forged charters, where the expertise of the Sultan's secretaries may have been needed.

freehold in any absolute sense, I now doubt. Ultimately all belonged to the sultan; hence the care of the estate-owners to have their estates renewed by the new sultan; yes, they were owned and heritable, but ultimately the state decided.

Secondly, there is a demographic factor that I under-estimated earlier. If Darfur was truly a sparsely-populated land in the seventeenth and eighteenth centuries as it seems reasonable to assume, then the issue of pioneering, of opening up new land—in Islamic legal terminology *ihya al-mawat*, "making the dead [that is, land] alive"—becomes a factor. In the court hearing quoted above, the plaintiffs open their plea thus,

This land is Khiriban and near this is Kurku, the riverbed [*wadi*] and the *qoz* [sandy soil alongside the banks]. Sultan Musa settled [*sakkana*] my ancestors (*ajdadi*) there, who opened it up [*ahiuha*] by hoe and fire [*bi'l-fas wa'l-nar*] by permission from the sultan and they made a well [*biran*] there ....[4]

These two *caveat*s seem to me to be crucial to the discussion that follows, which must be regarded as open-ended.

Thus, while not entirely rejecting what I have written before, I wish somewhat to reinterpret it. If one goes through the catalogue of documents on the Web, one is soon struck by the sequences of charters accumulated over the generations by, especially, holy families. The operative verb in the second and subsequent documents in any given sequence is *tamma*, which I have usually translated as "confirmed", but I now feel that "renewed" or "executed" is a more accurate translation, as emphasising the usufructary and provisional nature of the grants. I regard my interpretation of the evolution of *jah*-rights, in the catalogue translated as "privileged status", into estate (*hakura*) rights as still valid, but would now place more emphasis on the usufructary nature of all these grants.

My earlier interpretation was too static and legalistic, influenced too much by the language of the lawbooks and by British and post-independence Sudanese administrative attitudes towards the issue, both of which took an essentially static view of the system. I also under-

---

4   Ibid.; the theme of *ihya al-mawat* comes out very clearly in a group of documents from northern Kordofan published in my (1986), 43-63.

estimated the dynamics behind the land-management aspect of the system described here. This latter aspect comes out particularly in the documents of Sultan 'Ali Dinar (see Chapter Thirteen). The point is important in that the actors in the present crisis insist that land-rights are non-negotiable and that every tribal *dar* or *hakura* is immutable.[5]

A final comment to this *mea culpa*: when I photographed the documents in the early 1970s, they were sources to delight a young historian, but otherwise only of concern to their owners; today they are weapons of war. The change has been both semantic and substantive; the term, *hakura*, originally meaning an estate granted by the sultan to a specific group of people or to a person, is now used in the context of the present conflict by all sides to mean inalienable tribal homelands; thus,

In the sparsely settled south, the Fur sultans gave a large *hakura* to each of the four main Baggara groups, Ta'aisha, Beni Halba, Habbaniya and Rizei-gat. Their Abbala [camel nomads, in this context Janjawid] cousins, moving as nomads in the densely administered northern provinces, occasionally received small estates, but had no jurisdiction over huge swathes of territory. To this day, many Abbala Arabs explain their involvement in the current conflict in terms of this 250-year-old search for land, granted to the Baggara but denied to them.[6]

This fantasy history has no basis in fact, but is believed by all, while *hakura* has become a battle-cry of the Janjawid. The battle of the documents has turned murderous; in an attack on Umm (Am) Boru in Dar Zaghawa in January 2004, a group of such documents as are described and analysed below were destroyed by the Janjawid,

Dans sa maison d'El Fasher, le melik Ali Mohammaden [of Am Boru] montre à Jérôme [Tubiana] un parchemin vieux de deux cent dix ans, qui fixe l'une des frontières de son territoire. Dans sa fuite, le vieux chef n'avait

---

5   The unalterable nature of the *hakura* has been a leitmotif of every conversation I have had with Darfurians of all camps these last three years.

6   Flint and De Waal (2005), 9. In the Darfur Peace Agreement of May 2006, *hakura* is used to mean inalienable tribal territory. When, in Abuja, I explained that this was inaccurate, everyone agreed that I was right, but continued to use it in that meaning.

emporté que son Coran dans lequel il avait oublié ce manuscrit. Tous ses autres documents ont brûlé.[7]

In no other area of Darfur's past, except perhaps for the evolving concepts of ethnicity, have the past and the present so collided as in land.

The estate system

Land was never a scarce resource (and still is not) in Darfur, but its disposition and management was a fundamental prerogative of the state. However circumscribed by local custom and tradition, the move towards the codification and organisation of land and land-use marked a break or development from the notion of land as a commodity of only local or communal concern. This break or development came when the sultans began to grant rights over land and people, rights that came to be embodied in written charters, the earliest dating from about 1700. As the state came to be ruled by a diversely recruited elite, directly dependent upon the sultan and based largely at court or in its environs, so the estate system expanded to cater to its needs at the expense of the locally or ethnically based chiefs and their communities. Thus there was imposed upon agriculturally or strategically favoured regions a grid of estates that increasingly submerged the older chiefly order. Similarly, grants of land or privilege were used to accommodate newcomers, pre-eminently the *fuqara* and merchants.

Rainland agriculture, diffuse rather than concentrated and involving greater stress on communal rights and labour than on rigidly defined and protected areas of land and small units of production, was elastic enough to cater to a variety of forms of use. But vagaries of climate and variations in soil types, *qoz* sandy soil and *tin* black clay soil for example, and the needs of grazing required a high level of

---

7   Tubiana (2006), 205. Fortunately Madame Tubiana and her husband had photographed them in 1965 and they are published in O'Fahey and Abu Salim (1983), 79-99.

resource management.[8] Although in areas like southwestern Darfur or around al-Fashir competition for estates led to the submergence of the *dimlij*s (*dilmong* in Fur) or sub-district chiefs, elsewhere accommodation between the local community and its chiefs and their overlord was more characteristic.[9] The estate system, as it developed in Darfur, was a patron-client relationship defined by land or community rather than a thoroughgoing exploitative system comparable to the irrigation-based systems of the Middle East and the Nile Valley. Underlying the estate system was the fact that people were more valuable than land; nevertheless the land itself was deemed sufficiently important for the sultans to decide who should exploit it and to write their decisions down. And the language and legal terminology used in their charters, derived from the lawbooks, owed its origin to irrigation-based societies, a fact that makes their interpretation difficult without the exegesis of oral tradition. Here one may contrast the charters, generally uninformative beyond names, dates and boundaries, with the *sijillat* or court transcripts which are replete with inter- and intra-communal disputes.

A question that I can only raise but cannot answer is whether behind the estate system there lay a conscious policy of land or resource management. One reason for my being unable to answer is that at the time of my research I did not ask the question. But there are indications that in one sense there was an element of management.[10] The estates were carefully delineated by reference to trees and natural features; their owners were very careful of their boundaries and frequently went to court to defend them. Two other factors need emphasising: the recipients' families were very careful to hold on to

---

8   Tothill (1948), 814-51 is still the best introduction to agricultural practice in Darfur before the present cataclysm.

9   Adelberger (1990), 40-2 and 186-93, the latter a list of the estates or *hawakir* in western and southwestern Darfur. On this topic, Adelberger's and my researches complement each other; he focused on western Darfur and the Fur, I on the al-Fashir and northern Darfur areas.

10 It did occur to me at the time to try and measure an estate on the ground from the description given in the charters, but since I was largely dependent on others for transport, I never had the opportunity. There was also a question of not wanting to be too intrusive.

their documents, while the British were very loath to interfere with the system. They mapped it and made notes about it but hardly ever interfered with it. My own feeling, for what it is worth, is that the sultans did have some sort of management policy; what were the principles behind it is a project for the future.

The estate system appears early in the sultanate's history and may have existed in Tunjur times if the Tunjur of Khiriban's traditions of receiving an estate from Shaw Dorshid are correct (see Chapter Two). Shuqayr ascribes the division of parts of Darfur into *hakura*s (pl. *hawakir*) to Sultan Musa.[11] No documents have come to light from Musa, but there are several references and two documents from Ahmad Bukr's time. Thus Bukr granted land to his son Muhammad Dawra at Kullu in Dobo in east-central Jabal Marra and to the *al-hajj* Zaydan at Shoba (not the Shoba of Tayrab's capital) southwest of al-Fashir. Furthermore, the two earliest charters so far discovered come either from Bukr or Dawra, being issued by the latter but with the stamp of the former's seal; they granted privileged status and land to various Awlad Jabir *fuqara* who had settled among the Zayyadiyya of the northeast. They must date from between 1700 and 1720.[12] Thus charters and the rights promulgated in them had probably come into use already by about 1700, not long after the emergence of the sultanate from the mountains.[13]

The estate system in Darfur has close parallels with that of Borno:

Titled officials and even untitled followers of the Shehu [the ruler of Borno] could be given or they could inherit, at the pleasure of the Shehu, rights

---

11 Shuqayr (1903), ii, 137. *Hakura* is the common spoken word for an estate; it appears occasionally in the documents, where the term, *iqta'*, is more usual. It does not appear to be used outside Darfur with this meaning. Lane (1984), ii, 616 gives as its meaning "A piece of land retained and enclosed by its proprietor", while Qasim (2002), 258 simply gives its usage as in Darfur.

12 AP1, 10/48, 141-2, Dawra's estate, and my (1991), 79-88. The two Bukr/ Dawra charters are published in my (1979b), 13-17.

13 There is a hiatus between the Bukr/Dawra charters and those of Tayrab, of which we have several. I saw in al-Fashir in 1974 a charter issued by Sultan Abu'l-Qasim, but stupidly failed to photograph it properly.

of revenue collection and adminstration in one or more settlements spread throughout the state.[14]

In Borno the estate-holder or *cima kura*/the "big lord", who held his rights directly from the Shehu could be granted either a territorial or an ethnic estate, the latter being a grant of rights over a group defined by birth irrespective of where they lived. The *cima kura* lived at court and administered his estates, which could number twenty or more, through *cima gana* or "junior lords". The latter were the crucial link between the *cima kura* and the local communities under their lineage chiefs. Similarly, in Darfur the titled officials were assigned rights to collect revenue from estates throughout the sultanate, administering them through stewards called *wakil* or *kursi* (literally "chair") or *sagal* in Fur. But there are differences between Borno and Darfur; the ethnic estate is not prominent in the latter, while the drastic subordination of the local chiefs to the estate-holders and their stewards, as described in Borno, did not go so far in Darfur.

There is a further parallel with Borno and indeed other Sudanic states; Condominium and oral sources distinguish between the practice of the sultans of assigning limited rights over extensive tracts of land or communities and the granting of exclusive rights over a much smaller estate, between *hakura* and *hakurat al-jah*.[15] The two types of grant differed in purpose; the former was a grant of administrative rights whereby the sultans paid their notables and through them maintained control over outlying areas, while the latter was a means of accommodating newcomers and of providing an income for members of the royal house.

The granting of privileged status, particularly to Muslim holy men, was nothing new in the Sudanic Belt; the rulers of Songhay on the Middle Niger appear to have made similar grants in the fifteenth and sixteenth centuries. Likewise the rulers of Kanem/Borno granted *mahram*s or immunities to a number of holy clans; the first

---

14 Cohen (1967), 25 and Brenner (1973), 105-10.

15 Bence Pembroke, *Darfur Province 1916*, ms. University of Khartoum; Rihaymat Allah al-Dadinqawi, al-Fashir, 7.6.1970, and Shuqayr (1903), ii, 137.

mahram is said to have been granted to Muhammad b. Mani and his descendants in the eleventh century, although it survives only in late and corrupt versions.[16] Whether such grants of privileged personal status owed their origin to any earlier Islamic precedent is unclear, although some in Darfur approach the *waqf* or pious endowment in intention.

The distinction between the two forms of grant was primarily one of scale. To the *fuqara*, merchants and members of the royal family the sultans granted exemptions from taxation over a demarcated area of land or a defined community; to the title-holders much larger estates were granted, which in turn often encompassed privileged communities or land. Unfortunately we know much more about the privileged communities than about the ruling elite above them, since the descendants of the *fuqara* especially are (or were) still sitting on their land with their charters and other documents.

There are some hints of a patron-client relationship, comparable to the ethnic estate in Borno, that existed between the holders of privileged status and the lords within whose lands they lived. In the late seventeenth century a Tunjur *faqih*, 'Abd Allah Matluq, migrated from the Tunjur centre of Jabal Hurayz to Kamala Keirei in the Khiriban district, northwest of al-Fashir. His people opened up land there and were later granted privileged status by Tayrab. Some fifty years later the Tunjur Sultan of Jabal Hurayz, Muhammad Shalabi b. 'Umar, wrote to the governor of the northern province, the *takanawi* Yahya b. Muhammad, to inform him that all the Tunjur of the north, including Matluq's descendants, had been placed under Shalabi's charge by Sultan Muhammad al-Fadl. Neither the *takanawi* nor any other official were to interfere with the *fuqara*, but nevertheless Shalabi would leave them under the *takanawi*'s jurisdiction (*dhimma*).[17] The land around al-Tawila, southwest of al-Fashir, was an estate attached to the office of the "Father Shaykh", and in a

---

16 Hunwick (1992), 133-48 and my (1981b), 19-25.

17 O'Fahey and Abu Salim (1983), 49. A neighbouring holy clan are said to have paid an informal tax to the *abbo daadinga* under whose jurisdiction they came, PA DP.K. 1(9) Gedid el Seil Omodia, note by C. Dupuis, 10.7.1928.

letter of the late 1850s or 60s the then *ab shaykh* 'Abd al-Qafa says of *al-hajj* Adam of Shoba, near al-Tawila, to an official, "His dwelling is my dwelling (*baytuhu bayti*); he is my servant (*khaddam*) and all of you are servants."[18]

In the absence of documents from the great families, al-Tunisi is our main source on their estates at the beginning of the nineteenth century and Nachtigal towards the end. The chronology is important because al-Tunisi stresses their military function,

The sultan does not give any of these dignatories any salary or pay but they all have an assignment (*iqta'*) from which they obtain their revenues. With these revenues they buy horses, arms, coats of mail and clothes and distribute them to their soldiers.[19]

And he continues that the estate-holders took neither *zaka* nor *fitr* taxes from their estates, these being reserved for the sultans, although a later source suggests that the estate-holders did receive a share of the canonical taxes.[20] The main benefits derived from the estates were the labour exacted from the tenants and the various customary taxes known collectively as *'awa'id*/"customs". The taxes are listed below, but among these communal obligations were *hamil*, the proceeds from the sale of stray slaves and animals, *diyafa*/"hospitality", *hukm*/"judgment", the fees and fines from rendering justice, and *dam*/"blood" (the chief or estate-holder's share of the blood money paid an injured party). Since in the charters of privilege, i.e. those that grant *jah*-rights, a distinction is consistently made between *al-ahkam al-shar'iyya*/"the canonical ordinances", namely *zaka* and *fitr*, and *al-subul al-'adiyya*/"the customary taxes", it would seem that in the administrative estates the grantee took the latter but not the former.

Given that needs determine form, it is probably safer not to describe the estate system in too structured a fashion; the large administrative estates, implied rather than described by al-Tunisi, appear to have given way in the nineteenth century to the small privileged

---

18 My (1991), 105-7 (79-112).

19 Al-Tunisi (1965), 184-5 (176-7 & 271-2).

20 Bence Pembroke, Darfur Province 1916 (University of Khartoum).

estate described below, designed to provide an income to the *fuqara*, petty *malik*s, courtiers with antique titles and royal sons and daughters clustered around the later Keira court. In the eighteenth century the need was for soldiers for both internal consolidation and external campaigning. Thus estate-holders were required to maintain, and bring to the annual parades (*'arda*) that followed the Drum Festival, a number of armed retainers; these were mustered and declared *tahsil*/"levied" if they and their equipment were passed as fit.[21] But generally throughout most of the nineteenth century it was the *maqdum*s who maintained what little military force was thought needed. Certain title-holders continued to hold extensive lands for military purposes; the *abbo daadinga* who commanded the *daadinga* regiment of slave troops held lands around Qoz Bayna south of al-Fashir where his men were quartered. The last pre-colonial *abbo daadinga*, Mahmud 'Ali, was estimated in 1915 to have had 200 men stationed in and around Qoz Bayna.[22]

A vivid example of the granting of lands, the fortunes of war and the necessities of administrative consolidation is provided by the career of Sulayman b. Ahmad Jaffal.[23] A Kinana Arab from Sinja on the Blue Nile, Sulayman came to Darfur in the time of Tayrab, whose favour he won by his skill in the treatment of horses, a vital military skill. He was first granted as a *hakura* the area between Marshing and Jabal Marra in the Birged country; later the region of Torba north of Malumm was added. Just before the invasion of Kordofan in around 1200/1785-86, Tayrab dismissed the Birged *shartay* of Shawnga, the area between Marshing and Torba. This move was probably connected to a revolt of Birged against Tayrab (see Chapter Three). He continued to amass further estates (see Chapter Three). The climax came in Muhammad al-Fadl's reign when the four chiefdoms were consolidated under Muhammad

---

21 Ibid.

22 MacMichael, *Notes on Darfur* (University of Khartoum); Rihaymat Allah al-Dadinqawi (al-Fashir, 7.6.1970), Mahmud al-Dadinqawi was at one time allocated the entire Zayyadiyya tribe as an estate.

23 In my earlier writings I gave the name as "Jafdal"; I had misread my fieldnotes.

Kubur b. Musa, Sulayman's grandson, as first *shartay* of Dar Birged Kajjar with its capital at Ghor Abeshei.[24]

In the nineteenth century the title-holders and others began to acquire smaller estates but in greater numbers; indeed under Muhammad al-Husayn, when the system reached its apogee, a great *malik* might have as many as twenty to thirty estates scattered around the country; the *abbo fore* is said to have held estates in every *shartaya* or district chieftaincy (of which there were about forty) except Dar Fia.[25] In 1317/1899-1900 'Ali Dinar issued a decree restoring his ancestral estates to the *maqdum* of the north, Muhammad Adam Sharif; they numbered seven, all located in north-central Darfur. These were the personal holdings of the *maqdum*'s family since, as Muhammad Adam Sharif's son later explained to a Condominium official, "the Magdumate was something entirely different and was more of a personal appointment than one giving any hereditary rights over the land included in its administrative command".[26] 'Ali Dinar, in fact, seems generally to have been reluctant to allow too great a proliferation, but he was willing to renew pre-existing estates as part of his policy of re-establishing communities on their pre-1874 lands (see Chapter Thirteen).[27]

The holders of administrative estates held neither exclusive rights to all taxes from their estates nor exclusive legal jurisdiction over their tenants; serious cases were usually referred to the *shartay*, with whom through his steward he shared any fines accruing from their judicial duties. Practice tended to vary according to time and place; in western Darfur the onus for the collection of *zaka* and *fitr* fell on the estate stewards. For example, in Zami Baya *shartaya* the stewards collected fines, *zaka* and *fitr*, taking a proportion each year to the

---

24 Sabil Adam Ya'qub (a descendant of Sulayman, al-Fashir, 1 and 4.6.970, and many other occasions).

25 AP2 10/48, 4-5, informant *shartay* Ahmaday of Dar Fia.

26 DF271.33/4; the estates are listed as Shayli, Umm Marahik, Karqa, Kelinet, Selei, Turra and Arabad, covering an extensive region north of al-Fashir; PA (al-Fashir majlis) DP.FD.66 K. 15 Azagarfa Omodia, note from Yusuf Muhammad Adam Sharif, 22.2.1931.

27 Bence Pembroke, Darfur Province 1916 (University of Khartoum).

shartay from whom in turn the sultan's emissaries collected a part for their master.[28] Nearer the capital the canonical taxes were collected directly by the *jabbayyin* or tax collectors.

Privilege and Immunity[29]

They have become privileged of God and His Prophet and as cripples to the *diwan*.[30]

The majority of the charters so far recovered grant either privileges or immunities or exclusive rights over land or people. The idea of privilege or immunity is expressed through a number of words: the most common is *jah*, but *hurma, karama, hurriyya* are also used, all expressing the notion of "free" or "elect". The privilege granted was essentially immunity from taxation and other other exactions of the state—or, more positively, the transfer of the right to tax a particular community from the sultan to the grantee. In some charters immunity is stressed, while in others the transfer of rights over people or land is given greater weight. Within the present *corpus* there appears to be an evolution from the earlier passive rights of immunity, which seem originally to have been developed to accommodate the *fuqara*, towards a standard grant of rights and immunities over an estate or community—commonly described as *iqta' tamm wa-hawz kamil/*"a full assignment and complete occupation"—granted to all categories within the ruling establishment. This standardisation appears to have developed under Muhammad al-Husayn whose long reign (thirty-five years) was itself a factor in the creation of a regular chancery issuing standardized charters granting codified rights. Speculatively, one may see this development as the result of the convergence of immunity for the *fuqara* with the grant of administrative rights to the notables.

---

28 PA (al-Fashir), *Western Darfur District Handbook.*

29 The wider Sudanic and Arabian context is discussed in my (1996b), 339-54.

30 S*aru jah allah wa-rasulihi wa-maksurin al-'azm min al-diwan*; from an undated charter of Muhammad al-Husayn transcribed in AP1, 4/16, 60-61. This is the commonest formula to describe privileged status.

Diagrams 6. THE CHARTERS OF THE AWLAD JABIR

Sultanic Sequence	Takanawī's Sequence	Other Charters	ʿAbd al-Ḥamīd al-Jābir and his Descendants
1. Muḥammad Dawra (undated) to…			ʿAbd al-Ḥamīd and his brothers
2. Muḥammad Tayrāb (undated) to…			Sons of ʿAbd al-Ḥamīd
			Muḥammad b. ʿAbd al-Ḥamīd
3. ʿAbd al-Raḥmān (seal, 1214/1799-800) to…		11. *malik* al-Ḥājj (undated) to…	Fāris b. ʿAbd al-Ḥamīd
4. Muḥammad al-Faḍl (seal, 1222/1807-8) to…		12. ʿAbd al-Bārī (seal, 1231/1815-16) to…	Sulaymān, a grandson of ʿAbd al-Ḥamīd
5. Muḥammad al-Ḥusayn (1279/1862-3) to…		13. Muḥammad al-Faḍl b. ʿAbd al-Bārī (undated) to…	ʿAbd al-Faraj b. Muḥammad
	6. Ādam Tinbuktī (undated) to…	14. *maqdūm* Ādam Iringa (1277/1806-1) to…	ʿIbrāhīm, a grandson of ʿAbd al-Ḥamīd
	7. Abū Bakr Muḥammad (grandson of Ādam) to…		
	8. Aḥmed b. Mūsā (1264/1847) to…		
	9. Muḥammad al-Arbāb (undated) to…		
	10. Muḥammad Sulaymān Ādam (1279/1862-3) to…		

146

Privileges or estates were obtained by grant or inheritance, by personal solicitation, or by converting occupancy or settlement (*hawz* or *hiyyaza*) into ownership (*milk*) through the obtaining of a charter. The hereditary principle was deeply rooted in Darfur and the production of a charter before the sultan seems usually to have led to confirmation of the previous charter, so that the *fuqara* families in particular came to acquire chains of charters from the sultans and provincial rulers (see Diagram 6 "The Charters of the Awlad Jabir". The *fuqara* seldom lost their land, but the notables were more vulnerable since estates were an integral part of the political spoils system. In the civil war between 'Abd al-Rahman and Ishaq (see Chapter Three), the former sought to alienate many of the latter's secret partisans in his own ranks by giving out that Ishaq intended to confiscate the estates of all those who opposed him. Later, in the crisis that followed 'Abd al-Rahman's death in 1215/1801, Muhammad Kurra bought off some of the notables opposed to the accession of his nominee, Muhammad al-Fadl, with gifts of "ten hawakir, 500 dollars and twenty horses with armour and weapons".[31]

Among the notables land and people changed hands regularly; the estate "Ni'ama" granted in 1263/1846-47 by Muhammad al-Husayn to his son-in-law *al-hajj* Ahmad b. 'Isa is listed as having previously belonged to the *malik* Kartakayla, *malik* 'Abd Allah Karqash, *maqdum* 'Abd al-'Aziz and the Sultan's grandmother, Umm Buza.[32] Rights over people were similarly transferable; one powerful Fur warlord, the Wazir Muhammad b. 'Ali Jami' Dokkumi, brought back a group of some fifty Arabs from Kordofan, apparently to act as herders, after one of his campaigns there in the 1790s. They had been granted him by 'Abd al-Rahman; later they were transferred to

---

31 Nachtigal (1971-87), iv, 290 and 299.

32 O'Fahey and Abu Salim (1983), 101-3. The charter is interesting in several respects; Ahmad b. 'Isa was married to the Sultan's daughter, Fatima Umm Dirays; halfway through the charter the masculine endings throughout become feminine, i.e. the charter appears to be in reality addressed to Fatima. Some years later, the Sultan confirms that his son-in-law has given the estate to his wife.

147

the Wazir Hamid by Muhammad al-Fadl in 1221/1806-7, probably not long after Dokkumi's death.[33]

The act of grant was a formal legal process. The aspiring grantee presented himself before the sultan: *talaba minni hakuratan*/"he asked me for an estate" or *hadara amamna*/"[they] came before us". Often the petitioner sought rights over land he and his people had cleared and settled. The opening up of virgin land became an important element in the estate system; for the pioneers their charters were title-deeds to their new land, for the sultans they were a means of encouraging new settlement. In a court case of 1224/1809 from Kordofan Shaykh Junayd w. Salama al-Shuwayhi describes how his grandfather, Najm b. Muhammad, went up to Umm Diraysa where he found the land neglected and unused save for some hunting. He cut down the trees and put the land under cultivation, receiving charters for it from the Funj rulers in Kordofan which were later endorsed by the Darfur sultans.[34]

Or the petitioner could ask for new land:

Sharif Thabit came and sought for himself an unoccupied land to be given him. So our lord Sultan Muhammad al-Fadl told Sharif Thabit to carve out for himself an estate and record its boundaries and present [the details of the estate] to him. So Sharif Thabit carved out a locality for himself in the Marbuta district.[35]

Groups of people like the Masamir Arabs granted to Dokkumi and estates like "Ni'ama" were apparently considered to have a corporate and legal existence independent of the person to whom they were granted.[36] Thus estates reverted to the sultan when the grant lapsed; in 1263/1846-47 the *faqih* 'Izz al-Din sought from the sultan the estate "Bayd" which, on the death of the *habboba* Umm Buza (Muhammad al-Fadl's mother), had "reverted to the House of Tribute

---

33 Ibid., 76-9.

34 See my (1986), 43-63.

35 DF278.37/1, 1261/1862-63.

36 The *khabir* Muhammad Kannuna received an estate at Kobbei that had formerly belonged to another merchant; six years later he sued one of his neighbours for concealing the fact that some nearby fields had formed part of the original estate; O'Fahey and Abu Salim (1983), 108-12.

(*bayt al-jibaya*)".[37] The failure to occupy an estate led also to its loss because, as the *amin* Yusuf b. Fatr ruled in court, "an estate needs to be taken possession of [to render it legally valid] just like any other gift, according to the predominant view [of the Maliki School]".[38]

The next step was the demarcation of the boundaries of the land granted, which was often done even when an established (*ma'luma*) estate was being re-granted or earlier rights of settlement confirmed. The grantee went to the area with a *falqanawi* (royal messenger) or *muwajjih*, the latter term used of an official charged with administrative or judicial duties. Since the *muwajjih* had to return with a written deposition of the boundaries, he was necessarily literate and usually a *faqih*. Some names appear more than once, for example *al-hajj* Amin al-Katakawi described as *shaykh al-Takarir*. In one charter, the bounds were beaten by the "Father Shaykh", in another by a *khabir*. Usually, two officials were present, one from the sultan, the other representing the district chief who was thus made formally cognisant of the grant.[39]

The boundaries were beaten by the officials, the grantee and the neighbours (*ahl al-hudud*) walking or riding around them and marking them by reference to hills, trees, stony outcrops and the like; in the Zalingei region dry-stone walls were often built to delimit the estates.[40] The oath was taken on the Qur'an before the party set out, "thirteen men were present [for] the testimony, they swore upon the

---

37 Ibid., 42-4.

38 *Li-an al-iqta' yaftaqira li-hiyyazat 'ala'l-mashhur kasa'ir al-'ataya*; ibid., 94-5.

39 Amin appears in O'Fahey and Abu Salim (1983), 50-1 and DF 63.8/1, dated 25 Rajab 1267/7 June 1851; he was probably from the Kotoko people, from the Logone/Shari region south of Lake Chad, who were widely settled in Darfur. His title may imply some wider authority over westerners in the sultanate (Burckhardt (1822), 437 refers to a *makk al-takarna* [like takarir, a plural form of takrur]) at al-Ubayyid. On the *ab shaykh* and the *khabir*, see O'Fahey and Abu Salim (1983), 4-44 & 96-8. The *qadi al-hajj* 'Izz al-Din writes to a Berti chief announcing the coming of his messenger to settle a disputed boundary and ordering the chief to be present; DF 188.18/48, undated.

40 I am grateful to Jonathon Hales for information on stone-walling. Davies (1957), 54-5 gives a humorous but insightful account of "beating the bounds" in Kordofan in the early twentieth century.

Qur'an and went around [the land]".[41] The deposition was taken back to the court and usually incorporated directly into the charter.

The earliest charters addressed to the *fuqara* stress privilege and exemption; thus Tayrab says of the Awlad Jabir *fuqara*, "Now I have exempted his sons and those who are their neighbours with them, for ever."[42] The privilege was deemed to cover the grantees, their relatives, dependents and followers and, by implication rather than explicit statement in the early charters, their land. In the long term the rural *fuqara* were to be the prime beneficiaries of the grants of privilege; better able to weather the political storms, living away from the political centre, and above all because they were not absentee landlords, they were able to keep what they had been granted. The motives for the grants to the *fuqara* may be related to the general growth of Islam within the sultanate (see Chapter Ten), but the charters are on occasion quite explicit. Tayrab, after assigning the land of al-Tamru to Ahmad and his brother, concludes his charter, "[There is] not [due] from them [anything] except intercessory prayer (*al-du'a*)".[43] Muhammad al-Fadl rewards 'Abd Allah b. Abu'l-Hasan with a grant of land for teaching the Qur'an to the Sultan's sons,

"What should be the reward for kindness if not kindness (Q. lv, 60)"? Therefore we sought for something [to reward] his kindness, so I considered the land and found that it endures until the end of time and found it the most worthy and suitable form of recompense.[44]

Descent from the Prophet, a powerful distinction in a newly-Islamised land, provides the motive in another charter which indicates that privileged status could be transferred from one state to another. A group of Barriyab *fuqara* from the Nile presented Sultan 'Abd al-Rahman with a charter issued by one of the 'Abdallab rulers, governors of the northern provinces of the Sinnar Sultanate. Because they were *ashraf* (descendants of the Prophet)—their genealogy is given

---

41 DF193.18/53, undated.

42 DF173.18/33, undated.

43 DF166.18/26 (seal-date 1171/1758-59); this phrase appears in several charters.

44 O'Fahey and Abu Salim (1983), 36.

at length in the charter—the Sultan duly issued a charter confirming their privilege within his dominions.[45] Nor seemingly did conquest, in this case of Kordofan by Darfur, necessarily invalidate privilege, as the above-quoted example of the Shuwayhat demonstrates. Only in one charter does the term *waqf* or endowment appear, although a number make it clear that the support of a mosque and Qur'anic school was among the motives for the grant. The *waqf* originated with Muhammad Dawra who granted land at Jadid al-Sayl (north of al-Fashir) to Muhammad 'Izz al-Din. By the time the grant was confirmed by Muhammad al-Fadl in 1221/1807, it was described as "a perpetual endowment so that they can use its land tax for the mosque".[46] The same purpose was usually expressed differently, as in a Shuwayhat charter of 1220/1805,

All their *zaka* and *fitr* and blood money (*ahkam dima'ihim*) is to be paid to the aforementioned Shaykh al-Daw [as] a donation to him from us in support of the mosque.[47]

The emphasis on grants to individuals and their kin rather than the endowment of institutions reflects the personal and in many cases charismatic nature of the relations between the sultans and the holy men.

The *sijillat* or records of the court cases heard before the *qadi*s or other officials throw much light on the legal evolution of the estate system; legally, a community granted privileged status or land was treated as a partnership/*shirka*, and more specifically as an agricultural partnership/*muzara'a* or *shirka fi'l-zar'*.[48] The intra-community disputes which reached the courts revolved around inheritance and administration, or who held rights in the land and who held the right to dispose of the land. Behind the often complex and prolonged—

---

45 Two charters from 'Abd al-Rahman and Muhammad al-Husayn, formerly in the possession of Dardiri Ibrahim (copies in the NRO); see summary in Qasim (1996), i, 276-7.

46 *Waqfan mu'abbadan yasta'inu bi-kharajihi 'ala'l-masjid*; O'Fahey and Abu Salim (1983), 41.

47 See my (1986), 43-63; on the Shuwayhat, see Qasim (1996), iii, 1279.

48 On the Shari'a theory, see Schacht (1964), 155-64 and Santillana (1926), ii, 303-9.

over several generations—legal wrangles may be traced the history of a kinship-based community using its land communally but with authority vested in the male line of the original grantee through the *ras al-jah*.[49] The court cases clearly distinguish between an individual's legal right, acquired by inheritance under Islamic law, to a share of his community's land and the rights of administration and disposal held by the head of the community and his descendants on behalf of the whole community.[50]

Because land was not scarce, fragmentation, a problem in the Nile Valley, was not common. Shifting rainfed agriculture laid emphasis on rights within the community rather than on land *per se*. Nevertheless, estates were carefully demarcated and boundary disputes were not uncommon. It is possible to trace in the court records the evolution of communally-held rights, based on charters of privilege, into the standard estate granted to an individual and his immediate kin. To give one example, the Tunjur community established by 'Abd Allah Matluq at Kamala Keirei had its privileged status renewed by a number of sultans, the last being Muhammad al-Husayn in 1257/1841. A year later the same Sultan granted the same land to Muhammad b. Madani, a descendant of Matluq, as a "full assignment and in complete occupation". Twenty years later, in 1280/1863-64, a faction of the Kamala Keirei community sued Muhammad's brother, Muhammadayn, demanding the right to see the community's charters. From other court cases this demand seems to have betokened a challenge as to who was rightfully the leader of the community. The judge rejected the claim when

---

49 The commonest term is *wakil*; in one he is called *sahib hurma wa-sahib jah*/"owner of immunity and owner of privilege", see my (1991), 109 (79-112).

50 A similar distinction is noted by Miskin: "It was generally assumed that all the various people who had an interest in a plot had a share in the freehold, i.e. they were co-owners in the strict sense of the word. Now this may have been the case according to a precise definition of Shari'a law, but in practice and custom it was not so. Almost invariably then, and now, one or two people manage the plot on behalf of the other co-owners"; Miskin (1950), 282.

Muhammadayn produced his brother's charter, ruling that "[rights of] assignment take precedence over [rights of] cultivation".[51]

To sum up a complex and uneven development, collective and communal rights of privilege tended to give way to a form of private owenership granted by the sultan as *iqta' al-tamlik*, i.e. a concession of property rights (*milk*) which are comprehensively described in several charters as "[rights of] cultivation, causing to be cultivated, sale, demolition, building, alms and purchase".[52] How literally these "rights" were meant to be taken is an unanswered question; in the whole *corpus* there is only one reference to the sale of land.[53] Thus, under the long reigns of Muhammad al-Fadl and his son, the most common form of grant became the topographically defined estate transferred as a "gift" or "donation", *hiba* or *sadaqa*, which conceded both *milk* or property rights and immunity from taxation.

The acquisition of such grants and their legal definitions are one aspect, but their preservation against outsiders is another. All the charters end with sanctions directed particularly to the tax collectors. Muhammad al-Fadl's sanctions are often quite fearsome; "he who sprinkles them with cold water I shall splash with red blood". Despite such threats, the illegal seizure of taxes occasionally happened. Muhammad al-Fadl sternly reproves the *jabbay* Musa and his subordinates for levying taxes on the privileged Musabba'at community at Jugo Jugo (east of al-Fashir); "How can you then behave unjustly towards them and assess their grain and violate their sanctity (*karama*)?"[54]

If the evidence of the documents that have survived is not too misleading (because they are the records of communities that have

51 *Al-iqta' yajuz 'ala'l-ihya*; O'Fahey and Abu Salim (1983), 73, where pp. 45-75 give translations of most of the Kamala Keirei community's documents.

52 Ibid., 44 and 101.

53 My (1991), 88-93. Here I part company with La Rue (thesis, 1989), 393, who under the heading, "Towards the Commoditization of Land in Dar Fur", notes, "Documents directly concerning the sale or mortgage in Dar Fur are as yet rather rare. But documents referring indirectly to the sale of small parcels of land such as fields are so very matter-of-fact that the practice may well have been fairly common". One example is a frail basis for such a generalisation.

54 O'Fahey and Abu Shouk (1999), 55 (49-64).

survived), estate-holders had ready recourse to the courts to protect their rights. In several instances *fuqara* take members of the royal family to court for encroachment or trespass; a Fallata clan settled near Khiriban twice sued Muhammad Hud, evidently a rather truculent son of Muhammad al-Fadl, because his slaves trespassed on their land. At one point the judge asked of Hud,

Should the claim lie with the defence [i.e. with Hud] in the face of legal ownership, or [when you are] without a charter to support you in any way? [Hud] said, "No! However, don't pay any attention to their charters, don't move my slaves away.[55]

Hud lost the case.

Land and followers

The estate system arose in response to a need, the necessity for the sultans to provide for a burgeoning elite within an increasingly centralised state. But not all the sultanate was equally attractive; although no overall picture can yet be drawn, some trends can be discerned. Thus Dar Aba Diima contained some 200 estates; the province covered some 15,000 square miles and an average would give an estate of about 70 square miles.[56] But such calculations are misleading; given the variation in size, population and fertility of the *shartaya*s, the size of the estates cannot be known until they have been measured on the ground.[57] Estates in Dar Aba Diima and the three *shartaya*s west of the mountains, Fia, Madi and Kerne, were attractive by

---

55 DF63.8/1, 25 Rajab 1267/7 June 1851 and DF64.8/2, 6 Sha'ban 1268/6 June 1852. Another royal son, appropriately named 'Aqrab "scorpion", a son of 'Abd al-Rahman, was involved in disputes with both the Tunjur and Fallata fuqara of Khiriban; O'Fahey and Abu Salim (1983), 61-3 and DF68.8/7, 5 Jumada 1 1230/15 April 1815. But both families had close ties to the court, the Fallata supplying a number of prominent imams to the sultans.

56 Adelberger (1990), 186-93 lists them; they are given here in diagram 6. His discussion of the relationship between *hawakir* and *shartaya* (40-2) is fundamental.

57 Beaton (1948), 6, "Each fief was made up of the manors of half a dozen villages"; Beaton, whom I interviewed several times in 1966, knew Western Darfur and the Fur language very well.

Diagram 7. DIVISION OF DĀR ABA DIIMA INTO HAWAKIR
(according to the Western Darfur District Handbok)

Shartāya	Hawākīr	No.
Diima	divided into an unknown number of *hawākīr* from the time of Muḥammad al-Husayn	
Suro	Romatas, Fudi, Labada, Mogara, Keileik, Zigago, Gundobar, Tiro, Zoro, Wajikay, Dumbar Dulukuri	11
Nyoma	(part of Suro in Muḥammad al-Husayn's time) Murli, Wesing, Madi; Khantūra, Nyala, Abli, Wirwi	7
Kobara	Mittom, Fogli, Burnei, Faing, Um Haraz, Anderei	6
Fungoro	(formerly part of Kobora) (*a*) *Hawākīr* belonging to the sultan which were administered by the *abo fòre*: Kabar, Mulumaddi, Dimbola, Mutur, Malmalu Mugiir. (*b*) Others: Gelewi, Dumbar Dugo, Wejekay, Buru, Dumbar Durikuli	11
Zami Toya	Sunni, Jugma, Kerbi, Kuddum, Bindisi, Terim be, Kedery, Undu, Berbu, Garmie, Sinya, Zami Toya, Nyoma, Torozo, Berniyeel	15
Kulli	Balla, Gadara, Barigi, Sagay (belonging to the sultan), Wirwir (divided into 7 *hawākīr*)	11
Zami Baya	Buri, Bardi, Karima, Naiti, Zidiniba, Karsi, Sambinea, Galba Baarsa, Zidiya, Mgaile, Kasa, Berde, Zame, Zambiya, Marra, Kosa, Galbo, Barso, Taraba	19
Tebella	No names given	14
Tilni	No information	
Aribo	Divided into very small *hawākīr*	12
	Total	106+

155

reason of the fertility of the land and density of population, so that the estate-holders could expect a reasonably high revenue. Around al-Fashir proximity to the capital no doubt made estates there desirable, compensating in some measure for the poorness of the *qoz* soil and unreliable rainfall. Similar calculations applied when merchants sought estates between Kofod and Jabal Kobbei along the Wadi Kobbei. The commercial centre of Kobbei was in fact a series of such estates or households strung out along the riverbed. In contrast, Dar Daali in the east was unattractive because it was thinly populated and poorly watered, and because,

It was too remote for direct [tax] farming by the sultan and his underlings and the local leaders were bigger men, and there was tribal cohesion in the predominance of the Berti.[58]

Not all estate-holders were absentees; the *fuqara* were not, and royal women often came to live on the land granted them. Marsum Zaynaba, a daughter of Tayrab, settled at Kuume in the *shartaya* of Zami Baya, her steward Modila administering the estate on her behalf. Muhammad al-Husayn gave an estate in Dar Suwayni to his daughter Umm Dirays. After her death another sister took it over, installing one Muhammad to run it.[59] Generally the notables installed slaves as their stewards while the court *fuqara* preferred to employ relatives; the estates of Maliki b. 'Ali al-Futawi, Sultan 'Abd al-Rahman's Fulani friend, at Kerio were managed by his brother Ibrahim Bal.[60]

Those who held land as estates were considered to own it, as the term for them—*asyad al-tin*/"masters of the soil"—implies. Whoever came to settle on on their land had an obligation to pay the

---

58 PA (al-Fashir), some loose and untitled notes by G.D. Lampen, 1949. The *dimlij* Muhammad Salih Dash claimed he was dismissed by 'Ali Dinar for resisting "the sultan's habit of carving hakouras out of his Dar", PA (al-Fashir), DP 66. K. 1 Kiriu [Kerio] Omodia.

59 PA (al-Fashir), *Western Darfur District Handbook* and PA (Kutum) NDD 66 B 4/6, Dar Sweini, report of a majlis held 5.5.1924. This Umm Dirays may be the same whose affairs are documented in O'Fahey and Abu Salim (1985), 99-106.

60 Ahmad and Hamid Adam Abo, Kattal, 19.6.1970.

various taxes and dues to them. A distinction thus developed, still fundamental and contentious in Darfur, between *sid al-tin* or *sid al-hakura* on the one hand and *shaykh al-rijal/*"shaykh of people" on the other—between those who owned the land, however their rights to it may have originated, and those who administered people who had subsequently settled upon it.[61] A complex of overlapping rights, local customs and conventions covered the land. Muhammad al-Husayn gave an estate, Abu Mukhayr, in Dar Beira to a Zayyadi man, Mirni w. Salman, who had married his daughter, Umm Birayma. The estate was inherited by the Awlad Umm Badr shaykhs of the Zayyadiyya. Although Abu Mukhayr was some distance from the Zayyadiyya country, the Awlad Umm Badr were recognised as its *asyad al-tin*, which meant that they were entitled to two-thirds of all land taxes and dues, the other third going to the local chief. In the case of fines and judicial fees, the proportion was reversed; however, Zayyadiyya who settled at Abu Mukhayr were under the exclusive jurisdiction of their own chiefs.[62]

In practice the structure and function of the estates were determined as much by who owned them as by any particular or rigid legal formulation. For the *fuqara* and the merchants, the grants were security against harassment by the tax collectors and the notables. The most precious boon a sultan could grant was to tell his agents to keep away from the recipient of his favour; *la ahad yatarradu/*"let no one interfere": that interdiction runs like a thread through the charters. An enduring result of the grants to the rural *fuqara* was the growth throughout the sultanate of religious communities within whose hinterland the *fuqara* exercised an informal influence as teachers, mediators in local disputes, and writers of magical texts or *hijabat*.

The estates provided the notables and the Keira with revenue and followers. As we have seen, the charters distinguish between *al-ahkam* (or *al-ghilal*) *al-shar'iyya/*"the canonical ordinances or revenues" and

---

61 PA (Kutum) NDD 66 B 4/2/5, Tribal: Magdumate Area, Dar Anka-Beiri Boundaries, report 29.3.1938 and Rihaymat Allah Mahmud al-Dadinqawi, al-Fashir, 7.6.1970. See also Holy (1974), 116-53.

62 PA (al-Fashir) [number missing] Beira Omodia, note by District Commissioner, al-Fashir, 8.6.1938.

al-subul al-'adiyya/"the customary taxes". The former included fitr and zaka, in Darfur the basic grain and animal taxes, while the latter were the numerous (some thirty-five appear in the charters, see Diagram 9) "pains and penalties" exacted by the great from the lowly as well as various communal responsibilities. These taxes were paid to the estate-holder through his steward, whereupon,

The holders of hawakir either contracted to pay the sultan half of their rents or, if they were exempted from this obligation, according to their ability and at their discretion.[63]

Thus was reflected the difference between *hakura* and *hakurat al-jah*. The estate-holders were in any event expected to present a substantial gift (Ar. *salam*) to the sultan at the Drum Festival.[64] Revenues were paid in cattle, goats and sheep, dukhn, dhurra or honey, or in takkiyya or tob (classical Ar. *thawb*) rolls or pieces of cloth.

The estate-holders could also exact labour for their home fields from their tenants. In the Fur chiefdoms, each able-bodied man was under obligation to work seven days a year on his shartay's or estate-holder's land. However, the relationship was reciprocal, since the chief would kill a sheep or cow and have *marisa* or beer brewed by the women for the work party. As befitted his status, a holy man provided more meat but less beer for work parties on his land.[65] It was always in his interest for a chief or estate-holder to be generous to attract new settlers; land without people was useless. Settlers moving into an estate were granted *fas* or "hoe/axe" rights, namely land to cultivate; their communal head or sid al-fas was responsible for collecting the estate-holder's dues.[66]

---

63 Nachtigal (1971-87), iv, 359.

64 Ibid, and Shuqayr (1903), ii, 139.

65 PA (al-Fashir), *Western Darfur District Handbook*. The days were distributed thus: one day each for cleaning, planting, weeding, cutting, threshing, repairing the chief's house and rebuilding his compound or hosh.

66 DF190.18/50, 1279/1862-63 and 196.18/56, 1270/1853-54 are two long court hearings describing in detail "hoe" rights on an Awlad Jabir estate in Dar Zayyadiyya. While I was sitting in (10.6.1970) malik Rihaymat Allah al-Dadinaqawi's court, a case of "hoe" rights was heard; according to the *ajawid* or panel of elders, the rights were so called because the land sub-let had usually to be cleared by "fire and hoe", *bi-nar wa-fas*, and once granted,

Both sultans and notables used slaves on their estates; one very dubious source alleges that some of the great had 5-600 slaves on their land, which may be supported by Slatin's remark that 'Arafa, daughter of Muhammad al-Husayn and later wife of Muhammad Khalid Zuqal, a cousin of the Mahdi and first Mahdist governor in Darfur, owned several hundred slaves.[67] In 1263/1846-47 Muhammad al-Husayn granted a son-in-law an estate "with its slaves who number fifty".[68] Since Darfur was a major slave exporter, precisely because of raiding by the notables, it is difficult to imagine that the latter did not keep many of their captives for themselves. Moreover, some of the herders described below were probably considered to be of semi-servile status. A group of Korobat Arab traders had an estate from Muhammad al-Fadl at Gelli in Dar Konyir west of Jabal Marra; it was cultivated by their slaves. While the latter were obliged to subscribe to *diya* or blood compensation collections by the Konyir *shartay*, their owners were exempted.[69]

Since animals were among the few ways to conserve "capital", the notables needed herders. 'Abd al-Rahman granted a small group of nomads to Nur al-Din b. Yahya, a Zaghawi notable who had brought them back from Kordofan, as "herders for his camels". In 1268/1851-52, al-hajj Ahmad b. 'Isa presented to his daughter ten nomads "as her herders" on the occasion of the "shaving of her hair", *ziyanat rasha*, on the fortieth day after her birth; her grandfather, Muhammad al-Husayn, confirmed the gift.[70] Patronage, service and kinship could be intertwined; the same Nur al-Din was granted a group of his Zaghawa maternal kin by 'Abd al-Rahman. Muhammad al-Fadl, in confirming his father's grant, explains,

---

sub-tenancies were hereditary and could not be revoked by the estate-holder.

67 Zayn al-'Abidin (1981), 8-9 and Slatin (1896), 274. On Zuqal, see Hill (1967), 261-2 & 404.
68 O'Fahey and Abu Salim (1983), 101.
69 PA (Kutum) NDD 66, B, 8/2 Tribal: Dar Fia, note on Gelli, 23.4.1931.
70 O'Fahey and Abu Salim (1983), 80-1 and 103-4.

The sultan has granted them to Nur al-Din b. al-malik Yahya as his servants (*khuddamuhu*). They are to give all their customary taxes and their *zaka* and *fitr* to Nur al-Din. Thereby [the sultan] has given them inviolability and privilege ...[71]

Ahmad Bukr settled an estate at Bilio, north of Mellit, in Berti country on his son, Muhammad al-Hafiz; the latter's son Muham-mad Tur seems to have fought with 'Abd al-Rahman in the war against *al-hajj* Ishaq. Three of Tur's neighbours quarrelled with him, a dispute resolved by the Sultan giving the three men—and their land and descendants—to Tur in what appears to be a form of servitude or serfdom, distinguished in the documents from slavery:

They are to serve him in everything that he needs service for, service in sow-ing, service in his houses, or guardianship of his wealth, They, together with his slaves, are equally in his service (*fa-hum ma'a raqiqihi sawa' fi khidmatihi*) and their descendants are to serve the descendants of Hafiz after as their inheritance (*mirathan*).[72]

How successful was the estate system from the point of view of the notables? Commenting on an apparent decline in the prosperity of the sultanate in the 1860s and 70s, Nachtigal's travelling compan-ion, Ahmad Tangatanga, a shrewd merchant who knew Darfur well, ascribed it to the depredations of Zamzam and to the abuse of the estate system.[73] The causes of the decline, if decline there was, were more complex, but the estate system, whose original purpose was military—to maintain a fighting force—and administrative, had by the end of the first sultanate become a means of subsidising the elite, a subsidy from which the state got little return. Thus it may account for the seeming listlessness of the elite in the face of al-Zubayr's challenge to their survival in 1873-74. Whether tenants on the estates were more intensely exploited than those outside is problematical. Darfur was too thinly populated, and those dissatisfied with their lot could move away

---

71 Ibid., 84.

72 My (1992), 64 (57-93), where the complete archive is published. The distinction between "service" (*khidma*) and "slavery" (*riqq*) may be that the former could not be alienated from the estate.

73 Nachtigal (1971-87), iv, 316.

too easily, for any system to have been very exploitative. Both farmers and nomads probably gained from the patron-client ties created by the estate system, and especially from the partial immunity gained by settling on the land of an influential holy man.[74]

In fact the estates were probably not that profitable for the notables. Their owners could retire to them if political necessity demanded or if the cost of living at the capital became prohibitive. Estates in south-western Darfur may have been fertile, but "were not very profitable on account of the difficulties of transport in the mountainous regions and often the remoteness of the estates".[75] Agricultural produce was unlikely to contribute much to a notable's living expenses when a quantity of *dukhn* "sufficient for two horses and four men" cost a quarter of a dollar, and a horse 50 or more, a young male slave 30 and a Kashmir shawl, required by protocol at court, 150 (see Diagram ?). And on the shawls Nachtigal comments,

They are frequently sold dirt cheap for 5 to 10 dollars by dignatories who have worn them for only a short time, in their chronic financial difficulties.[76]

Estates were of value to the notables in the context of an eco-nomic cycle of which the Darfur end provided raw materials, slaves included, for the Egyptian market, which in turn provided the "cash" income with which to buy luxuries. Once the cycle was disrupted, as it was by the Bahhara traders south of Darfur from the 1860s on, the estates became less valuable.

The estate system undoubtedly had some impact on the tribal system by substituting a quasi-exploitative relationship for a com-munal or kinship one, by replacing chiefs "drawn from the people" by nominees from the centre, but only to a limited degree. It affected only parts of the sultanate, and never totally effaced the traditional administrative system described in the next chapter.

---

74 See my (1977b), 147-66 on relations between fuqara and their tenants.

75 Nachtigal (1971-87), iv, 341; see also, 365.

76 Ibid., 373-4.

8

SULTAN AND SUBJECT

The structure of administration

The sultanate grew outwards and away from the Fur homeland, Jabal Marra, and its environs to the west and southwest. As the Fur core was encompassed by new conquests, so the distinction between Fur and non-Fur blurred as the demands of the sultans fell upon all impartially. The Fur slipped even further away from the mainstream after the establishment at the end of the eighteenth century of the al-Fashir-Kobbei axis on the northeastern margins of the Fur lands. The Fur warlords like the *aba diimang* and *abbo uumo* who had loomed so large in the wars and dissensions of the eighteenth century were far less prominent in the next.

As new groups were incorporated into the state, an *ad hoc* administrative system grew up in which the new subjects were ruled largely through their own chiefs. However, incorporation under semi-autonomus local elites gave way under the impact of centralisation to an increasingly direct form of rule. The determination of the sultans to tighten their grip upon their state and to maximise profits led them to prefer commissioners to governors, emissaries to chiefs. However, these commissioners or emissaries did not replace the territorial chiefs, but simply sat on top of the old administration. And since they in their turn were subject to a law of ossification whereby commissioners became governors and emissaries acquired local interests, the sultans were forced constantly to renew their rule from the centre. 'Ali Dinar, faced with the restoration of order in a land ruined by twenty-four years of foreign rule, of necessity ruled through a handful of trusted and able men at the head of warbands.

Schematically the administrative structure was based on four provinces, each divided into a number of district chiefdoms or *shartaya*s. The provinces were,

1. *Dar* (or *ro* in Fur) *aba diima*, in the southwest;

2. *Dar abbo uumo*, in the southeast;

3. *Dar Daali* (or *Dar al-Sabah*), in the east, and

4. *Dar al-takanawi* (or *Dar al-rih*).

The chiefdoms west of Jabal Marra, although called collectively *Dar al-gharb*, were never administered as a province. According to Nachtigal, each province had originally been divided into twelve *shartaya*s, but this number was only to be found in the northern and southwestern provinces, while Dar Daali had only four and Dar abbo uumo five. Each *shartaya* was divided into a varying number of local or sub-chiefdoms, *dimlijiyya*s, administered by a *dimlij*. Some of the larger *shartaya*s had chiefs called *sambei* who acted as agents for the *shartay*s in dealing with the *dimlij*s; *sambei* means "barbed spear", and they were so called because through *sambei* the *shartay* was said to "spear" or control his *dimlij*s.[1]

Was this administrative structure a Fur creation—a Fur tribal system writ large—or was it older than the Keira? There is no certain answer, but rather tenuous indications that it may in part be a Tunjur legacy. Arkell argued that the quadrant-based provinces were a borrowing from Kanem-Borno.[2] However, his hypothesis of a Kanem-Borno interregnum in Darfur in the fifteenth or sixteenth centuries remains unproven, while the applicability of the quadrant notion to Borno itself has been doubted.[3] The tradition that Daali established the provinces radiating out from a sacred tree in Jabal Marra (see

---

1 Nachtigal (1971-87), iv, 324-5.
2 Arkell (1952a), 129-55; see O'Fahey and Spaulding (1974), 113-14.
3 Brenner (1973), 18-19.

Chapter Two) evidently telescopes a slow process of growth. Both Dar Diima and Dar Uumo were seemingly Fur chieftancies that grew by a process of accretion under the aegis of the Keira. The *aba diimang*s, discussed below, are a line of chiefs probably as ancient as the Keira. Dar al-Takanawi appears to correspond with the approximate area of Tunjur domination, while *takanawi* is but one variant of a widely-found title. It may not be too far-fetched to suggest that the northern governor was in origin a Tunjur viceroy on behalf a a newly-emergent Keira dynasty.[4]

Below the provincial level, indications of pre-Keira origins are largely linguistic. Of the various chiefly titles in use throughout the sultanate, few if any are undisputably Fur linguistically. The most likely etymology for *shartay* would link it with the Daju *chorte* meaning both "chief" and "drum"; the Fur for *shartay*—*kiiso* (pl. *kiisonga*)—bears the same double meaning. *Dimlij*, pl. *damalij* is probably from the Arabic for "bracelet, bangle" as al-Tunisi noted, for which the Fur equivalent (and presumably borrowing) is *dilmong*, pl. *dilmonga*.[5] And while *sambei* is used by the Fur, elsewhere such chiefs were more commonly called *qirqid*.[6] Similarly, *sagal* was the Fur term for the estate stewards elsewhere called *wakil* or *kursi* (the latter literally "chair"). While none of this is conclusive, it suggests that we are dealing with titles and, by implication, administrative practices that are far from simply being Fur in origin. And without pursuing etymologies and institutional parallels too far, the widespread currency well beyond Darfur of such titles as *mayram*, *takanawi* and *fashir* implies a floating stock of central Sudanic titles and terms that were inherited and adapted by the Keira to their own needs.[7] For the most

---

4 Tubiana (1985), 261-74.

5 Al-Tunisi (1965), 184 (176 & 271). Today *dimlijiyya* has been largely replaced by *'umudiyya*, which was never used in Darfur before colonial times.

6 AP2, 10/48, 221 and O'Fahey and Abu Salim (1983), 88

7 There is a parallel with Sinnar; Spaulding has identified titles and institutions inherited or appropriated by the Funj from Nubia. But there remains a stratum of titles that cannot be identified in terms of language. The Funj

part it is next to impossible to disentangle the different strands that contributed to the Keira administrative system.

There is one possible and important inheritance from the Tunjur that needs to be considered, the idea of Darfur itself. D'Anania's account of the kingdom of Uri, and the *waqf*s or endowments in Medina (see Chapter Two), describe an embryonic idea of Darfur (not yet, of course, with that name) already in the mid/late sixteenth century. The Keira traditions describing their expansion are surprisingly perfunctory: wars with Wadai and the western border states and a few tribal uprisings. But the implication of the traditions is that the Keira were expanding to take over a land already accustomed to some form of unitary rule, and that having through the royal myths established their right to rule, the legitimacy of Keira lordship over "Our Fur land"/*daruna al-furawiyya*, as it is called in one charter, was generally uncontested.[8] Both the loyalty shown by the Fur, but not only by them, to the "shadow sultans" in the years 1874 to 1891 (when 'Ali Dinar finally submitted to the Mahdists) and the ease with which 'Ali Dinar restored the sultanate in late 1898 are witness to this acceptance, to this sense of legitimacy. The contrast with Darfur's neighbours, Sinnar and Wadai, is striking; the Funj faced continual and ultimately uncontainable challenges from within to their authority, while Wadai was regularly torn apart as the Maba tribes fought over the royal succession even as the French were advancing in 1912. The Keira were never challenged from within their state, except possibly but doubtfully by Muhammad Kurra.

The Fur homeland

Whatever the sultans may have inherited from their predecessors, the strength of their state rested ultimately on the compact, fertile and relatively populous Fur lands. The Fur now (2006) probably number

---

as an identifiable ethnic group, if that was what they were, have gone; see further O'Fahey and Spaulding (1974), Part One.

8   O'Fahey and Abu Salim (1983), 39-40; *dawla* is the usual term for "state" in the documents.

about 1.5-2 million, by far the largest ethnic group in Darfur.[9] Today
the majority of the Fur live on the plains or in the foothills to the
south and west of the mountains, but this is probably a recent development due to administrative convenience and access to markets. In
the past the proportion of mountain to lowland Fur may have been
more equal.[10]

Fur traditions imply a process of southward expansion through the
peaceful incorporation of the autochthonous pagan, in Fur *majus-
inga*, peoples or through their expulsion, an expansion closely linked
to Islam.[11] The means were paradigmatically described by some Fur
elders to Arkell in 1935,

> They still speak of Western Darfur as "Dar el Fur". They say that originally
> the whole country was inhabited by tribes who have mostly been driven
> south and are now known as Fertit.

> [The first unnamed sultan] spread Islam and his empire further south, by
> sending in turn to the "king" of each hill and telling him, "Become Moslem,
> or I will fight you". Given such an alternative most of the people fled south
> and became Fertit, leaving much of Darfur uninhabited. The sultans used to
> bring people from the east to occupy the empty land.

A Fur song from the mid-nineteenth century puts the same senti-
ment in another way,

> *The people who live in Fartit (pirti) are slaves and yet go free.*

> *They know nothing at all, neither good nor evil.*

> *These heathens (abdienga; from Ar. 'abd "slave") who eat men are barbarians
> (adama)[12] and go around naked.*

---

9   Adelberger (1990), 11 suggests 720,000 Fur out of a total population for the
    province of 3,094, 000 (1983 Census). Assuming the current estimate of 6.5
    million for Darfur is correct, this would give an approximate figure of 1.5-2
    million for the Fur, but this is a guess at best.

10 Of course, as of this writing, a large percentage of Fur live in IDP camps or,
    increasingly, in Nyala.

11 Adelberger (1990), 35.

12 From the Ar. *adami*, "human being", often used in legal documents of
    slaves.

They cover their behinds with leaves; of clothes they know nothing. Or else they run around like cattle.

We Fur (fora) go and bring them among us and teach them our Islam,

And they live happily among us.[13]

"And became Fertit" in the first quotation means that they "became" pagan non-Fur, since Fartit was the generic name used to describe those pagans living along the southern fringes of the sultanate who were the legitimate prey of raiders from the north. As the song above says, the Fartit were by definition enslaveable. Here we encounter a complex of ideas into which were woven ethnicity, pride of religion and commercial self-interest. The equation of the south with paganism and of the north and east with Islam and an Arab identity, however perfunctorily assumed, is a commonplace in Darfur, as is the notion that Islam sunders ethnic ties or at least wipes the slate clean, rendering the land empty and fit for habitation by the believers. These notions are still very much alive and still very lethal, providing ideological justification for both ethnic cleansing and the trade in human beings.[14] But confronting this nexus of religious racism was an older set of realities which were acknowledged in the various "earth-owners", in the belief that some people "belonged" more than others, and in such tales as the Fur myth that Fir, "the begetter of the Fur", had a brother Firat, the progenitor of the Fartit.[15]

---

13 AP2, 10/48, 107, "Conversation with Abo Muhammad Ahmed and others at Kas", 17.12.1935, and Zyhlarz (1941-42), 177; the rest of the song continues with various derogatory remarks about various southern groups.

14 "They claim that these [Arab] immigrants found an empty land stretching from the Nile to Lake Chad, and say this should now be governed by their descendants—the present-day Abbala and Baggara Arab," from the so-called Qoreish 2 declaration of 1998-99 from the *al-tajammu' al-'Arabi/*"The Arab Gathering": in effect the blueprint or battle-plan of the Janjawid; Flint and De Waal (2005), 53. There is not much new in Darfur.

15 Among such examples are the *suuring sid/*"lord of the earth" among the Fur, who was apparently responsible for certain fertility rituals. In Zaghawa Kobe, the Mira, the original occupants of the land, provided the *takanyon* or second-in-command to the Kobe sultan, Tubiana (1964), 31-2; while among the Mileri of Dar Masalit some clans, the *ashab al-jabal/*"owners of the mountain",

Again Fur traditions imply rather than state that at one time most of Jabal Marra and the land south of the mountains as far as the Bahr al-'Arab was inhabited by peoples now found living in an arc south of Darfur stretching from the Western Bahr al-Ghazal through the northern part of the Central African Republic to Chad. Thus what is today the Fur heartland was historically a moving frontier which saw the progressive displacement or assimilation of such peoples as the Banda, Binga, Feroge, Shatt, Gula and Kara—peoples now mostly living several hundred miles to the south.[16] From at least the mid-seventeenth century, slave raiding—first under the aegis of the sultans and then under the Khartoum traders—was a key factor in precipitating migrations within the southern lands, as Fartit traditions stress.[17] Even earlier slave raiding, pushing ever southwards, had a cumulative part both in the growth of the Jabal Marra kingdom from the sixteenth century onwards and in the emergence of the marcher lordship of Dar Diima. A factor which probably intensified the differentiation of "Fur" from "Fartit" was the intrusion of the Baqqara from the west; they came to occupy a belt of land between Fur and Fartit, and both competed and co-operated with the former in exploiting the latter.

The transformation of "Fartit" into "Fur" was a function of the state-forming process, of slave raiding, forcible resettlement, Islamisation and conquest. Whatever the identity of the nuclear Fur and wherever their original homeland (which may have been in the north of the mountains around Jabal Si), the emergence of the Fur as the ethnically dominant group in the south must have gone hand in hand with the rise of the Keira. The course and dimensions of this

---

are considered to be "more Fartit" than the other Mileri, Hasan and O'Fahey (1970), 152-61. On Fir and Firat, Arkell (1951a), 52-3.

16　What follows is based on my (1982), 75-87.

17　On Fartit traditions in the Western Bahr al-Ghazal, see Santandrea (1964). On the traditions of emigration from the north among peoples now in the Central African Republic or the northern Congo, there are a number of articles; see Leyder (1932), 44-7, and Leyder (1936), 49-71, and Tanghe (1936), 361-91, idem (1943), 1-7, and idem (1944), 35-41. These need to be read with caution as being very speculative; see the critique in O'Fahey and Spaulding (1973), 505-8.

transformation or acculturation may be deduced from the numerous fragmentary traditions identifying present-day Fur mountain lineage groups (*orrenga*) as of Fartit origin; among such groups are the Kara of Jabal Si, the Daalinga of Dar Lewing who are said to be Gula, and the Hajaranga (="Mountain people") of Arwalla described as Shatt, itself a generic name. This list might be considerably prolonged.[18] A fundamental problem in evaluating these traditions is that the later sultans are known to have planted slave colonies throughout their dominions, including Jabal Marra, so that one cannot be certain to which period the traditions refer.

South of the mountains, Fur expansion seems linked to the "Lordship of Diima" in the early seventeenth century. Under the sultans Diima fluctuated, but was bounded by Jabal Marra in the north, the Masalit in the west, the Baqqara nomads in the south and Dar Uumo to the east.

Atim Muhammad Shatta, *shartay* of Dar Kerne, explained to MacMichael,

The Temurka [Fur] of Dár Abo Dima he regards as half Fur and half Fertit, the shartais chiefly the former and the common villagers the latter.[19]

In fact the vast area between the mountains and the Bahr al-'Arab, open to immigration by both Fur and Baqqara, was a veritable ethnic mosaic. In particular the Baqqara infiltration from the west led to the creation of a series of "territories" (*dar*s; from west to east, Ta'aisha, Bani Halba, Fallata, Habbaniyya, Ma'aliyya, Misiriyya and Rizayqat), whose "territories" conceal great ethnic heterogeneity.[20] One tradition alleges that the Rizayqat land was the original home of the

---

18 AP2, 10/48; this file of 238 ff. contains detailed notes by Arkell on almost every district in western Darfur. It is the single most important surviving source on the historical ethnography of the Fur; Adelberger and I have used much of it, but much more remains to be mined from it. See also MacMichael (1922), i, 94 and 97.

19 Ibid. Arkell was told the same, AP2, 10/48, 107. On the Feroge traditions from "the other side", see Santandrea (1957), 115-50, where the Feroge are said to have lived further north a century or so earlier.

20 Braukämper (1992), passim on this processs; the maps in this work are of especial relevance.

Shatt, themselves a mixture of a number of elements.[21] No reliable date can be given to the Baqqara movements, except that they probably occurred before the eighteenth century, perhaps a litle before the Fur moved into the region. That the coming of the Fur was later may be deduced from the shallowness of the genealogies of their *shartay*s and from positive traditions. Both the western chiefdoms of Tebella and southern Surro were originally peopled by Binga; indeed Surro is said to have been the original territory of the Binga where,

In Jebel Balgudi may still be seen the large *burma*s [pots] used by the Binga as hives and a stone well which they could conceal when attacked by enemy.[22]

Dar Fongoro, south of Dar Kobara, was the critical frontier between Fur and Baqqara, who between them transformed the region into a slaving cockpit.[23] By the eighteenth century Fur clans had apparently infiltrated into eastern Dar Fongoro, leaving the mountainous western parts in the hands of various peoples, among them the Gelege (or Gela), Muwanga, Suwanga and Kresh. Then the Ta'aisha moved into the area from the southwest, during Muhammad al-Fadl's reign. It was he or his successor who riposted by imposing some order over the region, first by removing the Gelege chief, secondly by expeditions against the nomads, and thirdly by parcelling out the land into estates—an example of the use of estates as a form of frontier consolidation. Five of the estates were earmarked for the sultan, being administered by his agent, the *fore*; they supplied the court with game, fish and honey.[24] Thereafter Fur and Arab control fluctuated while the Fartit, squeezed between both, were driven further into the less accessible and fertile western districts.[25] Dar

---

21 AP2, 10/48, 107; on the Shatt, see Tucker and Bryan (1956), 59-61.

22 AP2, 10/48, 105, and MacMichael (1922), i, 97.

23 Fresnel (1849-50), 19 and Lauture (1855-56), 100.

24 Game, in which southern Darfur was rich, may have formed an important item for the table of the sultan and his chiefs; one of the sultan's officials was the *malik al-jankaat, jankaat* being a hunter who uses pitfall traps, see Nachtigal (1971-87), iv, 330, n.2. On game, see Wilson (1979), 323-38.

25 AP2, 10/48, 181-95, note by A.C. Beaton on the Fur/Ta'aisha boundary, 9.2.1937. Beaton calls the Gelege chief, 'Abd al-Rahman Jokha, but there

Fongoro illustrates the close interaction between settlement patterns and political domination and between the latter and ethnic identity, since many of the Fartit simply became Fur in the process. Under the sultans the nomads were under some restraint, if only because their nomadic cycle took them far enough north to be vulnerable to the sultan's cavalry (see Chapter Four). The nomads could not encroach on the settled peoples if the latter had the support of a centralised state; today, sadly, the reverse is the case.

I give here only the barest sketch of the "migrations" and "transformations". The determinants of social and ethnic change can only be investigated at the village or camp level. Only at the same level can the ideological factor be evaluated, particularly the creation of the Muslim/pagan divide. Communities change less frequently than their labels. The appointment of a Fur *shartay* and the activities of the stewards on behalf of al-Fashir grandees could make a district "Fur" without any real ethnic change. Linguistic and religious acculturation followed political and economic integration, and the same community might bear different labels at different levels; on the Wadi Azum at Sulma there were (1969) two villages, one Fur, the other Tama. The Tama migrated to Sulma about a century ago because of famine in their homeland; today they speak Fur and intermarry freely with their neighbours.[26] A contrary example from further north in Jabal Si again illustrates the transparency of ethnic identity; a Fur community there is known locally as Kara (and distinguished from the Kara proper of Jabal Si), solely because its first chief was a Kara slave.[27]

Dar Diima was ruled by a line of hereditary chiefs, the *aba diimang* (in Arabic, *al-dimiqawi* or *al-dimijawi*), a title which Beaton suggests means simply "Lord of Diima".[28] They ruled their province autonomously until the early nineteenth century, when they were

---

may be a confusion here in that 'Abd al-Rahman Jokha appears in the lists as one of the lords of Diima (see below).

26 Ibrahim Ishaq and others, Sulma, 26.6.1969.

27 AP2, 10/48, 114.

28 Beaton (1948), 8-9; al-Tunisi's interpretation of the title as the sultan's "right hand" is metaphorical rather than literal and relates to his place in the warband to the right of the sultan; al-Tunisi (1965), 181-2 (173 & 267-8).

subordinated to but not superseded by the *maqdum*s of the south; they were restored by 'Ali Dinar, continued under the British and are still rulers of the Zalingei region, the present (2006) incumbent, Fadil Sissei Atim, being about the twentieth of his name. Their clan, the Morgenga,[29] is credited with a stranger ancestor, Ahmad (or in some versions, 'Abd al-Rahman) al-Barnawi, i.e. from Borno, who in one version, was

Going on pilgrimage in the time of Sultan Suliman. He stayed with the sultan and pleased him so much that he gave him a daughter in marriage. When he went on to Mecca he left the princess expecting a happy event. He gave her a paper in a leather case [*hijab*] to wear around her neck and told that if it was a son, she should give it to the boy, and eventually have it opened in front of the elders. When in due course the boy was born, the case was opened and the paper said that the boy's father was of the Murgi tribe of Bornu. The *fiki* died in Mecca and did not come back. His son became the original Dimingawi, because when he rode behind his grandfather, the sultan saw how brave he was.[30]

Wise strangers from Borno as founders of ruling lineages are not uncommon in Darfur—if Arkell's conjecture of a period of Kanem rule in Darfur remains unproven, the influence of the former on the central Sudanic states of Bagirmi, Wadai and Darfur is undoubted. Three Zaghawa clans—Awlad Diggayn, the Agaba and Dawra—descend from the sons of "*al-haj* Ali, a Bornawi who had been on pilgrimage three times, spoke Arabic fluently and had married a female relative of the Fur Sultan".[31] The chiefs of the Feroge living around Raga in the Western Bahr al-Ghazal claim descent from a Borno pilgrim who married the original Feroge chief's daughter.[32] In a variant

---

29 The name may appear as "Morga" in the list of peoples tributary to the king of Uri in the late sixteenth century, see D'Anania (1582), 349. An alternative identification as the Birged, who call themselves Murgi, is proposed by Lange and Berthoud (1972), 345, n.15. On the Morgenga clan or *orre*, see Adelberger (1990), 171-2.

30 AP2, 10/48, 102-3.

31 AP1, 5/21, 84-94, and PA (al-Fashir) DP 66 B 6, vol. 2, Tribal Affairs—General Zaghawa.

32 Santandrea (1957), 129-31. One may speculate that this is a memory of the origins of the lords of Diima carried southwards.

recorded by Beaton, the son of the holy man from Borno (who in this version marries the sultan's sister; the confusion of sister and daughter is common in "Wise Stranger" stories) is called Adam Morge and has his head shaved by the sultan, "Lo, I have shaved the head of the son of my sister, and will make him head over twelve Shartais".[33]

Beaton's version lays stress on the Borno "Wise Stranger's" fame as a rainmaker and ritual rainmakers played a part in the accession rituals of the lords of Diima. The rites have points of similarity with the installation of a new sultan; the *aba diimang* was accompanied to a sacred tree by ritual experts including old women—comparable to the *habbobat* of the sultan's accession. A goat, cow and bull were sacrificed and the party entered a cave (reminiscent of the entry into the Drum-house by the sultan), where the rain chief of Komoro prayed, "Do not reject your descendant, we have come to perform the rites (*awaida*) due to you". Thereafter a ritual meal was eaten, followed by the beating of the Diima lord's drum.[34]

After Adam Morge, there ruled eleven lords of Diima before Ahmad Titi who ruled in about 1830.[35] This suggests that the lords of Diima go back to the early seventeenth century and emerged more or less with the sultanate. Although as provincial rulers living away from the court they do not figure greatly in the records, there are indications of their warlike role as marcher lords. Their centres were located widely throughout their province, probably reflecting campaigns against the Fartit in the south and the Masalit in the west; Adam Morge, Ahmad Titi and possibly his predecessor 'Abd al-Rahman Jokha (namely the first, twelfth and eleventh) had their capitals at Umm Jadayn in the far south, while Ahmad Titi was for a

---

33 Cooke and Beaton (1939), 199.

34 Ibid., 200-1.

35 This approximate date is based on a letter by the French explorer in Ethiopia, Antoine d'Abbadie, in 1842 giving a Darfur itinerary from a Fallata shaykh who was born in Morocco, grew up in Darfur and lived at Massawa (Eritrea); part of the itinerary runs, "à Rodima [ro Diima] 2 jours—à Ahmed Thithi 5 jours—à Abou Omorig [Dar Uumo]"; see D'Abbadie (1842), 352. The genealogy of the lords of Diima is based on AP2, 10/48, 40, 53 and 102; PA (al-Fashir) *Western Darfur District Handbook*, and Sisei Muhammad Atim al-Diminqawi, Zalingei, 27.5.1969.

while based at Segali south of Nyala, and Khalil 'Abd al-Rahman (or Ahmad: the thirteenth *aba diimang*) had his main centre at Dergola in Bani Halba country. As commanders of the right flank, they took part in 'Umar Lel's ill-fated invasion of Wadai in about 1739, in Tayrab's successful conquest of Kordofan in 1785, in Muhammad al-Fadl's abortive attempt to reconquer the latter in 1821-22, and in his more successful, if short-lived, expedition in 1837 to impose a sultan on Wadai, when'Abd al-Rahman Kabbas (fourteenth in succession) was one of the leaders.[36] Not all were remembered only as warriors; the tenth lord, 'Isa Kull Barid, venerated as a rainmaker, owed his nickname, "all cool"—according to one version—to "his patience and his desire to see everybody happy". Another, perhaps more plausible, version alleges that it came from *akal barid* because he "ate [i.e. oppressed] his people and was "cold" or haughty towards them.[37]

The lords of Diima, who had their own home chiefdom of Dar Diima, ruled their province through ten or twelve *shartays*.[38] In contrast to the antiquity of the Morgenga lineage, few of the *shartay* families go back much beyond the eighteenth century; exceptional were the Daju *shartays* of Nyoma who traced their descent through ten generations to Nang (Fur, "millet"), so-called because he was found on a path by a millet plant. Nuqu, the first *shartay* of Kulli, was said to have come from the north and to have been installed by Muhammad Dawra (his brother Muqu is said to have been given the Jabal Marra *shartaya* of Wona at the same time, but the onomatopoeic names are suspect), while the first chief in Surro was an Arab

---

36 Nachtigal (1971-87), iv, 210; Cadalvène and Breuvery (1841), ii, 231 and AP2, 10/48, 108.

37 Cooke and Beaton (1939), 200 and AP2, 10/48, 102. Being *barid* ("cold" or "distant") was a common comment I have heard over the years from Darfurians about the British; it is ambiguous in meaning.

38 They were Diima, Surro, Nyoma (which separated from Surro), Kobara (which on occasion included Fongoro), Kulli, Zami Baya, Zami Toyo, Tebella, Aribo and Tilni. See further Adelberger (1990), 186-93 for a detailed analysis. In recent years there has been a proliferation of *shartayas* or would-be *shartayas*, to the confusion of all.

175

put in by Tayrab.[39] This heterogeneity seems to reflect a common Fur
pattern of relative instability among middle-ranking chiefs.

The power and prestige of the *shartays* varied greatly within the
sultanate; some, like those of Birged Kajjar and Kerne, were powerful
figures, while others controlled relatively small areas and few people.
The *shartays* of Diima, Uumo and the eight mountain chiefdoms of
Jabal Marra that made up *hakurat al-sultan* or the sultan's estate were
relatively modest figures, although again their chiefdoms varied in
size and wealth. Nevertheless the *shartays* were installed with some
ceremony and treated with respect, for the Fur compare their chiefs,
their parents and their wives' parents to the sun, "You cannot look
them in the face". Their accession rituals were modest versions of
those of the sultan or the lords of Diima; thus on the appointment of
a *shartay* in Dar Wona,

> He is taken to the *shartay*'s drum [*dinger*] and an *akhdar* [literally "green"
> meaning unmarked] ram is killed. The drum is smeared with ram's blood,
> and the *shartay* jumps over the ram's body and the drum is then beaten to
> announce the *shartay*'s appointment.[40]

The appointments, usually from among the brothers or sons of
the previous holder, were either made or confirmed by the sultan
who usually gave presents such as a carpet (Ar. *firsha*), a sword, an
ibriq ("pitcher", used for ritual ablutions before prayers), a horse
and saddlery.

The *shartay* was his ruler's representative to his people; his village was the district centre for taxation, justice and military levies.
His compound was a *fashir* writ small, within which was the *kerkera*
or *kiisonga diito/*"the *shartay*'s stone", where the chief sat to render
justice in cases brought before by the *dimlijs* and others.[41] Justice and
taxation were his main concerns; other duties included the allocation
of land to newcomers and grazing and livestock migration routes.
In time of war he would summon one or two men from each village

---

39 PA (al-Fashir), *Western Darfur District Handbook*, and AP2, 10/48, 40-9.

40 AP2, 10/48, 83-98, notes on Dar Wona.

41 Ibid., for a detailed description by Arkell of *shartay* 'Ali 'Abd al-Jalil's
    compound at Kalokitting in Wona.

for the season's campaigning or raiding. His revenues came from a proportion of the fines and blood money (*dam*) he could impose and from his land to which his people were obliged to contribute labour.

Before the transformation of so much of Diima into estates, each *shartaya* was divided into a varying number of *dimlijiyyas*. Each comprised a number of villages; in the 1930s the five *dimlijiyya*s of Wona averaged five to six villages, each village with between twenty to forty inhabitants. The *dimlij* was a minor functionary, essentially the *shartay*'s man in the locality, responsible for the payment of taxes, the maintenance of order and the forwarding of cases to his superior. Thus it was not difficult for the estate stewards to take over these functions.[42]

In practice the cohesive pattern of Fur village life provided whatever institutions of self-regulation were needed, just as through the *jurenga* they provided for their own defence. The *eling wakil* or headman relied on the *darang tebu* or head of the village mess (an unwalled shelter; *rakuba* in Sudanese Ar.) where the men ate and socialised to carry out whatever orders came from above.[43] The recording of taxes and the writing of petitions was the province of probably the only literate member of the community, the *faqih* or *goni*.[44] It is perhaps characteristic of the relative weakness of institutional links and offices in Fur society that the *fuqara* played so prominent a role in the local administration; elsewhere they were not so visible.

I have described here the administration of the Fur in Diima, in the cone of territory stretching southwest from Jabal Marra. Less is known of Dar Uumo or of the *shartaya*s due west of the mountains. Al-Tunisi metaphorically describes the *abbo uumo* as the sultan's

---

42 Ibid. Beaton (1948), 5-6 gives two explanations for *dimlij*, one that he was a local chief later partially submerged by the estate stewards, the other that he was primarily a rain chief; the two are not mutually exclusive. Detailed breakdowns for each *shartaya* are given in the *Western Darfur District Handbook*.

43 Beaton (1941), 184, the *darang tebu* "is an elderly man among the group of males eating in common food provided by their wives or mothers".

44 The distinction is one of reputation; the *goni* (a word of Kanuri origin [spoken in Kanem/Borno, i.e. present-day western Chad] would be known throughout a district, the *faqih* or imam only locally.

"backbone" and as the commander of the rearguard in time of war, although the title appears to come from the Fur for fontanelle. Little is known about the ruling lineage or the extent of its domain, although it was evidently less powerful than its western neighbour, no doubt because of the comparative diversity and poverty of its command. The *abbo uumo*s came from the Meiringa Fur and had their centre at Jabal Kedinger.[45] At one time Uumo had included most of eastern Jabal Marra south of Turra, divided into several *shartaya*s: the Daju and Beigo in the southeast stretching into Dar Rizayqat, parts of Dar Birged, and the lowland Fur around modern Nyala. At best it was an amorphous province, lacking the cohesion of Diima. Thus the Birged came to be consolidated under the *shartay*s of Birged Kajjar; the Rizayqat were effectively outside the Keira state, and the whole region came to form the heartland of the southern *maqdum*ate.

The four *shartaya*s of Konyir, Kerne, Fia and Made, reaching westwards from the mountains towards what is now the Chad/Sudan border, were a frontier zone between Fur and Masalit. Of what is now Dar Masalit, the south was theoretically part of Diima and the north was divided between Kerne and Fia. These latter were the two largest Fur chiefdoms, ruled by closely-related lineages and answerable directly to the sultan.[46]

Frontiers, provinces and tributaries

Within the sultanate's inner core of the four provinces, the distinction between Fur and others was of little importance, except insofar as the former were concentrated in the two southern provinces; nor did administrative practice vary greatly. Equally, the notion of a compact tribal homeland is misleading. Dar Berti contained more or less than

---

45 Adelberger (1990), 169-70. On the title, see al-Tunisi (1965), 151 (137 & 225), his reference to the *abo uumo* ruling the Masalit probably refers to the Masalit (otherwise, Masalat) of southern Darfur. The statement in Nachtigal (1971-87), iv, 324 that the abo uumo belonged to the Baldanga is not supported by later sources; see MacMichael. *Darfur 1915* (University of Khartoum), and AP2, 10/48, 124 & 215-16.

46 Nachtigal (1971-87), iv, 324-5 and PA (al-Fashir), *Western Darfur District Handbook*.

simply the Berti: more in that most tribal chiefdoms contained other communities within their borders, and less in that, for example, Berti settlements were to be found far outside their tribal homeland. There were few ethnically homogeneous areas in the sultanate, even among the Fur, and this is still very much the case today.

Like other Sudanic states the sultanate may be seen structurally as a series of zones radiating out from the centre, in each of which the nature and strength of the ruler's authority varied. This is not simply to say that the further from al-Fashir the weaker was the sultan's writ because, although distance was a determinant, centre-periphery relations were defined by ecology and political factors. Force, embodied in cavalry but restrained by law and custom, defined the vulnerability of the settled communities to overlords. By contrast, while mutual concerns like slave raiding, livestock migration and the caravan trade may have brought sultan and nomad together, the latter's herds and their political turbulence were a recurring temptation and challenge. Within the core or zone of taxation the sultan's authority was legitimised by tradition; beyond it, in the raiding zone, force more overtly defined relations—a distinction made formally by the sultans when they delegated some of their authority to the *sultan al-ghazwa* or slave-raiding chief (see Chapter Eleven). A major difference between the two zones lay in the nature of the taxes levied, whether in people or in kind. But the transition was never abrupt and peoples could be transferred from one zone to another, the emancipation of the Beigo being an example (see Chapter Three).

Two at least of the sultanate's frontiers were geographically defined; the northern frontier marched with the South Libyan Desert, a fearsome and desolate waste that provided little refuge for nomads however hardy. The southern frontier was a complex of overlapping zones; administratively the Baqqara Belt marked the southern limit of the sultanate, but the raiding zone passed through and far beyond the nomads' lands, and therein lay a continual source of tension between the cattle nomads and the sultans.

Both the eastern and western frontier zones had complex histories which illustrate several Sudanic realities, not least that foreign policy was much concerned with frontiers and with control over or access

179

to resources beyond the frontiers. Neither zone was geographically or ethnically clear-cut. In the late seventeenth and early eighteenth centuries successive sultans had with little success contested control of the western marches with Wadai; these wars were legitimised in Darfur by the sultanate's claim to be the senior successor-state to the Tunjur and thus entitled to tribute from Wadai. In the course of three or four wars Darfur made little headway and Tayrab, possibly realising that his country's future lay in the east, is said to have made peace with Sultan Joda of Wadai.[47] But the first delimitation of a frontier between the two states may have made even earlier; when crossing the no man's land between Darfur and Wadai in about 1811, al-Tunisi saw several large iron spikes driven into a series of trees. He was told that these had been put up to mark the frontier by Sulayman and Salih, respective founders of the two states. Later sources describe two small parallel ranges of hills as the two *tirja*s or "barriers" formally marking the border.[48] But the "barriers" accounted for only the central section of the frontier, the land of the Masalit; both to the north and the south lay states that were fought over by their more powerful neighbours.

Of the frontiers the eastern was the most porous, expanding and contracting until some stability was imposed upon it by the Turco-Egyptians after their conquest of Kordofan in 1821 (see Chapter Four). The sultans did not create a new province in Kordofan but extended eastwards the provinces of the north and east. The northern governors were based at al-Ubayyid or Bara, while southern Kordofan was administered as part of Dar Abbo Shaykh Daali. However, in about 1805 the administration of Kordofan was unified under Musallim, who remained sole governor until his death before Bara (18 August 1821) at the hands of the Turco-Egyptians.[49] Kordofan was a prosperous region; Danaqla and Ja'aliyyin traders from the

---

47 Al-Tunisi (1851), 91; see further O'Fahey and Spaulding (1974), 125-34.

48 Al-Tunisi (1851), 76-7 and Nachtigal (1971-87), iv, 238 and note.

49 O'Fahey and Spaulding (1974), 331, n.73, and PA (al-Fashir), DP FD 66 K 15, Azagarfa Omodia. An undated charter issued in northern Darfur by the *malik* al-Hajj, "deputy of the malik Musallim", appears to confirm these arrangements.

Nile had built up trading networks based on al-Ubayyid and Bara dealing in gum arabic, ivory, slaves and alluvial gold. The Darfur governors appear to have encouraged commerce, so that Darfur's rule was later favourably contrasted with the rapacity of the Turco-Egyptians.[50] It was no doubt Kordofan's very size and prosperity that led to both Kurra and Musallim being suspected of seeking to make themselves independent there, in other words to emulate Hashim al-Musabba'awi. The virtual closure of the eastern frontier after the Turco-Egyptian occupation was to cause a concentration of Darfur's external trade along the Forty Days Road, to Kordofan's loss and Asyut's gain.[51]

Within the provincial core, administrative practice was more or less uniform, although the three tiers of chiefs bore different titles in different regions—*shartay* and *malik al-'urban* for the nomads; shaykh, *dimlij*, *kursi* or *firsha* (common in the far west) below them, and shaykh again at the lowest level. Titles were a matter of self-esteem; one who was a *malik* to his people might simply be addressed as *shartay* by the sultan.[52]

Both within and on the margins of the provinces a number of tribes, or more accurately tribal territories, preserved their identity and a degree of administrative autonomy. Among the most important were the Qimr and Tama in the west; Kobe and the other Zaghawa chiefdoms, the Meidob, Zayyadiyya and Berti forming an arc across the north; the Birged, Tunjur and Mima of the centre and east, and the Daju and Beigo of the south, beyond whom lay the Baqqara and the Fartit.[53] The history of the incorporation of these peoples

---

50 Cuny (1862), 177, Pallme (1846), 12-14 and Lejean (1862), 854-82.

51 Kropacek (1970), 73-8 and Walz (1978b), 113-26.

52 Exaggeration was a form of flattery; a chief's daughter would be addressed as *iiya* in imitation of the royal women. Titles could be debased (a commonplace in colonial times). *'Aqid* (Fur, *ornang*) was in origin a war chief, in colonial times the leader of a hunting party, today it is used of the field commanders of the various rebel factions. See Beaton (1941), 181-8. By contrast, official documents are precise, often listing three or four titles before the official's name.

53 For surveys, see al-Tunisi (1965), 132-53 (126-38 & 205-27), Lauture (1855-56), 94-8, and Nachtigal (1971-87), iv, 346-61.

is only sketchily known, and that largely from the viewpoint of the sultans. Of greater interest are the formal and informal mechanisms whereby relations between sultan and tributary were maintained or adjusted—the marriage alliances, the giving of gifts, the bestowal of drums and titles, or the sending of cavalry to collect tribute. The distance between centre and tributary had not only a political dimension; central peoples like the Birged, Berti, Tunjur and Mima were acculturated to an Arabic-based Islamic culture spread under the aegis of the sultans to a much greater degree than the Fur, Meidob or Zaghawa. Both the Birged and Berti have lost their own languages, while Fur, Meidob and Zaghawa still thrive. But distance was never the sole factor; the camel nomads of the north lacked the escape routes and marshes that protected the Baqqara, and the Meidob were simply off the beaten track.

Expansion west and northwestwards in the early eighteenth century brought the Keira into contact with, among others, the Qimr, Zaghawa and Tama. The Qimr sultans, like those of Wadai, claimed to be of Ja'ali origin, from al-Matamma on the Nile; the eponymous ancestor, Qimr Hasab Allah, is said to have led a band of Arabs (Ja'aliyyin, Korobat, Sa'ada, Hotiyyya and Tarjam) to the area and to have established a state around Jabal Nokat, now in Dar Tama. The Qimr were conquered in a series of campaigns led by Bukr and Dawra. Although the Qimr kept their sultan, who was indeed honoured above other tributaries by being allowed to retain his royal carpet, some Qimr irreconcilables seem to have sought refuge at the court of Sinnar. A later Qimr Sultan, Hashim b. 'Umar (d. 1935), married a daughter of Muhammad al-Husayn.[54]

Of all the tributaries, it was the Zaghawa who had the most lasting and intimate relationship with the Keira; the relationship of Fur and Zaghawa is as vital now as in the eighteenth century, since the great

---

54 PA (al-Fashir) DP 1 D 3 5, note on Dar Qimr by E.A.V. de Candole; Nachtigal (1971-87), iv, 280-1; MacMichael, *Darfur 1915* (University of Khartoum), 56-8; idem (1922), i, 84-5 and Abu Sinn (1968), 70-1. On the soi-disant "Sultan of Qimr" Muhammad in Sinnar, see Spaulding and Abu Salim (1989), 80-108 where he appears on some royal charters as a witness.

non-Arab divide in Darfur is between Fur and Zaghawa.[55] Generally
the Keira only intervened in the mêlée of Zaghawa politics when
absolutely necessary. Relations were largely reciprocal; each year, after the rains, a caravan left Dar Kobe taking horses, cattle and sheep
as tribute; in return the Keira Sultan sent imported war horses and
fine clothes.[56] Some Zaghawa resisted the Keira advance; Muhammad Fa'it, the most influential chief of his day in Galla, Tuer and
Artag, rebelled against Bukr. He was eventually defeated and killed
by Dawra, who, to weaken Fa'it's Agaba Zaghawa, took from them
the Anka wells and gave them to the Beiri *shartay*s. Another chief,
Ubayd (or 'Ubayd) chose flight and led a section of the Awlad Dawra
to Kajmar in northern Kordofan where their descendants still live.[57]

Tama, to the west of Qimr, was never comfortably part of Darfur
or of Wadai, but oscillated between the two, as we have seen (see
Chapter Four).

Political subordination and hierarchy within the sultanate found
their most characteristic expression in the drums, specifically the
nahas or copper kettle drums which were the paramount symbol of
autonomous authority throughout Darfur and beyond. At the apex of
the drum hierarchy were naturally the Keira *nahas*, housed within the
fashir and ceremonially renewed each year in a ritual which mystically
identified them with the sultan's authority and wellbeing. Among
the seven royal drums, some regarded as male and others as female,
were *al-bayda*/"the white [one]" and *al-mansura*/"the victorious",
the latter, female, being the smallest and most sacred of all.[58] The

---

55 From conversations I have had in recent years with many of the actors,
both Zaghawa and Fur leaders are well aware of the historical dimension,
going back to the war between 'Abd al-Rahman and Ishaq. Jérôme Tubiana
tells me that he has had a very similar experience. This historical dimension
eloquently informs every page of 'Uthman (2006).

56 Tubiana (1964), 32.

57 AP1, 84-94; Lejean (1865a), 301-2 and MacMichael (1912), 109-12.

58 AP1, 3/13, 38-43 and Shuqayr (1903), ii, 145. The original *al-mansura* was
captured by al-Zubayr at Manawashi and later came into the hands of the
Khalifa. 'Ali Dinar asked for its return but was told by the Condominium
authorities that it had been taken to Europe. They sent him instead two very
large drums that now stand in the police headquarters. The sultan named

nahas were a rallying point in time of war and the ultimate symbol of legitimacy, as an episode recounted by Nachtigal illustrates. There was considerable opposition to Muhammad al-Husayn's accession in 1837; among the discontented was the former Wazir 'Abd al-Bari who was sitting drinking with his cronies when a slave said,

We sit here in the *bayt al-kabir* [the great or old palace, south of Rahad Tandalti] with our *nahas*, and the king sits yonder in Tombasi [the new palace] with Adam Tarbush. What if we were set up another ruler here in the old palace?[59]

The granting (or withdrawal) of one or more *nahas* was a way to regulate and regularise relations between sultan and tributary. *Shartays* and even powerful Fur chiefs such as the *aba diimang* held only the *dinger* or wooden drum, since the Keira *nahas* were considered to serve all the Fur. But the tributary chiefs could be granted *nahas* either in recognition of their autonomy or to mark a shift of power within a tribe. Bukr is said to have promoted Ta b. Kwore of Zaghawa Kobe by granting him the *nahas* in replacement of his *dinger*, while Tayrab recognised a transfer of paramountcy among the Zayyadiyya from the Awlad Jabir to the Jarbu'a by granting *nahas* to the latter's shaykh, Umm Badr.[60]

According to a British report of 1922 the sultans maintained "a system of decentralization with the proviso that the Fur ascendancy in public affairs was to be maintained at all costs"; Fur here meant the Keira and the court elite, not the Fur people.[61] The bestowal of drums, robes of honour, arms and armour, estates and honorifics such as "sultan", as well as the education of chiefly sons at court,

---

them *al-dar 'amir/*"the land is prosperous" and *'ata al-mawla/*"the gift of the lord" and had them inscribed with magical formulae (*hijab*). PHOTO

59 Nachtigal (1971-87), iv, 307; see also ibid., 286 for *al-mansura* as a rallying point in battle.

60 PA (al-Fashir) 66 B 29/1; Tubiana (1964), 27 and shartay Hasab Allah Abu'l-Bashr (Tarni, 9.4.1974) who listed thirteen tribes as having the right to *nahas*. The drum is usually represented in the *wasm* or brand of the ruling section of a tribe; see Arkell (1951b), 218-25 and MacMichael (1913) for examples.

61 (Bence Pembroke), *Darfur Province 1916* (ms. University of Khartoum).

were all instruments of this policy. Opposition could arise when the legitimacy of the relationship was threatened, as the example of the Birged girls illustrates (Chapter Three). Flight or migration was a more realistic alternative for the nomads, and both the Mahamid and the Zayyadiyya oscillated between Wadai and Darfur and between Kordofan and Darfur respectively, as advantage dictated.

For their own purposes the Condominium files portray a static society in which all knew their place and kept it. The reality was more fluid; tribal ruling lineages were not so ancient, nor tribal boundaries so inviolable under the sultans as they were to become under the British or are considered to be today. Sultans frequently interfered with chiefly succession; even in remote Meidob, Keira intervention led to a dynastic shift, while attempts to impose order on the Zaghawa were seemingly as frequent as they were fruitless.[62] Cavalry and the tax collectors as well as the intangibles of ideology and religion bound the village communities of the savanna to their rulers; the nomads forced the sultans to create new institutions of control, essentially the *maqdum*s and their successors.

Maqdums, Wazirs and Mandubs

The title *maqdum* first appears in about 1800 as a new official who functioned outside the old titled hierarchy. A commissioner or viceroy appointed for a specific task, to govern a particular area or to lead a campaign, the *maqdum* "in some measure represents the person of the king", this being symbolised by the granting to him on appointment of royal insignia, Qur'an, carpet, *kurkur* or stool, and lances but not the *nahas*. The appointee could be either servile or free and on completion of his assignment he reverted to his former rank.[63]

---

62 Lampen (1928), 55-67, "the story is that the wakil of the last king of this line [of the Shelkota lineage] bribed the reigning Fur sultan to give him the throne". The situation among the Zaghawa seemed to them so confused that the British tried to undo the settlement that 'Ali Dinar had made (see 'Uthman (2006), 286-300) and actually cancelled charters granting land and chiefly powers. This simply compounded the confusion.

63 Nachtigal (1971-87), iv, 309 & 326.

The emergence of the *maqdum*s was one response among several to a complex of developments. The end by the 1820s of the sultanate's expansion to the east and west and the intensification of the trade with Egypt and of the slave trade, both for export and internal consumption, focused attention on the northern and southern frontiers, i.e. on the nomads. The slaving grounds could only be reached by passing through the Baqqara; the Forty Days Road passed through the lands of the camel nomads. And although direct evidence of any extensive nomad involvement in the long-distance trade is meagre, from comparisons elsewhere in the Sudanic Belt they must have played a role as carriers in the north and as fellow raiders in the south. Within a broader context, the trade and raid boom of 1800 to 1850 and the elite that profited from it began to modify relations between ruler and ruled within the state; the *maqdum*ate and the estate system were perhaps the most obvious symptoms of this change.

Although there is little direct evidence to link the emergence of the *maqdum*s to the nomad problem, they were in time to become very closely tied. In the north, where the nomads were never a serious problem, the *maqdum*s soon settled down as hereditary governors. In the south they were never given a chance; wars with the Baqqara both took their toll of the *maqdum*s sent against them and turned the south into a warring frontier, which remained as such until the 1920s.

In the north the lack of serious conflict led to the hardening of the *maqdum*ate into a territorial command at the expense of the *takanawi*s, the earlier governors of the north. In about 1810, for reasons that are unknown but which may be linked to the conflicts with the camel nomads, Hasan Segerre (Ar. Siqiri) was appointed *maqdum* in the north; his family was remotely of Arab origin and long settled in Jabal Meidob. They held the Fur honorific title of *iringa*/"exalted" and owned land in the Wana Hills northwest of al-Fashir. The *maqdum*ate soon became hereditary within the family; Hasan died about 1855-56 and was followed by his son Muhammad, who in turn was succeeded by a grandson, or possibly another son, Adam. The family survived the Mahdiyya, and by a decree of 1899 'Ali Dinar restored the title and estates to the family in the person of Muhammad Sharif

Adam, who had come back to Darfur with him from Omdurman.[64] The *maqdum*s of Dar al-Rih, based at Kutum, had simply replaced the *takanawi*s, who survived as intermediary chiefs between the new masters of the north and the *shartay*s.

The disastrous campaigns against the Baqqara had the effect of consolidating a southern *maqdum* governorate, which has survived to this day, but the toll on the commissioners—two died in battle—ensured that it did not become hereditary until British times. The command included the lands of the *abbo uumo*[65] and *aba diimang* and had its capital at Dara with a forward base at al-Shakka in the Rizayqat country just north of the Bahr al-'Arab. The *maqdum*s were first and foremost warlords moving around with their troops to the areas of conflict, whether in the south or in the west along the Masalit and Dar Sila borders. They collected taxes, or rather summoned the chiefs to bring in the taxes, primarily to maintain their own forces, and could impose the death penalty, hitherto the sole prerogative of the sultans. On occasion *maqdum*s were also appointed in the west and east, and thus for a time Dar al-Gharb was administered by 'Abd Allah Runga, a Dinka slave, operating from Kabkabiyya and al-Tiniyyat.[66] But the *maqdum*ate never formally coalesced into a rank of provincial governor over and above the old quadrant system.

A number of *maqdum*s held the title of *wazir* which, according to Nachtigal, was the Arabic equivalent of the Fur *abbo kotingo*, a slave title attached to the old palace in al-Fashir, *bayt al-qadim*.[67] This may be too precise, since *wazir* appears to be more an honorific than an office; the closest parallel to the classical Islamic *wazir* was

---

64 On the history of the family, PA (al-Fashir) DP FD 66 K 15, Azagarfa Omodia; Lauture (1855-56), 95; Cuny (1858), 13; Lejean (1865b); Nachtigal (1971-87), iv, 306, 310 and 330-1, and 'Uthman (2006), 287. The decree (DF269.33/2) is dated 22 Jumada I 1317/28 September 1899.

65 PA (al-Fashir) *Nyala District Handbook*; the British in 1916 intended to establish their southern headquarters at Dara, but the wells had failed there and Nyala was chosen instead.

66 PA (Kutum) NDD 66 b 8/2, Dar Fia. The best known *maqdum* in the east, Rahma Gomo, was also *ab shaykh* and was thus ex officio governor of the east; see O'Fahey (1991), 79-112.

67 Nachtigal (1971-87), iv, 332-4.

THE DARFUR SULTANATE

Diagram 8

THE MAQDUMS OF THE SOUTH

Name	Tribal Affiliation	Other Titles	Comments
1. Saʿīd b. Muḥammad	Berti/ Rizayqāt	*soming dogala*	campaigned against Rizayqāt c.1818-20
2. Ramadān b. *al-sulṭān* ʿAbd al-Rahmān	Keira/Fur	*baasi*	
3. ʿAbd al-ʿAzīz	Fur	*soming dogala*	campaigned in early 1840's against the Rizayqāt and Habbāniyya
4. Khalīl b. ʿAbd al-Sīd (son of a *maqdūm*)	Fur	*malik kórkwa*	campaigned against Rizayqāt c. 1854
5. Ādam Bōsh	Meidobi/slave	*wazir al-aʿzam*	killed by Rizayqāt in 1856
6. Ahmad Shatta b.ʿAbd al-ʿAziz (son of 3)	Fur	*malik saaringa, wazir*	*maqdūm*, 1856-73

Under ʿAlī Dīnār, 1898-1916
(Held office for short periods only)

7. Qamr al-Dīn	Berti		
8. Adam ʿAlī	Fur		
9. Maḥmūd al-Dādinqāwī	Fur	*abbo daadinga ; also acted as* Alī Dīnār's *wazir*	
10. Tibn b. Saʿd al-Nūr	Konyunga/ Fur	*soming dogala, malik al-nahās*	
11. Muḥammad Kebkebe	Beigo	"Sultan" of the Beigo	

the *ab shaykh daali*. But the precise use of *maqdum, wazir, wazir al-a'zam* is of less moment than the fact that they describe a pattern of semi-autonomous and highly mobile warlords operating over and above the old-established territorial administration. Their strength lay in the warbands they led and in the fact that many held powerful positions within the hierarchy in their own right (see Diagram 7). Few were slaves suddenly elevated from the ranks. This flexible pattern evidently arose in response to military needs, which the older structures of command were inadequate to meet. External threats were to conceal the potential threat of the *maqdum*ate to the sultans, although *maqdum* Ahmad Shatta's march in 1873 on al-Fashir with his southern forces, in an unsuccessful bid to put his candidate on the throne was a portent of what might have been.

The ruination that 'Ali Dinar faced in late 1898 on his return to Darfur left him little choice but to rule through slaves, generals and confidants sent out with warbands on an *ad hoc* basis. These were sometimes called *mandub*s or "agents", possibly a borrowing from Mahdist practice, but *maqdum* continued in use in its original meaning of "commissioner".[68] Thus Diima and Dar Kerne were administered in the space of ten years by four *maqdum*s, Mustafa Qalgham for a year, Mahmud 'Ali al-Dadinqawi for two years, the *baasi* Abbo for five and Ahmad wad al-Mayram for two.[69] But 'Ali Dinar's *maqdum*s and *mandub*s were, with a few trusted exceptions like Mahmud al-Dadinqawi, much smaller men than those of the previous century and were kept on a much tighter rein by the sultan.

68 Lampen (1950), 204.
69 AP2, 10/48, 54-7, "Administration of Dar Kerne and Dar Abu Dima under Sultan Aly Dinar".

9

GOVERNMENT AND COMMUNITY

The boundaries of state power

The sultans have left a collective description of their ruling elite in a phrase that appears in their charters describing the chiefs and officials to whom the documents are addressed: "And all those oppressive [officials] who are overbearing with the rights of the Muslims".[1] Its very ambiguity is a warning against seeing the evolution and functioning of the elite within the state within a simple model of exploitation. The social and political divide between *khassa* and *'amma*, between "elect" and "commoner", between participants and non-participants in decision-making, was bridged by both upward and downward mobility and by kin and communal loyalties.[2]

A fundamental aspect of a centralising sultanate was the increasing control over the state's resources exercised by the "elect". Some of the means have already been described: the concentration of power and people at court, the granting of estates or rights over people, and the creation of new offices that overrode the tribal order. All these innovations may be characterised as the more effective exploitation of the ruled by their rulers, whereby the latter used both force and material inducements, whether land or goods, to attract followers

---

1   *Wa-jumlat al-tughat al-mutamarradin bi-huquq al-muslimin*; see O'Fahey and Abu Salim (1983), 32.

2   The stereotypical phrase, *'awwam wa-khawass*, introduces the listing of witnesses in a number of judicial transcripts.

and clients who in turn could work more land, herd more livestock or raid for more slaves.[3]

However, neither the degree of exploitation nor the value of this model should be exaggerated; both were mitigated by the inertia of poor communications, by communal solidarity, by the role of traditional and Islamic beliefs in cementing social bonds, and by the ruler's own conception of legitimacy. Such sultanic honorifics and epithets as "the servant of the Law and Religion" or "who spreads the banner of justice over the heads of the people", common in the charters, were not simply rodomontade, but in some degree ideological statements of intent. Darfur was not a Japan or China; there did not exist an arcane court culture expressed in a language incomprehensible to ordinary people. Shared beliefs and prejudices, state rituals and public worship served to reinforce the bonds of society; commoners participated in the state festivals, the sultans helped local local communities build permanent mosques of red brick, 'Ali Dinar decreed prayers for rain, and preparations for war included exhortations by the sultans for recitations of the Qur'an by the *fuqara*.[4] Islam, whether through the Shari'a or popular Sufism mediated by the *fuqara*, increasingly provided the referent for social norms.

The needs of their rulers impinged upon the local community unevenly. Local communities under their village or nomad shaykhs were

---

3 Informants (both in the Condominium files and to me) contrasted "the good old days" under Muhammad al-Fadl and his son with the grim years that followed; insecurity and disorder were always worse than grasping rulers. 'Ali Dinar, however tough he may have been, is well remembered precisely for his restoration of order. Likewise the British are positively remembered despite being "cold", *barid*, i.e. unfriendly, because they stuck to the rules, unlike what happens under the present dispensation.

4 The intertribal gatherings, *'arda*, a continuation of sultanic practice focusing on horses and horse-racing, which continued under the British and indeed were encouraged by them, survived into the early 1970s (I was present at several). They were fun, had the atmosphere of a gymkhana, and were crucial in interethnic problem-solving. Dr Al-Waleed Madibbu is currently trying to revive them; an *'arda* was recently held at al-Da'ayn. DF225.28/6, 'Ali Dinar to *shartay* al-Doma Muhammad of Dar Simiyat: the rains are late, which the Sultan attributes to his people's wickedness. All are to pray for rain. On Qur'anic recitations, see O'Fahey and Abu Salim (1983), 42.

self-governing, and their ideal of good government (from outside the community) was probably as little as possible, a view no doubt reciprocated by the ruling institution once its demands had been met. The communities' main contact with their rulers was confined to war, justice in matters such as homicide that could not be settled within the community, and taxation. Within these spheres the sultanate was, without doubt, efficiently administered in the sense that the elite could reasonably expect their orders and demands to reach down and be enforced at the local level; in turn, their subjects could expect a measure of justice and not too much *zulm*, "oppression". The limited expectations on both sides of the political fence should be borne in mind in the following pages.

Warfare

The making of war was a fundamental activity of the state, but in the Sudanic Belt its scale was limited by factors such as distance and climate. For example, almost the only time when armies could move was in the rainy season and a little after (approximately June to October) when water supplies were reasonably certain and widespread. By the beginning of the nineteenth century, Darfur had ceased to be a regular warmaking state; foreign expeditions were a thing of the past, save the expedition to Wadai in 1837 and the attempted invasion of Kordofan in 1821-22 which came to nought. War or the use of force had, above all, become a matter of raiding for slaves, a stylised form of warfare with little military content. The inadequacies of the state's military forces were to be cruelly exposed in the wars of the 1840s and 50s against the Baqqara, and underscored, despite much heroism, by al-Zubayr's invasion and the subsequent resistance.

It is unlikely that a kingdom born in the mountains began its career of conquest using horsemen. In fact, it is possible to guess at three—and to describe two in some detail—of the stages in the military evolution of the Keira state: the Fur people under arms, the dominance within the savannas of mounted and armed elites, and a final desperate scramble to equip and train bodies of slaves in the use of rifles.

193

Of the three stages the first is the most speculative, but the evidence suggests that until Tayrab's reign the state was geared for war in the sense of the sultan waging a more or less regular annual campaign. By contrast, after the conquest of Kordofan and civil war between 'Abd al-Rahman and Ishaq, no sultan went campaigning in person until Ibrahim Qarad's fatal encounter with al-Zubayr at Manawashi. Nor, after the restoration, did 'Ali Dinar go to war himself, being content to leave campaigning—even against the British—to his generals. The early sultans campaigned regularly; Sulayman, appropriately for the state's progenitor, is credited with leading no less than thirty-three expeditions. In these early campaigns, mainly against the western border states and Wadai, the Keira army fought as a hierarchy of warbands where each of the great terriorial chiefs had his appointed position within the order of march, a hierarchy clearly described by al-Tunisi (see diagram 3). These early armies were composed of tribal levies called out *en masse* under their chiefs. A hint of how they were mobilised comes from Beaton's account of youth organisation among the Fur; the *jurenga*, youths who had been circumcised but not yet married, were banded together in each district or *dimlijiyya* largely for social purposes, most commonly dancing. But in time of war they could be called out under the leadership of an'*aqid* (Ar.) or *ornang* (Fur), an older man appointed by the elders of the district.[5]

As well as the usual weapons—spear (*kor* or *sambei*) and shield (*kebi*), the latter made of buffalo, elephant (from the ear) or bull hide—some western Fur groups were accustomed to use the iron throwing knife (*sambal*), the wartime version of the common wooden hunting-stick (*safarog* or *dorma*). Shaped like a large question mark with sharpened edges and wings to ensure straight flight, it was carried three or four at a time in a holster over the shoulder and was a formidable weapon, but required great skill to be effective. However, in one of the crucial battles of the civil war between Ishaq and 'Abd

5   Beaton (1941), 181-3; compare Nachtigal's description of youth organisations in Wadai; (1971-87), iv, 188-9.

al-Rahman at Tabaldiyya (northeast of Nyala), the latter's victory
was ascribed to the skilful use of the wooden stick by his men.[6]

By the eighteenth century, down on the plains the horsemen was
supreme, a supremacy that was much more than a military phenomenon. The needs of an extensive empire and the ethos of its elite led
to the rise of the leavily armoured *fursan*, meaning "horseman" but
with something of the same overtones as "knight", who terrorised the
farmers, raided for slaves and upheld their honour in single combat.
Along the Nile, in the confusion of the dying Funj Sultanate, the
exploits of the *fursan* gave rise to heroic poetry in such sagas as that
of Sha' al-Din of the Shukriyya.[7] Less is heard of such heroics in
Darfur, although al-Tunisi's account of the death of Kurra and his
adopted son, Shaylfut, breathes the spirit of Sudanic chivalry,

The [*ab*] shaykh's adopted son, Shaylfut, returned [from another part of the
battlefield] thinking that he would find [Kurra] alive and rescue him, but
he found him killed. He unsheathed his sword and drove towards them and
killed a number of their heroes, crying all the while, "Vengeance for *al-abu
al-shaykh* Muhammad Kurra!" At the end they rushed together and he was
killed after he had killed more than twenty of their distinguished men.

And something of the horsemen's arrogance is captured in a song
of a raiding party preparing to ride south:

O Youths!
Come, seek wealth [for your brides]
With the raiding party of Daldang wad Binayya;
They have reined in their horses at Kerio,
[Ride] to the party of Daldang wad Binaya.[8]

---

6 Al-Tunisi (1965), 104-6 (92-3 & 162-3). On the throwing knife, see Thomas
   (1924), 129-45, Olderogge (1934), 106-7 and Arkell (1939a), 251-68.

7 On this poetry, see 'Abd al-Mahmud (n.d. 1965), passim, al-Shush (1962),
   30-35 and 'Abidin (1967), 195-8.

8 Al-Tunisi (1965), 71-2 (53-54 & 109-10), Shaylfut and ibid., 236 (233 &
   339); something of the terror engendered comes out in a description of a
   Rizayqat raiding party among the Dinka in 1909, Greenwood (1941), 189-
   95. The Janjawid of today have simply modernised an old practice.

Much has been written on the failure of Sudanic rulers to adopt firearms systematically despite a long acquaintance with them, but for controlling large areas a man on a horse was much more effective than a man with a gun. Mobility—not only during but between battles—was of more moment than firepower. Firearms only became vital when confronted by an organised enemy armed with them, by which time it was usually too late. Horsemen were also "cost effective" in that they were not needed in great numbers; only sixty were needed to chastise the Mahriyya and Mahamid; Kurra took only 200 "mounted on mares covered with red cloth" to drive Hashim al-Musabba'awi from Kordofan, while a report from 1862 estimated that of the 3,000 horsemen that the sultanate could mobilise, only 600 to 1,000 were heavily armed.[9]

Because both their horses and armour were imported, the *fursan* were expensive and were largely a monopoly of the sultans. The history of the horse and of horse-breeding has yet to be studied, but the fact that "horse" both in Fur (*murta*) and in a number of other languages spoken in Darfur appears to be a Nubian loanword suggests a long history.[10] Of the two breeds found in Darfur, the smaller Kordofani (in fact commoner in Darfur) and the larger Dunqulawi (Dongola), the latter was required because of the weight of armour for warfare.[11] Since the larger and heavier breed tends to degenerate in Sudanic conditions, constant imports were needed, but evidence for importation as opposed to internal trading in horses is scanty. It seems difficult to think of horses being imported along the Forty Days Road, so that the Dongola Reach along the Nile—an area

---

9   Browne (1806), 345; Cadalvène and Breuvery (1841), ii, 211 and Heuglin (1863), 97-114. The garrison in Kordofan consisted of some 500 horsemen, Burckhardt (1822), 482; a generation earlier, Muhammad Abu Likaylik had operated there with a 1,000 horsemen, Bruce (1790), iv, 479.

10 Within the Darfur region there is an as yet undefined linguistic boundary between those languages where "horse" seems to be a Nubian loanword and those where it comes from Arabic.

11 On the wider history of the horse in Africa, see Epstein (1971) and within the Sudanic Belt Fisher (1972-73). For Darfur, see Tothill (1948), 646-9.

famed for horses—seems the most likely source.[12] The scarcity and difficulty of importation explains their very high prices exemplified in the slave/horse price ratio (see Diagram 8), while Nachtigal's comment that horses "mostly had to be purchased with slaves" suggests a specialised trade in two causally related commodities.[13] Their value is illustrated vividly in a hastily written note of about 1800 by a Funj commander of a war party (*harba*) of an encounter "on the road" with a Darfur or Musabba'at war party, "Our warriors, God be Praised, are safe and our horses (*khayluna*) are safe. There escaped from the Kunjara but four men."[14]

A fully equipped *faris* (sing. of *fursan*) was a very expensive being; one may guess that with horse, imported weapons and armour, grooms and maintenance, the cost may well have been above a hundred slaves. German swordblades and chainmail—and horse armour, some also made in Germany—were staples of the Forty Days Road trade.[15] Both rider and horse were protected by quilted cotton (Ar. *libis*) made locally by a Fur section, the Kuuringa, over which was worn a suit of mail (Ar. *dira'*). In addition the rider wore greaves (Ar. *buraka*). Over the chainmail a silk coat (*shahiyya*, referring to a type of imported silk) was worn, while a turban whose ends hung down over the shoulders was wound around the helmet (Ar. *talli*). The favoured weapons of the horsemen included the long straight-bladed sword (Fur *saar*), preferably from Solingen in Germany, the mace (Ar. *dabbus*), and the long heavy-bladed lance (Ar. *salatiyya*) that gave its name to the raiding parties. Nor was it uncommon for

---

12 Nachtigal (1971-87), iv, 254 and 378 (merchants bringing Dongola horses to al-Fashir from Kordofan); on horsebreeding in Dongola, see Cailliaud (1823), i, 108 and Werne (1852), 201.

13 Nachtigal (1971-87), iv, 254. Lyons (1821), 121 noted the same link between horse and slave prices in the Fezzan.

14 Spaulding and O'Fahey (1980), 42-6.

15 On the imports, Browne (1806), 302-4. On the role of armour and swords in the Sudan generally, see Bruce (1790), iv, 479, Parkyns (1851), 254-7 and Werne (1852), 37 and 173.

Diagram 9. HORSE, SLAVE AND OTHER PRICES, c. 1800-1914

No attempt has been made to standardize the values, although the dollar is, in most cases, the Maria Theresa dollar. One may note the horse/slave price ratio and the increasing price inflation during the century.

Date	Horse	Slave	Other	Source
c. 1793		15 piastres (Kobbei)		Browne (1806), 220.
c. 1805		sudasī= 10 M.T. dollars	or in equivalent values, 30 takkiyyas / or 6 strips, blue cloth / or 8 strips, white cloth / or 6 cows	al-Tūnisī (196) 298 (315-16).
1837	10-30 slaves	"good slave"= 5-6 dollars		Abdin Archives, box 262.
c. 1850		female slave	= 3 thwab turunba plus 1 taqq al-ʿartis plus 3 takkiyyas } cloth = 8 cows	122.13/7.
1862		male slave		170.18/30.
1874	good horse = 150 dollars	sudasī= 30 dollars		Nachtigal (1971), 373 & 254.
1879 (in Dara)	good horse = 300-400 dollars[a] horse= 50-60 dollars		ox= 3-6 dollars / sheep= ¾ dollar / goat= ½ dollar / riding camel=50-70 dollars / pack camel= 25-30 dollars	
c. 1900		"concubines"= 50-150 dollars		Felkin (1885-86), 251.
1910		female slave= 12 majīdī dollars		Muhammad ʿAbd al-Rahīm (1935), 80. 77.10/2.
1914		female slave= 72 dollars		76.10/1.

(a) The exceptionally high price may be due to the difficulties of transport and maintenance in southern Dār Fūr. It should not be assumed from the diagram here that horses, slaves, livestock, cloth etc., were freely convertible; each item had its own appropriate economic sphere. takkiyyas were probably rarely used to buy slaves.

the *fursan* to use firearms, early carbines, as personal sidearms in the Mamluk fashion.[16]

The *fursan* were not a class but a type, bands of horsemen led by chiefs who were responsible for equipping and maintaining their men and whose fame attracted more followers. Occasionally there are echoes of Mamluk Egypt as in the story of the Birged lad who courted one of Tayrab's slave girls—a very dangerous pastime, as the castration of Kurra and Musallim testified—and who was rewarded for his fearlessness with

A warhorse (*jawad*), weapons, two slaves, marriage to the slave and by being placed in the ranks of [the sultan's] horsemen[17]

—a princely and costly promotion.

The sultans and some of their chiefs maintained regiments or bands of armed slaves. Both the sultan and the notables were guarded or attended by *korkwa* (Fur, sing *kordungo*, "spearmen"), armed pages rather than soldiers, recruited from the *som* and commanded by a number of *malik*s, of whom Browne has left a description,

The place he [the sultan] sat in was spread with small Turkey carpets. The Meleks were seated on the right and left, and behind them a line of guards, with caps ornamented in front with a small piece of copper and a black ostrich feather. Each bore a spear in his hand, and a target [a small round shield] of the hide of the hippopotamus on the opposite arm. Their dress consisted only of a cotton shirt of the manufacture of the country.[18]

Other quasi-military slaves within the *fashir* included the *korayat* or grooms and the *kotingo* or slaves, a kind of police force, of the *abbo kotingo*, a slave eunuch title-holder responsible for law and order in the "Old Palace". Around al-Fashir were stationed several substantial slave regiments, the most important being the *daadinga*, the forces of the *abbo daadinga*, who were divided into the "Black Shields" (*kebi*

---

16 Nachtigal (1971-87), iv, 341-44; Cuny (1856), 111, and AP1, 3/13, 77-8 on the making of armour locally. See also Adelberger (1990), 166.

17 Shuqayr (1903), ii, 118-19.

18 Browne (1806), 235-6; see also Nachtigal (1971-87), iv, 333 and 335. 'Ali Dinar was accompanied to the mosque each Friday by forty or fifty youths as *korkwa*, AP1, 3/13, 38-43.

diko) and the "Red Shields" (*kebi fuka*), and the *saaringa*, the "Swords-men" under the *malik saaringa*. These regiments were destined to die with Qarad at Manawashi in October 1874.[19] Other groups included the *andanga* or "scouts", but our information is too limited for any real estimate of how these forces were armed or organised.[20]

Thus by the early nineteenth century the sultanate's armed force consisted of a small but probably efficient core of cavalry and some slave regiments supported by a swarm of ill-armed levies called out as and when needed.[21] As long as warfare was a matter of slave raiding and occasional punitive forays and no external challenges loomed, there was little necessity for change, but the forces' inadequacies were laid bare by the campaigns of the 1840s and 50s against the Baqqara (see Chapter Four).

Too late the Keira began urgently to react to the new military realities around them by attempting to create bodies of slaves trained to use firearms. The use of guns and indeed cannon was nothing new; a trickle of guns were regularly imported, but they seem to have been used as much for hunting as for war.[22] Cannon appear intermittently; Bukr is said to have used one in his campaigns against Dar Qimr, Musallim had two at Bara and Shatta one at al-Shakka.[23] Although by the 1830s Muhammad al-Fadl's guards had "about four hundred muskets, of various shapes and sizes", firearms were still expensive

---

19 Nachtigal (1971-87), iv, 332-3, PA (al-Fashir, majlis), DP FD 66 K 1/5, Tawila Omodia, and Rihaymat Allah al-Dadinqawi, al-Fashir, 7.6.1970. See also Adelberger (1990), 148-49.

20 Ibid., 142-3.

21 We have some rather doubtful figures: al-Tunisi (1845) 154 [not given in the Arabic text] lists what purports to be a partial census of armsbearing males totalling 50,050; Heuglin (1863), 97-114 gives 70,000 infantry and 3,000 horse, while Hartmann (1863), Anhänge, 17 estimated the sultanate's forces at 100,000 of whom 20,000 were horsemen.

22 Browne (1806), 347, Cuny (1856), 113, Figari (1864-65), 442 and Nachtigal (1876-77), 314-15. The Egyptian musketeer who killed Ishaq was a hunter; al-Tunisi (1965), 110 (99 & 170).

23 Nachtigal (1971-87), iv, 281 and 312, and Douin (1944), i, 205. See also Mengin (1823), ii, 233.

and unreliable exotica with no technological or tactical back-up.[24] The real revolution, namely their organised use, began in the 1850s and 60s and was a tardy and indirect response to the military innovations of the Turco-Egyptians in Kordofan and the *Bahhara* traders in the south.

Of the three basic requirements for the transformation, raw manpower was not a problem but trained manpower was, as also were firearms and ammunition. The main agents in the diffusion of firearms in the Eastern Sudanic Belt, both by example—as at the massacre at Bara in 1821—and by wastage and desertion from their garrisons, were the Turco-Egyptians. But they were well aware of the need to preserve their monopoly, since Muhammad 'Ali's conquest of the Sudan had been largely prompted by his desire to acquire the men and money needed to sustain his own military revolution in Egypt and his ambitions in the Middle East. Thus in 1835 Muhammad 'Ali wrote to the governor of Asyut, the northern end of the Forty Days Road, that he had heard that the traders there were taking pistols, muskets and powder to Darfur. Anyone caught in the act was to be killed.[25]

The monopoly failed and guns were imported, and just as there was a fertile interchange of weapons and personnel between the army of occupation and the *Bahhara*, so this also happened in Darfur. Muhammad Nadi Pasha, an Egyptian officer sent in 1867 to al-Fashir as a spy, reported back that Ahmad Shatta's slave troops were being trained in the use of firearms by one Fadl Musa, "a sergeant of the black troops", who had fled to Darfur after the defeat of 'Uthman Bey al-Sinnari at Jabal Taqali in Kordofan in 1856. Shatta's motive was said to be the desire to avenge the death of his father, the *maqdum* 'Abd al-'Aziz, at the hands of the Rizayqat. Another deserter, Muhammad al-Takruri (from his name possibly a West African), who had fought in the Hijaz, was training 400 men for 'Abd al-Razzaq, the *maqdum* and *ab shaykh daali*, or as Nadi Bey describes

---

24 Pallme (1846), 352. See further Fisher and Rowland (1971), 215-39.

25 Muhammad 'Ali to Husayn Bey, mudir of Asyut, 29 Dhu'l-hijja 1250/28 April 1835, Abdin Archives (Cairo), register 60, maiya turki, 193 (a reference I owe to Richard Hill).

him "chief of the *aghas* of the harim" and a sworn enemy of Shatta. 'Abd al-Razzaq's forces consisted of 500 horsemen and 2,000 men with muskets (*silah al-daraba*) of whom the 400 under training had rifles (*bunduqiyya*).[26] A great variety of guns and powder were being imported, while some ball and powder were manufactured locally.[27] Thus by about 1870 the sultanate was beginning to build up the sort of forces and armaments that the *Bahhara*, pre-eminently al-Zubayr, had perfected.

But it was too late; as al-Zubayr moved north in early 1874 for his final assault on the sultanate, he brought with him some 7,000 *bazinqir* or slave troops. When in January or February he defeated Shatta near Dara, he also broke up the embryo army that the latter had been trying to create. At the final rout at Manawashi on the road to al-Fashir on 25 October 1874, Ibrahim Qarad had only his household troops with him and died leading a furious old-style cavalry charge.

But the Keira soon learned; in 1879 the "shadow sultan" Harun b. Sayf al-Din was reported as having 17,000 men of whom 6,000 were armed with rifles.[28] But Darfur in the years following the invasion was to pay a high price for the influx of guns, just as today.

Taxation and revenue

Warfare in Darfur tended towards specialisation, towards the lessening of involvement by the community. Taxation involved the community comprehensively, being a communal rather than an individual responsibility in that below the district level it was the community that collected its taxes together for the sultan's agents to take away. Generally in the pre-1874 sultanate a proportion of the

---

26 *Taqrir Nadi Bey*, 20 Safar 1284/23 June 1867. I am grateful to the late al-Shatir Busayli 'Abd al-Jalil for a copy of ths report.

27 Pallme (1846), 253, balls made of copper. A Fur section nicknamed Bandaqa made powder near Kutum, 'Abd al-Rahman Nurayn, Khartoum, 14.3.1970.

28 Messedaglia (1886), 9. A Darfur account of al-Zubayr's invasion stresses the role of firearms; AP1, 3/13, 48-50.

revenues was retained and stored locally, while under 'Ali Dinar at least from the districts around al-Fashir the centre absorbed a major part directly. There are two issues that can be raised here, but not properly documented: how far the estate system (see Chapter Seven) served to localise food supplies, and how much was actually stored for "a rainy day". In other words, to what degree did the sultans have a conscious resource management and "food" policy? Some circulars from 'Ali Dinar point in this direction; in one he notes that the rains have come and orders that an extra field must be prepared and a report sent in on its size; in another, he orders the erection of a storage enclosure (*zariba mashhayyina*) on some deserted land.[29] But it is difficult to say more.

The collection and storage of the revenues (Ar. *jibaya*) throughout the state was the administrative responsibility of the *abu'l-jabbayyin*, who from the late eighteenth century came from a Musabba'at clan living around Tarni southwest of al-Fashir. He was one of the greatest of the state officials and controlled an extensive hierarchy of subordinates, the *jabbayyin* (Fur, *jubanga* or *jafanga*) who were found in every *shartaya*.[30] The visits of the *jabbayyin* "of the grain, cotton and seed", as they are called in several charters, to the villages and markets, were regarded with some dread, as a Fur song recalls:

> At Dirbat market the jafanga have ruined me;
> I will go and pay the home of the apes a visit

—"the home of the apes" being the singer's fields laid waste by baboons in his absence.[31] Resented also were the exceptionally large containers used by the *jabbayyin* to measure the grain tax, one reason why the use of money was later preferred.[32] The *jabbayyin* did not

---

29 DF24.6/9, 23 Muharram 118/28 May 1900 and 25.6/10, 19 Muharram 1319/8 May 1901.

30 Al-Tunisi (1965), 106 and 184 (106 & 163 and 175 & 270-71); Nachtigal (1971-87), iv, 331 who says he came from the Koranga Fur (on whom, Adelberger (1990), 164), and shartay Hasab Allah Abu'l-Bashar, Tarni, 9.4.1974.

31 Beaton (1940), 322-3.

32 PA (al-Fashir), Western Darfur District Handbook.

collect the taxes and other dues from the sultan's estates; they were sent directly to the palace's "narrow gate" where they were distributed to the women by the *abbo jode*, a senior slave eunuch. Nor did the *jabbayyin* collect the market dues and customs tolls, *maks* and *khidma*. These were the responsibility of the *abbo daadinga*, who in this guise was called *malik al-qawwarin* (or *al-makkasin*) and whose officials, the *makkasin*, delivered the tolls to him.[33]

The fundamental household taxes were *fitr* and *zaka*; the former was a poll-tax paid usually at the end of Ramadan at the rate of one *midd* (approximately eight litres capacity measure) per head. *Zaka* in Darfur was in fact an *'ushr* or tithe and was the basic grain and animal tax. The grain tax was most commonly called *umm thalathin*/"mother of thirty" since the tax was usually assessed at a rate of three *midd* in every thirty. Thus an average field yielding 300 *midd* would pay thirty *midd* or one *umm thalathin*, a unit known elsewhere in the Sudan as a *rayka*. In fact it seems that a harvest below 300 *midd* was not taxed at all. *Zaka* and *fitr*, whether in grain or animals, were collected by the *dimlij*'s men, who came to the village or camp and, after swearing the shaykh and *faqih* of the community on the Qur'an, took the taxes to the *dimlij* who forwarded them to the *shartay*, who in turn kept them for collection by the *jabbayyin*.[34]

The other major household tax was the *takkiyya*, so called because it was levied in *takkiyya* (pl. *takaki*), concisely described by Browne as

Cotton cloths, of five, six or eight yards long, and eighteen to twenty-two inches wide; they are strong but coarse, and form the covering of all the lower classes of both sexes.[35]

The basis on which it was assessed is not certain; it may have been a household land tax, assessed on fields under cultivation, or a communal levy, where each community was assessed to pay so many

---

33 Al-Tunisi (1965), 183-4 (175 & 270-1); Nachtigal (1971-87), iv, 358; PA2, 10/48, 111, and Rihaymat Allah al-Dadinqawi, al-Fashir, 7.6.1970.

34 Browne (1806), 345-6; al-Tunisi (1965), 184 (176 & 271); Nachtigal (1971-87), iv, 358; PA (al-Fashir), *Western Darfur District Handbook*, and Muhammad and Ibrahim 'Abd Allah 'Abd al-Rasul, al-Tawila, 31.7.1976.

35 Browne (1806), 269.

*takkiyya*s.[36] Whatever the basis it was in effect a "money" tax since the *takkiyya* was the most widely-used medium or unit of exchange in the sultanate; other units such rock salt, hoes, copper and the like tended to have only a local circulation. Some light is thrown on the tax's scale by a letter from the *takanawi* Adam Tinbuki to two Zayyadiyya chiefs ordering them to return eight *takkiyya*s to a *faqih* 'Abd Allah, who had complained that they had taken ten instead of the two which were the "established custom". Nachtigal, who had access to some of the tax returns, estimated that this levy yielded about 100,000 pieces of cloth.[37]

Nachtigal also describes a general levy imposed every four years called *diwan*, a term which appears in a number of documents as a synonym for *jibaya* or "revenue"; hence the relationship between what I have described above and what Nachtigal describes here is unclear. Even so, his account of the *diwan* is worth describing *in extenso* since it gives a good indication of the variety of produce and products brought in by taxation,

[The *diwan*] varied according to the occupation of the tribes and the yield of the region; cattle rearing tribes paid in horses or camels up to 130 head. Other tribes, e.g. the Sulla [Sila], Bego [Beigo], Daju, Gulla [probably Gula in Dar Fongoro] etc., paid in slaves. It was also paid in donkey loads of wheat, *durra* and *dukhn*, in *teqaqi* [*takaki*], tobacco [Ar. *tombak*], honey and salt [Fur, *falgo*], which in some districts in the Marra range and the north is obtained by washing saliferous earth, and in [clarified, i.e. *semn*, used for cooking] butter. The butter tax was very productive; several thousand jars were collected, each of which might hold up to 20 pounds, from the Arab tribes of the Beni Holba [Halba], Missiriya, Torjem [Tarjam], Ta'aisha, Habaniya and Rezeqat, but chiefly from the hawakir assigned to the officials, many of which had to deliver 50, 100 up to 200 jars.[38]

---

36 Nachtigal (1971-87), iv, 358 distinguishes between *takkiyya* and *tugandi*, describing the latter as a land tax paid in takkiyya (dugundi elsewhere in the Sudan is a ground rent paid to the landlord on land already cleared; see Qasim (2002), 342).

37 176.18/36, undated, late eighteenth century, and Nachtigal (1971-87), iv, 359.

38 Ibid.; my daughter-in-law pointed out to me that *semn* is still a very expensive and prized commodity in the Sudan.

To these national taxes may be added what the charters describe as "the customary ways", a flock of local imposts, communal dues, fines, obligations and exactions, some of which were also in use in the Funj Sultanate; many of the charters list these in detail, and although in several cases their meaning is far from certain, they give a vivid picture of the scale of the demands a community might be called upon to bear (see Diagram 9).

From the perspective of the rulers, revenues were a fluctuating resource. Food shortage or famine was always possibly around the corner; even in good years, taxation in kind could not, with the exception of grain, be easily stored or converted into more durable goods, and had to be utilised directly. A treasury could not be stocked with clarified butter for too long. Thus a maze of transactions directed resources to satisfy particular needs: food to feed soldiers, cloth to clothe them, slaves to provide manpower on the sultanic estates and to pay for imports. It is within this context that the estate system served to transform part of the tax system into a patron-client relationship in which taxes and labour went directly to maintain the elite. How burdensome to the local community this particular transformation was it is impossible to say, but it was presumably only possible because central needs could be satisfied in other ways despite a theoretical diminution in the inflow of resources.

Within the maze of transactions whereby resources were reallocated, a number of paths can be picked out which together formed a fundamental nexus within the sultanate's political and economic order. The grain and animal taxes tended to be kept within the locality of their origin, the former being stored in granaries (Ar. *matmura*, pl. *matamir*) which in Jabal Marra were built in stone; only the accounting (Ar. *taliba*) was sent to al-Fashir.[39] Although tax records were evidently kept before 1874, none have been found and it is to 'Ali Dinar's reign that one must turn for analogous examples of how grain and other resources were disbursed and to whom, with the proviso that affairs were undoubtedly more leisurely and less centralised under his predecessors. In 1899 'Ali Dinar orders al-Doma

---

39 Ibid., 332.

Diagram 10

TAXES AND COMMUNAL OBLIGATIONS

(The following is based on the charters; in many cases, the precise meaning is unknown)

Name	Definitions and Comparisons
1. *ʿāda*, pl. *ʿawāʾid*	"custom(s)"; general term. In Sinnar, "first-fruits" or obligatory labour, MacMichael (1922), ii, 79, and Abū Salīm (1967), 32.
2. *ʿāna*	"assistance"
3. *dam kabīr*	"big blood and litle blood"; levy by sultan's representative on a
and	community where a homicide or injury has occurred. After its payment,
4. *dam ṣaghīr*	blood-money can be arranged.
5. *dihn*	"oil, butter"
6. *ḍiyāfa*	"hospitality", a levy for official travellers
7. *dugundi*	land tax
8. *fisq*	"sinfulness", a fine for adultery
9. *fiṭr*	poll-tax at the rate of one *midd* per head
10. *hāmil*	"stray"; dues from the sale of stray slaves and animals
11. *ḥukm*	"judgement"; fee for the rendering of justice
12. *jibāyat ʿaysh wa-qutun*	i.e. *zakā*
13. *kabsh*	"sheep"
14. *kayl*	a measure of capacity
15. *khidma*	"service"; obligatory labour for estate-holder or chief
16. *manṣāṣ*	"stipulated"?
17. *nār*	"fire"; fine for causing bush fires
18. *nūba*	"opportunity"
19. *quwwār*	"custom"; market-dues, see MacMichael (1922). ii, 79
20. *rabṭa*	"thong" or "thread"
21. *raḥl*	"burden"
22. *shaqq*	"half, moiety", possibly *shaqqa* "camel-hide"
23. *shayl*	"burden"
24. *shayl al-daraqa*	"burden of the shield", possibly military service
25. *shōba*	"warband"?
26. *sūq daraqa*	"market shield"?
27. *sirwāl*	"trousers"; a type of cloth
28. *suwal*	"presents", hospitality tax
29. *takkiyya*	cloth, as a tax see p.102
30. *thawb takākī*	i.e. *takkiyya* tax
31. *t.q. al-baqar*	tax or levy paid in "cattle"
32. *tūr* (classical Ar. *thawr*)	"bull", see MacMichael, ii, 79.
33. *ulūq*	forage-tax; "a gift to feed the beasts of a great man and his retinue when at a village", *ibid*
34. *umm thalāthīn*	"mother of thirty", *zakā*
35. *zakā*	the basic tithe tax
36. *zarība*	"thorn enclosure"
37. *zinā*	"fornication", fine for making an unmarried girl pregnant

Muhammad, *shartay* of Dar Simiyat (east of al-Fashir; the Simiyat are a separate ethnic group related to the Berti), to send 50 *ardabb*s (*c.* 9,900 litres capacity measure) because so many visitors have come to the palace; in the same year ʾAli Najm al-Din of Jadid al-Sayl is ordered to give five *ardabb*s (*c* 990 litres) to Adam Rijal, ʾAli Dinar's

207

leading general.[40] Some idea of the scale and frequency of 'Ali Dinar's demands upon the two communities of Simiyat and Jadid al-Sayl, which probably had a combined population of just over 7-8,000, can be seen from Diagram 10.[41] These two districts lay near to al-Fashir and the times were atypical, but nevertheless they were expected to provide a flow of grain for the soldiers and the palace, cloth, money (probably an innovation under 'Ali Dinar), livestock, and wood for weapons and saddles. And under 'Ali Dinar they could expect to have to pay *musa'ada/*"assistance" or enforced "presents", which was probably a Mahdist novelty.

Human revenues were more versatile and accordingly more prized. The sultans received a regular flow of slaves and captives, both as formal tribute from those Fartit tribes who paid slaves as a form of "protection money" to avoid being raided, and from the raids themselves, where a tenth of the captives brought back were owed to the sultan.[42] The use of royal slaves within the *fashir* has already been discussed, but as elsewhere in the Sudanic Belt royal slaves or *'abidiyya* were dispersed in settlements throughout the sultanate under the general authority of the *malik al-'abidiyya*.[43] War and raiding ensured a constant supply; Tayrab settled slaves around Shoba and later brought in Turuj Nuba from the Daju Hills in Kordofan, who were settled among the Daju near Tayrab's later capital at Ril. 'Abd al-Rahman brought back with him Nuba captives from Kordofan.[44] The origin of one small *'abidiyya* community may serve as a further example; in 1924 a community of forty men living at Fashil in Dar Kobe described themselves as being of Shatt origin from the Western Bahr al-Ghazal, their ancestors having been settled there by Mu-

---

40 241.28/20, 22 Dhu'l-Qa'da 1316/3 April 1899 and 61.7/34, 18 Sha'ban 1317/22 December 1899.

41 Sudan Census 1955/56: Notes on Omodiyya Map, gives 11,870 for Simiyat and 687 for Jadid al-Sayl.

42 Browne (1806), 343.

43 Al-Tunisi (1851), 439-40.

44 AP1, 3/13, 186 and 6/25, 5; AP2, 10/48, 115; see also al-Tunisi (1965), 93-98 (76-85 & 142-52) and MacMichael (1922), i, 89-90. On the Turuj, see Tucker and Bryan (1956), 72.

hammad al-Fadl.[45] In function these settlements were similar to the Fulani *rumada* of northern Nigeria or the princely estates of Songhai, servile agricultural settlements, and are described in a French report of about 1798,

[The slaves] are given some land to cultivate; there they marry and pay to the king, since the land is his domain, an annual tribute, consisting of a certain number of their children born from their marriages and *dhurra* or millet grain from their cultivations.[46]

Some of these settlements had specialised functions like the *daad-inga* and *saaringa* soldiers, and the *kuuringa*, the makers of padded cotton armour described above.

These settlements not only lay outside local jurisdiction but in some sense partook of the royal prestige; the Turuj, settled by Tayrab among the Daju, are said to have taken over the chieftaincy from the latter precisely because they were royal slaves, while in a form of inverse snobbery a Kara commnunity in Dar Inga was so called not because its people were Kara but because their first chief was a Kara slave placed over them by one of the sultans.[47] Unlike other slave owners, the sultan combined both sovereign and ownership rights over his slaves. The Shatt community at Fashil

Paid no dues on land or anything else except to the sultans. [The ruler of] Kobbe was obliged to accept them as the sultan's personal following and could not come down on them for anything.

Not surprisingly, the *'abidiyya* could be tiresome neighbours; in a court case of 1261/1845-46 a *faqih* complained of trespass by a gang

---

45 PA (Kutum) NDD 66 B 4/3, Tribal: Magdumate Area: Dar Sereif, and NDD 66 B 7/3/6, Tribal: Zaghawa: Dar Galla: boundaries.

46 P.J. G[irard] in Denon (1809), ii, cclxviii. Girard locates the settlement at "karrantîn-dar-êl-saïd", presumably somewhere in southern Darfur.

47 AP2, 10/48, 114; the close identity between master and slave led in a number of instances to the slaves taking their royal or chiefly owners' clan names; thus the slaves of the Berti chiefs were, like their masters, called Basanga, Holy (1974), 54.

Diagram 11

REVENUE DEMANDS UPON TWO COMMUNITIES. 1841-1904 (a)

Date	Jadīd Al-Sayl		Date	Dār Simiyāt	
1898: 16.11	"Milk camels" 100 wooden poles to be cut and sent	Receipt acknowledged "To re-stock the weapons".	30.11	Confiscation of all guns and ammunition, even from the sultan's sons	
1899: 6.7	4 ardabbs (= c.1,450 lb.)	To be debited from revenues and given to Mūsā's party	3.4	50 ardabbs (= c.18,000 lb.)	for the palace, to feed visitors.
8.7	100 poles	Demand repeated, with a warning.	9.11	Unspecified	Upon arrival of tax-collector, revenue to be stored and demand (taliba) completed
14.8	100 poles	Demand repeated, messengers sent.			
21.12	grain	Ordered by amīn of the "Narrow gate".			
26.12	50 riyāls a month. (b)	In addition to normal taxes			
27.12	3 ardabbs (= 1,080 lb.)	From the revenues, to be paid to a military commander (rās al-mī'a).			
1900:			28.5	Rains have come; an extra field to be prepared for sultan and its size reported	
			20.6	Wood and supplies	A saddle-maker is coming with 15 men to make saddles for "racing camels".

	Date	Amount	Notes
Undated demand for 50 *ardabbs* (= 18,000 lb.)	20.7	100 *thawb dammur* (roles of coarse cloth)	
1901:	8.9	10 *ardabbs* (=c.3,600 lb)	To be paid to the people of two of the sultan's sons.
	24.5	10 *ardabbs*	to be given to bearers.
1902:	mid-Jan.	60 *riyals* (b)	to be paid to bearer.
	12.6	50 *thawbs*	To be paid to a war leader (ʿArabī Dafallāh).
1903:	mid-Jan. 1903/4	60 *riyals* (b) 300 *ardabbs* (=c.108,000 lb.)	Repeated demand.
1904:	31.8	"emergency provisions"	To be brought to al-Fāshir a month in advance; for a campaign.

(a) Drawn from Archives 6,7 and 28, from documents addressed to Ali Najm al-Dīn of Jadid al-Sayl, and al-Dōma Muhammad, *shartay* of Dār Simiyāt. These are in no way complete administrative records.

(b) Since the addressee's name has been written in seperately, these are evidently general demands addressed to those districts attached to the palace. The *riyāl* here is the Turkish *riyāl majīdī* valued at 20 piastres; see Theobald (1965), 210.

of *'abidiyya* and later received an injunction from the Sultan restrain-
ing the slaves' leader.[48]

The redirection of revenues served not only economic purposes;
slaves, like horses and armour, made excellent marks of royal esteem,
as the anecdote of Adam Bosh and his nickname illustrates. 'Ali
Dinar reciprocated some presents from a Majabra merchant from
Libya with a slave girl "pleasing of looks" and some fine cloth; while
the progress of the Tunisian travellers 'Umar al-Tunisi and his son
Muhammad through Sinnar, Darfur and Wadai was marked, as
befitted the father's status as an al-Azhar *'alim*, by gifts of slaves.[49]
Similarly with customs tolls: incoming caravans from Egypt halted
first at Suwayni, where the tolls were evaluated and received before
being allowed to proceed to Kobbei. Customs rates varied, although
Nachtigal quotes five *maqta turunba* (units of cloth). Outgoing caravans paid their tolls on arrival in Egypt to the sultan's representative,
who then used the money to make purchases for his master.[50]

Law and justice: Fur and Islamic

A constant source of revenue for the chiefs were fines, the lynchpin
of Fur law. Fur tradition ascribes its system of law to the quasi-legen-
dary Sultan Daali, of the late fifteenth or early sixteenth century, who
is said to have codified it in the so-called *kitab* or *qanun* Daali. But
whether the code was actually ever reduced to writing is uncertain.

Nachtigal gained the impression that the *kitab daali* contained
"the basic principles of the administration and of the system of justice"; that it was a species of code of criminal law in no way based
on the Shari'a, prescribing fines payable in cattle or *takaki* and which
had as its main purpose "to assure power and an adequate income

---

48 See above n. 44, and O'Fahey and Abu Salim (1983), 65-9.

49 82.10/7, Muharram 1323/April-May 1905, and al-Tunisi (1965), 31 and
    65-6 (13 and 47-8 & 46 and 99-100). See also Nachtigal (1971-87), iv, 247,
    365 and 367.

50 Ibid., 359; Browne (1806), 343, Browne's caravan was assessed to pay 3,000
    mahbubs to the *khabir* upon arrival in Egypt, and Frank in Denon (1809), ii,
    ccxxxvii.

for the ruler and his officials and to bind the two closely together."
He associates the *kitab* with the *ab shaykh*, recording that the first *ab shaykh*, called Khalifa, was responsible for drawing up the code under Sultan Daali. Thus appreciating its importance, Nachtigal tried to borrow the code from the *ab shaykh* at the time of his visit, 'Abd al-Razzaq, but failed to obtain it from him; he then asked Sultan Ibrahim, who promised "to have a search made for the Dali book and to lend it to me".[51] However, Nachtigal does not allude to the subject again; either the Sultan was unwilling to show him the code, although the traveller was shown other state papers, or it did not in fact exist in written form.

More recent attempts to find the *kitab daali* have proved equally unsuccessful; if it ever existed in written form, it appears to be no longer extant. It seems, however, that parts of Fur and other tribal law were committed to writing, which may suggest that *kitab daali* was simply a generic term for Fur legal custom (Ar. *'urf* or *'ada*) in relation to the Shari'a.[52] The coexistence of two systems of law side-by-side is noted by Nachtigal,

Right up to the most recent times any one could, in relation to specific cases, be judged according to his wish, either by the religious laws of Islam or by *siesa* [*siyasa*], i.e. the old customs of the country.[53]

In fact, nowhere else is the divide between the Fur and the Islamic dimension more explicit than in law and justice. Customary law and its practitioners, the chiefs and the elders—the latter an integral part of any Darfur court—coexisted with the Shari'a and its exponents,

---

51 Nachtigal (1971-87), iv, 273, 277, 328 and 369-70. See further my (1977a), 110-24.

52 Shuqayr (1903), ii, 137-9 takes the existence of the *kitab daali* as a written document for granted, linking it to the Fur word "tongue", *daali* pl. *kalinta*; so does Felkin (1885-86), 220 who asserts that it was written down more than 300 years before. See also Arkell (1952a), 145-6. The latter, in the 1920s, made a determined effort to find the code and collected several manuscripts that are indeed records of customary law presented to Arkell as being the *kitab daali*, AP2, 4/17, 1-88. I likewise tried to find the code in the early 1970s; I failed, but was assured by several informants that it had existed in written form.

53 Nachtigal (1971-87), iv, 330.

the *fuqara* and *qadi*s. The general practice in what can be loosely regarded as criminal matters, was for the *shartay* to judge with the advice of the *fuqara*, but according to customary law. In matters regarded in Darfur as pertaining more directly to the Shari'a—marriage and divorce, maintenance and inheritance—the *qadi*'s jurisdiction was more substantive, although even here on certain issues, such as female rights of inheritance, custom prevailed over the Shari'a. In practice, much depended on the personalities of the chief and the *faqih*; in some cases, litigants dissatisfied with the chief's judgment or *hukm* were allowed to appeal to the *qadi*.[54] The further one went up the administrative ladder, the more prominent was the role of the *fuqara*; the sultans and the *maqdum*s rarely gave judgment without a chorus of *'ulama* in attendance.

At the level of the local community, justice and the resolution of conflict were matters of internal regulation, of "agreement, reproof or the award of compensaton" as a British report put it, with expulsion, *muruj min al-ahl*, the ultimate communal sanction.[55] Beyond the village, local chiefs, *dimlij*s and *shartay*s meted out justice from which indeed they garnered the greater part of their income. Among the Fur, fines were commonly calculated in units called *toni* (Ar. *thaniyya*) bearing a conventional but varying relationship to the barter value of a female calf of three years; thus a *toni* could equal eight *takkiyya*s, four sheep or thirty *midd*s of grain, the precise equivalents differing from district to district. Full compensation for homicide in Diima could be up to ten *toni* units; in the north around Kutum it could be as much as fifty. For adultery the usual fine was between two to three *toni*, for theft two, for assault or insult a few *takkiyya*s; the fine for insult, of which a part went to the injured party as compensation, was called in Fur *utang jaaso*/"wiping the mouth". Fines were divided up along the chiefly ladder; thus if a fine of thirty *takkiyya*s (approximately two *toni*s) was imposed for adultery, fifteen

54 PA (al-Fashir), *Western Darfur District Handbook*; for examples of the conflict between Shari'a and custom, see al-Mufti (1387/1959), i, 60-1.
55 On the administration of justice among the Berti, see Holy (1974), 120-51. Local conflicts and their resolution among the Zayyadiyya are analysed in El-Hakim (thesis, 1972).

would be shared among the *shartay*, the estate steward or *dimlij* and the *aba diimang*, the other fifteen going to the *maqdum*. The village shaykh would sometimes receive a *takkiyya* as a *haqq* or "right" or "fee". The scale of fines varied from *shartaya* to *shartaya*, as did their division among the chiefs; among the highland Fur fines were much heavier than in the lowlands because the former were said to be much richer—in contrast to the situation in the 1940s. The items with which the fines were paid also varied according to the ecology of the region; around Kutum they were commonly paid in animals and around Zalingei in grain.[56]

We have some snapshots of justice being administered locally from the documents; one is the entertaining tale of the slave, Bakhit, jointly owned by four women. Bakhit apparently found this intolerable and wanted to become the slave of the *faqih* Ibrahim. To achieve this, he made a cut in the ear of Adam, Ibrahim's son, to signal his determination to exchange four mistresses for one master. The matter ended up in court, where the judge ruled that the four ladies had to compensate Ibrahim with four cows for the injury to his son. In the end, Bakhit was handed over to Ibrahim in compensation, presumably to Bakhit's satisfaction.[57]

Despite *diya* and *sadaqa*, extra-judicial procedures designed to restore inter-communal (*diya*) or communal (*sadaqa*) harmony after violence, homicide and serious affray were considered to concern the state. In such cases a levy called *dam kabir* or *dam saghir*, "big blood" and "little blood", was imposed by the *shartay* on the offender's community.[58] Again the amount and procedure varied; sometimes several cows or a *takkiyya* were taken from each household, a burdensome fine. But it seems that not infrequently those guilty of culpable homicide were sent to al-Fashir where they were either beaten to death by the *abbo daadinga*'s men or, under 'Ali Dinar, hanged. The

---

56 PA (al-Fashir), *Western Darfur District Handbook*, and SAD, P.J. Sandison's Papers, where details are given for each shartaya.

57 My (1981a), 44-53 and Kapteijns (1981), 54-5. O'Fahey and Harir (1986), 30-42, three mid-nineteenth century court cases concernng husbands being sued for desertion and a girl being married off as a "ward of court".

58 On *diya* among the Berti see Holy (1967), 466-79.

centre appears to have intervened even in seemingly small matters; Muhammad al-Husayn writes to the *takanawi* Muhammad ordering him to investigate an affray between two *fuqara* clans (perhaps their status warranted sultanic involvement) that had led to the theft of two donkeys and six waterskins, while 'Ali Dinar writes to al-Doma Muhammad of Dar Simiyat that he has forgiven a man the blood-price for a killing and that neither the *shartay* nor the dead man's family are to intervene.[59]

Within the judicial system the sultan stood at the apex. Access to him was obtained at the public audiences held before the palace, while he rode to the Friday prayers across al-Fashir, or by means of a petition—Browne had a petition seeking permission to leave Darfur written for him by the *khatib/*"scribe" 'Ali—presented by a notable or in person.[60] Surrounding the sultan was an informal panel of advisers, mainly *fuqara*, but including some of the notables; in the two transcripts we have of hearings before the sultan, he gives judgment following the counsel of the *'ulama*. Thus in a case concerning a forged charter Muhammad al-Husayn rules,

However, we discovered it [the disputed charter] to be a forgery both in its writing and seal, so we rendered it null and void and expunged it at the court hearing (*al-majlis*) ... I have given judgment ... after consulting with the *'ulama* and with their agreement after an examination of the ruling in the light of the provisions of the Law and the stipulations of the [Maliki] School.[61]

On occasion the sultan directed cases to particular officials; thus Browne, who got into a dispute over a slave girl, had his case referred by the Sultan to the *malik al-jallaba*, "under whose appropriate jurisdiction are all foreign merchants", since the traveller was regarded as a species of foreign trader.[62] In other cases the sultan was the final

---

59 O'Fahey and Abu Salim (1983), 64-5, and 221.28/2, undated.

60 Browne (1806), 256 and Cuny (1854), 93.

61 Text and translation in my (1991), 82-7, dated 1271/1854-55 and witnessed by both *'ulama* and *muluk*, with the former as always being listed first. Unlike Funj practice where the witness lists form an elaborate hierarchy, in Darfur documents they are very ad hoc.

62 Browne (1806), 239.

court of appeal; in a hearing before the *maqdum* Rahma in 1289/1872 the plaintiff, the *faqih* Muhammadayn, alleges that a son of Sultan Muhammad al-Fadl, Muhammad Hud, has seized his land. Both parties to the dispute produce charters, the *faqih*'s granting rights of privilege (*jah*), the Sultan's son's estate (*iqta'*) rights. The *maqdum* appears to feel that the latter outweigh the former, an interpretation supported by other court hearings, but refers the case to the Sultan. The sultan replies, presumably in writing, that Muhammad Hud must leave the *faqih*'s land.[63]

The pattern of the sultan and his chiefs administering justice in concert with the *fuqara* and wih increasing reference to the Shari'a was only partly modified by the appointment of some of the latter as *qadi*s. These were mainly attached to the entourage of the *maqdum*s and governors. Before 'Ali Dinar, who inherited and developed a regional network of *qadi*s and deputy judges (*na'ib*) from the Mahdist administration,[64] there was no question of a formal judicial hierarchy except perhaps at Kobbei; rather, a number of *fuqara* clans provided *qadi*s over several generations to serve the sultans and their title-holders—an aspect, therefore, of the unobtrusive intermeshing of Islam and its protagonists with the administration of the state. We know of the *qadi*s almost solely from the transcripts of their judgments, since oral sources stress the advisory role of the *fuqara*. From the *sijillat*, those *fuqara* who are described as *qadi*s may be divided into those operating at a local level and whose judicial functions were but part of their general role within the community; others who were part of the entourage of one of the great state functionaries; and a few who were distinguished by such titles as *qadi al-qudat*, *shaykh al-Islam* or *shaykh qudat al-Islam*.

Of the latter group, such men as Muhammad Ishaq, Muhammad al-Harith and *al-hajj* 'Izz al-Din al-Jami' evidently held fairly independent positions, judging by their titles and honorifics but also from the *sijillat*, where they are not described by the usual formula of

---

63 O'Fahey and Abu Salim (1983), 74-5.

64 Thus in an elaborately written document 'Ali Dinar appoints Hamad 'Abd al-Qadir deputy judge of Jadid al-Sayl; 33.7/6, 1316/1898-99.

judging "on behalf of" (*bi–niyaba*) the sultan or one of the notables. *Al–hajj* 'Izz al-Din was an influential figure between about 1780 and 1810; described by al-Tunisi as *qadi al-qudat*, he was the son of a Jawami'a immigrant from Kordofan and was renowned for his *baraka* or religious charisma. He lies buried in the mosque built by 'Abd al-Rahman at Jadid al-Sayl.[65] But the more usual pattern was for the *qadi* to judge on another's behalf; thus the *qadi* 'Uthman was appointed (*bi–tahkim*) by the Wazir Adam Bosh to try a case in the council or court (*majlis*) of the *malik* 'Atiyya, a Berti chief who was a follower of Bosh.[66] The chain of authority may be seen in the judicial entourage of the *iiya baasi* Zamzam; in the first of three surviving court cases, the *faqih* Baraq judges on her behalf; in the second he does the same but is now called her *orrengdulung* or chamberlain, while in the third a *qadi* Muhammad, son of the *qadi* Khalil, "from the following of the lady Zamzam" gives judgment on behalf of the *qadi* Muhammad Abu'l-Qasim.[67]

The majority of the court transcripts so far found concern mainly land and its administration (the reason for their survival), and occasionally disputes over slaves or questions of inheritance. The transcripts underscore the general analysis here and in the preceding chapters of an evolving territorial elite exploiting the local communities, but with the sultans able to control both elements through the *jabbayyin* and *maqdum*s and through their personal agents, the *kursi*s and *falqanawi*s (Fur, *folgoni*), who "kept a watching brief on behalf of their royal master".[68] Growing official literacy, a contribution of the *fuqara* who wrote the letters, charters and transcripts, further strengthened the centre's grip; and if the evolution of more bureaucratic ways led to greater exploitation, it did allow for a social order in which the positional rigidities characteristic of so many African

---

65 Nasr al-Din 'Izz al-Din, al-Fashir 24.3.1974; Ahmad 'Abd al-Hakam, al-Fashir, 27.3.1974 and *al-hajj* Abu Bakr Mahmud, a series of interviews, al-Fashir March 1974. See also al-Zayn (1971), 21-3 and my (1977a), 120-1.

66 63.8/1, 25 Rajab 1267/5 June 1851; see also Nachtigal (1971-87), iv, 311.

67 196.18/56, 1270/1853-54; 190.18./50, 21 Ramadan 1289/22 November 1872 and 159.18/19, 1260/1844-45; see further my (1977a), 123-4.

68 Bence Pembroke, *Darfur Province 1916* (ms., University of Khartoum).

kingdoms gave way to mobility and achieved status. Specific skills or talents and proximity to the court tended to counterbalance heredi- tary status or title. The destruction of the title-holding elite struc- tured within a state that had legitimacy in the wars of the Turkiyya and Mahdiyya meant that the sultanate of 1898 to 1916 saw a stark confrontation between 'Ali Dinar, his generals and their warbands, and the re-emergent tribal chieftaincies. The loss of a supra-tribal legitimacy is still a factor in Darfur.

10
ISLAM, STATE AND SOCIETY

The fuqara: a portrait

Any assessment of the impact of Islam on Darfur and its peoples must begin with the *fuqara* or Muslim holy men. Almost all the leading *fuqara* lineages of Darfur claim a foreign ancestry, tracing their origin to an immigrant from beyond the sultanate's borders. The Islamisation of Darfur was thus largely brought about by the missionary activities, broadly defined, of immigrant holy men and their descendants moving into an Islamic frontier, a migration made possible by the security and inducements provided by the sultans. Without the state, Islamisation would have been much slower. But the relationship that developed between the sultans and the holy men was a complex and ambiguous one. The Islamic frontier, the scattered populations, the emergence of new centres of power, all attracted and created a distinctive missionary type, the peripatetic individualist holy man, propagating an Islam imbued both with the remote images of the Sufi or mystical Islam of the heartlands and with an "African" sense of the nearness of the Divine. The further one went into the frontier, the greater was the emphasis on miracles (Ar. *karama*), magic and hereditary spiritual charisma (*baraka*) and the less the emphasis on the Law and its institutions. But these generalisations need qualification; all Muslims believed in the possibility of *karamat*/"signs of God's favour", while the transmission of

221

learning, but not necessarily within an institutional framework, was an integral part of African Islam.[1]

Along the Nile in the centuries (fifteenth to seventeenth) following the breakdown of medieval Nubia, the *faqih* emerged as the key protagonist of Islam. Into a disintegrating society where Christianity was slowly dying came such figures as Ghulam Allah b. 'A'id,

[who] went out with his sons to the territory of Dongola, for it was in extreme perplexity and confusion for lack of learned men. When he settled there, he built mosques, and taught the Qur'an and the religious sciences.[2]

With the emergence of the Funj Sultanate in the sixteenth century, the Islamic frontier moved south under the aegis of a state prepared to accept Islam, at least in part.[3] By the eighteenth century much of the history of Sinnar may seen in terms of *faqih* and *faris*. As the warbands of the latter tore the state apart, the clans and settlements of the former increasingly provided a refuge and new focus of loyalty for the peasants; the Majadhib of al-Damar (al-Damir) near the junction of the Nile and Atbara and the Al 'Isa of Kutranj on the Blue Nile are famous but by no means unique examples.[4] In the nineteenth century, with the destruction of the old ruling elites by the Turco-Egyptian regime (1821-85), the *fuqara* clans increasingly joined the newly emergent *tariqa*s,[5] Sammaniyya, Khatmiyya and Isma'iliyya, which came to provide the only institutions to which the

---

1   On miracles in Islam, see Gramlich (1987) and on the transmission of learning in Muslim Africa, Reese (2004).

2   Holt (1973), 89.

3   The earliest account of an encounter between Muslim holy man and king in the Sudan are the reminiscences of a self-styled sharif or descendant of the Prophet at the court of the first Funj king, an account not the less revealing for being written by a Jewish would-be Messiah, see Hillelsen (1933), 55-66.

4   On the Majadhib, see Burckhardt (1822), 235-40 and the modern study by Hofheinz (thesis, 1996); on the Al 'Isa, McHugh (1996). Such families are still important in the northern Sudan and are disproportionately represented among the educated elite.

5   *Tariqa* (pl. *turuq*), a "mystical way"; a specific Sufi or mystical tradition that became institutionalised and perpetuated under the name of its putative founder. For an overview, see Trimingham (1971).

Sudanese could turn—a development that culminated in the revolt of Muhammad Ahmad, the Mahdi (1844-85).[6]

In Darfur the patterns of Islamisation developed differently. The rural holy lineages were not subsumed into organised *tariqa*s until much later and then only partially, while a strong court, as the fountain of patronage and employment, attracted to it the better-educated *fuqara*, whose skills and reputation were of interest to the sultans. These court *fuqara* used the sultans' favour to plant settlements throughout the state, and these came to exercise a wide and informal influence over their religious hinterlands. The village or rural holy men were of much humbler status. But the differences and the accusations of self-interest that were directed at the court *fuqara* were kept under control by the dominance of the sultans. The "royal dilemma" which Spaulding has proposed for Sinnar, whereby an African king faces the loss of the mystical prestige that binds his people to him as Islam brings in a new legitimacy, did not happen in Darfur.[7] Rather the sultans broadcast their pre-eminence anew through Islam and, in so doing, took on some of the characteristics of the holy men; Sultan 'Abd al-Rahman, before his accession at the age of about fifty, had lived for many years as a *faqih* at Kerio with his friend Maliki al-Futawi, while Muhammad al-Husayn was noted for his piety and generosity to visiting scholars.[8] 'Ali Dinar projected a consciously Muslim image—I am in no way impugning his sincerity—by a variety of means, among them the publication in Omdurman of a volume of *mada'ih* (sing. *madih*) or praise-poems to the Prophet, the dispatch of a *mahmal* or symbolic cover for the Ka'ba to Mecca, and sending an account of his miracles for publication in the Khartoum newspaper, *The Sudan Times* (see Chapter Thirteen).

The "stranger ancestors" of the great holy lineages of Darfur were of diverse origins and attainments. Representative figures include Hamid w. Faris,

---

6 On the coming of the brotherhoods, see Karrar (1992).

7 O'Fahey and Spaulding (1974), 85-8 and Spaulding (1977), 408-26.

8 On Kerio, see my (1977b), 147-66.

Who is said to have been a native of Barabra [i.e.from Berber on the Nile], and to have preached the Islam, made many converts, and died in Fur.[9]

Another was Abu Zayd (or Abzayd) al-Shaykh 'Abd al-Qadir, a pupil of one of the sons of Muhammad Sughayrun of the Awlad Jabir, the reputed descendants of the Ghulam Allah mentioned above and one of the oldest and most influential of the holy clans of the northern Sudan; Abu Zayd travelled in Darfur, where he built a mosque, and in Wadai in the late seventeenth century.[10] As we have seen, a branch of the Awlad Jabir seems to have settled among the Zayyadiyya in the early eighteenth century and became a major section of the tribe. From further afield came Muhammad Salih al-Kinani, who came from the Hijaz in Arabia in the early eighteenth century and became *imam* to Muhammad Dawra, who built him a mosque at Terjil between Kas and Nyala.[11]

Contributing to the diversity of Islam in Darfur was the fact that so many of the holy men came from the west. Indeed, although the evidence is sparse, it would seem that the earliest wave of immigrants were from the west, beginning as early as the sixteenth century when Darfur was still ruled by the Tunjur, and that only in the eighteenth century did Darfur become a missionary field for holy men from the Nile Valley. This surmise would fit the sultanate's political history of increasing involvement in the affairs of the northern Sudan. There are some tantalising early hints and many concrete later examples; among the former is an Arabic manuscript in Paris of a commentary on the most widely used Maliki lawbook in Darfur, *Sharh Mukhtasar Khalil* by Bahram b. 'Abd Allah al-Damiri, which was allegedly written for a Sultan of Darfur, Ibrahim b. Bakaw, who died in 1050/1640-41, i.e. possibly in Tunjur times. Neither the sultan nor the date can be confirmed, but what is of interest is that the manuscript is written in the Maghribi or western script which is not used in any

---

9   Browne (1806), 319. He may have been from the Awlad Jabir, since the name Faris (uncommon in Darfur) appears frequently in their documents.

10 Dayf Allah (1971), 73 and 106 and MacMichael (1922), ii, 229. On Sughayrun and the Awlad Jabir, see Holt (1973), 120-33.

11 My (1973c), 51.

of the later documents.[12] Among the earliest western immigrants were probably the "Wise Stranger" ancestor of the *aba diimang*s, two brothers from Bagirmi, Muhammad Tamr and Hammad, and 'Ali b. Yusuf al-Futawi from Futa Toro in Senegal, progenitor of the Awlad 'Ali clan, who became particularly influential and prosperous through their reputation as miracle workers.[13] But not all who came prospered, as the unhappy story of Muhammad al-Bulalawi demonstrates (see Chapter Twelve).

Darfur thus became the meeting ground of several different African Islamic traditions, from Egypt via the Forty Days Road, from the northern Sudan and from West Africa. As diverse as their origins were the motives of the holy men in coming; missionary zeal could be combined with the hope of material gain and greater prestige on the frontier. The religious migratory urge, whether a "shaykh seeking" or the search for a *hadith* or "Tradition" of the Prophet with a shorter chain of transmission (thus strengthening its authenticity), was as old as Islam itself.[14] The doubtful Zayn al-'Abidin explains his perilous journey from Cairo through Kordofan, Darfur and Wadai as motivated by the search in exotic lands for knowledge of the "science of talismans, of the names of God and of *tanqir* [meaning not known]".[15] The shorter migrations, e.g. from Kordofan to Darfur, were often the result of political moves. 'Izz al-Din, the famous *qadi al-qudat* of Jadid al-Sayl, accompanied a party of Musabba'at chiefs who wished to make their peace with Tayrab and was instrumental in obtaining land for them at Jugo Jugo. 'Izz al-Din's journey had a mystical element in that he is said to have brought his father's body

---

12 The manuscript is BN. mss. Arabes 4553. A page is reproduced in Vajda (1958) plate 60. I have checked a microfilm of the ms. and cannot find the reference to Darfur, but Vajda, a careful scholar, may have had other sources of information.

13 My (1977b), 147-66 is an account of the Awlad 'Ali based largely on oral tradition from the lineage, collected with the help of two former students of mine, Ibrahim Musa Muhammad and Muhammad Bidayn, both members of the lineage.

14 See the studies in Eickelman and Piscatori (1990).

15 Zayn al-'Abidin (1981), 3.

in a pannier on a camel, the other pannier containing an enormous Qur'an of great *baraka*.[16] The combination of miracle-working and the more prosaic attractions of trade are well illustrated in the story of how 'Ali b. Ramli from Upper Egypt came to settle in Darfur (see Chapter Eleven). The traditions concerning immigrants from the west stress that the lineage ancestors came on pilgrimage and were enticed by the sultans to settle in Darfur on their return; thus 'Ali al-Futawi is said to have met Ahmad Bukr in western Darfur and to have been promised land there if he would return from Mecca and settle in the sultanate. 'Ali went on his way and, returning from Mecca, settled on the Nile near Omdurman for some years before finally going to Darfur to claim his estate.[17]

The positive inducements offered to the holy men by the sultans—prestige, privilege or immunity, land and people—have already been described. Under one aspect, particularly since so many of the holy men travelled with their families and bands of followers, the active encouragement of the sultans was but one more facet of a comprehensive immigration policy that at its other extreme embraced the slave raids to the south and southwest. All were aspects of a policy designed to draw people into a sparsely-peopled land, or, as 'Ali Dinar describes it, in the context of the restoration of 1898: "Our desire is for the restoration of the country and the revival of the former places and lands".[18]

The working out of the policy can be seen in the settlement patterns of the holy clans, which in some respects parallel the slave settlements. In the Fur areas the settlement pattern is less marked in the sense that *fuqara*, like the slaves, were assimilated into the village communities, but in eastern and central Darfur, especially around al-Fashir, a series of settlements dominated by holy men grew up, each with its religious hinterland and network of economic relationships. Privileges granted to holy men attracted followers. The people of Kerio are said to have initially been hostile to Maliki al-Futawi when he was granted the area

---

16 O'Fahey and Abu Shouk (1999), 49-64.

17 My (1977b), 151-2.

18 In 75.9/2, 23 Jumada II 1320/27 September 1902.

by 'Abd al-Rahman, but he soon won them over by granting them sub-tenancy (or *fas*) rights and thereafter the district filled up with immigrant communities—Zaghawa, Fulani, Kotoko and Bornawi. Maliki's economic base was further strengthened by his role as patron to the Fulani, both nomad and settled, throughout the sultanate; in return for protection at court, he received cattle and grain. A number of Maliki's sons went into slave raiding and trading, and by the 1850s Kerio was a major staging-post for raiding parties going south (see the song of Wad Binayya in Chapter Nine). A tendency developed for holy families to bifurcate, one line keeping to its primary religious functions, the other moving over to secular leadership positions; both at Kerio and nearby Shawa descendants of Maliki became *shartay*s and *dimlij*s.[19] Another tendency was for the *fuqara*, or at least the more powerful lineages, simply to encroach upon the prerogatives of local chiefs; 'Ali Dinar writes to al-Doma Muhammad of Simiyat ordering him to warn off the holy men of Jadid al-Sayl from illegally taking taxes outside their estate.[20]

Apart from the attractions of land and security, the *fuqara* settlements offered a variety of spiritual, medical and educational services. For the poorer *fuqara* the sale of *hijab*s or amulets in the form of leather pouches containing prophylatic verses from the Qur'an, and of their medical services, were their major source of income.[21] The sultanate was, as Darfur still is, covered by networks of itinerant *fuqara*, of different ethnic groups and offering different specialised services, travelling from community to community selling their skills and their wares, operating on the principle that the prayers and potions of someone else's holy man are likely to prove more efficacious

---

19 My (1977b), 153-5.

20 233.28/14, date missing.

21 On *hijab*, see Tom (1985), 414-31. Amulets are an important aspect of popular Islam in Darfur and are universally found in the Islamic world; on amulets and the numerology associated with them, see Kriss and Kriss-Heinrrich (1962), ii, 1-139. There is much on medical practices in Darfur and Wadai in both of al-Tunisi's books (1965 and 1851). This is not surprising in that he later had a distinguished career at the School of Medicine at Abu Za'bal in Cairo, where he translated or wrote a number of works on surgery and pharmacology; these latter are listed in my (1994), 69-70.

than those of the local man. The Fulani in particular enjoy a reputation for being especially potent outsiders. In the 1960s and 70s such figures with their pouches of herbs, mixing bowls and the like could still be met on the road; I have no more recent information, but judging by the general upsurge in "traditional" medicine in other parts of Africa following the breakdown of colonial and postcolonial medical services, I doubt that today Darfur is any different in this respect.[22]

The community *faqih* operated within the framework of two institutions: the mosque, usually an enclosure marked out on the ground by stones, and the Qur'anic school (Fur *som*; Ar. *khalwa* or *masid*) under a shady tree. The status of the school depended on that of the *faqih*; the village school recruited its pupils up to the age of about ten, where they were taught to write verses from the Qur'an on their wooden writing-boards (Ar. *loh* or *lawh*) and to chant or sing the sacred text *hizb* by *hizb* (a thirtieth portion of the Qur'an).[23] When a boy had mastered a chapter or section of the Qur'an and had written it out neatly, his parents usually gave a present to the teacher. A *faqih*, distinguished by the title *goni*, whose reputation transcended his own community, usually because his miracles and learning had been noised abroad or his *hijabs* reputed especially effective, might attract as many as 200 pupils often of mature age, known as *muhajirin*/ "emigrants", since they studied at some distance from their homes. In return for their lessons, the students worked upon their teach-

---

22 Largely based on personal observation in Darfur and more recently (and much earlier) on the East African coast. As a teenager in Mombasa, I studied Islam with a prominent young scholar of the Jamal al-Layl 'Alawi clan, Sharif Khitamy (d. 2005); in his later career he became famous throughout East Africa as a herbal healer. Ahmad b. Idris (see below) was interested in medicine, judging by comments in his letters; see Thomassen and Radtke (1993), 17-19. See also Trimingham (1949), 126-82 on popular practices in the Sudan generally and "Mohammedanism in Darfur" (1917), 278-82, despite its unsympathetic tone. A very useful survey of Sudanese medical practice is al-Safi (1970).

23 *Hizb* singing is a high musical form among the Fur, which in an interesting if idiosyncratic way was incorporated into a mass by the English composer, David Fanshawe, in a work (subsequently recorded) called "African Sanctus". In his book of the same name (1975), 132-46 he describes *hizb* musically.

er's lands.[24] At this level the education offered was more complex; Qur'anic recitation, the composition of *hijab*s, and the study of some of the basic Maliki legal texts, principally the *Mukhtasar* of Khalil b. Ishaq (d. 776/1374) and the *Risala* of Ibn Abi Zayd al-Qayrawani (d. 386/996). From Darfur a small trickle of students made their way to al-Azhar in Cairo, where at some time in the nineteenth century a modest Darfur *riwaq* or hostel was established. Evidently by the 1830s there were enough students from the sultanate to start a small riot (see Chapter Four); a more peaceful role for the students was to provide information about their homeland to European travellers. The hostel survived into the twentieth century, although by 1925 there were only four students.[25]

Sultanic support for the *fuqara* was not confined to the granting of lands and privileges; the sultans actively financed the building of mosques. From the time of the establishment of al-Fashir, the capital was ringed by a series of red-brick mosques built under the patronage of the sultans; Kerio, Jadid al-Sayl (well preserved in the 1970s), Arari, Azagarfa, al-Firsh and Manawashi are only some.[26] It was part of 'Ali Dinar's religious policy to encourage the restoration of the mosques and the settlements associated with them, or, as the Sultan put it, "our rule begins with the restoration of the mosques and the revival of the religious ceremonies". To judge from the number of specific decrees on this topic, this was no mere rhetoric.[27]   Not all

24 Abdul-Jalil (thesis, 1974).

25 On the hostel, see Husayn (1935), ii, 513-15. However, the *riwaq* is not listed in Mubarak (1306/1888), iv, 22-4, although the Wadai hostel is. Seetzen interviewed a Darfur student in 1811, Seetzen (1813), 145. See also Lauture (1855-56), 93 and Shuqayr (1903), ii, 132-3. On the four in 1925, see the papers of Sir Gordon James Lethem, Rhodes House Library, Oxford, II/2, f. 2, letter to H.R. Palmer, 4 August 1925, from Cairo. In 1935 there were five students under Shaykh Sulayman Ibrahim; Husayn, op.cit. It was still active in the 1940s, see 'Abd Allah (1973), i, 27-8.

26 Muhammad 'Abd al-Rahim, *al-Durr al-manthur*, ms. NRO, Khartoum, gives a detailed list of the main mosques of the sultanate.

27 299.43/3, 17 Dhu'l-hijja 1317/18 April 1900. See O'Fahey and Ahmed (1972), for texts and translation of documents concerning the rebuilding of the mosque and tomb of the *wali* Muhammad Haduj al-Kinani at al-Firsh. On the *waqf* at Jadid al-Sayl, see O'Fahey and Abu Salim (1983), 37-45.

holy men would accept royal patronage; doubts as to the propriety of accepting worldly office and favour is a theme common in Islam. Sa'id al-Futawi is said to have refused to eat with his brother, Maliki, because the latter lived in luxury at court serving the sultan. One *faqih*, Hasan al-Kaw, publicly defied and humiliated an *ab shaykh*.[28] However, at the level of the court the holy men were definitely a subordinate element, even if a respected one; at the local level a more reciprocal relationship prevailed—*faqih* and chief operated within different orders of authority, complementing each other, the former as the exponent of a local orthodoxy, the latter as the representative of political authority.

Islam and the state

The Islamisation of the peoples of Darfur was a very uneven process. In the heartlands of the sultanate, where the holy clans exercised great influence, where the *qadi*s sat in judgment, where caravans passed by, conversion was accompanied by acculturation—a process that can be charted by the displacement of local languages (Berti and Birged are just two examples) by Arabic. Further from the centre or in mountainous areas, away from the trade routes or administrative centres, earlier patterns of belief were hardly disturbed by nominal conversion to Islam. From nominal conversion, via the insinuation of Islamic practices or norms, to an acceptance of Islamic/Arabic culture, but not necessarily identity, represents an almost infinite gradation, conceptually but not in practice susceptible to analysis. From the *qadi al-qudat al-hajj* 'Izz al-Din, whose elegant court transcripts would not have disgraced al-Azhar, to the Bideyat chiefs of the 1880s described by Slatin, who took Muslim names and proclaimed *Allah* when meeting Muslims but who worshipped before a sacred tree at home, is a very broad spectrum.[29]

The Bideyat lived on the northernmost margins of the state, practically outside its authority. The Fur lived encapsulated within it, their apparent cultural homogeneity concealing a long history of

---

28 My (1977b), 154-5 and al-Tunisi (1965), 254 (255-6 & 362-3).

29 Slatin (1896), 114-17.

immigration and assimilation of other groups. All Fur are Muslim, but although the Fur life-cycle, as described by Beaton in the 1940s, is marked by occasions when Islam in the person of the local *faqih* intervenes—naming, circumcision (but not female circumcision as practised along the Nile), marriage and death—Fur society exhibits few specifically Islamic traits.[30] The observation that the Fur had by the early twentieth century hardly moved beyond an undifferentiated and formal commitment to Islam would seem to support the notion that Islam spread from the ruling institution outwards and down-wards. If the key external factor was the coming of the holy men, the crucial internal commitment came from the rulers, a commitment dramatised in the Islamisation of the myths of origin of the ruling Keira dynasty and their predecessors.

The "Wise Strangers" who orchestrated the transition from Daju to Tunjur and from Tunjur to Keira are presented as Muslim and more equivocally as Arab. Islamisation by pedigree was not taken as far in Darfur as in some of its neighbours, where elaborate gene-alogies were forged and such claims were broadcast upon sultanic seals. As in Wadai, but in contrast to the Funj dynasts who claimed Umayyad descent, the Keira laid claim to 'Abbasid descent, and in his letters 'Ali Dinar occasionally calls himself "the Hashimite, the 'Abbasid", thus claiming descent from the family of the Prophet.[31] More relevant are the traditions that emphasise Sulayman's role in spreading Islam, building mosques and personally circumcising new converts.[32] It would thus seem that Islam and Keira expanded to-

---

30 Beaton (1948), 1-39. I cannot see that much had changed by the time of the description of Fur culture by Abdul-Jalil and Khatir (1977). Doornbos (1984), 139-87 begins to observe change in the early 1980s, especially among Fur traders in the towns.

31 For Sinnar, see Hasan (1965), 27-32 (repr. Hasan (2003), 49-56. Two sultanic letters from Wadai (85.10/10, 1320/1902-3 and 86.10/11, 1319/1901-2) bear seals whose inscriptions end in al-'Abbasi. On 'Abbasid descent in Darfur, see Shuqayr (1903), ii, 111-13. Shuqayr's informant, Muhammad al-Tayyib, a Fallata *faqih* from the community at Khiriban, probably laid more emphasis than the sultans on this.

32 On Sulayman's proselytising role, see Lauture (1855-56), 79, Nachtigal (1971-87), iv, 279 and Shuqayr (1903), ii, 113.

gether from the beginning and that, over time, the religion served as a catalyst transmuting ethnic solidarity into a centralised yet institutionally diversified monarchy. This top-down process of Islamisation and the practice of students being taught as *muhajirin* away from their homes led to a uniformity of religious practice among the different peoples of Darfur.[33]

One way of analysing Islam's impact on the sultanate is to look at the progressive adoption by the sultans of Muslim institutions and practices to articulate developments that in their inception had little to do with Islam. The move from territorially-based chiefly rule to a court elite in al-Fashir, the concomitant emergence of the estate system, the growing literacy in Arabic of the administration, and the use of slaves and "new men" were all factors in a process of centralisation; alongside this process, and because of it, Islam became the dominant cultural and religious force within the sultanate.[34] The coexistence of the Islamic and Fur dimensions began to seem incompatible at court; 'Abd al-Rahman's abolished the seclusion ritual, explaining to his courtiers, "The custom is bad; it is found neither in the Book of God nor in the Custom of the Prophet".[35] Some of the Fur establishment seemingly looked askance at the changes; al-Tunisi reports that some of 'Abd al-Rahman's courtiers complained among themselves about their Sultan's preference for the company of the *'ulama*, saying that next time they should take care that they had a sultan who could neither read nor write. Their remarks were repeated to a furious Sultan by one of the court buffoons. Earlier, the *iiya kuuri* Kinana is said to have told Tayrab that while she was willing to serve food to the notables—part of the duties of the royal women —she refused

---

33 This is an important point: during the early phases (late 2003 to mid-2004) of the present conflict the Janjawid attempted to insert a religious divide between themselves and those they were attacking by burning mosques, killing imams and desecrating Qu'rans, but there is no difference in the practice of Islam among the peoples of Darfur.

34 There seems never to have been any attempt to reduce Fur or any other language in Darfur to writing in the Arabic script, unlike some West African languages such as Wolof and Hausa and. on the East African coast, Swahili.

35 Al-Tunisi (1965), 102 (89-90 & 158-9).

to serve the *fuqara*; they failed to appreciate the cuisine. When the Sultan pointed out that she would receive blessings for doing so, she retorted: "I have no need of their blessings (*baraka*)".[36]

Yet Islam was too dynamic and too universal a force to be subservient. The story of 'Umar Lel attempting to abdicate because he felt he could not rule justly may conceal a clash of ideologies (see Chapter Three). Some sixty years later, 'Abd al-Rahman banned the drinking of *marissa* or beer; although the ban was widely ignored, even by his own women, it indicates how Islam was becoming the norm.[37] Nachtigal has a revealing story of the 1850s or 60s: his merchant friend, *al-hajj* Ahmad Tangatanga, was travelling once in western Darfur with a Fur chief. At the chief's request they made a detour to his village, where the merchant cooled his heels for several days until at the prompting of the chief's son he sneaked into the chief's hut to find him worshipping a cat, "for he was a Muslim in name only and had remained in fact a pagan". The sequel is significant; the chief was denounced by his son to the Sultan who stripped him of his office, "which was later conferred on his perfidious son".[38] The normative power of Islam and the growth of learning at both al-Fashir and Kobbei are well described by al-Tunisi, who mentions various books and subjects taught by his father, an al-Azhar graduate, in Kobbei and al-Fashir both to the *fuqara* and to Sultan 'Abd al-Rahman; the subjects included *hadith*, the Traditions of the Prophet, and *fiqh* or jurisprudence, and among the books were al-Bukhari's (d. c. 870) *Sahih*, one of the canonical collections of Traditions, and the *Mukhtasar* of Khalil b. Ishaq, on which 'Umar al-Tunisi wrote a com-

---

36 Ibid., 191-2 (182-3 & 281). As in most of Sudanic Africa, the divide between Islamic and indigenous beliefs (in Fur, *aadinga*) became gender-based, expressed in the spirit possession cults (*zar*, *tambura* and others). There is a considerable literature on this theme, but not from Darfur; see as one example Kenyon (1991).

37 On the banning of beer, see Browne (1806), 211, Felkin (1884-85), 215 and Shuqayr (1903), ii, 138-9.

38 Nachtigal (1971-87), iv, 367-8. The cat may be a garbled reference to the *damzogha*, spirits that can enter animate or inaninate objects to cause mischief; the totemic role of animals is attested in Darfur, for example the hyena among the Masalit.

mentary for the Sultan, *al-Durr al-awfaq 'ala matn al-'allama Khalil ibn Ishaq*.[39] Books were imported; we have seen that Tayrab ordered a copy of the great dictionary, *Taj al-'Arus* (see Chapter Four), and the French traveller Charles Cuny met at Khandaq in 1858 a Shaykh Muhammad of the Shaiqiyya who was taking a number of lawbooks to Muhammad al-Husayn, a gift of the eunuchs of the Egyptian ruler, 'Abbas I (1849-54).[40]

Thus by the nineteenth century the sultans were encompassed by the full panoply of Islamic orthodoxy as understood in Sudanic Africa. They built numerous mosques, sought the prayers of their holy men in time of peril, consulted with their *qadi*s on points of law, made a formal procession each Friday from the palace to the mosque, and sent a *mahmal* to Mecca.[41] The sultans had succeeded by the mid-nineteenth century in presenting their African kingdom, in its external dealings at least, as a remote but acceptable member of *Dar al-Islam*. Their Sudanic Islamic tradition, to use Lidwien Kapteijns' felicitous description, was to be challenged by Egyptian imperialism which in turn brought forth a new, at least for Eastern Sudanic Africa, form of Islamic messianism, Mahdism.

Sufism: new impulses

Just as Mahdism was influenced by new ideas, so Darfur was beginning to be touched, however lightly, by the new ways of thinking, specifically "neo-Sufism", a somewhat controversial term used to describe Sufi *tariqa*s founded in the period.[42] Two key figures here were North Africans, Ahmad al-Tijani (d. 1815), an Algerian from whom stemmed the most Pan-African of Sufi orders, the Tijaniyya, and Ahmad ibn Idris (d.1837), a Moroccan whose influence and students

---

39 Al-Tunisi (1965), 116-17 (106-7 & 178-81). 'Umar al-Tunisi apparently wrote several works for 'Abd al-Rahman; none appear to be extant.

40 Cuny (1863), 309 and Nachtigal (1971-87), iv, 289.

41 Ibid., 335-56 (procession) and al-Naqar (1972), xx, *mahmal*.

42 O'Fahey and Radtke (1993), 52-87 and my (1990b) study of Ibn Idris and his wider impact. See above also for the earlier contacts with the Indian scholar al-Zabidi.

stretched from Albania to Malaysia, but whose deepest influence was to be felt in the Sudan, with whose people he seems to have had a special affinity; his descendants later settled there. Whether what the two Ahmads were preaching was new or not is a matter of controversy, but where and to whom they preached, especially the latter point, is perhaps more significant.

But it was from another figure within neo-Sufism, Muhammad b. 'Abd al-Karim al-Samman (d. 1775), that the first trace of it came in Darfur. Al-Samman, a Medinan scholar and Sufi, had among his students one from the northern Sudan, Ahmad al-Tayyib w. al-Bashir (d. 1824), who took his teacher's "way" back to the Sudan where it spread widely; it is still a vibrant part of Sudanese Sufi life. In a hagiography of Wad al-Bashir by his grandson, the latter lists his grandfather's students; one of these, Muhammad b. Musa al-Shakitabi, travelled in Darfur, where he died and was buried at Sani Karaw. Among those that al-Shakitabi appointed as *khalifa*s of the Sammaniyya in Darfur was Muhammad w. 'Ali Karrar al-Ta'aishi, almost certainly the father of the Khalifa 'Abdullahi (1846-99).[43] The identification is an interesting one in that membership of the Sammaniyya may have been a bond between the Mahdi and the Khalifa.

Of the direct and indirect students of the two Ahmads one stayed in Darfur, the second may well have been from Darfur, while a third came from neighbouring Kordofan. The first, Muhammad b. al-Mukhtar al-Shinqiti (d. 1881-82), came from Mauritania and travelled eastwards as both merchant and Tijani missionary, having been initiated into the way by a student of al-Tijani himself; he was an honoured guest of Sultan Muhammad al-Husayn, serving as an envoy of the Sultan to Egypt, returning in 1858 with a

---

43 Nur al-Da'im (1973), 327. The author of this work, written early in the twentieth century, almost certainly knew who Muhammad w. 'Ali al-Ta'aishi was, but seemingly chose not to identify him as such. I have always been surprised that neither of my former mentors, Abu Salim and Holt, both of whom had assuredly read Nur al-Da'im, ever made this connection. Perhaps I am wrong, but I do not think so. Madame A. Yagi, in an unpublished typescript, pushes the Sammani connection a generation further back by recording a tradition that 'Ali al-Ta'aishi, the Khalifa's grandfather, was initiated into the Sammaniyya.

present from the Viceroy of a carriage and horses. What the Sultan made of this "innovation" is not recorded! Al-Shinqiti, in addition to his Sufi writings, wrote an account of his travels from West Africa, which sadly seems not to have survived. My impression is that by the mid- or late nineteenth century the Tijaniyya was beginning to be implanted in Darfur, especially among the Fulani communities.[44] A possible Darfurian student of Ibn Idris was 'Abd Allah al-Mawarzi (d. 1860-61) from the Ma'aliyya; he joined Ibn Idris in Mecca and was with him in 'Asir (now in Saudi Arabia) when he died in 1837. Al-Mawarzi has a special place in the Idrisi tradition in that the notes he took down from the master's teachings were written up and later printed by an Afghan student of the tradition, Isma'il al-Nawwab al-Kabuli, a striking example of internationalism in neo-Sufism.[45] Thereafter al-Mawarzi travelled throughout the Middle East before returning to the Sudan where he joined the grandfather of our third figure below, Isma'il al-Wali (d. 1863), founder of the Isma'iliyya, an Ibn Idris-inspired order, in Kordofan, with whom he worked as a missionary among the Nuba there.[46] The third figure, also seemingly a guest of Muhammad al-Husayn, was Isma'il b. 'Abd al-Qadir al-Kurdufani (d. 1897) from the family of Isma'il al-Wali; he studied at al-Azhar and returned via the Forty Days Road to Darfur, where the Sultan persuaded him to stay for a period with presents of money and slaves. Al-Kurdufani became under the Khalifa 'Abdullahi, the successor of the Mahdi, the "official" biographer of the Mahdi, but fell out of favour and died in exile at al-Rajjaf in the southern Sudan, the Siberia of the Mahdist state.[47]

After 1874 these impulses were to be a factor in the emergence of Sudanic tradition in opposition to Mahdist faith, of which an

---

44 On al-Shinqiti, see my (1994), 287-8, but see additionally Qasim (1996), v, 2212-14.

45 The compilation, *al-'Iqd al-nafis fi nazm jawahir al-tadris ...al-sayyid Ahmad ibn Idris*, has been continuously in print since about 1880.

46 See my (1994), 142-3. Ibrahim (1993), 368 says he was from Kordofan, but in the nineteenth century the majority of the Ma'aliyya were in eastern Darfur.

47 My (1994), 241-2.

important expression was the creation of the Masalit Sultanate and 'Ali Dinar's restatement of his state's Islamic stance (see Chapter Thirteen). The tension between an Islam based on a putative Arab identity, whether Sufi, Wahhabi or Mahdist, and an Islam shaped by Sudanic norms but also responsive to Sufi impulses was to dominate Darfur in the twentieth century, as it does today.

11

RAIDING AND TRADING

Patterns of trade

The imports of arms and armour, firearms and horses and a great range of consumer goods were paid for by the export of slaves and other items to Egypt along the Forty Days Road. How crucial to the elite was this trade? Any answer must raise the much-discussed topic of the interaction between long-distance trade and state formation in Africa and elsewhere. In the context of early Darfur the connection may reasonably be assumed, but can hardly be documented; the few sixteenth and seventeenth-century references to Darfur that derived from the trade route itself cannot be taken as proof that the sultanate simply arose to supply a foreign market. Local, regional and specialised trade, for example the trade in western Darfur in salt cones (Fur, *falgo*) or locally-produced cloth, was probably as significant factor as the luxury trade across the desert. It is, however, difficult to measure the relative importance of the different trade networks.

If trading was conducted north, west and east, raiding went southwards and southwestwards, while diplomacy, meaning here the interaction between states and peoples, was like trading latitudinal. Bagirmi, Wadai, Darfur and Sinnar, and indeed the other states of the Bilad al-Sudan, recognised each other and each other's subjects as members of *Dar al-Islam*. Hashim al-Musabba'awi could search for allies along the Nile or in Sinnar; Wadai and Darfur, after fighting each other to a standstill, could negotiate a settlement with each

other, but continue to meddle in each other's affairs (just like the Sudan and Chad today), and holy men could transfer their status from
one state to another. War and diplomacy were latitudinal activities.[1]

By the nineteenth century the raiding/trading cycle had probably
become crucial in maintaining the elite in the style to which they
had become accustomed, but the foundation of their position still
lay in the lands, herds and people they held within the sultanate. The
raiding/trading cycle did, however, serve to cushion the sultanate's
core from the full cost of the elite by directing the latter's energies
outwards. It was the sultanate's southern neighbours who paid for
the state's growth, who provided the elite with its most prized and
versatile resource, human beings, both for export and for use within
the sultanate. This cushioning effect was underscored when the cycle
was interrupted and then taken over by al-Zubayr,

The effect of this [al-Zubayr's control of the south] on the luxury-loving
Darfurians was painfully evident. They saw their main supply of ivory and
slave supplies cut off, and to meet Government expenditure increased taxation was enforced, which resulted in widespread discontent.[2]

The disappearance of the income from long-distance trade is probably why our sources, both written and oral, emphasise how much
more ruthless revenue collection was under 'Ali Dinar. His subjects
were now the sole source of revenue, an unusual state of affairs for a
Sudanic kingdom.

Related to the earlier question on the link between trade and state-
formation is the relationship between the long-distance cycle and
local and regional trading networks. The latter largely exploited ecological variations and exchanges and the former political inequalities,
but it does not follow that long-distance trade was based solely upon
the import of exotic luxuries for consumption by the court without
regard to wider economic factors. Although the trade along the Forty
Days Road ultimately served the state—e.g. the import of weapons,

---

1   The style of Sudanic diplomacy, albeit in a period of crisis, is vividly illustrated
in the correspondence between the rulers of the states of eastern Chad and
Darfur presented in Kapteijns and Spaulding (1988).
2   Slatin (1896), 48; see also Nachtigal (1971-87), iv, 365-6.

the role of the royal merchants as suppliers of specialised goods and as a diplomatic link to the outside world—it was also seemingly responsive to market forces and was largely under the control of the merchants themselves.[3] We lack any real quantative data, but when the demand for slaves declined in Egypt from the mid-nineteenth century on, ivory and gum arabic began to fill the gap. Conversely, slaves were a staple for whom there was a secure and stable home market; the Fartit were never hunted solely for export.

The caravan trade operated through the interplay of a number of groups; the raiders supplied the slaves, while the *jallaba* or itinerant merchants collected export items from local markets, for example gum arabic from the gum gardens of eastern Darfur and western Kordofan. The sultan and his officials provided the political and administrative framework and access to the would-be exports. A small group of large-scale operators, the *khabir*s, controlled the trade from Kobbei to Asyut, where they dealt with and were often financed by merchants there specialising in the Sudan trade. Essentially the caravan trade was controlled by an informal alliance of rulers and traders, the former providing the exports and protection, the latter supplying the know-how and capital and carrying on the actual day-to-day trading.

The internal commerce was dominated by Jabal Marra, the flanks of which were encircled by a series of markets where highland produce was exchanged or sold for onward distribution. Among the main products of the mountains were wheat, grown for export rather consumption, rock salt, cotton and a variety of vegetables.[4] The markets were the nodal points for wide-ranging transactions which brought together farmers, nomads and itinerant traders, and their taxes provided a valuable income for the chiefs within whose territory they lay, for as a report of 1933 noted,

---

3   It is for this reason that I am hesitant to use Polanyi's notion of "administered trade" since it implies an absence of the market, which I believe not to be the case in Darfur; see Polanyi (1968).

4   On wheat, see Wickens (1976), 3-4.

At each step in the attempt of the native to buy the money for his taxes, by exchange of grain for raw cotton, of raw cotton for salt and of salt for money, he pays a tithe to the lord of the market.[5]

Thus at Umm Haraz in Dar Kerne rock salt and cotton were sold in part for export further west to Dar Masalit via Murnei on the Wadi Azum, or to the north via Kabkabiyya. Directly south of the mountains the markets at Nebagai and Kas were outlets for wheat, rock salt, cotton, chillies and the like to al-Fashir and the southeast. Beyond the immediate range of the mountains, markets such as Garsila on the Wadi Debarei and Umm Haraz in Dar Kobara brought nomad and farmer together. Garsila dealt in salt and other mountain products, grain from the surrounding countryside, and raw cotton from Dar Sila and Dar Masalit, as well as dried fish from Mogororo in the far southwest and palm fibre mats. Umm Haraz in Kobara was on the summer grazing route of the Rizayqat, so that ghee could easily be exchanged for salt and grain.[6]

Each region or market network had its own particular specialities which served as the local units of exchange or reckoning; as al-Tunisi remarks, "everyone buys with what he has", underlining the point by giving some equivalent values for a male slave—thirty *takkiyya*s (coarse local cloth), six strips of blue cloth, or eight of white, or six cows, or ten French dollars (*abu madfa'*) (see Diagram 8).[7] But coins were little used internally, and although the *takkiyya*, cow and slave (the latter only in more substantial transactions) were probably the most widely used units of exchange, there were many others: chewing tobacco (*tombak*) from the Kusa region, which used to supply the best quality to al-Fashir; rock salt from Dar Lewing in Jabal Marra; and *harish* or strings of beads at Kabkabiyya and Kobbei.[8] Several of these units functioned virtually as a currency in that they came to be reck-

---

5   SAD, P.J. Sandison's Papers, Notes on the Geography and Trade of the [Zalingei] Emirate, 20.1.1933.

6   Ibid.

7   Al-Tunisi (1965), 298 (315-16 & 426); the slave in question was a *sudasi*, i.e. "a sixer", one who from the heel to the lower ear lobe measured six spans (*shibr*, span of the hand).

8   Ibid., 297-302 (315-21 & 424-34).

oned at a conventional rather than real value: for example, the *tarni* or rings of tin, of which there were two varieties of differing value; or the copper bracelets, *dimlij*, used in western Darfur and made from copper brought from the mines of Hufrat al-Nahas on the borders of Dar Fartit. This process of reducing, both physically and metaphorically, a unit of exchange to a conventional currency, an immense step forward in easing the flow of trade, is well illustrated by the *hashasha* or small iron hoes that al-Tunisi noted as in use in Jadid al-Fil market in eastern Darfur. They were apparently introduced into Kordofan by the sultans or traders, but by the time Pallme came to describe them in the late 1830s they were so small (and of so little value) that he failed to realise the significance of their shape:

It is a small piece of iron, from two to three inches in length, and of an obtuse bibrachial anchor. 150 of these pieces were formerly considered the equivalent to one dollar; they subsequently fell in value to 250, and their present currency is 800 to the dollar, or one *para* each.[9]

Local networks linked up with not only the highly organised trans-Saharan trade out of Kobbei, but also trans-Sudanic routes. Moreover, the northern nomads traded across the desert on their own account; both the Zaghawa and Zayyadiyya took animal skins, ostrich feathers, and some ivory as well as natron from Bir Natrun in the far north in small caravans directly to Egypt. This nomadic enterprise is not matched by any certain evidence of their involvement in the great annual or semi-annual Kobbei caravans either through their animals or as specialised personnel, although it seems likely.[10] The trans-Sudanic routes are less easy to describe than the desert crossings precisely because they passed through populated lands. How far a merchant travelled along them and what he dealt in were matters of personal strategy; the scale of investment of course varied—from Nachtigal's affluent friend, Ahmad Tangatanga, moving from court to court and trading in the costliest of all goods, horses, to impoverished pilgrims who eked out their journey with petty trading

---

9 Pallme (1846), 303.

10 Cuny (1854), 85-6 emphasises the small scale of these nomad caravans; see also Slatin (1896), 106.

is a wide spectrum.[11] Trade in specialised products went far; copper from Hufrat al-Nahas went to Hausaland (Northern Nigeria), eunuchs were a noted export from Bagirmi to Darfur and beyond, ivory and slaves were exported from the sultanate to Kordofan, Sinnar and beyond. Muhammad Bello, writing in Hausaland in the early nineteenth century, praises Darfur for its hospitality to pilgrims from West Africa and, as we have seen, Muhammad al-Husayn employed a Shinqiti scholar from Mauritania as his ambassador to Egypt (see Chapter Ten). Islam and Arabic were and still are the ties that bind in Sudanic Africa.[12]

Slave raiding and trading

Slaves were the sultanate's staple export and their capture was the most characteristic involvement of the elite in the trading cycle.[13] The slave raid, called *ghazwa*/"raid" or *salatiyya*/"spear" for reasons given below, formalised the difference between Fur and Fartit, between Muslim and non-Muslim, and between military might and political "know-how" on one side and, on the other, the acephalous societies that were the slavers' victims. The slave raid was, in effect, a mobile Sudanic state.[14]

---

11 Al-Naqar (1972), Works (1976), Birks (1978), and Yamba (1995) provide a wealth of detail on pilgrims across the savanna. On Tangatanga, see Nachtigal (1971-87), iv, under index.

12 On copper exports, see Barth (1857-59), iii, 339 and on eunuchs, Gaden (1907), 436-47. Darfur had traded eastwards since the late seventeenth century; see Krump (1710), 285; Prudhoe (1835), 46-7 on the sale of Darfur slaves at al-Masallamiyya near the Blue Nile; Holroyd (1839), 163-91 and Müller (1851), 275-89 on trade with Kordofan. Finally, see Muhammad Bello (1957), 4-5.

13 Much, mostly self-serving, has been written about slavery in the Sudan since Victorian times. For a balanced assessment, see al-Nuqud (1995) and on its legacy my (2002).

14 Unless otherwise indicated, what follows is based on al-Tunisi (1851), 467-95. Much of al-Tunisi's account of the raiding system, based on his own participation in a raid, was confirmed by informants; see further my (1973a), 29-43 and (1985), 81-101.

The granting of the right to raid into the Fartit country became as formalized a procedure as the granting of estates. To those who made application and gave a suitable present, the sultan issued a letter of marque together with a spear of the *salatiyya* type (a long broad-bladed lance particularly used by the Baqqara),

... We have given him a *salatiyya* in order to lead an expedition into Dar Fartit and to make a raid in the direction of such-and-such a tribe.[15]

Although there was evidently a class of professional slavers—al-Tunisi mentions one Ahmad Tiktik who led twenty such expeditions—nobles and others regularly mounted such expeditions, for example Muhammad Daldang, a grandson of Tayrab whose prowess was celebrated in a song already quoted (see Chapter Ten). Raiding could be a way out for a notable from a dangerous political position; 'Abd al-Fattah, who had opposed Muhammad al-Husayn's accession, though it prudent to go raiding, with the sultan's permission, for a few months.[16]

The raiding expedition was a carefully organised commercial operation in which violent capture played only a limited part. The expedition's leader would begin by gathering followers around him—the number depending on his reputation—and negotiating with the merchants. A credit system operated whereby the traders would supply the slavers with goods for use on the raid in exchange for slaves to be captured. A slaver with a good reputation could obtain goods on credit worth as much as five to six hundred slaves. But the merchants covered their risks, particularly the risk of some of the slaves dying on their way from the south, by a system of differential credit; if they accompanied the *ghazwa* to the south and took payment there, they received five to six slaves for goods valued at one slave at al-Fashir prices; if they were content to wait until the slavers had returned,

---

15 Al-Tunisi (1851), 468-9 reproduces a model letter or *farman* from Muhammad al-Fadl; it follows the charters closely in form.

16 Professional raiders are alluded to in Girard (1824), xvii, 278. On raiding by members of the royal family, see Lapanouse (1799-1800), iv, 82-3 and on raiding by a faqih, O'Fahey (1977b), 163-4. On 'Abd al-Fattah, Nachtigal (1971-87), iv, 307; the Sultan, nevertheless, allegedly had him poisoned.

they received only two to three slaves for the same quantity of goods. These transactions were confirmed in writing.

The raiders usually set out after the rains (June to July) to ensure pasture for their horses. The sultan was said to have granted permission to between sixty and seventy expeditions each year, which seems exaggerated; Ahmad Tiktik told al-Tunisi that he had once seen seven bands set off at the same time.[17] Each party was given a particular route to follow and a particular tribe to raid.

Once all the members of the party had met at the agreed rendezvous on the southern border, the leader took the title of *sultan al-ghazwa*, and now that he was outside the authority of the state, he took on the attributes and powers of the sultan, giving his close companions titles associated with the court, *abbo soming dogala, aba diimang* etc., and they acted out towards him their assigned roles. The leader kept his position until the party returned once more to the land and authority of the real sultan. His position was thus closely parallel to those of the *maqdum* and *khabir*, all three received direct but limited commissions from the sultan, whom in some measure they were felt to represent.[18]

All slaves given as presents by the local chiefs or taken without resistance became the property of the *sultan al-ghazwa*; if he died, all the slaves went to the real sultan, so the "courtiers" had an incentive to keep their "sultan" alive. At intervals during the raid, which could last three months or more, a *jibaya* or "levy" was held.[19] A *zariba* or thorn enclosure was constructed to which all the members of the party brought the slaves they had so far captured. The *sultan al-ghazwa* sat in the centre dividing the booty; his proportion varied between a third and a half depending on his rank and investment.

---

17 Al-Tunisi (1851), 481. Lapanouse (1799-1800), iv, 82 says the sultan ordered raids every two to three months.

18 This mimicry of the state has parallels with the *baramka* tea-drinking associations, which likewise imitate the political hierarchy, among the Baqqara; see Cunnison (1966), 122-8.

19 Al-Tunisi accompanied a raiding party under the *malik* 'Abd al-Karim b. Khamis 'Arman, who owed him money; the party stayed in the south for three months, (1965), 329 (357 & 469-70).

After the *jibaya* those merchants who had accompanied the raiding party were paid, while after an interval a further another "levy" would be held.

The raids described here were the high point in the relentless southward pressure of the Fur and their state (see Chapter Eight). The next stage in the southward advance was to be the coming in the mid-nineteenth century of the rifle-using *kubaniyya*s or trading/raiding companies that could penetrate where horses could not go because of the tsetse fly. There were similarities between *ghazwa* and *kubaniyya*; both were in effect joint stock ventures, both were phenomena of the frontier, both used superior military technology, horse and gun. The irony was the *kubaniyya* were to destroy the state that sent the *ghazwa* southwards.

The royally-sanctioned slaving parties were not the only people hunting for slaves; the Baqqara and others were frequent if opportunistic kidnappers, stealing a boy here, a girl there,

They lie in ambush and as soon as one of the children is within reach, they seize it, mount their horses and ride away at full gallop.[20]

It is probable that kidnapping and small-scale raiding by nomads were cumulatively as significant as the more spectacular state-sponsored raiding parties. Some slaves were sold north, others were incorporated into the Mandala servile communities settled in Baqqara territory. The nomads used their slaves both as herders—as did many of the notables—and to produce food as a "cushion" against want within the nomadic cycle. Indeed the cattle and cattle nomads were probably more nomadic in the nineteenth century than they are today (when the distinction between nomad and farmer is fast fading), precisely because they had slaves: "Ideally the Hababin [of central

---

20 Pallme (1844); on Dinka attitudes to Arab slave raiding, see Deng (1978), 139-41. The numerous reports put out by Amnesty International and Human Rights Watch over the last twenty years echo the nineteenth-century travel literature. Thus from Human Rights Watch (1996), 307, "The practice of government soldiers, officers and militia (Popular Defense Forces) who take women and children captive, to be used or sold as household slaves, has persisted almost since the beginning of the war …".

Kordofan] would prefer to return to their pre-Mahdiyya system of animal husbandry with cultivation mainly by slaves".[21]

By the nineteenth century the inner hunting grounds of the slavers lay immediately south and southwest of the sultanate; here the Fartit included (from west to east) the Runga, Kara, Yulu, Kresh, Binga, Banda, Feroge, Shatt and a number of small groups around the copper-mining area of Hufrat al-Nahas and Jabal Dango, the effective southern limit of the sultanate.[22] Within this inner arc relations between raided and raider became stabilised in a formal tributary status, where the *sultan al-ghazwa* was empowered to accept or reject as quasi-tributaries those Fartit who wished to become so and who paid over slaves as tribute.[23] Hence from the perspective of the notables slave-raiding was a form of tax-farming.

Dar Fartit grew or fluctuated as the raiders penetrated ever further south. In fact the main thrust was towards the southwest, open savanna land largely free of tsetse, rather than directly south, though a land corridor leading beyond the Mbomu River into the Ubangi/Shari Basin.[24] One of the great rivers of this region, either the Mbomu or the Ubangi, had been reached by the early eighteenth century; the

---

21 Hill (1968), 58-70. See also Cunnison (1966), 40, 66 and 80, and on the Mandala, Hebbert (1925), 187-94.

22 Mengin (1823), ii, 234 lists the tribes from whom slaves were taken; Rong (Runga), Befeg (?), Chal (Shala), Feroukah (Feroge), el-Hofrah (people around Hufrat al-Nahas, probably Kresh), Danq (Dango or Dongo), Kar (Kara), Youl (Yulu), el-Nabeh (?), and Bonoud (Ar. pl. form of Banda?). On the historical traditions of most of these peoples, see Santandrea (1964) and my (1982), 75-87. The implication of the list is that the raiders generally did not go that far south and tended to go southwest (see MAP 3). The most detailed map is that in Tucker and Bryan (1956) at the end.

23 Al-Tunisi (1965), 141 (130 & 216) lists the Runga, Fongoro, Bandala (Mandala), Binga and Shala as tributary Fartit people; to them may be added the Daju of Dar Sila, the Beigo and Gula, according to Nachtigal (1971-87), iv, 359. On "secondary state formation" in this region, see my (1982), 75-87 and the literature cited there.

24 On the speculative earlier history of Muslim/Sudanic penetration into the northern equatorial region, see Birmingham in Oliver (1977), iii, 565-6, Kalck (1971), 1-25 and Cordell (1985), 7-30. The movement of raiders and refugees as of this writing between Darfur, Chad and the CAR seems to mirror this pattern.

faqih Madani told al-Tunisi of a party of raiders who tried to go as far south as possible. They travelled for six months until they came to a great stretch of water which they could not cross, but on the other side of which they saw men dressed in red. The *faqih* had once talked to an old man who had reached this lake or river in 'Umar Lel's reign (c.1730-39).[25] A hundred years later, c. 1840, a great expedition led by the *maqdum* 'Abd al-Sid passed through the Shala and Binga lands south of Wadai and penetrated further south for another thirty days towards the Ubangi.[26] These raids were to open up the south to numerous *jallaba* immigrants who settled around Hufrat al-Nahas, Shakka and Dara, when they ventured south on small-scale trading journeys perilous enough to warrant taking their burial shrouds with them.[27] This opening up of the southern borderlands and beyond and the extension of the trading networks were to pave the way for al-Zubayr and his competitors.

Slaves brought north for export or sale locally were as carefully classified as ivory or ostrich feathers, and as with the latter, so with slaves an elaborate terminology was developed, as al-Tunisi describes.[28] Apart from such common trade terms as *sudasi*/"six-span" to describe a male slave by height, those slaves in the south taken without resistance were called "*denguyeh*", probably from *jaang*, the Nuer name for Dinka and other foreigners that became almost as common as "Fartit" as a label along the southern borderlands. This may suggest that "*denguyeh*" were slaves that had already enslaved in the south. Slaves captured in the mountains after resistance were called "*fekk al-djebâl*" (? "of the mountains"), referring presumably to people enslaved in the mountainous regions between Wadai and Darfur and in Kordo-

---

25 Al-Tunisi (1851), 274-6. Other journeys or expeditions to the south of 30 to 40 days duration are referred in Browne (1806), xv; Cadalvène and Breuvery (1841), ii, 236; Brun-Rollet (1855), 131-2; and Barth (1853), 120-2, the last-cited giving a detailed itinerary. The extent of these journeys is discussed in Dampierre (1967), 59-60.

26 Bizemont (1871), 120-30.

27 Nachtigal (1971-87), iv, 353-4 and Brun-Rollet (1855), 130-2 (on the shrouds).

28 Al-Tunisi (1851), 483-4 and 725.

fan who were otherwise known as *jabalawiyyin*/"mountain folk", a term almost synonymous with pagan. From another perspective, the most valuable slaves were those already acclimatised and acculturated, "*mougeddeh*" (Ar.?), in contrast to the less valuable newcomers called "*foutyr*" (possibly from *fatir* which has the meaning, applied to a person, of "immature" in Sudanese Arabic).[29]

These terms and others and references throughout this book underline the fact that Darfur was a slave-owning as well as a slave raiding/trading society. Discussion of domestic slavery within Sudanic Africa has been skewed by the over-emphasis on the Atlantic and Middle Eastern slave trades out of Africa. In the case of Darfur, the majority of slaves brought into the sultanate were probably destined for domestic consumption. We know something about the royal slave settlements and royal military slaves and slaves on the estates of the notables, but much less is known about the use and distribution of slaves at a more local and modest level. Here, I suspect the use of slaves was much more widespread than can be documented, as was said of neighbouring Kordofan by the German traveller A.E. Brehm: "Just as the Kordofani ladies have their slave women so do the men have their slaves" (*Die Frauen Kordofahns haben ebensogut ihre Sklavinnen als die Männer ihre Sklaven*).[30] In the relatively few legal documents concerning slaves that have survived from the Nilotic Sudan (there are very few from Darfur), the slaves have Muslim names, which presumably were given them upon capture.[31] The at-

---

29 A suggestion I owe to Dr Abdel Ghaffer Muhammad Ahmad.

30 Brehm (1975), 206. McLoughlin (1962) 361, estimated that slaves formed 20-30% of the total population in the northern Sudan; although the figure appears reasonable, he provides little evidence to support it. More recent studies have not really added much.

31 The question of the unlawful enslaving of Muslims does not appear in Darfur as an issue, as it did in West Africa. For a treatise on the issue by the great scholar of Timbuktu, Ahmad Baba (d. 1627), see Hunwick and Harrak (2000). Slavery in Darfur is placed within its wider Muslim context in Clarence-Smith (2006), 11-13 and 202. Occasionally, "joke" names appear— Limuna ("Lemon"), Sabah al-Khayr ("Good Morning"), Salamatuhu ("His Comfort")—but most slaves that appear in legal documents have Muslim names.

titudes arising from the widespread ownership of slaves, reinforced by a "frontier mentality", served to produce a complex of ideas and opinions, ethnic and religious prejudices, economic patterns and expectations that pervaded all aspects of society and which survive in attenuated form to this day. Of the few recorded court cases concerning slaves from Darfur, two involve slave girls who had run away from a chief to a *faqih*, while one of the categories of slaves brought back from the south were the "strays"/*hamil*, which suggests the existence of a "freedom road".[32]

Kobbei and the Forty Days Road

As the southern terminus of the Forty Days Road most of the sultanate's trade with Egypt passed through Kobbei. The desert crossing of nearly 1,100 miles was long and arduous, the more so going to Egypt when the caravans were slowed by slaves; the "forty days" refers to the number of days of march, not to the total time taken, although this still seems very fast. The caravans stole across the desert from oasis to oasis, the main stages from Kobbei being Jabal Meidob, Bir Natrun, Laqiya, Salima, al-Shabb, Kharja to Asyut (see Map 1).[33] Despite occasional raids by the Kababish nomads of Kordofan along the southern stages and the 'Ababda and Magharba in the north, the caravans were at little risk from man. It was the natural dangers in crossing the Sahara at its most desolate, and the organisational and financial backing needed to transport relatively bulky items such as slaves, ivory and gum Arabic, that caused the trade to be concentrated at Kobbei under the effective control of a small group of big traders.

Kobbei was a town of the Nile Valley set down in the savannas, a reflection of the urban or semi-urban background of its merchant inhabitants. Now more or less deserted, partly because the wells have

32 For one, see my (1991), 93-102 (79-113); the other is 175.18/35, 1290/187374, where Jum'a is sued by malik Abbakr for the return of the runaway girl Sa'da.
33 For modern descriptions see Shaw (1929), 63-71 and the vivid account of Asher (1984); among the earlier descriptions are Browne (1806), 194-238; al-Tunisi (1965), 48-54 (28-35 & 71-9); Denon (1809), i, 280-1 and Cuny (1854), 87-8.

dried up and partly because of the disappearance of the caravans, Kobbei was probably Darfur's largest town with a population in its heyday of 6-8,000.[34] Even its physical configuration was reminiscent of the Nile Valley: it consisted of a long, narrow strip of settlement along the Wadi Kobbei between Kofod and Jabal Kobbei, a prominent landmark; outlying villages lay on either side of the main settlement whose length Browne estimated at more than two miles, since

The houses, each of which occupies within its enclosure a large portion of ground, are divided by considerable waste. The principal, or possibly the only view of convenience by which the natives appear to have been governed in their choice of situation and mode of building, must have been that of having the residence near the spot rented or inherited by them for the purpose of cultivation.[35]

Kobbei was the creation of immigrants from Upper Egypt and the northern Sudan, Ja'afiriyya, Hawwara and others from the former, Danaqla (sing. Dunqulawi) and Mahas Nubians and Ja'aliyyin from the latter. The motives and causes of what had been termed (in recognition of its commercial basis) the *jallaba* diaspora throughout the savanna lands into Wadai, Darfur, Kordofan, the Gezira (between the two Niles) and the Ethiopian borderlands are less clear than its consequences, which were profound.[36] As uncertain as its causes is the chronology of the diaspora. Its first waves may well reach back to and be associated with the prosperity of the Christian Nubian states in Fatimid times (tenth and eleventh centuries). As regards the Darfur/Wadai region, the traders appear to have already pioneered the routes by about the mid-sixteenth century; Sultan Shaw's endow-

---

34 PA (al-Fashir) DP FD 66 K 1/27 Arab Omodias, and Sarsfield-Hall (1922), 362. The decline was rapid: Nachtigal (1971-87), iv, 255-6 noted many empty houses in 1874 and six years later only 80-100 out of an estimated total of 4-500 houses were still inhabited, Fraccaroli (1880), 205-6. Browne (1806), 324 estimated its population at about 6,000 ("of these the greater proportion are slaves"); Perron at about 8,000 compared with 30,000 males at al-Fashir, which latter seems exaggerated; al-Tunisi (1845), 154 (not in Ar. text), and Nachtigal (1971-87), iv, 253 at "about 2,000 hearths".

35 Browne (1806), 265; on estates at Kobbei, see O'Fahey and Abu Salim (1983), 106-18.

36 On the diaspora, see Bjørkelo (1989), 137-47.

ment of 1576 made through Hawwara traders, D'Anania's notice
of Uri in about 1580, and Wansleben's accurate description of the
Forty Days Road confirm this (see Chapter Two). It was because of
this enterprise that the trade in black slaves (as opposed to that in
white slaves), which had been so important in early medieval Egypt
under the Fatimids, revived in the seventeenth century, a revival signalled by the building of the *wakalat al-jallaba/*"the caravanserai of
the travelling merchants" in Cairo as a centre for those merchants
dealing in Sudanic products.[37]

The trading community at Kobbei was cosmopolitan; Browne
noted merchants from Upper Egypt, Tunis, Tripoli, Dongola, Nubia and Kordofan, whose main business was the long-distance trade
centred on the market held twice a week.[38] Merchants settling in
the district built up their own settlements and farms to which they
welcomed their compatriots, thus creating a patchwork of immigrant
communities. The merchants were divided not only by community
but also by status, into *jallaba* and *khabir.* The former were hardy
itinerant small-scale traders or peddlers who sought a modest profit
wherever and in whatever trade they could, and whose assets varied
from a few hundred to 1,000 piastres, invested in cloths of various
types, beads, razors, perfumes, paper and a few slaves.[39] By contrast
there were merchants like *khabir* 'Ali b. Ibrahim who on occasion
gave Muhammad al-Husayn presents worth 9,000 piastres (see
Chapter Six).

Khabir, usually with the more modest meaning of "leader" or
"guide", became an official title borne by a small number of the big
merchants, of whom some twenty to thirty operated out of Kobbei in the mid-nineteenth century. They were a heterogeneous
group; among the more prominent figures were the brothers Hamza

---

37 See Walz (1978), 66-9 et passim.

38 Browne (1806), 271-4 says the market was held on Mondays and Fridays;
according to Nachtigal (1971-87), iv, 253 they were on Monday and
Thursday.

39 Cuny (1863), 283 gives a detailed breakdown of the type of goods a travelling
merchant was taking to Darfur; their total value was 2,203 piastres. On the
scale of the financial transactions, see Walz (1978), 108-9 et passim.

and Muhammad al-Imam, of Dunqulawi origin, and Abbakr al-Khandaqawi from Khandaq on the Sudanese Nile.[40] Others included Idris al-Mahasi, 'Ali b. Ibrahim, Mahmud al-Shafi'i, a Ja'ali, and several families from the Tirayfiyya, a section of the Jawami'a people of central Kordofan; Aqbash al-Jayyari from Upper Egypt; and, of an earlier generation, 'Ali b. Ramli, a Mashaykhi from Asyut.[41] The latter's story illustrates a common and constant Sudanic theme, the intertwining of the two faces of external contact, religion and trade. 'Ali b. Ramli came to Darfur in Sultan Tayrab's time as a trader, but for some unremembered reason was imprisoned in Jabal Marra. So assiduous a Muslim was he in performing his ablutions before prayer that a melon sprang up out of season from the water thus spilt. This miracle or *karama* was reported to the Sultan, who ordered 'Ali's release and granted him land at Kofod near Kobbei. 'Ali married into a prominent Bidayriyya clan settled at Kofod and his son Mahmud, a *khabir* at Kobbei, received a charter for the land from Muhammad al-Fadl in 1233/1817-18. Mahmud's great-grandson was *al-hajj* Badawi, a merchant whose encounter with 'Ali Dinar is described elsewhere (see Chapter Six).[42] Several charters survive granting land to merchants in Kobbei region, but, as Browne's comment above suggests, there seems to have been a market in land there; 'Ali b. Ibrahim is reported as having bought land there.[43]

The Kobbei community seems to have been largely self-governing, dealing with the sultans through one of their number appointed as *malik al-jallaba*.[44] His functions were both administrative and judi-

---

40 On the al-Imam brothers, see Hill (1967), 150-1 and on Abbakr, Bjørkelo (1989), 125.

41 Muhammad 'Abd al-Rahim, *al-Durr al-manthur*, ms. NRO, Khartoum, gives a partial list of the most prominent traders.

42 'Ali al-hajj Badawi, al-Fashir, 13.8.1976; the grant was confirmed by 'Ali Dinar in 1328/1910-11 (278.35.1).

43 For the charters, see O'Fahey and Abu Salim (1983), 106-18 and PA (al-Fashir) Beira Omodia file.

44 Browne (1806), 293 and Nachtigal (1971-87), iv, 340. In a court transcript from Kobbei discussed here (photographed in Asyut from the original in the possession of the Jawhari family by T. Walz, who kindly gave me a copy), the holder of this position, Imam 'Abd al-Hafiz, is called *shahbandar*

cial, the registration of contracts and debts and of the property of deceased merchants so that the details could be forwarded to Egypt, the settlement of internal disputes, and the making of representations to the sultan when necessary. His judicial role was supplemented by a *qadi*; in the 1860s he was the *imam* Ahmad w. Taha, described in a court transcript as "the legal official (*al-hakim*) of the city of Kobbei".[45] One way in which the sultans kept watch over the merchants was through a system of guarantees which obliged every newcomer to stay with a local sponsor who acted as his agent in dealing with the authorities.[46]

Both Cuny and Nachtigal praise the generosity and graciousness of the merchants of Kobbei and their combination of trading acumen with religious learning, a tradition far from moribund in Darfur today.[47] Cuny met in Kordofan a Shaykh Muhammad who was taking various legal works to Muhammad al-Husayn, while 'Ali b. Ibrahim maintained a mosque at Kobbei to serve his people.[48] The strength of the merchant community lay in its expertise and financial connections in Cairo and Asyut with such firms as that of Shinuda al-Jawhari, a leading Coptic merchant in Asyut, or the Greek Nikopoulos. By the 1850s Asyut had entered a boom period based on its trade with Darfur, a boom reflected in court and commercial circles within the sultanate in increasing opulence and a growing familiarity with money.[49] The links between the travelling merchants, largely of

---

al-tujjar in imitation of Ottoman practice; see Gibb and Bowen (1950-57), i/1, 303.

45 In the document described in n.42 above. See further Browne (1806), 275 and on Ahmad w. Taha, Shuqayr (1903), ii, 146.

46 Browne (1806), 223 and al-Tunisi (1965), 63-6 (45-8 & 95-6).

47 The Ma'ali student of Ahmad b. Idris, al-Mawarzi, combined trading with missionary work; see Chapter Ten. The late al-Tayyib and Ibrahim Muhammad Nur, Fulani merchants and brothers, were my patrons in al-Fashir in the 70s. Their shop was my base and they showed a keen and very knowledgeable interest in my research. They both spoke French and had trading connections in Chad and the CAR.

48 Cuny (1862), 309 and Shuqayr (1903), ii, 146.

49 On al-Jawhari, Cuny (1854), 94-5; on Nikopoulos, Hartmann (1863), 67-70. On the Shinudas and the boom, see Walz (1978b), 113-26 and the older

northern Sudanese origin, and their Egyptian partners are well illustrated in a court case of 1862; *al-hajj* Salim Abu Saba'a, described as one of the *jallaba*, borrowed 320 *mahbub*s from Shinuda al-Jawhari in Dongola and was given in return a note of hand (*tamassuk*). When he later repaid the loan in Asyut, Shinuda claimed he had mislaid the note. Some time later, Shinuda's son produced the note and demanded and received payment from a friend of *al-hajj* Salim in Asyut. However, in order to clear the matter up, another merchant was sent to Darfur where the dispute was settled before the *qadi* Ahmad w. Taha.[50]

From the perspective of Darfur, the merchants were, together with the *fuqara*, the intermediaries between the wider world of commerce, of Islam and of new ideas and products and the encapsulated world of the Sudanic kingdom. In the decades immediately before the destruction of the first sultanate, the informal alliance between the merchants and the sultan became more and more intimate (see Chapter Six); on one occasion Muhammad al-Husayn invited the al-Jawhari family to send a representative to Darfur, an intimacy that provoked opposition from the more traditionally-minded members of the Keira clan.[51] Paradoxically, within the world of African exploration of the time Darfur gained a wholly undeserved reputation as an inhospitable land; when Josef Natterer, Austro-Hungarian Consul in Khartoum between 1860 and 1862, wrote to the Sultan to enquire about the death of Charles Cuny in al-Fashir in 1858 (it was rumoured that he had been murdered at the Sultan's orders), the Sultan wrote an indignant reply, asserting that his state was open and hospitable and that Cuny had died of natural causes shortly after his arrival in al-Fashir.[52]

---

study by Dehérain (1901), 65-72.

50 See n. 42.

51 Cuny (1854), 94-5. A number of Copts traded in Darfur, but risked persecution, see Browne (1806), 229-30.

52 A translation of the letter, dated 7 Dhu'l-hijja 1278/5 June 1862, in Cuny (1862), 221-4. The letter is undoubtedly authentic.

A detailed analysis of the trade and its fluctuations between Egypt and Darfur lies beyond the scope of this book, but its scale was significant to both countries:

Exports from Egypt to Darfur c. 1796 (in *nisf fidda*), 19,765,750

[Exports to Sinnar c. 1796, 3,792,375]

Imports from Darfur to Egypt c. 1796 (in *nisf fidda*), 50,285,625

[Imports from Sinnar, c. 1796, 12,053,600].[53]

I give these figures impressionistically; to understand and contextualise them, one must read Walz's analysis. Three obvious comments: the sultanate enjoyed a very favourable balance of trade with Egypt, it was increasingly linked to the global economy. and it was much richer than Sinnar. Nor did Darfur trade solely with Egypt; apart from the trans-Sudanic routes, caravans also went intermittently to North Africa, especially Tunis.[54] But Egypt was always Darfur's major trading partner. Whatever its destination, the sultans controlled and profited by the trade, not only indirectly through customs duties and the like but also by directly commissioning the *khabir*s to organise and lead the great annual or semi-annual caravans; without the ruler's consent no caravan, great or small, could enter or leave Kobbei.[55] In this sense Browne's description of the sultan as trader is accurate:

The king is chief merchant in the country, and not only dispatches with every caravan to Egypt a great quantity of his own merchandise, but also

---

53 Walz (1978), 36—listing the main categories of exports, slaves (38.8%), camels (19%), gum (13.3%), ivory (about 6%; here Sinnar was a significantly large exporter) etc.—and 43, listing imports with two main categories, cloth and metalware. Walz's various writings are fundamental to an understanding of the sultanate's trade with Egypt.

54 On slaves from Darfur in Tunis see al-Hashayshi (1903), 227 and Valensi (1967), 1267-88. In the early twentieth century, trade with Libya was important, while one of the leading families in al-Fashir was the Abu Sufita from the Fezzan. Their business papers were still extant in al-Fashir in the 70s, but I could never find the man who had the key to the safe.

55 Browne (1806), 249-50 where 'Abd al- Rahman controls the trade by refusing permission for the caravans to leave.

employs his slaves and dependents to trade with the goods of Egypt, on his own account, in the countries adjacent to Soudan.[56]

The size and frequency of the caravans naturally fluctuated, both in response to the rise and fall of demand in the Egyptian markets and for political reasons; thus the trade was interrupted both by the rapacity of the Mamluk rulers of Egypt in the 1780s and by the attempts at monopoly by Muhammad 'Ali in the 1820s and 30s.[57] According to Browne, "a caravan of 2,000 camels and 1,000 slaves was considered rather larger than normal", although an exceptionally large caravan (because of a gap of several years) is said to have brought 12,000 slaves to Egypt in 1798.[58] Slaves were always the basic export until the mid-nineteenth century at least; French sources of the period 1798-1801 estimated that 5-6,000 slaves were brought to Egypt each year.[59] Other exports included the pack animals themselves, overwhelmingly camels, and ivory (of growing importance from the 1840s onwards), alluvial gold (mainly from Kordofan), gum arabic (from eastern Darfur and western Kordofan), rhinoceros horn, ostrich feathers (a major item), and some copper from Hufrat al-Nahas.[60] Naturally the caravans took pilgrims as well as the *mahmal* or decorated covering sent by the sultans to the Ka'ba at the time of the great pilgrimage, a symbol of their independent place among the polities of the Muslim world.[61]

Once the caravans were under way, the authority of the *khabir* was absolute, symbolised by his use of drums in the chiefly manner

---

56 Ibid., 346.

57 Walz (1978), 61-4. On the number and frequency of caravans, see La Rue (1989, thesis), 159 and 165-6.

58 Browne (1806), 282.

59 These figures are discussed in Walz (1978), 124-30 and 173-221. Here Walz is elegantly analysing data collected by the French savants brought to Egypt by Napoleon, many of them intellectuals of high calibre, against local contemporary records from the Wakalat al-jallaba, a combination that makes his material of exceptional interest.

60 See n. 53.

61 Al-Naqar (1972), xx; a photograph of 'Ali Dinar's *mahmal* is given in Gleichen (1905-6), i, opp. p. 189.

to transmit his orders and the routine of the day's march along the line of the caravan; even on arrival at Asyut the other merchants were obliged to wait until he had given permission to begin trading. The organisation of the larger caravans in particular must have been a formidable undertaking and their passage through the desert a spectacular sight.[62]

The caravan, like the *ghazwa*, was the state outside the state; the *khabir*, like the *sultan al-ghazwa*, was an agent of the state beyond the state. The sultans came to profit from the raiding/raiding cycle, not so much by running it themselves, as they had probably tended to do in the time of Tayrab and 'Abd al-Rahman, but by incorporating into the elite the key personnel at both ends of the cycle.

---

62 I have a vivid memory of Tony Arkell describing to me how he organised the movement of 18,000 camels from Darfur, across Kordofan and the Gezira to the Sudanese/Ethiopian border; between 1941 and 1944 he was Chief Transport Officer in connection with the British invasion and occupation of Italian-held Ethiopia.

PART III
THE END OF INDEPENDENCE

12
THE CONQUEST OF DARFUR
1873-1874

Introduction

The conquest of the Keira Sultanate of Darfur in 1874 by al-Zubayr Pasha (d. 1913) marked not only the beginning of the end of the Keira sultanate's existence as an independent state continuing since the sixteenth century, but was also a climacteric in modern Sudanese history. Although the Keira dynasts put up a heroic resistance throughout the 1870s and 80s and although their last Sultan, 'Ali Dinar b. Zakariyya (d. 1916), was able formally to restore the sultanate between 1898 and 1916, after 1874 Darfur was regarded by its overlords, be they Egyptian, Mahdist or British, as a part of "The Sudan", with all the implications that has had until today. The issue of Darfur's separate identity, not to speak of independence, did not again enter the international arena until the Abuja negotiations between the Khartoum Government and the various Darfur rebel groups opened under the auspices of the African Union in 2004. As of this writing the issue of Darfur's place within the Sudan remains unresolved.

Al-Zubayr was the product of a quasi-colonial frontier expansion making use of new technology, in this case boats and guns. The breakthrough by Salim Qapudan beyond the *sadd* or swamps on the White Nile into the southern Sudan in 1839 led to the rapid incorporation of parts of the southern Sudan into a raiding/trading cycle which, while operating in a different ecology, was not too removed from the Darfur model described in Chapter Eleven; the difference lay in the technology. By the 1850s a wave of European, Egyptian and Levantine, and then Sudanese adventurers moved by boat along the western river tributaries into the Western Bahr al-Ghazal to create networks of *zariba*s or stockades, joint-stock companies or *kubaniyya*s and slave armies to exploit the region's two most valuable resources, human beings and elephants.[1] The whole system was to be rationalised by one man, al-Zubayr Rahma al-Mansur.

Al-Zubayr arrived in the Bahr al-Ghazal in 1856.[2] A man of great determination and ability,[3] he rapidly built up a trading empire based organisationally on the *kubaniyya* or joint-stock trading company and geographically on a network of armed camps (*zariba*) garrisoned by slave troops armed with firearms, usually double-barrelled Remingtons, and linked by boats using the numerous rivers of the

1 There is a very considerable literature; useful works include Gray (1961) and Stiansen (thesis, 1993).

2 Al-Zubayr's autobiography until 1875 is published in Shuqayr (1903), iii, 60-84; this is an "improved" version, from a literary point of view, of the original manuscript to be found in SAD Ar. 110/3/1, ms. 18 ff., dictated in October 1876. Shuqayr's version was translated by Thilo (1921). Two further relevant accounts are Shaw (1887), 333-49, 564-85 & 658-83, based on interviews held through an interpreter between Flora Shaw (later Lady Lugard) and al-Zubayr during the latter's exile in Gibraltar (where he stayed 1885-87), and Jackson (1913), which is little more than an imaginative translation of the account in Shuqayr. In most instances, I have preferred the account in Shuqayr, but have crosschecked it with the original manuscript in Durham.

3 Al-Zubayr has entered into mainstream Sudanese history as a major figure, in part because of his role in the Victorian myth-making around Gordon, in part as a northern Sudanese state-builder and, paradoxically, a loyal servant of Egypt; both themes are evident in his son's hagiography, al-Zubayr (1952) and, more critically, in Warburg (1992). Despite having a street named after him in downtown Khartoum, al-Zubayr was essentially a slave-trader, a fact of which he makes no secret in his autobiography.

region. The main trade item was ivory, but slaves both for internal use, as soldiers and as labourers to grow food for the encampments, and as exports to the savannas to the north were the other staple. By 1865, al-Zubayr virtually controlled the whole Bahr al-Ghazal, having killed off or incorporated his rivals, but as his empire grew he came into conflict with the Khedive Isma'il; Turco-Egyptian anti-slavery measures blocked his outlets through the White Nile and made the overland routes to the north vital.[4] These were routes that passed through the various tribal territories of the Baqqara or cattle-nomads, whose lands lay between the sultanate and the area controlled by al-Zubayr.

As we have seen, the Darfur sultans had never successfully managed to control the Baqqara, although much of the sultanate's trade in slaves and ivory passed through their territory. In the 1840s and 50s the sultans had mounted a series of campaigns in a fruitless attempt to impose their rule on the nomads, probably in order to secure their southern flank from the potential threat of the trading companies in the Bahr al-Ghazal. Indeed 1856, the year al-Zubayr arrived in the Bahr al-Ghazal, had seen the defeat and death at the hands of the Rizayqat of the Wazir Adam Bosh at the head of a large army (see Chapter Four). It was to these same Rizayqat that al-Zubayr now turned.

There is no evidence that al-Zubayr had at this stage any long-term ambitions against the sultanate, but in Shawwal 1282/February-March 1866 he made an agreement with the Rizayqat that was to lead indirectly to the downfall of Darfur.[5] At a meeting with some eighty Rizayqat shaykhs, the trader agreed to pay a toll on his caravans passing through their territory in exchange for safe passage. This rationalisation of the trading networks of the region struck a severe blow at the commercial basis of the sultanate; al-Zubayr now

---

4 See further, Shukry (1938), 222-3.

5 Shuqayr (1903) iii, 66-7 (a misprint here and elsewhere: Zirayqat for Rizayqat); Shaw, 584-5 dates the agreement to 1868, while Shukry (1938), 222-3 has March 1860 (no doubt also a misprint).

controlled not only the sultanate's economic hinterland but also all access to and from it.[6]

An interlude: al-Zubayr and al-Bulalawi

The sultanate, however, gained a temporary respite in the form of a rival to al-Zubayr's position in the Bahr al-Ghazal. This was a central Sudanic adventurer, Muhammad al-Bulalawi,[7] who turned up in al-Zubayr's domains in 1869 with the backing of Khartoum. Al-Bulalawi was in origin a *faqih* from the Bulala people of the Lake Fitri region in modern Chad, and claimed to be a member of their ruling family.[8] He had spent some years at the court of the pious Sultan Muhammad al-Husayn who treated him well, as he did all visiting holy men, and who gave him an estate in southern Darfur. But the *faqih* quarrelled with the powerful Wazir Ahmad Shatta (whose nickname, *shatta* "red pepper", reflected his temper) who coveted the estate, and with the Sultan's sister, the *iiya baasi* Zamzam, and he was forced to flee the sultanate. He then went to the Turco-Egyptian authorities in Kordofan and Khartoum and pretended that he had a claim to Darfur and Wadai because of his royal Bulala blood; he is also said to have claimed ownership of the copper mines at Hufrat al-Nahas in southern Darfur.[9] These claims were wildly improbable; nevertheless, the Governor, Ja'far Pasha Mazhar, gave him a few regular troops to support his own Takarir or West African followers and sent him to try conclusions with al-Zubayr. But al-Zubayr was too strong and three years later in 1872, after much manuoevring, al-Bulalawi was killed and his troops

---

6   On the Kordofan routes at this period, see Gray (1961), 66.

7   There has been some confusion over his correct *nisba* or family name; see my (1973d), 197.

8   The following is based on Nachtigal (1971-87) iv, 316-17; Slatin (1896), 48-9; Shuqayr (1903), ii, 67-8, and Shukry (1938), 152. The Bulala had in the fourteenth and fifteenth centuries ruled Kanem and much of Wadai; see Hagenbucher (1967), 39-76.

9   Gray (1961), 121.

incorporated into the former's forces.[10] The Ja'ali was now undisputed master of all the lands south of the sultanate.

The beginning of the conquest

By 1873 al-Zubayr's agreement with the Rizayqat had broken down. The German traveller Gustav Nachtigal, who arrived in Darfur from Wadai in March of the following year, records that Muhammad al-Husayn, at last realising the danger from al-Zubayr and the Bahhara (i.e. the traders of the Bahr al-Ghazal) induced some of the nomads to break their agreement.[11] The Rizayqat, with no central leadership, were split into two factions, one under Madibbu b. 'Ali and 'Uqayl w. al-Janqawi supporting al-Zubayr, the other, led by Munzal and 'Ulayyan, supporting the sultanate.[12] One of al-Zubayr's caravans was attacked and several of his relatives killed, while the Sultan placed an embargo on the export of grain to the south.[13] Al-Zubayr, before retaliating, wrote to the Sultan on 1 Jumada 1290/27 June 1873; this was the first of a sequence of five letters written between June 1873 and August 1874 to the Sultan, in which the trader sought to justify his actions (see further below, The Diplomatic and Propaganda War).[14] It is a subtle production; the trader, addressing the Sultan respectfully, writes as a servant of the Khedive (fa-nahnu 'abid af-fandina) who has been engaged in the conquest of the country of the slaves (bilad al-'abid) or the land of the Fartit (bilad al-faratit) since 1270/1853-4.[15] He had then established a route to Kordofan via al-Shakka passing through the Rizayqat country, whose security he had entrusted to the nomads by agreement. But they had reneged and

---

10 Shaw (1887), 658-62; Shuqayr (1903), iii, 67-8, and a manuscript autobiography of al-Nur Bey Muhammad 'Anqara in the possession of Sayyid 'Abd Allah Amir Isma'il of Omdurman. There is a copy among my papers.

11 Nachtigal (1971-87), iv, 319-20.

12 After the disappearance from the scene of Munzal and 'Ulayyan, 'Uqayl and Madibbu split. For the background, see Abu Salim (1979), 35-113.

13 Hill (1884), xxxix.

14 Al-Zubayr in al-'Ubayd (1995), 2-3.

15 This date seems too early, since al-Zubayr seems to have first entered the Bahr al-Ghazal in 1856, although the latter date is not entirely established.

attacked the caravans, "Spilling the blood of Muslims and seizing their property without any legal justification." He then launches into an historical aside recounting the sorry history of the sultanate's previous encounters with the Rizayqat, noting that among other leaders 'Abd al-'Aziz, father of the current *maqdum* of southern Darfur Ahmad Shatta, had been killed by them in the early 1840s as had the father of the present Wazir Bakhit, Adam Bosh, in 1856. He concludes that he had attacked the nomads and had the right to do so "since they have been outside your control for thirty years"—brutally said, but true.

The letter was addressed to Sultan Ibrahim Qarad, since the old Sultan had died in April 1873, probably before the Rizayqat raid. Before his death Muhammad al-Husayn had arranged with his confidants that Ibrahim should succeed him (see Chapters Four and Six). The new Sultan, described by Nachtigal as "A man of forty, and in many respects resembled his dead father. He had the same mildness and intelligent complaisance, but was, however, on the one hand less clever and learned, on the other, more manly and decisive,"[16] now had to deal with al-Zubayr. He began by sending Ahmad Shatta back to Dara, the southern capital of the sultanate, as *maqdum*. In the meantime al-Zubayr, having received no reply to his letter, moved into Dar Rizayqat where he was joined by Madibbu and 'Uqayl and occupied al-Shakka on 1 Rajab 1290/25 August 1873.

Two weeks later Al-Zubayr wrote again to al-Fashir, on 15 Rajab 1290/8 September 1873; the letter was addressed both to the Sultan and to his uncle, the *amir* (described as *faqih*) Hasab Allah b. Muhammad al-Fadl. In it he announces his occupation of al-Shakka after a great battle with the nomads. He notes that Munzal and 'Ulayyan had fled to the Sultan, whom he counsels against listening to their evil words. The Egyptian state's intentions are honourable and al-Zubayr is writing to prevent any disputes between the two states (*al-fitan bayn al-dawlatayn*). He reminds Ibrahim of the good relations that had existed between his father and the Khedive and requests that the fugitive Rizayqat shaykhs be delivered up to him in

---

16 Nachtigal (1971-87), iv, 320.

shay'bas (wooden shackling yokes used in the transport of slaves) and irons.[17] The tone is sharper than in his first letter and is interesting in two respects; al-Zubayr emphasises his role as a faithful servant of the ruler of Egypt, but at the same time acknowledges that Darfur is a state (*al-dawla al-furawiyya*). The trader again received no answer, learning instead that Ibrahim had written to Madibbu threatening to wreak vengeance on al-Zubayr, whom he contemptuously described as a "petty trader", *jallabi*. The trader wrote a third letter on 21 Ramadan/12 November; the tone was now considerably stiffer—Why had the Sultan not answered his two earlier letters? He, al-Zubayr, an 'Abbasid and a Hashimite by descent,[18] would not be threatened or insulted; and he added, ominously, that the Sultan should submit to the Khedive.[19] A few days later, on 1 Shawwal/22 November, al-Zubayr learned that he had been appointed *mudir* or governor of al-Shakka and the Bahr al-Ghazal with the title of Bey.[20] We know very little of the internal policies of the Turco-Egyptian administration at this time; events would suggest an opportunistic decision to back al-Zubayr in his attempt to conquer the sultanate, providing him with a figleaf of legitimacy and staking Egypt's claims.

The conquest of the sultanate

In fact, the conquest of the sultanate took nearly a year; the immense distances—from al-Shakka to al-Fashir is over 400 kilometres as the crow flies—and the difficulties of supply precluded any rapid campaigning. The conquest demonstrated al-Zubayr's great mastery of this form of warfare and the complete inadequacy of the sultanate's military organisation (see Chapter Nine).

---

17 Al-Zubayr in al-'Ubayd (1995), 4-5.

18 Al-Zubayr was very proud of his claimed 'Abbasid descent, a claim common to all Ja'aliyyin, and frequently signed his letters "al-Zubayr Rahma al-'Abbasi", although in his letters to the Sultan he uses the *nisba* al-Jimi'abi, one of the sub-tribes of the Ja'aliyyin.

19 Al-Zubayr in al-'Ubayd (1995), 6-10.

20 Shuqayr (1903), iii, 73-4.

The opposing forces were woefully mismatched. Al-Zubayr, in nearly twenty years (1856-73) of hard campaigning in very difficult terrain, had built up an unrivalled irregular army of slave troops (known as *bazinqir,* later as *jihadiyya*), whose rank and file were recruited from the tribes of the Bahr al-Ghazal and beyond, especially from the Azande, and whose officers, many of whom like al-Nur Muhammad 'Anqara had served in the Egyptian forces, had as much fighting experience as their leader.[21] Among his officers were a number who later became famous as Mahdist generals, Hamdan Abu 'Anja, al-Nur 'Anqara, al-Zaki Tamal and 'Abd al-Rahman w. al-Nujumi,[22] and another who was to have an even greater career of conquest than his master, Rabih Fadl Allah (d.1900).[23] Against such experience and expertise the sultanate had little with which to respond. The sultanate had long since ceased to be an expansionist power and attempts by Shatta and others to create new military units like the *bazinqir* were simply too late.

However, it was the sultanate that moved first; Ahmad Shatta together with the *malik al-nahas* Sa'd al-Nur b. Ibrahim Ramad advanced into Dar Rizayqat, where in about December 1873 they defeated a detachment of al-Zubayr's forces under al-Nur Muhammad 'Anqara. Despite this success, Shatta found it expedient to write a conciliatory letter to al-Zubayr and apparently to try and open negotiations.[24] Eventually, the reluctant *maqdum*, urged on by the Sultan and compelled by his men, attacked al-Zubayr somewhere between al-Shakka and Dara in January or February 1874. In the second of two battles, Shatta, Sa'd al-Nur, the *maqdum* 'Abd Al-

---

21 After serving in the irregular cavalry on the Ethiopian frontier in the 1850s, al-Nur deserted together with forty companions (plus their weapons) and took service with al-Zubayr; from his manuscript autobiography. A vivid visual image is provided by the Ausrian photographer Richard Buchta in a picture of such troops; it is reproduced in Zaccaria (1999), 134. On military slavery of this period, see Johnson (1992).

22 See their biographies in Hill (1967).

23 For whose career, see Hallam (1977); what is interesting about Rabih's career of conquest was that he did it in his own name, unlike al-Zubayr.

24 Nachtigal (1971-87), iv, 321 and Slatin (1896), 52. Neither al-Zubayr nor al-Nur Muhammad 'Anqara mention the defeat.

lah Runga, a Dinka slave who administered western Darfur, and the *amin* 'Abd al-Bari, were among those killed. Al-Zubayr occupied Dara on 23 Dhu'l-hijja 1290/11 February 1874.[25] Despite a lull of several months, the battle sealed the fate of the sultanate for several reasons; Shatta probably had with him the few slave troops the sultanate possessed who were armed with Remingtons, while al-Zubayr now began to bring up considerable reinforcements from his *zaribas* in the Bahr al-Ghazal until he had some 7,000 men armed with rifles with him, and the Turco-Egyptian authorities began to move.[26]

Khartoum and Cairo had both been following al-Zubayr's progress with some anxiety and now began to act, if not to forestall him at the least to rob him of his gains. In February 1874, the Khedive Isma'il declared war on the sultanate, "The pretext was the aggression of the sultan and the determination of the Khedive to suppress the slave trade, reasons which must have struck the sultan as peculiar".[27] The Governor-general, Isma'il Ayyub Pasha, was ordered to concentrate his forces in western Kordofan preparatory to an invasion of Darfur.

Despite his victory and the occupation of Dara, al-Zubayr was still being pressed by the sultanate's forces; *shartay* Ahmad Nimr b. Tayrab, ruler of the Birged people living north of Dara (Dar Birged Kajjar), collected together the remnants of Shatta's army and tried to hem al-Zubayr in at Dara to give the Sultan time to collect another army.[28]

The diplomatic and propaganda war

As we have already seen, al-Zubayr sent a number of letters to the Sultan in the course of the campaign. These served several purposes, to delegitimise the authority of the Sultan, to destabilise his state by winning over key establishment figures within the sultanate, and,

---

25 Nachtigal (1971-87), iv, 321; Slatin (1896), 52, and Shuqayr (1903), iii, 75, who gives 4 February 1874 for the *hijriyya* date, as does Shukry (1938), 228.
26 Nachtigal (1971-87), iv, 312, and Gray (1961), 122.
27 Hill (1958) 1958, 137, and Shukry (1938), 228.
28 Shuqayr (1903), iii, 76, Jackson (1913), 62, and Sabil Adam Ya'qub, al-Fashir 1.1.1970.

a sensitive issue, to justify his actions in attacking a Muslim state. After his fatal move to Cairo in 1875 he had the letters published in a lithographed pamphlet of 22 pages entitled *al-Ajwiba al-sadida fi-indhar wa-tahdid ahl al-makida*, "Pertinent Letters of warning and admonishment to the people of intrigue".[29] Seven of the eight letters are addressed to the Sultan, but one, dated 1 Muharram 1291/18 February 1874, is addressed "to the *'ulama* of Darfur occupied with the Sunna and the Book".[30]

It is an unctuous epistle; those *'ulama* mentioned by name include Muhammad Salama b. Maliki al-Futawi, Fakhr al-Din b. Muhammad Salim, one Salim (unidentified; perhaps the father), al-Daw b. *al-imam* al-Masri, and one Fakhr al-Din (unidentified). Interestingly they all appear to be Fulani, mainly of the Awlad 'Ali lineage. Why al-Zubayr should be writing to these figures is unexplained.

He opens the letter by presenting himself as a tireless and disinterested missionary for Islam among the pagans of the south,

We were fighting (*mujahidin*) all the unbelieving oppressors (*al-tughat al-ka-fara*) and the polytheists (*al-mushrikin*) until we had reduced them to obedience and had forbidden them to offend against the law or to behave indecently. We turned them away from the worship of idols (*al-awthan*) and many entered the community of Islam (*millat al-Islam*) by saying the profession of faith, "There is no god but God; Muhammad is the Messenger of God".

He continues that he had then peacefully opened up the routes between Darfur and the Egyptian Sudan to all Muslims, but that in 1288/1871-72 he learned that the Rizayqat were raiding the routes. He was thus forced to occupy Dar Rizayqat and to punish the nomads, being well aware that "A Muslim is not allowed to make war against another Muslim except for a compelling reason or because of disobedience to the Shari'a". He then concentrates on the culpability of Sultan Ibrahim in sheltering the evil shaykhs, Munzal and 'Ulayyan, and says that he had sent five letters to the Sultan urging concerted action against the nomads. He was writing to the *'ulama*

---

29 Cairo, n.d., n.p.; it is reproduced from an original lithograph in the Egyptian Archives in al-'Ubayd (1995).

30 Al-Zubayr in al-'Ubayd (1995), 12-15.

because of "The offences of Sultan Ibrahim against us and because he was making war against us without us having offended him or having disobeyed the Shari'a." He concludes by asking the 'ulama to explain to him why their Sultan was making war on him.

Seven months after he had written to the 'ulama, al-Zubayr sent a final letter, dated 3 Rajab 1291/16 August 1874, to the Sultan.[31] He recapitulates his past dealings with the sultan over the Rizayqat and then baldly announces his intention to annex the sultanate in the name of the Khedive,

God Most High has imposed upon us the duty to fight with you in order that you and those with you who are among the evildoers of this earth should be set aright. When we encountered your armies, God gave us victory over them and we entered the town of Dara. Now we have formed the intention (wa-sara 'l-qasd) to lead you and your country to submit to the Khedivial government. O! Prince, if you consider yourself to be God's slave and are convinced that, "Surely the earth is God's and He bequeaths it to whom He will among His servants (K. 7: 128, Arberry's translation)", then make haste to renounce your kingship (al-mulk) by submitting to my master.

He concludes by assuring that the sultan that his property and treasure will remain his and that he will enjoy an honoured status, but if not, "You will be accountable to God for the blood of the Muslims".

Al-Zubayr's arguments are thus a mixture of religious platitudes and *Realpolitik*—this because he said that the Sultan in effect had forfeited the right to rule because he had failed to control the nomads, with the trader casting himself in the role of the Khedive's most loyal servant. Al-Zubayr does not really or honestly address, although he was evidently aware of the problem, the issue of the right of a Muslim to make war on another Muslim.

Ibrahim apparently ignored al-Zubayr's letters—there was little else he could do—judging by the latter's constant complaints that he never received any answers to them. On the issue of the Rizayqat there was little the Sultan could say; he lacked the means to control the nomads. Apart from the battlefield, the Sultan's response was twofold, spiritual and diplomatic. A brief letter from Ibrahim—in fact the only extant

---

31 Ibid., 19-22.

document from him in which he uses the throne-name *al-mu'tasim bi
'llahi*, "Safe-guarded in God"—has survived. In this letter (no doubt
originally one of many) addressed to the Awlad Jabir holy clan near
Mellit, he requests them to make a thousand complete recitations
(*khatma*) of the Koran, "For victory over the enemy".[32]

The other response was diplomatic; Gustav Nachtigal, who left al-
Fashir on 2 July 1874, volunteered to take a letter to the Ottoman
Grand Vizier, after the Sultan had stressed to him that there were two
Ottoman *farman*s, one from Sultan 'Abd al-Majid (reigned 1839-61),
the other from 'Abd al-'Aziz (1861-76), "Which guaranteed the king
of Darfur his territory and autonomy". To which *farman*s the Sultan
was referring presents a puzzle that will only be resolved in the archives
of Istanbul. On 13 February 1841, 'Abd al-Majid issued two *farman*s to
Muhammad 'Ali Pasha; the second, concerning the Sudan, specifically
includes Darfur as a dependency of Egypt. These *farman*s were confirmed and extended by 'Abd al-'Aziz in a *farman* dated 8 June 1867.[33]
If it is to these *farman*s that Sultan Ibrahim was referring—documents
of which he seems to have had copies—it is hard to see how he could
have interpreted them as guaranteeing his independence.

Darfur does seem to have had occasional diplomatic contact with
the Ottoman state. Thus, as we have seen, 'Abd al-Rahman is said
to have sent presents to the Ottoman Sultan (probably Salim III,
reigned 1789-1807) who in reply bestowed upon him the honorific
al-Rashid, which appeared on the Darfur ruler's seals. Some sixty years
later, in 1855, Charles Cuny reported that when the Wadai Sultan
Muhammad Sharif sought and obtained from the Ottoman Sultan
"*l'investiture de sa souveraineté*", Muhammad al-Husayn, "*Qui rédoute
l'Egypte*", obtained the same; the document announcing this was officially received in al-Fashir with great ceremony.[34] This may be one of
the documents to which Sultan Ibrahim was referring.

---

32 DF 156.18/16. A similarly-worded letter from Sultan Muhammad al-
Husayn survives, although the occasion for it is unknown; see O'Fahey and
Abu Salim (1983), 42.

33 See Hurewitz (1956), i, 120, and Douin (1933-41), i, 442-3.

34 Cuny (1858), 15.

The Sultan did not rely entirely on alleged Ottoman guarantees; he also sought to conciliate the Khedive. He sent a humble letter of submission, dated 4 Rajab 1291/17 August 1874, to Cairo with the merchant, *al-hajj* Hamza.[35] It was, of course, of no avail.

But Darfur's claim to be an independent and sovereign Muslim state, a claim stoutly asserted by Sultan Muhammad al-Fadl to Muhammad 'Ali Pasha some fifty years before (see Chapter Four), counted for nothing in the eyes of al-Zubayr, nor in the eyes of Khartoum and Cairo.

The campaign continued

Meanwhile, the campaign continued; a small force under Rabih Fadl Allah sallied forth from Dara and killed the Birged *shartay*. Despite this success, al-Zubayr stayed in the Dara region, probably waiting for the rainy season to begin in July/August. Nachtigal describes the indecision in al-Fashir,

The king himself did not appear to have made up his mind about what he ought to do. Should he march against the Baharina [*Bahhara*]? Should he send others? Or should he allow them to remain undisturbed in the south as long as they did not threaten him? Most of his advisors and the distinguished men of the capital laboured under the most arrogant self-deception, telling each other and the king of their conviction that God could not possibly agree that their beautiful, great, powerful Darfur, so favoured by God, should fall into the hands of the Turks.[36]

Sometime in July or August, the Sultan did send another army south under his uncle, the *amir* Hasab Allah b. Muhammad al-Fadl.[37] Hasab Allah's army marched south and attempted to besiege

---

35 It is reproduced in Deny (193, plate liii); Deny notes (p. 549) that there were other letters from Sultan Ibrahim in the 'Abdin Archives.

36 Nachtigal (1971-87), iv, 374 & 322.

37 Shuqayr (1903), iii, 77; al-Zubayr says, no doubt rhetorically, that it was 100,000 strong, but shows his knowledge of the sultanate's military and administrative system by giving the names and titles of its commanders: 'Ali al-Tamawi, described as *ra'is al-dadat* al-sultan, i.e. as *abbo daadinga* commander of the *daadinga* slave regiment; Rahma Gomo, who had succeeded Shatta as maqdum with responsiblity for southern Darfur; Hasan b. Abele, *maqdum* in succession to 'Abd Allah Runga, and 'Ali b. Ibrahim

al-Zubayr in Dara—al-Zubayr's tactics were essentially defensive, which gave great advantage to his trained firepower. The sultanate's forces pressed him hard but a night attack drove off Hasab Allah's men, and although they rallied, a second defeat forced the *amir* to retreat northwards.[38]

Ibrahim finally marched south, having "appointed his eldest son Mohammed to rule at El Fasher, after extracting an oath from each of the chief ministers of state to appoint his own son as his representative (*khalifa*)."[39] The Sultan reached Dara on 5 Ramadan 1291/16 October 1874, but in what was to be the decisive battle of the campaign the furious Darfur onslaught was shattered by the rifle-fire of al-Zubayr's men; "At that time the people [of Darfur] did not know of war with rifles".[40] Ibrahim began to withdraw with the remnants of his army towards Jabal Marra, the ancestral home of the dynasty. Nine days later, he had reached as far as Manawashi when al-Zubayr caught up with him; on 14 Ramadan 1291/25 October, in a last stand with virtually only his bodyguard around him, Ibrahim was defeated and killed and the sacred drum, *al-mansura* "The victorious", was captured.[41] On the orders of al-Zubayr, the Sultan's body was honourably buried in the mosque of Shaykh Tahir Abu Jamus at Manawashi.[42]

The downfall of the sultanate was greeted with celebrations in Khartoum and Berber.[43]

Wir, the *abbo daadinga*, to whom the phrase *ra'is dadat* should refer (there is a misprint, Dir for Wir; the confusion is compounded by the fact that the *abbo daadinga* lineage is of Tama origin).

38 Shuqayr (1903), iii, 77-8 and Jackson (1913), 63-5; among the spoils al-Zubayr says he took from Hasab Allah were eight cannon.

39 Jackson (1913), 65-6 and Shuqayr (1903) iii, 79.

40 AP, 3/13, 48-50, a brief Arabic note on the battle.

41 Ibid.; the Sultan had with him only his household troops, the *korkwa* and *soming dogala*.

42 Shuqayr (1903), iii, 79-80 and Jackson (1913, 67-8. Some of the spoils taken at Manawashi are described in Thomas (1923), 1-36 & 137-85.

43 Chaillé-Long (1876), 219-20 and Marno (1874), 10.

13
DARFUR, 1874 TO 1916

Umm Kwakiyya:[1] the beginnings of resistance

Al-Zubayr Pasha destroyed the Darfur Sultanate and killed the Sultan, Ibrahim Qarad, at a final battle at Manawashi on 25 October 1874. He thus brought to an end the existence of an independent African Muslim state that had emerged in the mid-seventeenth century, but which was heir to a state-forming tradition going back, probably, to the twelfth century.

From 1874 until the outbreak of the Mahdist Revolution in 1882, Darfur was theoretically a part of the Turco-Egyptian Sudan. However, throughout these years the cause of the Keira dynasty was kept alive in Jabal Marra and the Fur lands, where the Fur clung to their old patrimony from the days of the first great ruler of the dynasty who had brought them down from the mountains, Sulayman Solongdungo. This Jabal Marra state, or focus of resistance, was to be nearly swamped by the Mahdist cataclysm, but never entirely extinguished. The idea of Darfur in some sense survived.

A week after Manawashi al-Zubayr entered al-Fashir, where he was joined a few days later by Isma'il Pasha, the Turco-Egyptian governor of the Sudan, who had advanced slowly across eastern Darfur

---

1   A term used by a number of my informants of the period from Manawashi to the restoration, 1874-98 (*kawakiyya* may mean "gunfire").

from Kordofan.[2] The Pasha soon began to organise the new province, dividing it into four *mudiriyya*s or sub-provinces, roughly following the old *maqdum*ate commands, under a Governor-General. Plans to suppress slavery and impose a poll-tax were to cause trouble, but very soon an administration of sorts, staffed in many cases by personnel from the sultanate, was in being. Among those who joined the new administration were two prominent merchants based at the sultanate's commercial capital of Kobbei, the brothers Hamza, who had taken Ibrahim's letter to Cairo, and Muhammad b. Imam, and two of the *'ulama* to whom al-Zubayr had written, Muhammad Salama and al-Daw al-Masri.[3]

The superstructure of the Keira state had seemingly collapsed overnight, but the appearance was illusory. Among the Keira there were, inevitably, both collaborators and resisters; thus 'Abd al-Rahman Shattut, a brother of Sultan Ibrahim, soon made his peace with Ayyub and ended up as a pensioner in Cairo, while a number of Keira royal women married into the new elite.[4] Thus, al-Nur 'Anqara married Bakhita, a daughter of Muhammad al-Husayn, while Muhammad Khalid Zuqal (a cousin of the future Mahdi), who was to play a key role in the Mahdist take-over of Darfur, married another daughter, 'Arafa; according to Slatin, "This good lady had hundreds of male and female slaves, and kept up her state in true Sudanese fashion."[5] The most famous example of intermarriage was the Mahdi himself who married Maqbula bt. Muhammad Nurayn, the latter a

---

2 Shukry (1938), 229-31 contrives to present Ayyub as the real conqueror of Darfur, but this is farfetched. It is hard to see how, for example, his capture of Umm Shanqa in September 1874 can be said to have relieved al-Zubayr at Dara, several hundred kilometres to the south.

3 For the two brothers, see Hill (1967), 150-1, and for Muhammad Salama, Ahmad Amin 'Abd al-Hamid, al-Fashir 7.5. 1970. Al-Daw appears as a witness to a judicial record of a lawsuit concerning a land dispute heard before Isma'il Pasha dated 30 Rabi' I 1292/6 May 1875. In it, the Pasha confirms a charter issued by Sultan Muhammad al-Husayn; DF 12.3/1, the only Turkiyya document so far found in Darfur.

4 Shukry (1938), 232 and Chaillé-Long (1876), 294-5.

5 Slatin (1896), 274, and Muhammad 'Abd al-Rahim, *al-Durr al-manthur*, (ms. NRO, Khartoum), p. 213.

son of Sultan Muhammad al-Fadl; Maqbula became the mother of Sayyid 'Abd al-Rahman al-Mahdi.[6]

The first leader of the resistance was the *amir* Hasab Allah who retreated into the Marra Mountains to continue the struggle. Here began a divergence in interests and policy between al-Zubayr and Ayyub; the former followed the *amir* into the mountains and captured him together with many of Sultan Ibrahim's family and notables without resistance. Al-Zubayr proposed that Hasab Allah be allowed to govern Darfur on behalf of the Khedive on payment of a regular tribute, a policy that might have avoided much of the later bloodshed.[7] Ayyub rejected this plan and sent Hasab Allah and Muhammad al-Fadl b. Ibrahim, his father's nominated successor, to Cairo, where he also wrote suggesting that al-Zubayr's power was quite extensive enough and that he need be given no share in governing Darfur.[8]

But Keira resistance was only beginning; Bosh, a son of Sultan Muhammad al-Fadl, proclaimed himself sultan and he and his brother, Sayf al-Din, soon controlled Jabal Marra. Al-Zubayr marched back into the mountains and forced the brothers to retreat towards Kabkabiyya, where they were both killed.[9] Al-Zubayr continued his progress westwards as far as the borders of the Wadai sultanate, spreading terror and destruction wherever he went. Upon his return, the rift with Ayyub deepened, allegedly over the question of taxation; al-Zubayr, enraged at his treatment, went in June 1875 to Cairo to complain.[10] It was the slave trader's greatest blunder, for he was not allowed to return to the Sudan until 1899.

While Darfur was being "opened up" by the new regime and its motley collection of European officials and "experts", Keira resist-

---

6   SAD, Sandison's Papers. A letter survives from Muhammad Nurayn; Bergen, DF195.18/55, undated.

7   Shuqayr (1903), iii, 81-2, and Jackson (1913), 70-2.

8   Shukry (1938), 232-4.

9   Shuqayr (1903), iii, 82, and Slatin (1896), 55-6. Al-Zubayr's campaigning in the mountains are said to have depopulated several valleys; PA (al-Fashir), *Western Darfur District Handbook*.

10 Shaw (1887), 671-5, and Shuqayr (1903), iii, 84-5.

ance coalesced in 1876-77 around Muhammad Harun al-Rashid b. Sayf al-Din, who kept up the struggle until his death in 1880.[11] Muhammad Harun al-Rashid based himself at Jabal Nurnya towards the southern and more thickly-populated end of Jabal Marra, and was supported by most of the Fur *shartays*; his writ ran as far as Dar Kerne in the west, while he had supporters as far east as al-Tuwaysha.[12] By 1879 G.B. Messedaglia, the Italian *mudir* at Dara, credited him with 17,000 men, of whom 6,000 were armed with Remingtons.[13] The Keira had learnt quickly.

Harun al-Rashid soon controlled Jabal Si to the north, laid siege to al-Fashir and threatened Dara. His activities were the more ominous in that he apparently planned to join forces with al-Zubayr's son, Sulayman, who was operating in the south with most of his father's men and provided a second focus of opposition to the Turco-Egyptians.[14]

These were the years remembered in Darfur as *umm kwakiyya* or years of banditry and misery; the province was in a state of chaos with bands of slave troops and nomads roaming at will, a bankrupt administration and continual warfare. Even before he reached Darfur, Gordon (Governor-General of the Sudan, 1877-80), on his way to make his first visit in 1877, opined that, "I would not try to reconquer

---

11 Much has been written on the fighting with Muhammad Harun al-Rashid and subsequent events by the various European officials involved. The most useful account is Messedaglia (1886), of which a translation was made by the Sudan Intelligence Department, Khartoum January 1916, NRO, Khartoum. Messedaglia's assertion that Muhammad Harun al-Rashid was not a Keira but a Fallati is without foundation. A useful survey of this period is Zach (1987), 157-69.

12 The former sultans had a "summer" *fashir* or palace at Jabal Nurnya; Messedaglia (1888), 45. In his (1886), transl. p. 9, he lists the *shartays*, while PA, (al-Fashir), *Western Darfur District Handbook* confirms that Muhammad Harun al-Rashid regularly appointed and dismissed *shartays* and *dimlijs*.

13 Messedaglia (1886), transl., 7 & 9 for the arrest of people at Kobbei and al-Tuwaysha for supplying Harun al-Rashid with gunpowder. A letter from the Sultan to *shartay* Tahir written in the normal Keira chancery style and dated 16 Shawwal 1296/3 October 1879 is reproduced in Messedaglia (1935), opp. p. 202; see also Abu Salim (1975), 140-1.

14 Holt (1970), 38-9 and Zaccaria (2001), 115-34.

Darfour - it is quite worthless." By the time of a second tour in 1879, his opinion was, "The only hope is to restore the old regime as soon as possible."[15] He wrote to Cairo asking for a suitable member of the Keira pensioned there to be sent down, and released from prison in Sawakin the former *maqdum* Rahma Gomo, to act as regent.[16] But these plans came to nothing.

The revolt of the *Bahhara* was crushed and Sulayman was shot in July 1879 by the Italian Romolo Gessi. Thereafter Messedaglia and the Austrians Francesco Emiliani dei Danziger and R.C. Slatin gradually wore Harun al-Rashid down, driving him further into the mountains; eventually in March 1880 he and his dwindling band of followers were trapped and killed by al-Nur Bey Muhammad 'An-qara, now in service with the new regime.[17]

Despite Harun al-Rashid's death, the Keira were by no means finished and 'Abd Allah Dud Banja b. Abi Bakr, a grandson of Sul-tan Muhammad al-Fadl, emerged, apparently after some internal conflict, as sultan in Jabal Marra.[18] And so he remained until the province was engulfed by the Mahdist Revolution in 1882.

These political conflicts were played out against a backdrop of internal refugees, raid and counter-raid, displacement of peoples and famine. The following are from a note on Kabkabiyya written in 1936,

When Zubair having disposed of Ibrahim turned his attention to the west for slaves and booty. Hussain was Ali wad Magdum [*maqdum*] in Kebkebia. He in company with the 4 Shartais (Adam Hanafi of Fia, Abbakr Daldum of Madi, Othman Muzammil of Kerni [Kerne] and ..... [*sic* in original] of Kuniar [Konyir] were persuaded to meet at Kulkul near Birket Saira and were all put to death on the spot.

---

15 Hill (1884), 238 & 350; Gordon's letters in 1877 and 1879 (233-90 and 340-71) give a vivid picture of the pitiable state of the province.

16 Ibid., 355 and Messedaglia (1935), 126-7.

17 The details of the fighting with Harun al-Rashid can be found in Messedaglia (1886), Slatin (1896), 56-85, and Messedaglia (1950), 89-100. On Gessi and Sulayman, see Gessi (1989), 253-78.

18 al-Hasan (1970), 39-40.

During his [Adam effendi 'Umar, the Turco-Eygptian governor of Kabka-biyya] "rule" the whole area was practically depopulated; those who had es-caped the clutches of Zubair had fled west to Tama and Bergo [Wadai].[19]

The Mahdiyya[20] in Darfur[21]

The history of the Mahdist period in Darfur is complex and multi-sided. Mahdism, that is the belief in a divinely-guided being who will restore the kingdom of God on earth, in this case embodied in the figure of Muhammad Ahmad b. 'Abd Allah (1844-85), ap-pears to have had very little appeal to the non-Arab communities in Darfur. Why is a complex question: linguistic issues may well have been important—who spoke Arabic and who did not; the lack of penetration among the settled farmers of the neo-Sufi movements that in the Nile Valley and, to a lesser degree, among the nomads, laid the foundations for the later success of the Mahdiyya (Chapter Ten). The Fur, Masalit and others still lived encapsulated in their own worlds.

The Mahdist *da'wa* or "call" found its greatest resonance among the nomads. Here, there may have been two impulses of importance: one, the role of the Sammaniyya *tariqa* among the cattle-nomads and the other, the role of various influential Fulani holy families, who in turn may well have been influenced by the Fulani *jihad* of Usuman dan Fodio (d. 1817) in the area that later became Northern Nigeria and the messianic and eschatological impulses it gave rise to throughout the central Sudanic belt (this may in part explain why al-Zubayr wrote to the Fulani *'ulama*). In regard to Darfur, the Mah-diyya has a twofold significance; it enmeshed the region in the wider politics of the Sudan and ultimately the imperialist designs of the

---

19 PA (Kutum), NDD 66. b. 8/2 Tribal, Dar Fia: Fur. De Waal (2005), 62-6 well describes the famines and miseries of these years, but his understanding of 'Ali Dinar's role (he was certainly no millenarian) is flawed.

20 Mahdiyya is used here both of the period 1882-98 and of the movement. On the idea of a Mahdi in both the wider Islamic and particular Sudanese context, see Abu Salim (2004).

21 Al-Hasan (1970) is still the standard work on the subject.

British, and it defined a cleavage between two different conceptions of Islam, "Mahdist faith" and "Sudanic tradition"—that is, between a holistic, not to say totalitarian, understanding of Islam's role in society and an understanding of Islam as being accommodating to a local context. Mahdism was to draw Darfur into the Sudan, not so much in the Mahdist period but later, in the 1920s and 30s, through the movement Hasan Ahmad Ibrahim calls neo-Mahdism; by contrast Sudanic faith was responsible for the emergence of a new state in the region, the Masalit Sultanate, and was a force behind the restoration of the Keira Sultanate under 'Ali Dinar (r.1898-1916). These two tendencies are still operative in the Sudan today.

The Mahdi's agent in Darfur was his cousin, Muhammad Khalid Zuqal who was married to 'Arafa, a daughter of Sultan Muhammad al-Husayn, and who had been a trader in both Darfur and Wadai and was now an official in the Turco-Egyptian administration.[22] Zuqal successfully began to mobilise support for the Mahdi especially among the Baqqara, but the turning point came outside Darfur with the battle of Shaykan (north of al-Ubayyid in Kordofan) in November 1883, when the Mahdi's army destroyed an Egyptian army under a British general, William Hicks. Shaykan made the Egyptian position in Darfur untenable; by January 1884 Slatin and the Egyptian garrisons in Dara and al-Fashir had surrendered, as did 'Abd Allah Dud Banja later that year.[23]

The Mahdi died in June 1885 a few months after the fall of Khartoum and the death of Charles Gordon; he was succeeded by the Khalifa 'Abdullahi b. Muhammad, a Ta'aishi from southwestern Darfur.[24] Darfur was now part of the Mahdist state, but in a state of

---

22 Qasim (1996), ii, 1019.

23 Al-Hasan (1970), 68. Dud Banja became an enthusiastic Mahdist and died fighting the Ethiopians. Slatin converted to Islam in order to rally his troops, but to no avail; see Hill (1965), 17-20.

24 On the Darfur and West African dimensions to the Khalifa's accession, see Abu Manga, Hunwick et al. (1998), 85-108. The first to swear allegiance to the Khalifa, in what appears to have been a carefully stage-managed event, was an aged Fulani holy man, Muhammad al-Dadari, who had served many decades before in the jihad of Dan Fodio. There is a specifically Darfurian Fulani dimension to the Mahdiyya that invites further research.

utter ruin, while Keira ambitions were far from dormant. When the Khalifa, still feeling somewhat insecure, summoned the fomentor of Mahdism in Darfur to join him in Omdurman, Muhammad Khalid Zuqal left his nephew by marriage Yusuf, a son of Sultan Ibrahim Qarad, behind to govern the province. Almost immediately Yusuf began to restore the sultanate and by 1887 was openly defiant of Mahdist authority. He revived the *maqdum*s and was able to mobilise substantial forces. Darfur was, however, vital to the Khalifa and he sent his young but able kinsman, 'Uthman Adam Jano, to reconquer the province. Jano, whose ruthlessness is still remembered in Darfur, crushed Yusuf in a series of battles and the Sultan was finally trapped and killed in February 1888.[25]

It was at this time in the early and mid-1880s that the Masalit began to be unified by two figures, Hajjam Hasab Allah in the Egyptian period and Isma'il 'Abd al-Nabi (d. 1889); it is from the latter that the present sultans of Dar Masalit descend.[26] But Yusuf's death and the beginnings of what became the Masalit state were only part of the prelude to the messianic rising of Abu Jummayza. What Abu Jummayza, whose real name was Muhammad Zayn, claimed to be religiously is a complicated question, but Kapteijns' informants, as well as Mahdist sources, were of the opinion that he claimed the position of the *khalifa*ship of 'Uthman b. 'Affan, which the Mahdi had offered to Muhammad al-Mahdi al-Sanusi (d.1902), the head of the Sanusiyya brotherhood in Libya, an offer ignored by the latter.[27]

---

25 Al-Hasan (1970), 100-9 and 116-23.

26 Kapteijns (1985) is an authoritative account of the rise and history of the Masalit Sultanate.

27 Kapteijns (1985), 83-99, al-Hasan (1970), 147-80 and Holt (1970), 157-8 quoting a letter from Jano to the Khalifa. The acting out by the Mahdi of the *sira* or sacred biography of the Prophet involved appointing of three of his closest followers to fill the positions held by the first three orthodox caliphs in succession to the Prophet; thus the Khalifa 'Abdullahi "became" the Caliph Abu Bakr (632-34), while the fourth *khalifa*ship, that of 'Uthman b. 'Affan (644-56), was offered to the Sanusi leader; see ibid., 119-20. Muhammad al-Mahdi in a letter to the Egyptian ruler does not allude to this, but makes clear his opposition to the Mahdi's claims; see Abu Salim (2004), 521-2. On the involvement of the Zaghawa in the Abu Jummayza movement, see 'Uthman (2006), 258-69.

Whatever his actual claims, Abu Jummayza seems to have had the
authority and charisma to unite behind him most of the disaffected
groups in Darfur. At the head of a host, he marched against Jano.
Among Abu Jummayza's allies were the Masalit, Fur irreconcilables
led by Yusuf's successor as nominal Sultan, Abu'l-Khayrat b. Ibrahim
Qarad, the Zaghawa and other western tribes. Abu Jummayza carried all before him, but died before the final battle in February 1889
just outside al-Fashir. With Abu Jummayza's death and the dispersal
(rather than defeat) of his followers, Abu'l-Khayrat fled for refuge to
the Daju state of Dar Sila in the far west (in modern Chad).

"We were scattered among the trees"

Abu'l-Khayrat was forced to leave Dar Sila and returned to Jabal
Marra where in late 1890 or early 1891 he was murdered in mysterious circumstances.[28] He was succeeded as titular Sultan by 'Ali
Dinar, a grandson by an unremarkable father of Sultan Muhammad
al-Fadl. In his brief *apologia*, 'Ali Dinar describes the bitterness of
the times:

Such was the desolation of Darfur that we were scattered among the trees,
wilderness and mountains.

He continues by implicitly rebutting the accusation of complicity
in Abu'l-Khayrat's murder.

Yusuf died and was succeeded by his brother, Abu'l-Khayrat. We were not
involved in this matter but stayed in the swamps, forest and wilderness where
none of us owned even a chicken. Then his slaves and servants betrayed him
and deliberately stabbed him to death upon the ground. They then agreed
among themselves to appoint me to succeed, I, the humble slave [of God]; I
reminded them of my faults, which I had committed in the world. But they
called me—this slave—and told me, "We hated Abu'l-Khayrat; we propose
to make you sultan over us". But I told them, "I don't want it; I am unqua-
lified in such matters. Truthfully, I am finished, insignificant and poor. Do

---

28 According to Boustead (1939), 149-53, he was murdered at 'Ali Dinar's
orders. Not surprisingly, this is denied by the latter's relatives, see Theobald
(1965), 27-8. A less partisan account which exonerates 'Ali Dinar is given
by Abu'l-Khayrat's brother, 'Abd al-Hamid b. Ibrahim Qarad, see SAD,
511/4, P.J. Sandison's Papers.

not give the kingdom to any save a brother [of the previous Sultan]. I own nothing, not a goat, nothing." I went on and on in this vein until my speech was exhausted. "By God", they said, "You shall be with us in this affair, or we shall kill you". The orderlies were standing by me with weapons as a precaution; they were threatening me with words, "You know that we killed Abu'l-Khayrat." I saw them persisting with these words against me and said, "Protected is the believer in himself, better it is if you kill me". But I stayed with them, accepting their decision until God should judge the matter.

This was how I succeeded to the rule over them, just as God commanded; and thus does God ordain His eternal affairs according to His judgment; He alone knows, no other knows. I then assembled the people of the country and they told me, "Go to the Mahdiyya."[29]

'Ali Dinar had little choice and on 13 October 1891, after desultory negotiations, he and his dwindling band rode into al-Fashir. Here he surrendered to the Mahdist governor, 'Abd al-Qadir Dalil.[30] According to the Sultan, 'Abd al-Qadir's father had been a slave of his aunt, Zamzam Umm al-Nasr, the formidable daughter of Sultan Muhammad al-Fadl. The humiliation he felt comes through vividly in his brief autobiography, especially when, as he claims, he was tricked into drinking wine, imprisoned and stripped of his property, women and slaves. After thirty days' imprisonment he was released and later escorted to Omdurman, where he spent the next six years half-prisoner, half-reluctant Mahdist and a casual acquaintance of another Mahdist prisoner, R.C. Slatin.[31]

In the meantime the Masalit under Abbakr Isma'il were consolidating themselves in Dar Masalit and the Zaghawa were effectively outside anyone's control. But the situation in Darfur was so desperate that 'Uthman Adam Jano held a great tribal gathering in Dara in about June 1889, where he attempted in effect to set up a system of

---

29 From an untitled autobiographical fragment by 'Ali Dinar, of which two versions are known to the present writer. One is a photocopy in 17ff. of an untraced original in the library of the NRO, Khartoum and which is dated 9 Ramadan 1330/23 August 1912. The other of 11ff., which has only small lexical and stylistic variations, is in AP1, 3/13, ff. 1-11. An English précis is given as "A fragment from Ali Dinar", (1953), 114-16.

30 Theobald (1965), 28-9.

31 Hill (1965), 93.

indirect rule; the Mahdists effectively controlled the area bounded by Jabal Meidob in the north, al-Fashir, al-Tuwaysha in the east and Dara in the south. Western Darfur was outside the Mahdist state; only around al-Fashir, and probably Dara, was there any semblance of administration.[32]

The restoration of the Sultanate: 'Ali Dinar, 1898-1916[33]

Listen, in every part of my country where I find a hyena who kills someone's animal, a lion that eats someone's animal, a man of the people who seizes his brother's property, or something like this happening in my land, then I shall arouse myself against this. Thus, with God's support, the wild beasts will not kill the livestock; the hobbled camel will go from Fashir to Kutum without anything happening to it; the thief will neither interfere with nor touch it. The well-dressed woman will be able to go wherever she wishes without anyone bothering her. There will be true security, not partial security.

'Ali Dinar[34]

Then God imposed the English Government upon [the Mahdists]. God dispersed the Khalifa's group and people and God scattered them all.[35]

'Ali Dinar

---

32 Holt (1970), 165; a brief glimpse of the Mahdist day-to-day administration under Jano's successor, Mahmud Ahmad who ruled from 1891 to 1897, is given in Hunwick (2002), 21-5.

33 In what follows I have chosen to focus on two aspects of 'Ali Dinar's rule, his religious policies and his efforts to rebuild the state. The wider aspects of British imperial policies, British and French rivalries in the Central Sudan and Darfur's very marginal role in the politics of the First World War are not my concern here. If I may venture a personal judgment, based on having read most of 'Ali Dinar's writings, I have a sense that he was well aware of his ultimate powerlessness in the face of the forces around him.

34 A speech by Sultan 'Ali Dinar as remembered by *al-hajj* Muhammad al-Bideyati and as recorded in the unpublished *Eléments pour une histoire du Dar-Fur au temps d'Ali Dinar* by Isa Hasan Khayar, Marie-José et Joseph Tubiana.

35 'Ali Dinar, NRO ms., f 8.

As Kitchener approached Omdurman in August 1898, 'Ali Dinar was evidently planning his return to Darfur. Either immediately before or after the battle of Karari, the sultan escaped south to Tur'at al-Khadra, the region just north of Kosti, where his followers seized some of the Khalifa's camels before turning west to Kajmar to link up with various followers from Darfur.[36] It was no wild solo dash; 'Ali Dinar had with him a group of notables who between them represented a good part of the old sultanate's "establishment".[37]

With this support, he was able to brush aside a local pretender, Abu Kawda, the Mahdist garrison in al-Fashir under Ambadda al-Raddi, and a dilatory claimant, 'Ali, a son of Ibrahim Qarad who had the theoretical support of Kitchener.[38] By late October 'Ali Dinar was firmly esconced in al-Fashir.

But this was only the beginning; Darfur was in chaos and still overrun by remnants of the Mahdist regime; 'Arabi Daf' Allah was at large in the south, the fervent Mahdist *faqih* Sanin Husayn was entrenched at Kabkabiyya on the vital route through Jabal Marra, and on the western borders the Masalit had created their own sultanate in imitation of their former Keira masters. Theobald has described the measures taken by the Sultan to rid himself of the surviving

---

36 Shuqayr (1903), iii, 672. The inconclusive evidence on the timing of his departure is discussed in Theobald (1965), 30-1, and Zulfu (1973), 419-20. My own feeling is that the whole affair was well planned.

37 Their names are given in a letter from the pretender Abu Kawda to 'Ali Dinar while the latter was en route to al-Fashir; the letter survives in two versions (4.4/1 and DF251.28). Both are modern versions that have been written down following oral transmission of the lost original. Among the notables with 'Ali Dinar were Amin 'Abd al-Hamid (Fallata; of the Awlad 'Ali lineage), Mahmud 'Ali al-Dadinqawi (Fur), Mustafa w. Bahr (Aqaba Zaghawa), Khatir Ibrahim (Fur), al-Doma Salih (Simiyat), al-Zayn Salih Dunqus (Bideyat), Ahmad Rashid (Tunjur), Muhammad Kebkebe (Beigo) and Abbakr 'Umar (Borqu). The absence of Arab names may or may not be significant.

38 Theobald (1965), 31-2. Little is known about Abu Kawda; he was deposed by 'Ali Dinar who is said to have made him *malik al-hadadin* or "king of the blacksmiths"—blacksmiths being a despised endogamous group in Darfur. He was "in power" long enough to issue at least one charter confirming an estate just south of al-Fashir, dated 2 Jumada II 1316/18 October 1898 (DF1.1/1). See Lampen (1950), 196.

Mahdists and to preserve distant relations with the Condominium regime in Khartoum, paying an annual tribute to avoid trouble.[39] Equally important was a series of costly campaigns in the south to push back the cattle nomads who had profited from the preceding quarter century of anarchy to encroach on the lands of the settled peoples. All these actions were based on the twin policies of asserting the Sultan's authority as widely as possible in Darfur and fending off Kitchener, Slatin and Wingate in Khartoum. It took time and was never completely successful—the Sultan was forced to accept the Masalit *fait accompli* and the Baqqara were only partially contained, while the Rizayqat under Musa Madibbu (d. 1920), armed by and allied to the British from Kordofan, were completely outside the Sultan's sway, while the Kababish of northern Kordofan and the Meidob were involved in constant cross-border raids. Nevertheless, by 1916, the year of the British invasion, 'Ali Dinar had consolidated his control over the sultanate's core lands.[40]

A general comment: by comparison with that of his forefathers, 'Ali Dinar's rule was autocratic; he had to be, Darfur was in too great a mess to have reverted overnight to the ordered hierarchy of the old sultanate. Oral sources in al-Fashir, reflecting an uncomfortable closeness, emphasise the Sultan's self-will and sternness. With a mixture of necessity and personality, 'Ali Dinar ruled his state directly. This directness comes out in all his policies and actions. To strengthen his authority as Sultan, he had to emphasise continuity with the past, while the threat of messianism forced him into somewhat paradoxical religious policies. Since Mahdism had reverberated down to the Sudanese undergrowth, it had to be fought both by

---

39 Theobald (1965), 33-55. There is nothing to suggest that 'Ali Dinar felt that he owed his throne to the British or that he was their *mandub* or "agent" (as Wingate described him). He paid tribute because, "It was only agreed upon by certain friends and advisors out of pity on the worshippers of God, to avoid friction and trouble", SAD, 128/1, 'Ali Dinar to Wingate (transl. only), 1916; see Theobald (1965), 143.

40 There is absolutely no factual basis for Wingate's expectation of "The disintegration of Darfur which is groaning under him—as the Sudan groaned under the Khalifa"; SAD 127/2, Wingate to Kitchener, 15 March 1916.

asserting orthodoxy and by arrogating to the Sultan himself the attributes of a *wali* or saint.

The Sultan's methods and the ideology articulating them can be
traced in some detail through his surviving correspondence. He soon
reconstituted his court and central administration, calling in various
chiefs to assist him; thus on 2 November 1898 he wrote to al-Doma
Muhammad, chief of Dar Simiyat, to come to al-Fashir with his
elders: "They were to assist him in deliberations and consultations."[41]
Others needed no invitation; there was a veritable rush in 1898-99 of
holders of estates or privileged status to have their pre-1874 charters
renewed.[42] In the preamble to these charters, the Sultan explicitly
sets forth the principles of the restoration; emphasis is laid on his
desire to follow in his ancestors' footsteps.

You are well aware of the constancy and good qualities of [our] late fathers
and grandfathers—May God's favour be upon them all and may He show
them benevolence and favour—to all who were in their state (*dawla*) and
to whosoever sought their mercy and assistance, whether by [gifts of] land,
almsgiving or abundant donations. They were our fathers—without boast-
ing—and we are, like them, of equal generosity and [and intend to follow]
in their ways and footsteps, God Willing, so that He will not deny us our
reward [in heaven].[43]

---

41 DF17.6/2, 17 Jumada II 1316.

42 Among examples of the "rush", we have:
(a) DF18/26/1; 24 Jumada II 1316/9 November 1898—an estate near al-
Fashir.
(b) 30.7/3; 28 Jumada II 1316/15 November 1898—*jah*-status for 'Ali Najm
al-Din of Jadid al-Sayl.
(c) 130.14/5; 4 Sha'ban 1316/18 December 1898—an estate at Jadid al-Sayl.
(d) 91.11/5; 5 Sha'ban 1316/19 December 1898—*jah*-status for some Berti holy
men.
(e) 138.16/1; 14 Dhu'l-qa'da 1316/4 April 1899—an estate at al-Tawila.
(f) 112.12/20; 2 Safar 1317/12 June 1899—an estate at Kamala Keirei.
(g) 6.1/6; Rajab 1317/November-December 1899—an estate at al-Firsh.
(h) 144.18/4; 1316/1898-99 —*jah*-status in Dar Zayyadiyya.
(i) 287.38/7; 24 Dhu'l-hijja 1317/1899-1900—*jah*-status in Nyala district.

43 DF32.7/5; 24 Dhu'l-hijja 1318/14 April 1901—a charter granting an estate
to Hamad 'Abd al-Qadir.

Equally stressed was the theme of physical restoration. 'Abd al-Rahman w. Makki was a leading member of the Fallata Juba clan who had supplied a number of imams to the sultans since the time of Sultan Muhammad Tayrab. Like so many others, 'Abd al-Rahman had fled to Wadai during the Mahdiyya; on his return he was offered the position of imam by the Sultan, but declined it on the grounds of old age. The Sultan then commissioned him to resettle Qoz Kubra,

Inasmuch as [our] purpose is the care of the people and the rebuilding of every district with its people.[44]

Two years later, in 1902, the Sultan confirmed 'Abd al-Rahman's rights over some deserted land (*bobaya*) at al-Shawa Kasa, since the latter had

Revived it after [it had become] deserted land (*kharab*) and restored it, so that its former inhabitants have prospered there…. And in accordance with our desire for the restoration of the lands and the revivification of the former districts and country, we have confirmed for 'Abd al-Rahman Makki ownership (*milk*) of the deserted land (*bobaya*).[45]

A little later come various decrees appointing chiefs; for example, on 13 July 1900 Muhammad 'Ali Salih was appointed chief of the 'Irayqat Arabs, while nearly a year before, on 28 September 1899, Muhammad Adam Sharif was appointed *maqdum* or governor of the northern province. A year later, the *maqdum*'s estates in the north, to the number of seven, were restored to him.[46]

One obvious priority was the creation of a functioning judicial system. 'Ali Dinar sought to provide for legal continuity, issuing a general decree that all those who had cases pending from the Mahdiyya or Abu Kawda's brief "reign" should present them to their local chiefs.[47] The Sultan, however, broke with tradition by appointing a *qadi al-qudat*; in the pre-1874 sultanate there had been senior judges

---

44 DF74.9/1; 17 Dhu'l-hijja 1317/16 April 1900. On 'Abd al-Rahmn, see Bidayn (1995), 68-9.

45 DF75.9/2; 23 Jumada II 1320/27 September 1902.

46 DF15.5/1; 15 Rabi' I 1318 ('Irayqat). The *maqdum*'s two letters are DF266.33/1; 22 Jumada II 1317 & DF269.33/4; 1318/1899-1900.

47 DF232.28/3; 5 Ramadan 1316/17 January 1899.

but no clearly-defined head of the judicial hierarchy. He now appointed the Dunqulawi, Idris 'Abd Allah, as *qadi 'umum Dar Fur*, a position he retained until the conquest of 1916.[48] He also reappointed the former Mahdist judge Hamad 'Abd al-Qadir as deputy judge (*na'ib shar'i*) of the Dar Simiyat and Jadid al-Sayl region.[49] But to what extent he retained the Mahdist judiciary in the areas he controlled is not yet known.

These remarks are impressionistic; nothing has been said of the Sultan's taxation or military reforms.[50] Here he was more innovatory, borrowing freely from what he had seen in Omdurman; one no doubt unwelcome innovation was the Mahdist levy in cash (mus'ada). His armed forces were organised along Mahdist lines, their core being slave troops or *jihadiyyya* armed with rifles. As in all matters, he combined old and new in an ongoing effort to restore his state. He was even more original in his religious policies.

"The revival of religion"

The old sultans had lived hedged about by rituals that were much more Fur than Islamic (see Chapter Five). If 'Ali Dinar decisively rejected the easygoing *takhlit* or "mixed" Islam of his forefathers, he was as vehemently opposed to Mahdism, preferring a combination of an al-Azhar type of "establishment" Islam, with a due subordination of "church" to state, and Sufism. The real significance of the Mahdiyya for 'Ali Dinar was that it led him to formulate a conscious external and internal religious policy, even to producing an interpretation of Darfur's past for the benefit of the Ottoman Sultan:

We are related to the Prophet through his uncle El Abbas. God had willed that my grandfather [probably, *jaddi*, "ancestor"] should emigrate to Darfur and be a mercy to the Furs in preaching Islam to them, which they

48 As he is entitled in two surviving letters from him; DF29.7/2; 16 Rabi' I 1319/3 July 1901 and DF182.18/42; 25 Rabi' I 1329/26 March 1911. Both are letters confirming that certain *fuqara* had valid sultanic charters. See also al-Mufti (1387/1959), i, 70-1.

49 DF33.7/6; 1316/1898-99.

50 See Theobald (1965), 208-19.

embraced abandoning their former worship of heathenism—they had worshipped stones and trees, and he brought them the light; God granted unto his descendants the sceptre of royalty over the Fur country. Many of the Furs became Fikis and Ulemas and ascetics, who preached and founded Islam. The above facts are true and are recorded in our history—it took place since 870 years, long before Constantinople was conquered.[51]

At the outset he was still influenced by Mahdist ways; his secretaries whom he inherited from the Mahdist authorities continued for the first few years to use the Mahdist greeting, *habibi* (pl. *ahbabuna*), "dear one, friend". His slave troops were called *ansar* or "Companions" (in imitation of Prophetic practice).[52] But *habibi* was soon dropped and the older forms re-emerged, though in a more religious guise.[53] A significant innovation was the incorporation of the claim to 'Abbasid descent into his formal titles (see the quotation above); the old sultans had vaguely claimed such descent, but they scarcely referred to it in their documents, even when they had not blushed to use such Mamluk or Ottoman titles as *khadim al-haramayn al-sharifayn*, "Servant of the Two Holy Places (i.e. Mecca and Medina)", or *sultan al-bahrayn wa'l-barrayn*, "Sultan of the Two Seas and Lands".[54]

A practical expression of the Sultan's policy was "The rebuilding of mosques and the revival of religious ceremonies".[55] Mosques were built or rebuilt in red brick at al-Fashir, his birthplace Shawaya (near Malumm in the south), Dara and al-Firsh (south of al-Fashir).[56] In al-Fashir he built not only a mosque but also a *qubba* or domed tomb for his father, Zakariyya, to which was attached a small mosque, and a school for the sons of leading chiefs and *fuqara*. The Kinana fuqara

---

51 SAD 129/3, 'Ali Dinar to the Ottoman Sultan (transl. only), 8 Jumada I 1334/14 March 1916.

52 DF218.26/1, 24 Jumada II 1316/9 November 1898.

53 Documents from the pre-1874 sultans rarely opened with a basmala—"In the name of God, the Compassionate, the Merciful"; those of 'Ali Dinar always did.

54 "al-'Abbasi, al-Hashimi" appears in DF32.7/5; 24 Dhu'l-hijja 1318/14 April 1901.

55 DF299.43/3; 17 *Dhu'l-'ijja* 1317/18 April 1900.

56 Shawaya, see Muhammad 'Abd al-Rahim, *al-Durr al-manthur*, ms., NRO, Khartoum; Dara, DF299.43/3 to DF301.43/5 and al-Firsh, DF7.1/7.

of al-Firsh had approached the pretender Abu Kawda in October 1898 for help in rebuilding their mosque. They repeated their request to 'Ali Dinar who responded with a decree giving permission

To the said 'Abd Allah [leader of the al-Firsh community] that he could build and maintain [the mosque] and collect in it the people .... [lacuna in the original] their followers who had disappeared.[57]

The *fuqara* of al-Firsh were further recommended to 'Ali Dinar's leading general, Adam Rijal, and the instructions were repeated in a letter to a local official,

Since the intention is to build mosques for the remembrance of God and to light the fires of the Qur'an in all the mosques.[58]

But evidently the officials did not always share their master's zeal; after Mahmud w. Adam made the long journey from Dara to al-Fashir to complain of obstruction of his efforts to rebuild the former's mosque, the Sultan issued a fierce decree warning his officials to obey his orders.[59]

The rebuilding programme was paralleled by a very tight control over the *fuqara*. In effect, the Sultan treated the fuqara of his kingdom as members of a Sufi brotherhood of which he was the shaykh. The *fuqara* of each district were organised under a *muqaddam* who was responsible for their behaviour.[60] The *muqaddam's* most important responsibility, presumably apart from general surveillance, was to bring their charges to al-Fashir to spend Ramadan, fasting and praying with their ruler. This was bureaucratically organised; letters were sent out in mid-Rajab, ordering the holy men to be in al-Fashir

---

57 DF2.1/2, undated.

58 DF7.1/7; 28 Dh'l-hijja 1317/19 May 1900. "Lighting the fire of the Qur'an" is a common Sudanese expression.

59 DF299.43/3 (see above n. 35).

60 Examples include Ahmad Khalil, *muqaddam* of the *fuqara* of Dobo (eastern Jabal Marra); Mahmud w. Adam of those of Dara, and 'Ali Najm al-Din of those of Jadid al-Sayl.

by 15 Sha'ban, two weeks before the month of the fast.[61] The Sultan accepted neither excuse nor delay,

And none of the *fuqara* will be permitted to be late; and if one is ill, let him take refreshment from his desire [to be present] and delay not.[62]

Or,

If one of you *fuqara* delay, the patrol will go out and find him so that he will not escape from me.[63]

Or, most drastically, to Ahmad Khalil,

[If a faqih is late], he will be killed by hanging as a warning to the others: greetings.[64]

Such gatherings, whether for Ramadan or for the other religious festivals, were attended by the chiefs as well as the holy men; troops were reviewed, justice done and accounts rendered. Here 'Ali Dinar was reviving the old tradition centred around the great national festival of the *jalud al-nahas* (see Chapter Five), but once again within a more specifically Islamic context.[65] This tightness of control probably reflects the Sultan's fear of a resurgence of messianism or Mahdism.

This broadcasting of a Sudanic Islam—in contradistinction to the *thawra Ta'aishiyya* "The Ta'aisha upheaval", as he describes the Mahdiyya in his autobiographical memoir—reached the press. As befitted a *wali* or "saint", the Sultan perfomed *karamat* or miracles, which following custom were written down.[66] Among the miracles

---

61 Two examples are DF261/31/3; 14 Rajab 1328/22 July 1910 to Ahmad Khalil of Dobo, and DF298.43/2; 1324/1906-7, to Mahmud w. Adam of Dara.

62 DF298.43/2 (see above, n. 43).

63 DF297.43/1; 29 Rajab 1325/7 September 1907.

64 DF261.31/3, undated.

65 DF224.28/5, 2 Dhu'l-qa'da 1329/25 October 1911, ordering al-Doma Muhammad of Simiyat to bring all his warriors (*harub*), horses and weapons to al-Fashir by 20 Dhu'l-qa'da to celebate 'id al-dahiyya al-mubarika (= 10 Dhu'l-hijja = 'Id al-Hajj).Tax accounts were checked at 'id al-dahiyya; MacMichael, Notes on Darfur 1915, typescript, University of Khartoum.

66 The following is from Jureidini (1917), 409-14, which in turn derives from a translation of a manuscript apparently sent by the Sultan to the editor of the

so recorded were the making of rain in the Wadi Keila in Safar 1325/
March-April 1907 and several cures (of a difficult childbirth, fainting
fits and a stomach illness) resulting from sprinkling the sick with
water from his *'ibriq* or ablution bottle. In his *karamat*, 'Ali Dinar
records the execution of various would-be messianic figures; as in
the Condominium Sudan, so in the post-Mahdist years in Darfur
there were localised religious risings under *fuqara* proclaiming themselves to be the Prophet Jesus (*al-nabi 'Isa*), who would come after
the Mahdi.

A stranger who after several days visiting the mosque in al-Fashir
proclaimed himself *al-nabi 'Isa*, and a villager in Jabal Marra who
claimed to be the Prophet, were put to death. So was a would-be
Mahdi,

The sultan one day went out hunting, and a large multitude assembled In
their midst appeared a man brandishing a spear, who claimed he was the
looked-for Mahdi (presumably *al-mahdi al-muntazzar*), who would appear
at the end of time and would fill the world east and west with justice, in the
place of injustice. Our lord and master was then going out of the city with
his suite, when some of the attendants heard this man and his claims. They
ordered him to stop his utterances. He would not comply, but tried to attack
them and kill some of them with his spear. But through the blessing of our
lord and master, the man's hand was withered, and he could not move it.[67]

'Ali Dinar and Reginald Wingate (Governor-General of the
Sudan, 1902-17) could have compared notes on their neo-Mahdist
problem.

A final aspect of 'Ali Dinar's religious policies was his relationship
to the outside Muslim world. He had close relations by correspondence with several of the neo-Sufi orders, especially the Sanusiyya,
Khatmiyya and Isma'iliyya. Contacts with the Sanusiyya in Libya
were important in themselves and as a conduit to the Ottomans,

---

Sudan Times who forwarded it to Jureidini. I have been unable to trace the
original.

67 Ibid. In all three instances the Sultan emphasises that efforts were made
to determine that the pretenders were not insane (that legally they were
'aqil) before their execution. Kapteijns (1985), 203 reports a Masalit *nabi 'Isa*
executed in al-Fashir in 1905.

while in some extant letters to the shaykh of the Isma'iliyya in al-Ubayyid, Muhammad al-Makki (d.1905), 'Ali Dinar describes his efforts to promote religion in his state.[68] It was to Sayyid 'Ali al-Mirghani (d. 1968), head of the Khatmiyya order, that the Sultan most freely revealed his exasperation with what he saw as the duplicity of the Condominium Government, in a letter of 20 March 1915 just before the end.[69]

It was in 'Ali Dinar's time that the Tijaniyya order began to become widespread in Darfur. A Tijani shaykh from Masina (in present-day Mali), Muhammad Salma b. Fadigh (d. 1918-19) settled in al-Fashir and in 1905 was host there to one of the most prestigious West African Tijani leaders of the time, Hashim b. Ahmad al-Futi, also known as Alfa Hashim (d. 1932), when he passed through Darfur on his way to exile in Medina. Muhammad Salma established a *zawiya* or religious centre in the Tijaniyya quarter of al-Fashir, which is currently run by a grandson, Muhammad al-Ghali, and is now affiliated to the Nyasiyya branch of the Tijaniyya.[70] Another Tijani visitor to al-Fashir, the Hausa 'Umar Janbu was less fortunate; he "came under suspicion of using witchcraft to cause the sultan's illness and fled from Darfur in 1908".[71]

Among the external signs of orthodoxy was the intermittent sending of a *mahmal* or ceremonial covering for the Ka'ba in Mecca.[72]

---

68 Thirty letters exchanged between 'Ali Dinar and various Sanusi leaders are edited and translated with a very useful introduction in Spaulding and Kapteijns (1994), while the letters to Muhammad al-Makki are in the NRO, Khartoum (Isma'iliyya collection).

69 Theobald (1965), 140-2.

70 See my (1994), 300-1 and Sessemann (2000), 107-24, which corrects and amplifies my account.

71 Willis (1921), 183.

72 It was sent on at least three occasions, 1906, 1909 and 1913, in the charge of Muhammad al-Simawi; SAD 127/3, report, H.A. MacMichael 1915. In Rabi' II 1322/May-June 1905 'Ali Dinar writes to Muhammad al-Makki in al-Ubayyid to announce the coming of his son Salih, *muqaddam al-mahmal*; NRO, Khartoum, Misc. 1/82/1332. Muhammad al-Simawi met and was entertained by the Khedive 'Abbas Hilmi of Egypt in Mecca in 1909; SAD 127/3.

The Sultan continued the irregular support given to the small Darfur *riwaq* at al-Azhar, to which a trickle of students made their way (see above Chaper Ten). Other gestures included the sending of a short account of his life to the Dar al-Falah Library in Mecca and the publication in Khartoum of a *Diwan al-madih fi-madh al-nabi al-milih* or verses in praise of the Prophet.[73]

By 1915, 'Ali Dinar was more or less doomed. The Governor-General of the Sudan, Reginald Wingate, was pressuring Cairo and London for permission to "pinch out" Darfur before the French, hovering on the borders of Dar Masalit, were tempted to move in. Theobald describes at length the causes and course of the invasion of 1916, mainly from an uncritical British point of view.[74] Both parties produced their own propaganda. In what became almost a personal vendetta, Wingate's characterisation of the Sultan and justification for the invasion became steadily infected by the hysteria of the First World War, to whose operations he wanted his campaign to be linked. 'Ali Dinar, "the Kaiser's new ally", was no longer fit to rule because

He has murdered secretly many of the chief men among the people and replaced them by slaves, he has oppressed the poor, and whatever he has coveted he seized from its owner as a wild beast seizes its prey.[75]

Even the anti-German "handless baby" type of atrocity story was brought into play; writing to Kitchener on 27 April 1916, a month before the occupation of al-Fashir, Wingate reports, without citing any source,

A woman had the audacity to name her two weeks old baby Ali Dinar, and that the sultan in his fury sent for her and her baby, had the latter beaten to pulp in a large pestle and mortar and made the wretched woman eat the mess.[76]

---

73 The *Diwan* (of 24 pp.) was published by Matba'at al-Sudan in 1331/1913.

74 Theobald (1965), 118-207.

75 From a proclamation to the "people of Darfur", *ila ahali Dar Fur 'umuman*; SAD, 128/3, 1916.

76 SAD 128/1, Wingate to Kitchener, 27 April 1916. It was, of course, common in the sultanate for people to name their sons after the reigning sultan. For

By contrast, 'Ali Dinar's propaganda or justification, apart from his play on words in addressing Wingate as *sirr al-nar* "leader of fire" instead of *sirdar*, "Commander", is restrained and dignified. In 1915 he wrote a series of letters to various chiefs in Kordofan reproaching them for backsliding from Islam and for siding with the Christians, but still firmly distancing himself from Mahdism; thus to 'Ali al-Tom of the Kababish,

I do not tell you that I am a Mahdi or Khalifa as they before us thought they were, but I am a slave of God fulfilling his commands.[77]

The same orthodox position comes out in his formal declaration of war:

The Sultan of Islam [i.e. the Ottoman Sultan] has issued an order that the war is a religious one, and whosoever believeth in God, His Prophet and the Last Day, should rise and hasten to the "Jehad" in the path of God.

The same themes are summed up more personally in a letter to Wingate written early in 1916,

I am not a Dongolawi [an allusion to the Mahdi, whose family were from Dongola] nor Abdulla el Taaishi. I am by the mercy of God, a sultan and the son of a sultan. I rightly inherited the kingdom from generations and I am now seated in the throne of my fathers and forefathers by the will of the Great God.[78]

The rest is simply told; the British invaded Darfur; the Darfur forces were slaughtered just north of al-Fashir and 'Ali Dinar was hunted down and killed in November 1916. Thus ended the Keira Sultanate; it died with honour.

---

the "handless baby" First World War atrocity story, see A. Ponsonby (1928), 78-82 (a reference I owe to my colleague, Leif Mjeldheim). It is hard to believe that Wingate actually believed this rubbish.

77 SAD 127/8 and 127/2, quoted in MacMichael to Assistant Director of Intelligence; see Theobald (1965), 144-5.

78 Ibid. To the sources cited in Theobald may be added a pamphlet by an Egyptian Army officer, Hasan Qindil, *Fath Darfur sanat 1916*, n.p., n.d., which includes some interesting photographs. Among my possessions is a photograph of the dead Sultan, even in death an arresting figure. A proper biography of one of Darfur's greatest and most sympathetic figures needs to be written.

14

DARFUR SINCE 1916
A POSTSCRIPT

The annexation of Darfur to the Anglo-Egyptian Sudan in 1916 at first changed little in the new province. The fundamental principle behind the British colonial administration of the Sudan (1898-1956), for that is what it was whatever the name, was financially the most economical administration possible. Nowhere was this more so than in Darfur which was for forty years run by a handful of British officials, first military, later civilian. At the outset they encountered the same problems of grass-roots Mahdism as 'Ali Dinar had faced (Chapter Thirteen), culminating in the attack on Nyala in 1921 led by 'Abd Allah al-Suhayni in which two British officials, among many others, were killed. But by the mid-1920s Darfur was more or less pacified.

The British ruled Darfur as had the sultans, arrogating to themselves control over taxation, the death penalty and the right to appoint or dismiss chiefs, a right they used as sparingly as had the sultans. There was very little or no direct development. The principles of "Indirect Rule", i.e. rule by chiefs, guided the British in Darfur and appears to have suited both sides.[1] Probably the greatest long-term

---

1   Reading the Condominium files in al-Fashir and Kutum in the early 1970s, I was constantly struck by how keen the British were to find out what had been the practice under the sultans and how whenever possible they adhered to that practice. Change was rare. My *Darfur and the British. A Sourcebook* (forthcoming) presents various British documents from the British records in Darfur that illustrate how they administered the province and how they understood the way the sultans had ruled their state.

legacy of the British in Darfur was to codify and write down in their *Handbooks* what had been sultanic practice and to record local history and ethnography.

British rule in the Sudan did, however, have an enormous long-term indirect impact on Darfur, since in the central regions of the Sudan they set about establishing the political, economic and educational institutions or structures of a modernising colonial state. And this they did some two decades before most of their other African colonies—of which, of course, they did not consider the Sudan to be one. It is within this process that the loss of Darfur's independence has been most marked. Decisions about Darfur were taken by the British and their Northern Sudanese successors in Khartoum, not in Darfur.

In the northern and central provinces around Khartoum, the British built schools and what became a university; along the Sharia al-Nil on the banks of the Nile in Khartoum flanking the Governor-General's palace they built a series of magnificent buildings that became (as they still are) the ministries of the state. Atbara to the north became the headquarters of Sudan Railways, linking Khartoum to Cairo, to al-Ubayyid in Kordofan and eastwards to Port Sudan, like Atbara a colonial creation. In the 1920s the Gezira Scheme (between the Blue and White Niles) produced cotton which, together with gum arabic and livestock, provided the economic underpinnings of the state. By the mid/late 20s a new Western-educated Northern Sudanese elite, whose members largely had their roots along the Nile, was beginning to emerge.

These developments affected Darfur profoundly, if only because they did not happen in Darfur. The Darfur response to this process of marginalisation was out-migration by thousands of young Darfurian men, seeking to avoid taxation at home and looking for work in the Gezira Scheme or as builders or servants in the towns of the northern and central Sudan.[2] What little trade there was in Darfur came increasingly to be in the hands of Northern Sudanese *jallaba*.

---

2   On the process of marginalisation, see Mohamed (2006), 41-60.

Little changed with formal independence on 1 January 1956; a small northern Sudanese administrative elite replaced the British, ruling over by now the sons or grandsons of 'Ali Dinar's title-holders or *shartays*.[3] The railway was extended to Nyala in 1959, boosting the livestock trade, and in the early 1960s the Jabal Marra Project attempted to introduce cash-crop farming, tobacco and citrus fruits mainly, with some limited success. By the mid-60s there was some political activity, mainly among the Fur from disgruntled ex-soldiers, and in 1966 the Darfur Development Front was established, bringing together some of the more progressive chiefs and the small group of Darfurian students in Khartoum.

There are three deep-seated causes behind the present crisis.[4] The first is demographic; the population of Darfur has allegedly grown from about 1.5 million in 1956 to between 6.25 m. and 6.5 m. today. I say "allegedly" because, as I have argued in Chapter One, I am very sceptical about the latter figure. Demographic change, especially in the form of brutal and rapid urbanisation, whether of the towns or of the IDP camps (Kalmar, Abu Shok, Qirayda [Gereida], etc.), is the most immediately visible consequence of the present crisis. Urbanisation may in the long run be a positive response to the second cause, namely ecological, if serious development can be focused on the urban areas.

Darfur has, at least since 1980s, been through processes of desertification, soil erosion and loss of fertility, and problems of water availability, all exacerbated by population growth. Land, and who owns it, is now a deadly issue in Darfur, one reason why I have been

---

3   This fact, of course, made my research from 1969 to 1977 very easy and enjoyable, although it was tough to get around; I was writing down traditions and stories from people about their grandparents. In the 1970s Darfur was going through a relatively "good" cycle. I had little premonition of what was to come in the 1980s.

4   I see no point in repeating here some of the excellent journalistic accounts which describe the immediate origins or progress of the present crisis. The books that I have found most informative are Flint and De Waal (2005) and De Waal, ed (2007). A flood of new books is promised or threatened.

very careful in what I have written here (Chapter Seven).[5] Janjawid spokesmen frequently quote land as a crucial issue for them, given that the *abbala* or camel nomads of the north do not have clearly defined tribal *dar*s or homelands, while those sitting with clear title-deeds see no reason for any new dispensation.[6]

The third cause which has to be faced is that Khartoum has failed to establish its legitimacy in Darfur. In 1956 it assumed a legitimacy that it has never really had. Already in the 1960s it was the *hakuma/* "the government", something alien and "far away" (*ba'id*). This lack of legitimacy was compounded by the disastrous decision in 1971 by the then "modernising" regime (1969-85) of President Ja'far al-Numayri to abolish native administration as being old-fashioned and un-modern. The problem was that the chiefs were not replaced by any viable alternative administration, and the situation was worsened by the oil shortages of the early 1970s which effectively immobilised the administration.[7] In periods of democratic rule Darfur was only of importance as voting fodder, while during non-democratic regimes it was only of importance within the regional politics of Chad, Libya and Khartoum.[8]

The combination of these factors led by the early 1990s to the breakdown of any effective administration in Darfur except in the main towns. The countryside was effectively out of control and it was within this context that the politicisation of the conflict developed. By 2003 Darfur had become an "international" problem, about which the international community worries intermittently. To avoid the breakdown of the Sudan Peoples Liberation Army/Movement (SPLA/M) talks with the Khartoum government in 2004, which was then the main focus of international concern and which led to the Comprehensive Peace Agreement (CPA) of January 2005, the

---

5   It may be an obvious point to make, but all Darfurian actors use their understanding of the past to justify their present actions.

6   The need for a new land policy in Darfur is obvious to any well-informed outsider, but is fiercely resisted by many Darfurians.

7   On the consequences of the abolition of native administration, see Morton (1993).

8   On the regional politics, Prunier (2005) is especially useful.

Darfur problem was handed over to the newly-established African Union (AU). The AU responded by sending a small and inadequate peace-keeping force to Darfur and by sponsoring talks between the Khartoum government and the Darfur movements, the latter very much divided among themselves. In May 2006 at Abuja a Darfur Peace Agreement (DPA) was signed between Khartoum and one of the Darfur factions. The DPA is as of this writing (2007) effectively dead, as most parties involved now recognise.

Most recently, there has been a recognition that there needs to be a Darfur/Darfur Dialogue, that the Darfurians will have to come together and hammer out an agreement among themselves. This will not be easy; the Darfur traditional tribal leadership, although reinstated after the fall of al-Numayri in 1985, no longer has the same power and legitimacy that it had before 1971, not least because their appointments have been politicised by the Khartoum Government. Generally appointments have been made from Khartoum downwards with little regard paid to tribal opinion, and they have often been very disruptive. In the meantime the demographic and ecological problems have grown and intensified, while the young leaders of the Darfur "movements" are deeply divided and lack a clear programme or policy. So far no one of consequence has raised the notion of independence for Darfur, but if the situation in Darfur continues to deteriorate, it probably will come to the fore. Oil, which is beginning to be discovered in southern Darfur, will be a factor here.

This brief summary of political facts conceals a horrendous humanitarian tragedy, a tragedy taking place within a very fragile environment, whose deterioration it will be extremely difficult to reverse.[9] But Darfur does not have to be a failed state; it is my belief that Darfurians, with some outside help, can come to an agreement among themselves, especially if Khartoum is prepared to be constructive rather than, as hitherto, defensive and obstructive. Darfur, as an idea and identity, has existed since the 1570s if not before; in the nineteenth century ties, religious, linguistic and economic, brought Darfur closer to the riverain Sudan. An autonomous Darfur within a

---

9   On the humanitarian aspects, see Reeves (2007).

wider Sudan can be a very valuable partner, but only if it retains and develops its own identity.

GLOSSARY, SOURCES AND BIBLIOGRAPHY

GLOSSARY

(a) *Titles and Offices under the Sultans*

Nachtigal is still our main source on the central title holding hierarchy, but not all the titles he records can be fully identified. The following list is selective (compare with O'Fahey (1980), 149-55) and should be used in conjunction with Diagrams 2, 3 and 4.

The language of the titles is identified where it is reasonably certain (F. = Fur, A. = Arabic); one may note the large number of compound titles. Titles prefaced by *abbo* ("father") or *malik* ("king") are abbreviated and listed alphabetically under their last component.

Ab shaykh daali, F. and A.: "father shaykh daali" (*daali* is the F. for "tongue"); chief eunuch (slave or free), governor of the eastern province and guardian of the *fashir* upon the sultan's death.
Aba diimang, F.: "Lord of Diima"; hereditary governor of the southwestern province, from the Fur Morgenga lineage.
Aba kuuri, F.: "father of obeisance"; Fur title of the sultan.
Ari, F.: Fur title-holder who took the sultan's place on certain occasions. *Ari* ("exalted") was an archaic title of the sultan.
A. daadinga, F.: title-holder from a lineage of Tama origin, commander of the *daadinga* slave troops; also as *m. al-qawwarin* (*al-makkasin*), collector of customs and market tolls.
A. "dugo erre", F.: title-holder, "who had in his keeping the butter used each at the drum festival", Nachtigal (1971-87), iv, 336.
A. iringa, F.: "exalted"; title-holder, of Arab origin, holding lands in the north. The family later became hereditary *maqdum*s of the north.

305

A. irlingo, F.: title-holder who administered the Mima and Tunjur southeast of al-Fashir, and whose honorary task was to place the turban on the sultan during the accession ceremonies.

A. jinshinga, F.: (A. *junfas* "sackcloth, felt"): one of the "masters of the grooms", responsible for a Fur section making covers for horses, etc.

A. jode, F.: chief eunuch in charge of the "narrow gate" of the "Old Palace" (*bayt al-qadim*).

A. kotingo, F.: slave official of the "Old Palace"; commander of the *kotingo* slave troops.

A. kunjaara, F.: chief of the Kunjara Fur section, from which came the Keira.

A. uumo, F.: hereditary governor of the southeastern province; *uumo* is the F. for fontanelle.

Abu'l-korayat (F. *a. koriat*): one of the "masters of the grooms".

Amin, A.: "commander"; honorific rather than denoting specific office.

Amin al-takkiyya, A.: official responsible for the *takkiyya* tax.

'Aqid, A.: leader of a warband (F. *ornang*), later of a hunting party; now (2007) used of the field commanders of the Darfur "movements". Also, an eunuch of the "narrow gate", "overseer of buildings and of the servants", Nachtigal (1971-87), iv, 337.

'Aqid al-sabah, A.: "commander of the east"; governor of Wadai's eastern province bordering Darfur.

Awlad al-salatin, A.: "the sons of the sultans", F. *baasinga*.

Darang tebu, F.: "head of the mess", senior member of Fur village men's mess; village spokesman.

Dimlij (pl. *damalij*, A.; F. *dilmong*, pl. *dilmonga*): sub-district chief below a *shartay*, now largely replaced by *'umda*.

Eling wakil, F. and A.: village head in Fur areas.

Faqih, A., with the anomalous pl. *fuqara* (for *fuqaha*): Muslim holy man.

Firsha, A.: "carpet"; a title used in western Darfur and among some nomads for a subordinate chief.

Folgoni, F. (Arabicised as *falqanawi*, pl. *falaqna*): royal messengers and heralds, commanded by several *muluk al-falaqna*.

Forang aba, F.: "father of the Fur"; title-holder and guardian of Fur law and custom.

Forang eri, F.: "exalted [elsewhere, *iri*, *ari*] of the Fur"; title of the sultan.

Fore, F. "beard"; stewards of the royal estates in Dar Fongoro and elsewhere, under the authority of the *a. fore*, see *kamni*.

306

Fuqara, see *faqih*.

Goni (Kanuri in origin?): a senior or widely-reputed *faqih*.

Habboba, A. (Fur, *abo*, pl. *abonga*): "grandmother"; widows and female relatives of the sultan who, together with various slave women, had ritual functions; title of the sultan's mother.

Hakim, A.: commonly used in the court transcripts for a judicial official.

Iiya baasi, F.: "royal mother"; one of the sultan's full sisters appointed to the title who was responsible for discipline among the royal women; a position of considerable power.

Iiya kuuri, F.: "powerful mother"; sultan's premier wife, responsible for the preparation of food in the *fashir*.

Imam, A.: religious title, usually associated with a mosque.

Jabbayyin, sing. *jabbay*, A. (F. *jafanga* or *jubanga*): tax-collectors, under the authority of the *abu'l-jabbayyin*, who also commanded the cavalry advance guard.

Kamni (F. *a. fore*): "shadow sultan", who in early times was reputedly put to death when the sultan died. Later, overseer of the royal estates in Dar Fongoro and elsewhere.

Khabir, A.: "expert, leader"; caravan leader appointed by the sultan.

Khadim, A.: "servant"; several royal merchants are so described in the documents.

Khashm al-kalam, A.: "the mouth of speech"; the sultan's "voice" and interpreter.

Kiiso, F.: see *shartay*.

Koriat, F. (Arabicised to *korayat*): royal grooms; a group of title-holders (see Diagram 4) collectively called *muluk al-korayat*, "kings of the grooms", who also held individual titles.

Korkwa (sing. *kordungo*), F.: "spearmen"; royal guards and attendants, commanded by several chiefs under the *a. korkwa*.

Kursi, A.: "chair"; estate-steward; the Fur equivalent is *sagal*.

Lofenga, F.: "eunuchs".

M. al-'abidiyya, A.: "king of the slaves"; title-holder responsible for royal slave settlements throughout the state.

M. al-jallaba, A.: "king of the travelling merchants"; head of the foreign traders.

M. al-Nahas, A.: "king of the drums"; a title held by the head of the Fur Konyunga clan (also called *a. Konyunga*), concurrently with the title *a. soming dogala*.

M. orre baya, F. (A. *warabaya*): "king of the narrow gate"; in charge of the revenues from the royal estates which were delivered to the "narrow gate".

M. al-qawwarin (or *al-makkasin*), A.: see *a. daadinga*.

M. saaringa, A. and F.: "king of the swordsmen": eunuch of the "narrow gate".

M. al-'urban, A.: "king of the nomads"; the usual title for senior nomad chiefs.

Mandub (pl. *manadib*), A.: "agent"; a Mahdist title introduced by 'Ali Dinar; to some degree similar to the *maqdum* of the previous century.

Maqdum (pl. *maqadim*) A.: a commissioner or viceroy appointed for a fixed term or purpose; introduced in the late eighteenth century; the office tended to become static and hereditary.

Mayram (pl. *mayarim*; a word probably of Kanuri origin): daughter of a sultan; a *mayram*'s husband had few rights over his wife.

Mirong sagal, F.: see *sultan al-haddadin*.

Moge, F.: "adulator"; a corps of praise-singers, jesters and criers at the court under a *m. al-moge*.

Muwajjah, A.: official of varying rank sent out to demarcate boundaries, to take evidence in disputes, etc.

Na'ib qadi, A.: deputy judge.

Ornang, F.: see *'aqid*.

Orrengdulung, F.: "doorposts"; majordomo of the palace; ruled parts of Dar Birged.

Qadi, A. (F. *kaadinga*): judge.

Qirqid: see *sambei*.

Ras al-jah, A.: "head of the privilege"; head of a community possessing privileged status, responsible for administering the community's land.

Sagal (or *shagal*) F.: see *kursi*.

Sambei, F.: "barbed spear"; a district chief ranking between *shartay* and *dimlij*; in non-Fur areas called *qirqid*.

Shartay (pl. *sharati*, possibly of Daju origin): district chief of a *shartaya*; in Fur areas called *kiiso*, pl. *kiisonga*.

Shaykh al-rijal, A.: "shaykh of men", local chief with limited jurisdiction.

Sid al-fas (pl. *asyad al-fas*), A.: "master of the hoe"; head of a community granted occupancy rights by a chief or estate-holder.

Sid al-hakura A.: "master of the estate"; estate-holder.

Sid al-tin, A.: "master of the soil"; estate-holder.

Sultan al-ghazwa, A.: "sultan of the raid"; chief commissioned by the sultan to go slave raiding.

Sultan al-haddadin, A. (F. *mirong sagal*): "chief of the blacksmiths"; the blacksmiths, a despised but feared caste in Darfur as elsewhere in the Sudanic Belt, were under an obligation to provide hoes and weapons to the sultan.

Takanawi: hereditary governor of northern Darfur, originally of Tunjur origin. The office declined in the nineteenth century.

'Ulama (sing. *'alim*), A.: Muslim scholar.

Wakil, A.: "agent or deputy"; estate-steward.

Wazir, A.: an honorific rather than a specific office.

(b) *Other Terms*

Only the more frequently recurring terms are given here; all other terms are explained in the text. For the various taxes, see Diagram 9.

Aadinga, F. (A. *'awa'id*): "customs"; Fur and other traditional religious practices.

'Abidiyya, A.: slaves owned by the sultan.

'Arda, A.: "parade, review", held before the sultan, continued into Condominium and independence.

Baqqara, A.: "cattle people"; Arab tribes of southern Wadai, Darfur and Kordofan.

Bayt al-jibaya, A.: "the house of tribute", a common synonym for the palace or *fashir*.

Bayt al-nahas, A.: "the drum house", where the royal drums were housed within the *fashir*.

Bayt al-qadim, A.: "the old house"; original palace built by 'Abd al-Rahman by Tandalti, the seasonal lake in the centre of al-Fashir.

Dallal, A.: royal umbrella.

Darb al-arba'in, A.: "Forty Days road", desert route from Darfur to Egypt.

Dhurra, A.: common millet.

Diya, A.: blood compensation for homicide or injury.

Dukhn, A.: bullrush millet.

Fashir (of uncertain origin): the area in front of the sultan's compound where he gave audience; by extension, the whole court complex, and finally, al-Fashir.

Fursan, A. sing. *faris*: horseman, knight; now often used of the Janjawid.

309

Furusiyya, A.: "horsemanship, chivalry".

Fugokwa, F.: "mountain people", i.e. the Fur of Jabal Marra.

Hakura, A.: "estate".

Hakurat al-jah, A.: "estate of privilege"; land granted with tax immunities rather than with administrative rights.

Hawz (or *hiyyaza*), A.: rights of occupancy as opposed to *milk* or ownership rights.

Hiba, A.: "gift", usually for a religious motive.

Iqta', A.: "assignment"; used in Darfur as an equivalent to *hakura*.

Jah, A.: "dignity, honour"; privileged status concretely expressed in tax immunities. Among the comparable terms used in the charters are *hurma*, *karama* and *hurriyya*. *Jah* was used with the same meaning by the rulers of the Taqali kingdom in Kordofan.

Jallaba, A.: travelling merchant.

Jallud al-nahas, A.: the drum festival.

Jurenga (sing. *jurengdungo*), F.: "warriors, youths".

Kukur: seat or throne.

Kundanga (sing. *nunda*), F.: liver, entrails; name of festival.

Mahram, A.: "immunity"; the term used for tax immunities in Kanem/Borno.

al-Mansura, A.: "the victorious"; the name of the most sacred of the seven royal drums.

Nahas, A.: "copper"; copper kettle drums.

Orre baya, F.: "narrow gate"; the smaller of the two entraces to the *fashir*, used by women and eunuchs.

Orre de, F.: "men's gate"; the main entrance to the *fashir*.

Qoz, Ar.: stabilised sand-dune; light sandy soil.

Ro kuuri, F. (A. *hakurat al-sultan*): "the ruler's estate"; Jabal Marra, which was a royal domain.

Sadaqa, A.: offerings made in memory of the dead: "donation" (of land, etc.) usually for religious purposes; a particular form of blood compensation.

Safarog, F.: throwing stick.

Sahil, A.: "coast"; the semi-desert zone between the savannas and the true desert.

Sambal, F.: throwing knife.

Sijill, A.: transcript of court proceedings.

Som, F.: "school or meeting place", within the *fashir* where the *soming dogala*, "the cadets (literally, 'children') of the school", were educated

310

under the *abbo soming dogala*. One of the sultan's wives, *umm soming dogala* supervised the school.

Tombasi (corruption of F. *tong baasi*, "royal house"): palace built by Muhammad al-Fadl by the side of lake Tandalti in al-Fashir.

Waqf, A.: religious endowment.

BIBLIOGRAPHY AND SOURCES

Abbreviations

AP: Arkell Papers (SOAS, London).
BSG: *Bulletin de la société de géographie.*
JAH: *Journal of African History.*
JRGS: *Journal of the Royal Geographical Society.*
PM: *Pettermanns Mitteilungen.*
SAD: Sudan Archive, University of Durham.
SAJHS: *Sudanic Africa. A Journal of Historical Sources.*
SNR: *Sudan Notes and Records.*

An essay on sources

The sources on the history and cultures of Darfur are complex and variegated, and in some cases irretrievably lost. I discuss and list all that I have collected in the way of sources, even those that I have not used myself, as an aid to the next generation of Darfur historians; I have included here numerous references on Darfur in the twentieth century and beyond. Let me repeat what I have written in the preface; it is my intention to place upon the Web—http://www.smi.uib.no/darfur/— as much of the material, in Arabic, English and other languages, as I can.

The sources are complex and can divided into the following categories:

1. Oral
2. Arabic Documents and Manuscripts
3. Archival
4. Theses and Unpublished Papers
5. Travel Literature
6. Secondary Literature

311

Oral

If the copious notes made by Muhammad 'Abd al-Rahim[1] and A.J. Arkell in the 1920s and 30s are combined with my material, an extensive corpus of oral tradition has already been collected in Darfur. Even so, given the region's size and the difficulties of travel, only a fraction of the "possible" oral traditions has been recorded. Since my research, Adam al-Zayn for the Musabba'at, Kapteijns in Dar Masalit, Adelberger among the Fur, Braukämper among the Baqqara, Sabil Adam Ya'qub on Darfur in general, and 'Uthman for the Zaghawa have deepened and widened the corpus. And there are others; hopefully I have listed them all in the bibliography.

During my visits in 1969, 1970, 1974 and 1976 a body of material based on essentially informal interviews and discussions, conducted usually in Arabic and where necessary in Fur, with a wide range of informants was built up. Most of this material concerns local and family history, and much was recorded in exegesis of the Arabic documents photographed at the same time, which are described below. Relatively little was added to what may be termed the central traditions of the sultanate so effectively recorded by Arkell and 'Abd al-Rahim and in an earlier generation by Nachtigal, whose account of the sultanate's history provides the groundwork for all subsequent interpretations.

My material will in due course be deposited at the Sudan Archive, University of Durham.

A final body of oral materials relevant to Darfur in recent years has been created by journalists and scholars such as Julie Flint, Alex De Waal, Nicholas D. Kristof, Lydia Polgreen, Gérard Prunier, Eric Reeves and others; most of this exists on the web. All this may be supplemented by the huge outpouring of reports by both international agencies and human rights organisations, especially Human Rights Watch and Amnesty International. The problem is that the quantity gives no assurance of quality.

Pre-colonial Arabic documentation

Subsequent experience, both my own and that of other researchers (especially La Rue, 1989 thesis, pp. 531-34), have confirmed that I had a

---

1   On whom see Karrar, Ibrahim and O'Fahey (1996), 125-36.

"window of opportunity" in Darfur in the early 1970s, when I was able to photograph some 400 sultanic or related documents, dating between c. 1700 and 1916. I was not at the time aware of my good fortune, which I owe above all to *malik* Rihaymat Allah al-Dadinqawi, then president of the Native Court in al-Fashir, in whose courtyard I photographed most of them in 1970 and 1974.

How many of the originals of these documents and indeed others unseen by me have physically survived the present miseries is unknown; at least one collection from Dar Suwayni photographed by the Tubianas in the 60s has subsequently been deliberately destroyed (Tubiana (2005), 205); unbeknown to the Janjawid, the Tubianas, Abu Salim and I had published them back in 1983 (O'Fahey and Abu Salim (1983)). Other documents from the collection have been published by myself and others over the years. The documents have become sadly a factor in the present conflict with the cry on all sides for their land.

Like my notes, I intend to deposit the original photographs in Durham, but hopefully to make the entire collection available on the Web. Copies of the photographs were deposited in the 70s at National Records Office under the category "Miscellaneous", *Majmu'at Awfahi*. I have already put a detailed catalogue on the Web.

Archival

As with the Arabic documents described above, I likewise had another "window of opportunity" in al-Fashir in 1970. The British provincial archives were kept intact in a room that formed part of 'Ali Dinar's throne-room complex and became the *bashkatib*'s office (the province secretariat) under the British. The then governor, 'Uthman Muhammad Husayn, gave me *carte blanche* to go through them, letting me borrow his office ('Ali Dinar's throne-room with the Sultan's rather ghastly throne, all gilt and red velvet, behind the governor's desk), while he went on vacation to fox-hunt in Dorset with the last British governor, K.D.D. Henderson.

In 1970 and 1974 I went through some 600 files in al-Fashir and Kutum; they were a veritable treasure-trove of local information, the series of tribal or *dimlijiyya* files starting with the number 66 especially; I describe them in my book (1980), 186-7. There is no point in repeating here the description given there, because some time in the late 1970s they were more or less all destroyed. So far as I can piece the story together, the room in which they were housed was assigned to the use

313

of the al-Fashir branch of al-Numayri's Sudan Socialist Union (*Ittihad al-ishtiraki al-Sudani*), and the files were stored in some grass huts (*tukl*); came the rains, exeunt the files. The 300 pages of my notes are all that remain; unfortunately I was not interested in the British administration of Darfur and took notes mainly on their precolonial information; with the naivety of youth I assumed they would be there in the future.

There is one area where their loss will prove crucial to any attempt to write about the history of the British in Darfur. Among the files in both al-Fashir and Kutum were some 100-50 "tribal" or `umudiyya* files (the 66 series); these were detailed records, `umudiyya* or *nazirate* one-by-one. They were a major source on the precolonial period and were marvellously rich on the Condominium period, not least because they represented the interface between the British and the Darfurians (for example the "Zaghawa: General" file in Kutum comprised three thick volumes, including many Arabic letters). The detail in these volumes cannot be replaced by the general correspondence in the National Records Office in Khartoum, which essentially record British officials in Darfur writing to their counterparts in Khartoum.

In Khartoum at the NRO there is much on the sultanate under 'Ali Dinar and his relations with the Condominium; on this material, see Theobald (1965), 226-7. Much of it is self-serving and biased; the British had really very little idea of what 'Ali Dinar was about. Likewise, the British records from 1916 onwards are not very informative about Darfur realities. Martin Daly's introduction to Lea's memoirs of Kordofan in the early 1930s, emphasising British ignorance of local realities, applies equally to Darfur (Lea (1994), 1-8).

Again, copies of my notes will go to Durham. In the meantime, I am putting as much as I can on the Web at http://www.smi.uib.no/darfur/.

One source at the NRO that I was not able to use fully were the papers of Muhammad 'Abd al-Rahim, a self-taught but truly indefatigable Sudanese historian; these are a major source for nearly all aspects of Sudanese history. When I did my main research on Darfur in the 1970s, access to the papers was limited because of acrimonious disputes among members of the family; nevertheless, the late Dr Abu Salim let me read, as it were under the table, 'Abd al-Rahim's *Al-Durr al-manthur fi-tarikh bilad al-'Arab wa'l-Fur*, a work of some 120 pages which deserves publication. The papers also include annotations to al-Tunisi's travels derived from 'Abd al-Rahim's own travels in Darfur.

314

In the Sudan Collection, University of Khartoum, there were several valuable typescripts and manuscripts:

H.A. MacMichael, "Notes on the Tribes of Darfur", Khartoum 1915 and H.A. MacMichael, "The Darfur Who's Who", Khartoum 1915: two reports arising from MacMichael's intelligence work in preparation for the campaign of 1916;

(Bence Pembroke), "Darfur 1916: Geographical and Tribal Distribution on Reoccupation", a much more clear-eyed view of Darfur than anything MacMichael wrote;

P.J. Sandison, "Fur/English, English/Fur Vocabulary", partly but not completely incorporated into Beaton's grammar; Sandison's other papers are in Durham.

At the School of Oriental and African Studies are held the papers (hereafter AP) of the Rev. Dr A.J. Arkell, who served in the Sudan from 1921 to 1948 (see O'Fahey (1974), 172-4). The papers comprise 76 files (about 6,000 ff.); most are reading notes, but twenty-one files contain ethnographic and historical notes on Darfur, which are of unparalleled richness—AP[2], 10/48 of 234 ff., i.e. file 48, gives information on every district of the Fur lands.

The Sudan Archive at the University of Durham, founded by Richard Hill in the late 1950s, is a repository of official and private papers of British officials who served in the Condominium of Sudan (see its excellent Website). The Archives contain much that is relevant to Darfur.

I should mention the library of the Darfur Heritage Centre at the University of al-Fashir, which since being established in 1993 has made an excellent start on assembling materials on Darfur's past.

A final category of written sources are the records of the various reconciliation (*sulh* or *musallaha*) meetings held from 1989 onwards. However flawed these may be, they still contain much that is useful about present realities in Darfur. Again I propose to give these to the University of Durham.

Theses and unpublished papers

Abdul-Jalil, Musa Adam (1974), "Some Political and Economic Aspects of Koranic Schools in Jebel Si." BSc dissertation, University of Khartoum.

315

Bakhiet, G.M.A. (1965), "British Administration and Sudanese Nationalism, 1919-1939." PhD thesis, Cambridge University. Translated as *al-Idara al-Britaniyya wa'l-haraka al-wataniyya fi'l-Sudan, 1919-39.* Hinri Riyad, Khartoum 1972. Here I have preferred the English version.

Beaton, A.C. (n.d.) "A Grammar of the Fur Language." Typescript. A copy with handwritten corrections by the author is in my possession.

Bedin, Mohamed Ahmed (1970), "The Fulani in Darfur. A Historical survey of Fulani Groups." Honours dissertation, University of Khartoum.

Cudsi, A.S. (1969), "Sudanese Resistance to British Rule, 1900-1920." MSc Thesis, University of Khartoum.

El-Hakim, Sherif Mahmoud (1972), "Collective Decisions in a South Saharan Village." PhD, Johns Hopkins University.

Hale, G.A. (1966), "Cultivation Terraces in Western Darfur: a Study in an Agricultural Form and Practice." PhD, University of California, Los Angeles.

Hofheinz, A. (1996), "Internalizing Islam. Shaykh Muhammad Majdhub, Scriptural Islam and Local Context in Early Nineteenth-Century Sudan." Dr. philos, University of Bergen.

Isa Hasan Khayar, Marie-José Tubiana and Joseph Tubiana, "Eléments pour une histoire du Dar-Fur au temps d'Ali Dinar."Typescript.

Kurita, Y. (2000), "The Sudanese Diaspora in Politics: Felix Dar Fur, Dusé Muhammad 'Ali and 'Ali 'Abd al-Larif." Unpublished paper.

La Rue, G. (1989), "The Hakura System: Land and Social Stratification in the Social and Economic History of the Sultanate of Dar Fur (Sudan), ca. 1785-1875." PhD, Boston University.

O'Fahey, R.S. (1972), "The Growth and Development of the Keira Sultanate of Dar Fur." PhD, University of London.

Pettersen, W. (1986), "The Few and the Many. From Direct to Indirect Rule in Darfur, 1916-1936." Hovedfag [=MA] thesis, University of Bergen.

Stiansen, E. (1993), "Overture to Imperialism. European Trade and Economic Change in the Sudan in the Nineteenth Century." Dr. philos. thesis, University of Bergen.

Thelwell, R. (1981), "The Daju Language Group." PhD, New University of Ulster, Coleraine.

Tom, Abdullahi Osman El- (1983), "Religious Men and Literacy in Berti Society." PhD, University of St Andrews.

Primary sources

Barth, Heinrich (1853), "Account of Two Expeditions in Central Africa by the Furanys [Fur]", *JRGS*, xxiii, 120-2.
—— (1857-59), *Travels and Discoveries in Northern and Central Africa.* New York, 3 vols. (repr. London 1965).
Beltrame, G. (1879), *Il Sennaar e lo Sciangallah*, 2 vols. Verona.
Bizemont, H. de (1871), Letter in *BSG*, 6e série, i, 120-30.
Bovill, E.W. ed. (1966), *Missions to the Niger*, 4 vols. London.
Brehm, A.E. (1975), *Reisen im Sudan 1847 bis 1852*. Tübingen.
Brocchi, G. B. (1841-43), *Giornale delle Osservazioni fatte ne' Viaggi in Egitto, nella Siria e nella Nubia*, 5 vols. Bassano.
Browne, W.G. (1806), *Travels in Egypt, Syria and Africa*. London, 2nd edn.
Brun-Rollet, A. (1855), *Le Nil Blanc et le Soudan*. Paris.
Burckhardt, J.L. (1822), *Travels in Nubia*. London
Cadalvène, E. de, et Breuvery, J. de (1841), *L'Egypte et la Nubie*. Paris, 2nd ed., 2 vols. O'Fahey (1973b) "Kordofan in the Eighteenth Century", *SNR*, liv, 32-42, is an annotated transl. of the Kordofan/Darfur section of this work.
Cailliaud, F. (1823), *Voyage à Méroé, au Fleuve Blanc*. 4 vols., Paris.
Chaillé-Long, C. (1876), *Naked Truths of Naked People*. London.
Combes, E. (1846), *Voyage en Egypte, en Nubie, dans le Désert de Bayouda des Bischarys*. Paris, 2 vols.
Courrier de l'Egypte. Newspaper published by the French during their occupation of Egypt, 1798-1801.
Cuny, C. (1854), "Notice sur le Darfour", *BSG*, 4e série, viii, 81-120.
—— (1858), "Observations générales sur le Mémoire sur le Soudan de M. le Comte d'Escayrac de Lauture", *Nouvelles Annales des Voyages*, mars, 3-28.
—— (1862), "Journal de Voyage du Docteur Ch. Cuny de Siout à el-Obeid", *Nouvelles Annales des Voyages*, 6e série, iii and iv, 257-341, 22-85 and 175-225. Paris.
D'Abbadie, A. (1842), "Lettre à M. d'Avezac sur divers points de géographie éthiopienne", *BSG*, 2e série, xviii, 344-59.

D'Albano, G. (1961), *Historia della Missione Francescana in Alto-Egitto-Fungi-Etiopia*, ed. G. Giamberardini. Cairo.

D'Anania, G.L. (1582), *L'Universale Fabrica del Mondo, Overo Cosmografia*. Venice.

Dayf Allah, Muhammad al-Nur b. (1971), *Kitab al-Tabaqat fi-khusus al-awliya' wa'l-salihin wa'l-'ulama wa'l-shu'ara fi'l-Sudan*, ed. Yusuf Fadl Hasan, 1st. edn. Khartoum.

Denon, V. (1809), *Voyages dans la Basse et la Haute-Égypte pendant les Campagnes de Bonaparte*, 2 vols. London.

Felkin, R.W. (1884-85), "Notes on the For tribe of central Africa", *Proceedings of the Royal Society of Edinburgh*, xiii, 205-65.

Figari, C.A. (1864-66), *Studii Scientifici sull'Egitto e sue Adiancese*. 2 vols., Lucca.

Fresnel, F. (1848), "Notice sur le Waday", *BSG*, 3e série, ix, 245-54.

—— (1849-50), "Mémoire sur le Waday", *BSG*, 3e série, xi, 5-75; xiii, 82-116 & 341-59; xiv, 153-92 and 315-24.

Fraccaroli, A. (1880), "Gita commerciale del Cordofan e Darfur", *L'Esploratore*, 205-6.

Gessi, R. (1989), *Sette Anni nel Sudan Egiziano*. Milan (first publ. 1891).

Hartmann, R. (1863), *Reise des Freiherrn Adalbert von Barnim durch Nord-Ost-Afrika in den Jahren 1859 und 1860*. Berlin.

Al-Hashayshi, Muhammad b. 'Uthman (1903), *Voyage au Pays de Senousiyya*, trans. E. Serres. Paris.

Henniker, F. (1823), *Notes on Egypt, Nubia, the Oasis, Mount Sinai and Jerusalem*: London.

Heuglin, T. von (1863), "Berichte und arbeiten über Agyptischen Sudan und die länder westlich und südlich von Chartum", *PM*, 97-114.

Hill, G.B. ed. (1884), *Colonel Gordon in Central Africa, 1874-1879*, 3rd. edn., London.

Holroyd, A.T. (1839), "Notes on a Journey to Kordofan in 1836-7", *JRGS*, ix, 163-91.

Al-Jabarti, 'Abd al-Rahman (1879), *'Aja'ib al-athar fi'l-tarajim wa'l-akhbar*, 4 vols. Cairo.

Krump, T. (1710), *Hoher und Fruchtbarer Palm-Baum des Heiligen Evangelij*. Augsburg.

Lauture, P.H. S. D'Escayrac de (1855-56), *Mémoire sur le Soudan*. Paris.

Ledyard, J. (1817), *Historical Account of Discoveries and Travels in Africa*, 2 vols. Edinburgh.

Lejean, G.N. (1862), "Le Haut-Nil et le Soudan", *Revue de Deux Mondes*, 854-82.

—— (1865), "Voyage au Haraza", *Nouvelles Annales des Voyages*, 300-13.

Lyon, G.F. (1821), *Travels in Northern Africa*. London.

Makhtuta (1961), *Makhtuta katib al-shuna, fi-tarikh al-sultana al-Sinnariyya wa'l-idara Misriyya*, ed. Al-Shatir Busayli 'Abd al-Jalil. Cairo 1961.

Marno, E. (1874), *Reisen in Gebeite des Blauern und Weissen Nil, 1869-1873*. Vienna.

Mengin, F. (1839), *Histoire Sommaire de l'Egypte sous le Gouvernement de Mohammed-Aly*. 2 vols., Paris.

Messedaglia, G.B. (1886), *Diario Storico Militare delle Revolte al Sudan de 1878 in poi*. Alexandria. English transl. in NRO, Khartoum.

Mubarak, 'Ali Pasha (1306/1888), *al-Khitat al-tawfiqiyya al-jadida li-misr al-Qahira wa-muduniha al-qadima wa'l-shahira*. 14 vols., Cairo.

Muhammad Bello (1957), *Infaku'l Maisuri*, ed. C.E.J. Whitting. London.

Müller, J.W. von (1851), "Extract from Notes Taken during his Travels in Africa in the Years 1847-8-9", *JRGS*, xx, 275-89.

Murray, A. (1808), *Life and Writings of James Bruce*. Edinburgh.

Nachtigal, G. (1876-77), "Handel im Afrika", *Mitteilungen, Geographische Gesellschaft, Hamburg*, 305-26.

—— (1971-87), *Sahara and Sudan*, 4 vols., transl. A.G.B. and H.J. Fisher, London.

Nur al-Da'im, 'Abd al-Mahmud (1973), *Azahir al-riyad fi-manaqib qutb al-zaman ... Ahmad al-Tayyib b. al-Bashir*. Cairo.

Pallme, I. (1844), *Travels in Kordofan*. London.

Parkyns, M. (1851), "The Cubbabish Arabs between Dongola and Kordofan", *JRGS*, xx, 254-75.

Pièces Diverses et Correspondance Relatives aux Opérations de l'Armée d'Orient en Égypte. Messidor an ix/June 1801.

Prudhoe, Lord (1835), "Private Memoranda on a Journey from Cairo to Sennar, in 1829", *JRGS*, v, 38-58.

Al-Qalqashandi (1913-19), *Kitab sub' al-a'asha*. Cairo.

Qindil, Hasan (n.d.), *Fath Darfur 1916*. n.p.

Seetzen, U.J. von (1813), "Nouveau renseignemens [sic] sur l'intérieur de l'Afrique, III, notions sur le-Dar Four, du pays de Four, recueillies de la bouche d'un indigène", *Annales des Voyages de la Géographie et de l'Histoire*, xxi, 145-79.

—— (1816), "Wörterverzeichnis aus der Sprache der Neger von Dâr Fûr", in J.S. Vater, ed., *Proben Deutscher Volks-Mundarten*, Leipzig.

Shaw F. (1887), "The Story of Zebehr Pasha, as Told by Himself", *The Contemporary Review*, 52, 333-49, 564-85 & 658-83.

Slatin, R. (1896), *Fire and Sword in the Sudan*. London.

al-Tunisi, Muhammad b. 'Umar (1845), *Voyage au Darfour*, transl. N. Perron, Paris.

—— (1851), *Voyage au Ouadây*, transl. N. Perron, Paris.

—— (1965), *Tashhidh al-adhhan bi-sirat bilad al-'Arab wa'l-Sudan*, ed. Khalil Mahmud 'Asakir and Mustafa Muhammad Mus'ad, Cairo.

—— (1976), "Al-Tunisi Travels in Darfur. Translation, Collation and Annotation of Tashhidh al-Adhhan bi Sirat Bilad al-Arab wa-l-Sudan" H.S. Umar, MA thesis, Bayero University, Kano. [On the complicated relationship between the French version of al-Tunisi's Darfur volume (1845) and the Arabic version, first published as a lithograph by Perron in Paris in 1851, see my (1969), 66-74. It is by no means certain that Arabic precedes the French version.]

Vansleb or Wansleben, M.J. in H.E.G. Paulus, ed. (1792-98), *Sammlung der Markwurdigsten Reisen in den Orient*, 3 vols., Jena.

Werne, F. (1852), *African Wanderings*. London.

Zayn al-'Abidin, 'Ali ibn (1981), *Le Livre du Soudan*, transl. from Turkish by Marcel Grisard and Jean-Louis Bacqué-Grammont. Paris.

Al-Zubayr Pasha (n.d.), *al-Ajwiba al-sadida fi-indhar wa-tahdid ahl al-makida*. n.p. Reproduced in al-'Ubayd (1995), at end.

Secondary sources

Here I have listed only those works cited in the book here, but with some exceptions, mainly recent works in Arabic and English on Darfur (see also my (2007) forthcoming review article). In listing works in Arabic, I have given the author by the last given name and have ignored the definite article.

"A Fragment from Ali Dinar", *SNR*, xxxiv, 1953, 114-6.

Abbakr, 'Abd al-Rahman Musa (1992), "Fayliks Dar Fur: min ruwwad al-haraka al-wataniyya", *Majallat al-Dirasat al-Sudaniyya*, 12/1, 176-9.

'Abd Allah, Muhammad al-Mubarak (1973), *Ma'a'l-Ta'alim al-dini fi'l-Sudan.* vol. 1 (all published), Cairo.

Abdul-Jalil, Musa Adam and 'Abd Allah Adam Khatir (1977), *al-Turath al-sha'bi li-qabilat al-Fur.* Khartoum.

'Abd al-Jalil, al-Shatir Busayli (1955), *Ma'alim ta'rikh Sudan wadi al-Nil.* Cairo.

'Abd al-Mahmud, Sulayman Khalid (n.d.: 1965), *al-Furusiyya fi'l-shi'r al-sha'bi al-Sudani.* Alexandria.

'Abidin, 'Abd al-Majid (1967), *Ta'rikh al-thaqafa al-'Arabiyya fi'l-Sudan*, 2nd. edn. Beirut.

Abu Manga, Al-Amin, J.O. Hunwick, S. Kanya-Forstner, Paul Lovejoy and R.S. O'Fahey (1998), "Between Niger and Nile: new light on the Fulani Mahdist, Muhammad al-Dadari", *SAJHS*, 8, 85-108.

Abu Salim, Muhammad Ibrahim (1975), *Al-Fur wa'l-ard. Watha'iq tamlik.* Khartoum.

—— (1979), *Fi 'l-shakhsiyyat al-Sudaniyya.* Khartoum.

—— (2004), *al-Khusuma fi Mahdiyya al-Sudan.* Khartoum.

—— (and Knut S. Vikor): 1991), "The Man who Believed in the Mahdi", *SAJHS*, 2, 29-52.

Adelberger, Jörg (1990), *Vom Sultanate zur Republik: Veränderungen in der Sozialorganisation der Fur (Sudan).* Stuttgart.

—— (1991), "Urimelis", *SAJHS*, 2, 177-8.

Ahmed, Abdel Ghaffar M. and Leif Manger, eds (2006), *Understanding the Crisis in Darfur.* Bergen.

Ajayi, J.F.A. and M. Crowder, M., eds (1971), *History of West Africa.* London, 2 vols.

Arkell, A.J. (1936; 1937a; 1946a), "Darfur Antiquities", *SNR*, Part One, xix/1, 1936, 301-11; Part Two, xx/1, 1937a, 91-105; Part Three, xxvii/3, 1946a, 185-220.

—— (1939a), "Throwing Sticks and Throwing Knives in Darfur", *SNR*, xxii, 251-68.

—— (1951a and b, 1952a and b), "History of Darfur, A.D. 1200-1700", *SNR*, xxxii/1 and 2, 37-70 and 207-38; xxxiii/1 and 2, 129-53 and 244-75.

Asher, M. (1984), *In Search of the Forty Days Road.* London.

321

Auriant, A. (pseud.) (1926), "Histoire d'Ahmed Aga le Zantiote. Un projet de conquête (1796-99) du Darfour", *Revue de l'Histoire des Colonies Françaises*, xiv, 181-234.

Balfour-Paul, H.G. (1955), *History and Antiquities of Darfur*. Khartoum: Sudan Antiquities Service, Museum Pamphlet no. 3, 1955.

—— (2006), *Bagpipes in Babylon. A Lifetime in the Arab World and Beyond*. London.

Al-Baqir, Taha al-Shaykh (2004), *Mawsu'at Ahl al-Dhikr bi'l-Sudan*. Khartoum, 6 vols. (A biographical and geographical dictionary of Sufis and Sufi centres and schools; it is particularly rich on the twentieth century and contains many Darfur references.)

Barbour, K.M. (1954), "The Wadi Azum", *The Geographical Journal*, cxx, 172-82.

Barbour, K.M. (1961), *The Republic of the Sudan: a Regional Geography*. London.

Bayoumi, A. (1978), *The History of Sudan Health Services*. Nairobi.

Beaton, A.C. (1940), "Fur Dance Songs", *SNR*, xxiv, 305-29.

—— (1941), "Youth Organisation among the Fur", *SNR*, xxiv, 181-8.

—— (1948), "The Fur", *SNR*, xxix, 1-39.

—— (1968) *A Grammar of the Fur Language*. Khartoum: Sudan Research Unit, Linguistic Monograph Series, no. 1. But see above for a more reliable version.

Bidayn, Muhammad Ahmad (n.d. [1995]), *al-Fallata al-Fullaniyyin fi'l-Sudan*. Cairo.

Birks, J.S. (1978), *Across the Savannas to Mecca: the Overland Pilgrimage Route from West Africa*. London.

Bjørkelo, A. (1989), *Prelude to the Mahdiyya. Peasants and Traders in the Shendi Region, 1821-1885*. Cambridge.

Boustead, Hugh (1939), "The Youth and Last Days of Sultan Ali Dinar: a Fur View," *SNR*, xxii/1, 149-53.

—— (1971), *Wind of Morning*. London.

Braukämper, Ulrich (1992), *Migration und Ethnischer Wandel. Untersuchungen aus der Östlichen Sudanzone*. Stuttgart.

Brenner, Louis (1973), *The Shehus of Kukawa*, London.

Bryan, M.A. (1959), "The T/K languages: a New Substratum", *Africa*, xxiv/1, 1-21.

Al-Buhayri, Zaki (2006), *Mushkilat Darfur*. Cairo. (An Egyptian political scientist's interpretation of the current crisis; very well documented.)

Carbou, H. (1912), *La Région du Tchad et du Ouadai*, 2 vols., Paris.

Cattani, R. (1931), *Le Règne de Mohamed Ali d'après les Archives Russes en Egypte*. Cairo.

Clarence-Smith, W.G. (2006), *Islam and the Abolition of Slavery*. Oxford.

Cohen, R. (1966), "The Dynamics of Feudalism in Bornu", in *Boston University Papers on Africa*, II, ed. J. Butler. Boston, 87-105.

Cooke, R.C. and A.C. Beaton (1939), "Bari and Fur Rain Cults and Ceremonies", *SNR*, xxii/2, 186-203.

Cordell, D.D. (1985), *Dar al-Kuti and the Last Years of the Trans-Saharan Slave Trade*. Madison.

Cunnison, I. (1966), *Baggara Arabs*. London

—— (1971), "Classification by Genealogy: a Problem of the Baqqara Belt", in *Sudan in Africa*, ed. Yusuf Fadl Hasan, 186-96. Khartoum.

Dampierre, E. de (1967), *Un Ancien Royaume Bandia de Haut-Oubangui*. Paris.

Davidson, B. (1959), "Letter [on rock-gongs]", *Man*, no. 114, lix, 85.

Davies, H.R.J. (1983), "Population Change in the Sudan since Independence", *SNR*, lxiv, 23-35.

Davies, R. (1957), *The Camel's Back. Service in the Rural Sudan*. London.

Dawra, 'Abd al-Qadir Muhammad 'Abd al-Qadir (1994), *Ta'rikh mamlakat Taqali al-Islamiyya*. Khartoum.

Dehérain, H. (1901), *Études sur l'Afrique*. Paris.

Deny, J. (1930), *Sommaire des Archives Turques au Caire*. Cairo.

Department of Statistics, *First Population Census of Sudan 1955/56. Final Report*, 4 vols., Khartoum 1962.

De Waal, A. (2005), *Famine that Kills. Darfur, Sudan*. Oxford.

—— (ed.) (2007), *War in Darfur and the Search for Peace*. Harvard: Global Equity Initiative & Justice Africa

Doornbos, P. (1983), "Languages of Wadai-Darfur", in M. Lionel Bender, ed. *Nilo-Saharan Language Studies*, 43-79. East Lansing.

—— (1984), "Trade in Two Border Towns: Beida and Foro Boranga (Darfur Province)", in *Trade and Traders in the Sudan*, ed. Leif O. Manger, 139-87. Bergen.

Douin, G. (1933-41), *Histoire du Règne du Khédive Ismaïl*. 3 vols., Cairo.

—— (1944), *Histoire du Soudan égyptien*, vol. 1 (all completed). Cairo.

Driault, E. (1927), *La Formation de l'Empire de Mohamed Aly d'Arabie au Soudan.* Cairo.

Eickelman, D.F. and J. Piscatori, eds. (1990), *Muslim Travellers: Pilgrimage, Migration and the Religious Imagination.* London.

Epstein, H. (1971), *The Origin of the Domestic Animals of Africa.* 2 vols., New York.

Falla, J. (2005), *Poor Mercy.* Edinburgh. (A novel of famine in Darfur in the early 1990s.)

Fanshawe, David (1975), *African Sanctus. A Story of Travel and Music.* New York.

Fisher, H.J. (1972-73), "'He Swalloweth the Ground with Fierceness and Rage': the Horse in the Central Sudan", *JAH*, xiii/3, 367-88 and xiv/3, 353-79.

—— and V. Rowland (1971), "Firearms in the Central Sudan", *JAH*, xii/2, 215-39.

Flint, Julie and Alex De Waal (2005), *Darfur. A Short History of a Long War.* London.

Gaden, H. (1907), "Les états musulmans de l'Afrique centrale et leurs rapports avec la Mecque et Constantinople", *Questions Diplomatiques et Coloniales*, xxiv, 436-47.

Gibb, H.A.R. and H. Bowen (1950-57), *Islamic Society and the West*, 2 vols. London.

Gleichen, A.E.W. (1905-6), *The Anglo-Egyptian Sudan: a Compendium*, 2 vols. London.

Gramlich, R. (1987), *Die Wunder der Freunde Gottes.* Wiesbaden.

Gray, R. (1961), *A History of the Southern Sudan, 1839-1889.* London.

Greenberg, J. (1966), *The Languages of Africa.* The Hague.

Greeward, R.C. (1941), "Escape in the Grass", *SNR*, xxiv, 189-95.

Gros, R. (1951), "Histoire des Toundjours de Mondo," *DocCHEAM* 1774, Paris.

Haaland, G. (1969), "Economic Determinants in Ethnic Processes", in F. Barth, ed., *Ethnic Groups and Boundaries*, London, 58-73.

—— (1972), "Nomadism as an Economic Career among the Sedentaries of the Sudan Savannah Belt", in *Essays in Sudan Ethnography*, ed. I. Cunnison and W. James, 149-72. London.

—— (1980), *Problems of Savannah Development: the Sudan Case.* Bergen.

—— (2005), "The Darfur Conflict in Evolving Politico-economic and Socio-cultural Contexts", *The International Journal of Diversity*, 5.

Hagenbucher F. (1968), "Notes sur les Bilala du Fitri", *Cahiers d'O. R.S.T.O.M*, série sciences humaines, V/4, 39-76.

al-Hajj, Sulayman Hamid (2005), *Dar Fur. Wad'a al-niqat 'ala 'l-huruf*. Khartoum. (An analysis of the current crisis by a Communist intellectual.)

al-Hajj, Taj al-Sirr 'Uthman (2005), *Ta'rikh Sultana Dar Fur al-ijtima'i, 1445-1874*. Khartoum. (A brief social history of Darfur.)

Hakim, Sherif Mahmoud El (1976), "The Effects of Administrative Policy on Tribalism and Inter-tribal Conflict: the History and Present Condition of the Zeyadiya of Darfur", *SNR*, lvii, 10-20.

Hale, G.A. (1964), "Terraseagerbrug i Jebel Marra, Darfur, Sudan", *Kulturgeografi*, 6/16, 17-23 (in Danish).

Hallam, W.K.R. (1977), *The Life and Times of Rabih Fadl Allah*. Ilfracombe.

Hallet, R. (1964), ed., *Records of the African Association, 1780-1831*. London.

—— (1965), *The Penetration of Africa*. London.

Harir, Sharif (1994), "Recycling the Past in the Sudan", in *Short-cut to Decay. The Case of the Sudan*, ed. Sharif Harir and Terje Tvedt. Uppsala.

Hasan, Hasan Imam and R.S. O'Fahey (1970), "Notes on the Mileri of Jabal Mun", *SNR*, li, 152-61.

Al-Hasan, Musa al-Mubarak (1970), *Ta'rikh Darfur al-Siyasi*. Khartoum.

Hasan, Yusuf Fadl (1965), "The Umayyad Genealogy of the Funj", *SNR*, xlvi, 27-32: repr. Hasan (2003), 49-56.

—— (1967a), "The Sudanese Revolution of October 1964", *Journal of Modern African Studies*, 5/4, 491-509; repr. in Hasan (2003), 171-91.

—— (1967b), *The Arabs and the Sudan*. Edinburgh.

—— (ed. 1971) *Sudan in Africa: Studies Presented to the First International Conference, Khartoum 1968*. Khartoum.

—— (1970) "al-qatl al-taksi 'ind al-Funj", *Majallat al-dirasat al-Sudaniyya*, ii/1, 32-47.

—— (1976), *al-Shullukh*, Khartoum.

—— (2003), *Studies in Sudanese History*. Khartoum.

Hassoun, Isam Ahmad (1952), "'Western' Migration and Settlement in the Gezira", *SNR*, xxx/1, 60-112.

Hebbert, G.K.C. (1925), "The Mandala of the Bahr el Ghazal", *SNR*, viii, 187-94.

Hill, L.G. (1968), "Hababin Village Economy", *SNR*, xlix, 58-70.

Hill, Richard (1967), *A Biographical Dictionary of the Sudan*, 2nd.edn. London.

—— (1959) *Egypt in the Sudan*. London.

—— (1965), *Slatin Pasha*. London.

Hillelson, S. (1925), "Notes on the Dagu", *SNR*, viii, 59-71.

—— (1933), "David Reubeni, an Early Visitor to Sennar", *SNR*, xvi, 55-66.

Holt, P.M. (1966), *Egypt and Fertile Crescent 1516-1922*. London.

—— (1970), *The Mahdist State in the Sudan, 1881-1898*, 2nd edn. Oxford.

—— (1973), *Studies in the History of the Near East*. London.

—— and M. Daly (1988), *A History of the Sudan*, 4th edn. London.

Holy, Ladislav (1967), "Social Consequences of *Dia* among the Berti", *Africa*, xxxvii/4, 466-79.

—— (1974), *Neighbours and Kinsmen: a Study of the Berti People of Darfur*. London

—— (1980), "Drought and Change in a Tribal Economy: the Berti of Northern Darfur", *Disasters*, 4, 65-71.

—— (1983), "Strategies of Drought Management in a Dry Savannah Agricultural Society: Berti of Darfur", *SNR*, lxiv, 165-89.

Horowitz, M.M. (1967), "A reconsideration of the 'Eastern Sudan'", *Cahiers d'Etudes Africaines*, vii/3, 381-400.

Howell, J. ed. (1974), *Local Government and Politics in the Sudan*. Khartoum.

Human Rights Watch (1996), *Behind the Red Line. Political Repression in Sudan*. New York.

Hunwick, J.O. (1992), "Studies in the *Ta'rikh al-Fattash* II: An Alleged Charter of Privilege Issued by Askiya al-hajj Muhammad to the Descendants of Mori Hawgaro", *SAJHS*, 3, 133-48.

—— (2002), "A Mahdist Letter from Darfur", *SAJHS*, 13, 21-5.

Hunwick, J.O. and F. Harrak (2000), *Mi'raj al-Su'ud. Ahmad Baba's Replies on Slavery*. Rabat: Institute of African Studies.

Hunwick, J.O. and R.S. O'Fahey (1994—), *Arabic Literature of Africa*, 4 vols., in progress. Leiden.

Hurewitz, J.C. (1956), *Diplomacy in the Near and Middle East*. 2 vols., Princeton.

Husayn, 'Abd Allah (1935), *al-Sudan min al-ta'rikh al-qadim ila rihla al-ba'atha al-Misriyya*. 3 vols., Cairo.

Ibrahim, Ishaq Ibrahim (1996), *Hijrat al-Hillaliyyin min Jazirat al-'Arab ila Shamal Ifriqiyya wa-Bilad al-Sudan*. al-Riyad.

Ibrahim, Yahya Muhammad (1993), *Madrasat Ahmad ibn Idris w'atharuha f al-Sudan*. Beirut.

Jaku, Muhammad Sharif (1997), *al-'Alaqat al-siyasiyya wa'l-ijtima'iyya bayna jamhuriyyat Tshad wa-jamhuriyyat al-Sudan*. Cairo.

Johnson, D.H. (1992), "Recruitment and Entrapment in Private Slave Armies: the Structure of the *zara'ib* in the Southern Sudan", in E. Savage, ed., *The Human Commodity. Perspectives on the trans-Saharan Slave Trade*. London.

—— (2003), *The Root Causes of Sudan's Civil wars*. Oxford.

Jureidini, L.B. (1917), "The Miracles of Ali Dinar", *The Muslim World*, vi, 409-17.

Kalck, P. (1971), *The Central African Republic*. London.

Kapteijns, L. (1981), "The Case of Adam's Ear, or how the Slave Bakhit Succeeded in Changing Master", *STB*, iii, 54-5.

—— (1985), *Mahdist Faith and Sudanic Tradition. The History of the Masalit Sultanate*. London.

—— and Jay Spaulding (1988), *After the Millenium. Diplomatic Correspondence from War and Dar Fur on the Eve of Colonial Conquest, 1885-1916*. East Lansing.

Karrar, Ali Salih (1992), *The Sufi Brotherhoods of the Sudan*. London.

—— (1996) (with Yahya Muhammad Ibrahim and R.S. O'Fahey), "The Life and Writings of a Sudanese Historian: Muhammad 'Abd al-Rahim (1878-1966)", *SAJHS*, vi, 125-36.

Kenyon, S. (1991), *Five Women of Sennar. Culture and Change in Central Sudan*. Oxford.

Kriss, R. and H. Kriss-Heinrich (1962), *Volksglaube im Bereich des Islam*, 2 vols. Wiesbaden.

Kropacek, L. (1970), "The Confrontation of Darfur with the Turco-Egyptians under the Viceroyships of Muhammad 'Ali, 'Abbas I and Muhammad Sa'id", *Asian and African Studies*, v, 73-86 (Bratislava).

—— (1997) *'Ali 'Abd al-Latif wa-thawra 1924*.

Lampen, G.D. (1928), "A Short Account of Meidob", *SNR*, xi, 55-67.

—— (1950), "History of Darfur", *SNR*, xxxi, 177-209.

Lane, E.W. (1984), *Arabic-English Lexicon*, 2 vols. (repr. of 1863 edn). Cambridge.

Lange, D. (1977), *Le Diwan des Sultans du (Kanem-) Bornü: Chronologie et Histoire d'un Royaume Africain*. Wiesbaden.

Lange, D. and S. Berthoud (1972), "L'intérieur de l'Afrique Occidentale d'aprés Giovanni Lorenzo Anania (XVIe siècle), *Cahiers d'Histoire Mondiale*, 14/2, 299-351.

LaRue, G.M. (1984), *Khabir 'Ali at Home in Kubayh: a Brief Biography of a Dar Fur Caravan Leader*. Boston: African Studies Center.

Lea, C.A.E. (1994), *On Trek in Kordofan*. London.

Lebeuf, A.M. (1969), *Les Principautés Kotoko*. Paris.

Leyder, J. (1936), "Note préliminaire à l'étude des grandes migrations de l'Afrique centrale", *Revue de l'Institut de Sociologie de Bruxelles*, xiii/1, 44-7.

—— (1936), "De l'origine des Bwaka (Oubangui)", *Bulletin de la Société Belge de Géographie, lx, 49-71.*

MacMichael, H.A. (1912), *The Tribes of Northern and Central Kordofan*. London, repr. 1967.

—— (1913), *Camel Brands Used in Kordofan*. Cambridge.

—— (1922), *A History of the Arabs in the Sudan*. London, 2 vols.

—— (1926), "A Note on the Burial Place of the Fur Sultans at Tura in Jebel Marra", *SNR*, ix/2, 75-7.

—— (1956), *Sudan Political Service, 1899-1956*. Oxford.

McGregor, A.J. (2001), *Darfur (Sudan) in the Age of Stone Architecture c. AD 1000-1750. Problems in Historical Reconstruction.* Cambridge.

McHugh, N. (1996), *Holymen of the Blue Nile. The Making of an Arab-Islamic Community in the Nilotic Sudan, 1500-1850*. Evanston.

McLoughlin, P.F.M. (1962), "Economic Development and the Heritage of Slavery in the Sudan Republic", *Africa*, xxxii, 355-89.

Messedaglia, L. (1935), *Uomini d'Africa*. Bologna.

—— (1950), "Francesco Emiliani", *Cé Fastu. Rivista della Società Filologica Friulana*, xxvi, 89-100.

Miskin, A.B. (1950), "Land Registration", *SNR*, xxxi, 274-82.

Mohamed, Adam Azzain (2006), "The Problem of Uneven Regional Development in the Northern Sudan", *The Fletcher Forum of World Affairs*, 30/1, 41-59.

"Mohammedanism in Darfur" (1917), *The Moslem World*, vii, 278-82.

Morton, J. (1993), "Tribal administration or no administration", *Sudan Studies Series* (on line).

—— (1994), *The Poverty of Nations. The Aid Dilemma at the Heart of Africa*. London. (Largely based on the author's experience in Darfur.)

Al-Mufti, Husayn Sid Ahmad (1837/1959), *Tatawwur nizam al-qada' fi'l-Sudan*. Khartoum, vol. i (all published).

Muhammad, Adam al-Zayn and al-Tayyib Ibrahim Wadi, eds (1998), *al-Niza'at al-qabaliyya fi 'l-Sudan*. Khartoum. A collection of essays on tribal conflict, mainly in Darfur.

Muhammad, Farah 'Isa (1982), *al-Turath al-sha'bi li-qabilat al-Ta'aisha*. Khartoum: Institute of African and Asian Studies, Sudanese Heritage Series, no. 29.

Mus'ad, Mustafa Muhammad (1972), *al-Maktaba al-Sudaniyya al-'Arabiyya*. Cairo.

Al-Naqar, 'Umar (1972), *The Pilgrimage Tradition in West Africa*. Khartoum.

Al-Nuqud, Muhammad Ibrahim (1995), *'Alaqat al-riqq fi'l-Sudan*. Cairo.

O'Fahey, R.S. (1969), "Al-Tunisi's Travels in Darfur", *Bulletin of the Centre of Arabic Documentation, University of Ibadan*, v, 66-74.

—— (1971), "Religion and Trade in the Kayra Sultanate of Dar Fur", in *Sudan in Africa*, ed. Yusuf Fadl Hasan, 87-97. Khartoum.

—— (1972), "The Affair of Ahmad Aga", *SNR*, liii, 202-3.

—— (1973a), "Slavery and the Slave Trade in Dar Fur", *JAH*, xiv, 29-43.

—— (1973b), "Kordofan in the Eighteenth Century", *SNR*, liv, 32-42.

—— (1973c), "Saints and the Sultans: the Role of Muslim Holy Men in the Keira Sultanate of Dar Fur", in *Northern Africa: Islamisation and Modernisation*, ed. M. Brett, 49-56. London.

—— (1973d), "al-Bulalawi or al-Hilali", *SNR*, liv, 197.

—— (1974), "The Sudan Papers of the Rev. Dr. A.J. Arkell", *SNR*, lv, 172-4.

—— (1977a), "The Office of *qadi* in Dar Fur: a Preliminary Enquiry", *BSOAS*, lx, 110-24.

—— (1977b), "The Awlad 'Ali: a Fulani Family in Dar Fur", *Gedenkschrift Gustav Nachtigal, 1874-1974 = Veröffentlichungen aud dem Übersee-Museum Bremen*, reihe C, i, 147-66.

—— (1977c), "Land and Privilege in Dar Fur", in the *Central Bilad al-Südan: Tradition and Adaptation*, ed., Yusuf Fadl Hasan and Paul Dornbos, 262-82. Khartoum.

—— (1979a), "Islam, State and Society in Dar Fur", in *Conversion to Islam*, ed. N. Levtzion, 189-206. New York.

—— (1979b), "Two Early Dar Fur Charters", *Sudan Texts Bulletin*, Coleraine, i, 13-17.

—— (1980), *State and Society in Dar Fur*. London. Translated as *al-Dawla wa'l-mujtama' fi Dar Fur* (2001) transl. 'Abd al-Hafiz Sulayman 'Umar. Cairo.

—— (1981a), "The Case of Adam's Ear", *Sudan Texts Bulletin*, Coleraine, 44-53.

—— (1981b), "The Mahrams of Kanem-Borno", *Bulletin of Information, Fontes Historiae Africanae*, 6, 19-25.

—— (1982), "Fur and Fartit: the History of a Frontier", in *Culture History in the Southern Sudan*, ed. John Mack and Peter Robertshaw, 75-87. Nairobi.

—— (1983a), "The Tunjur: a Central Sudanic Mystery", *SNR*, lxi, 47-60.

—— (1983b), "The Question of Slavery in the Sudan", in *Slaveri og Avikling i Komparativ Perspektiv*, ed Ø.Andersen, 235-49. Trondheim.

—— (1985), "Slavery and Society in Dar Fur", *in Slaves and Slavery in Muslim Africa*, i, 81-101. London.

—— (1986), "Dar Fur in Kordofan. The Sultans and the Awlad Najm", *Sudan Texts Bulletin*, Coleraine, vii, 43-63.

—— (1990 & 1991), "The Archives of Shoba", *SAJHS*, 1, 71-83 (part one) & 2 (1991), 79-112 (part two).

—— (1990b), *Enigmatic Saint. Ahmad ibn Idris and the Idrisi Tradition*. London.

—— (1992), "A Prince and his Neighbours", *SAJHS*, 3, 57-93.

—— (1994), *The Writings of Eastern Sudanic Africa to c. 1900*, vol. 1 of *Arabic Literature of Africa*, ed. J.O. Hunwick and R.S. O'Fahey. Leiden.

—— (1995), "The Past in the Present? The Issue of the Sharia in Sudan", in *Religion and Politics in East Africa*, ed. Holger Bernt Hansen and Michael Twaddle. London, 32-44.

—— (1996a), "An Hitherto 'Unknown' Darfur King-list", *SAJHS*, 6, 157-69.

—— (1996b), "'They have Become Privileged of God and His Prophet': *Mahram* and *zawiya* in Sudanic Africa", in *The Cloth of Many Silks. Papers on History and Society, Ghanaian and Islamic in Honor of Ivor Wilks*, 339-54.

—— (1996c), "Islam and Ethnicity in the Sudan", *Journal of Religion in Africa*, xxvi/3, 258-67.

—— (1997), "Endowment, Privilege and Estate in the Central and Eastern Sudan", *Islamic Law and Society*, 4, 334-51.

—— (1998), "The Conquest of Darfur, 1873-82", *SNR*, N.S., 1, 47-67.

—— (2002), "'They are slaves, but yet go free'. Some reflections on Sudanese history", in *Religion and Conflict in Sudan*, ed. Yusuf Fadl Hasan and Richard Gray, 48-57. Nairobi.

—— (2006), *Darfur Historical Documents: A Catalogue*, located at, http://www.smi.uib.no/Darfur/

—— (2006), "Does Darfur have a future in the Sudan?", *The Fletcher Forum of World Affairs*, 30, 27-39.

—— (2007), "*Umm Kwakiyya* or the Damnation of Darfur", *African Affairs*, (forthcoming)

—— and Abdel Ghaffar Muhammad Ahmad (1972 & 1973), *Documents from Dar Fur*, occasional papers 1 (54 pp.) & 2 (63 pp.), Programme of Middle Eastern and African Studies, Department of History, University of Bergen.

—— and M.I. Abu Salim (1983), *Land in Dar Fur. Charters and Related Documents from the Dar Fur Sultanate*, Cambridge (repr. 2003).

—— and Ahmed Ibrahim Abu Shouk (1999), "The Musabba'at of Jugo Jugo: Three documents", *SAJHS*, 10, 49-64.

—— with J.O. Hunwick and D. Lange (1979), "Two Glosses concerning Bilad al-Südan on a Manuscript of al-Nuwayri's *Nihayat al-arab*", *Bulletin of Information, Fontes Historiae Africanae*, Cairo, v, 16-24.

—— and Bernd Radtke (1993), "Neo-Sufism Reconconsidered", *Der Islam*, 52-87.

—— and Sharif Harir (1986), "Two Husbands and a Daughter from Dar Fur", *Sudan Texts Bulletin*, Coleraine, vii, 30-42.

—— and J.L. Spaulding (1972), "Hashim and the Musabba'at", *BSOAS*, xxxv, 316-33.

—— and J.L. Spaulding (1973), "The Geographic Location of Gaoga", *JAH*, 14/3, 505-8.

—— with Jay Spaulding (1981), "A Sultanic Present", *Sudan Texts Bulletin*, Coleraine, iii, 38-43

Olderoggge, D. (1934), "Survivals of the Throwing Knife in Darfur", *Man*, 128, 106-7.

Oliver, R.A. ed. (1977), *The Cambridge History of Africa*, vol. ii, c 1050–c. 1600. Cambridge.

Palmer, H.R. (1928), *Sudanese Memoirs*. Lagos, 3 vols.

Petrácek, K. (1975), "Die sprachliche Stellung der Berti-(Siga) sprache in Dar Fur (Sudan)", *Asian and African Studies* (Bratislava), xi, 107-18.

—— (1978), "Berti and the Central Sudan Group", in *Aspects of Language in the Sudan*, ed. Robin Thelwell, 155-80.

Polanyi, K. (1968), *Primitive, Archaic and Modern Economies*. New York.

Ponsonby, A. (1928), *Falsehood in War-Time*. New York.

Prunier, Gérard (2005), *Darfur. The Ambiguous Genocide*. London.

Qasim, 'Awn al-Sharif (1996), *Mawsu'a al-qaba'il wa'l-ansab fi'l-Sudan*, 6 vols., Khartoum. (Many of the Darfur entries in this biographical and tribal dictionary by the late Dr Qasim are based on the unpublished papers of Muhammad 'Abd al-Rahim in the NRO.)

—— (2002), *al-Qamus al-lajna al-'ammiyya fi'l-Sudan*, 3rd edn. Khartoum.

Reese, Scott S. ed. (2004), *The Transmission of Learning in Islamic Africa*. Leiden.

Reeves, E. (2007), *A Long Day's Dying*. Ontario. (A detailed and precisely documented account of the human tragedy in Darfur.)

Reichmuth, S. (1999), "Murtada al-Zabidi (d. 1791) in Biographical and Autobiographical Accounts: Glimpses of Islamic Scholarship in the Eighteenth Century", *Die Welt des Islams*, 39, 64-102.

—— (2004) "Murtada al-Zabidi (1732-91) and the Africans: Islamic Discourse and Scholarly Networks in the Late Eighteenth Century", in Scott S. Reese, ed., *The Transmission of Learning in Islamic Africa*, 121-53. Leiden.

Roden, D. (1972), "Down-migration in the Moro Hills of Southern Kordofan", *SNR*, liii, 79-99.

Rouvreur, A. le (1962), *Sahariens et Sahéliens du Tchad*. Paris.

Rünger, M. (1987), *Land Law and Land Use Control in Western Sudan. The Case of Southern Darfur*. London.

Al-Safi, Ahmad (1970), *Native Medicine in the Sudan: Sources, Conception and Methods*. Khartoum.

Sanderson, L.P. (1986), *Female Genital Mutilation*. London: Anti-Slavery Society.

Santandrea, S. (1957), "A Ndogo-kindred Group", *Annali Lateranensi*, xxi, 115-50.

—— (1964), *A Tribal History of the Western Bahr el Ghazal*. Bologna.

Santillana, D. (1926), *Istituzioni de Diritto Musulmano Malachita*. 2 vols., Rome.

Sarsfield-Hall, E.G. (1922), "Darfur", *The Geographical Journal*, ix/5, 359-68.

—— (1975), *From Cork to Khartoum. Memoirs of Southern Ireland and the Anglo-Egyptian Sudan, 1886-1936*. Kendal.

El-Sayed El-Bushra (1971), "Towns in the Sudan in the Eighteenth and Nineteenth Centuries", *SNR*, lii, 63-70.

Schacht, J. (1964), *An Introduction to Islamic Law*. London.

Sessemann, R. (2000), "The Writings of the Sudanese Tijani Shaykh Ibrahim Sidi (1949-1999), *SAJHS*, 11, 107-24.

—— (2002), "Sufi Leaders and Social Welfare. Two Examples from Contemporary Sudan", in Holger Weiss, ed., *Social Welfare in Muslim Societies in Africa*, 98-117. Uppsala.

Al-Shahi, A.S. (1972), "Proverbs and Social Values in a Northern Sudanese Village", in *Essays in Sudan Ethnography*, 87-104, ed. I. Cunnison and W. James. London.

Sharfi, Husayn Muhammad Ahmad (1992), *Suwwar min al-ada' al-idari fi'l-Sudan, 1942-1973*. Khartoum.

Sharkey, Heather J. (2003), *Living with Colonialism: Nationalism and Culture in the Anglo-Egyptian Sudan*. California.

Shaw, W.B. K. (1929), "Darb el Araba'in", *SNR*, xii, 63-71.

Shukry, M.F. (1938), *The Khedive Ismail and Slavery in the Sudan*, Cairo.

Shuqayr, Na'um (1903), *Ta'rikh al-Sudan al-qadim wa'l-hadith wa-jughrafiyatuhu*. 3 vols., Cairo; repr. Beirut, 1968.

Al-Shush, Muhammad Ibrahim (1962), *al-Shi'r al-hadith fi'l-Sudan*. Khartoum.

Spaulding, Jay L. (1977), "The Evolution of the Islamic Judiciary in Sinnar", *International Journal of African Historical Studies*, x/3, 408-26.

—— (1985), *The Heroic Age in Sinnar*. East Lansing.

—— and M.I. Abu Salim (1989), *Public Documents from Sinnar*. East Lansing.

—— and Lidwien Kapteijns (1994), *An Islamic Alliance. 'Ali Dinar and the Sanusiyya, 1906-1916*. Evanston.

—— and R.S. O'Fahey (1980), "A Sudanese Battle in about 1800", *Sudan Texts Bulletin*, ii, 42-6.

Stiansen, E. and M. Kevane, eds (1998), *Kordofan Invaded. Peripheral Incorporation and Social Transformation in Islamic Africa*. Leiden.

Sudanese Media Center (2005), *Darfur. The Absent Truth*. Khartoum. (A presentation of the crisis from the point of view of the Khartoum Government.)

Taha, Faisal Abdel Rahman Ali (1979), "The Boundary between the Sudan, Chad and the Central African Pepublic", *SNR*, lx, 1-14.

Tanghe, B.O. (1938), "Histoire générale des migrations des peoples de l'Ubangui", *Congo: Revue Générale de la Colonie Belge*, ii/4, 361-91.

—— (1943), "Pages d'histoire africaine", *Aequatoria*, vi/1, 1-7.

—— (1944), "Pages d'histoire africaine", *Aequatoria*, vii, 33-41.

Al-Tayyib, al-Tayyib Muhammad (1991), *al-Masid*. Khartoum.

Theobald, A.B. (1965), *'Ali Dinar. Last Sultan of Darfur 1898-1916*. London.

Thilo, M. (1921), *Ez-Zibêr Rahmet Paschas Autobiographie: Ein Beitrag zur Geschichte des Sudan*. Bonn.

Thomas, E.S. (1923), "The Ethnographical Collection of the Royal Geographical Society, Cairo", *Bulletin de la Société Khédiviale de Géographie*, 12, 1-36 and 137-85.

—— (1924), "The African Throwing Knife", *Journal of the Royal Anthropological Insttute*, iv, 129-45.

Thomassen, E. and B. Radtke, eds (1993), *The Letters of Ahmad ibn Idris*. London.

Tobert, Natalie (1988), *The Ethnoarchaeology of the Zaghawa of Darfur (Sudan)*. Cambridge.

Tom, Abdullahi Osman El- (1982), "Berti Quranic Schools", *SNR*, lxvi, 1-19.

—— (1985), "Drinking the Koran: the Meaning of Koranic Verses in Berti Erasure", *Africa*, 55/4, 414-31.

Tothill, J.D., ed. (1948), *Agriculture in the Sudan*. London.

Trimingham, J.S. (1949), *Islam in the Sudan*. London.

—— (1971), *The Sufi Orders in Islam*. Oxford.

Tubiana, Jérôme (2005), "Le Darfour, un conflit indentitaire?", *Afrique Contemporaine*, 214, 165-205.

Tubiana, Joseph (2005), "Misère et terreur au Soudan. A l'origine des affrontements dans le Darfour", *Afrique Contemporaine*, 214, 207-26.

Tubiana, Marie-José (1964), *Survivances préislamiques en pays Zaghawa*. Paris.

—— (1985), "A la recherche du 'Tékényâouy': nouveaux aperçus sur la structure du pouvoir au Dar For", *Journal des Africanistes*, 55/1-2, 261-74.

—— (2005), *Carnet de route au Dar For (Soudan), 1965-70*. Saint-Maur-des-Fosses.

Tubiana, Marie-José and Joseph (1977), *The Zaghawa from an Ecological Perspective*. Rotterdam.

Tubiana, Marie-José, Issa Hassan Khayar and P. Deville (1978), *Abd el-Karim: Propogateur de l'Islam et Fondateur du Royaume du Ouaddaï*. Paris.

Tucker, A.N. and M.A. Bryan (1956), *The Non-Bantu Languages of North-Eastern Africa*. London.

Tutscheck, Karl (1921-30), "Sprachproben von der Sprache in Darfur, heruasgegeben von Carl Meinhof", *Zeitschrift für Eingeborenen Sprachen*, xxi, 81-97; xvi, 161-96, and xx, 81-91.

—— (1941-42), "Sprachproben von der Sprache in Darfur, auf Tutscheks Nachlass", *Zeitschrift für Eingeborenen Sprachen*, xxxii, 164-82.

Al-'Ubayd, Khalifa 'Abbas (1995), *al-Zubayr Basha Yarwa Siratahu fi-manfaihi bi-Jabal Tariq*. Cairo. A transl. of Shaw (1887).

Urvoy, Y. (1949), *Histoire de l'Empire du Bornou*. Paris.

'Uthman, 'Uthman 'Abd al-Jabbar (2006), *Ta'rikh al-Zaghawa fi'l-Sudan wa-Tshad*. Cairo.

Vajda, G. (1958), *Album de Paléographie Arabe*. Paris.

Valensi, L. (1967), "Esclaves chrétiens et esclaves noirs à Tunis au XVIIIe siècle", *Annales*, xxii/6, 1267-88.

Vantini, Giovanni (1975), *Oriental Sources Concerning Nubia*. Heidelberg and Warsaw.

Wallis, W. (2004), "The Black Book history or Darfur's darkest chapter", *The Financial Times*, 21 August.

Walz, Terence (1972), "Notes on the Organization of the African Trade in Cairo, 1800-1850", *Annales Islamologiques*, xi, 263-86.

—— (1977), "*Wakalat al-Gallaba*: the Market for Sudan Goods in Cairo", *Annales Islamologiques*, xiii, 217-45.

—— (1978a), *Trade between Egypt and Bilad as-Sudan*. Cairo.

—— (1978b), "Asyut in the 1260s (1844-53)", *Journal of the American Research Center in Egypt*, xv, 113-26.

Wansbrough, J. (1970), "Africa and the Arab Geographers", in *Language and History in Africa*, ed. D. Dalby, 89-101. London.

Warburg, G. (1971), *The Sudan under Wingate. Administration in the Anglo-Egyptian Sudan, 1899-1916*. London.

—— (1992), *Historical Discord in the Nile Valley*. London.

Wickens, G.E (1970), "The Early History of Jebel Marra and the Tora City of Kebeleh", *SNR*, li, 147-51.

—— (1976), *The Flora of Jebel Marra*. London.

Willis, C.A. (1921), "Religious Confraternities of the Sudan", *SNR*, iv/4, 175-94.

Wilson, R.T. (1979), "Wildlife in Southern Darfur, Sudan: Distribution and Status at Present and in the Recent Past", *Mammalia*, 43, 323-38.

—— (1980), "Wildlife in Northern Darfur, Sudan: Distribution and Status at Present and in the Recent Past", *Biological Conservation*, 17, 85-101.

Works Jr., J.A. (1976), *Pilgrims in a Strange Land*. New York.

Yamba, C. Bawa (1995), *Permanent Pilgrims. The Role of Pilgrimage in the Lives of West African Muslims in Sudan*. Washington.

Zaccaria, M. (1999), "*Il Flagello degli Schiavisti*". Romolo Gessi in Sudan *(1974-1881)*. Ravenna.

Zach, M. (1987), "Der Schädel 1081 des Naturhistorischen Museums in Wien - ein Beitrag zur Geschichte Darfurs 1874-1889", *Mitteilungen der Anthropologischen Gesellschaft in Wien*, 117, 157-69.

Al-Zayn, Adam (1971), *al-Turath al-sha'bi li-qabilat al-Musabba'at*. Khartoum.

Al-Zubayr, Sa'd al-Din (1952), *al-Zubayr Basha, rajul al-Sudan*. Cairo.

Zulfu, 'Ismat Hasan (1973), *Karari. Tahlil 'askari li-ma'rikat Ummdurman*. Khartoum.

Zyhlarz, E. (1941-42), "Sprachproben von der Sprache in Darfur. Eine Auslese aus Max Müllers Kondjarawerk", *Zeitschrift für Eingeborenen Sprachen*, xxxii, 81-9 and 164-82.

INDEX

For definitions of titles and other technical terms, see also glossary and diagrams. The abbreviations "b." and "w." stand for *ibn* and *walad* (or *wad*) "son of" and "bt." for *bint* "daughter of". The Arabic definite article *al-* is ignored. Not all titles and customary dues are indexed since they appear either in the glossary or diagrams.

'Abd Allah Runga (slave; *maq-dum*), 187, 268-9

'Abd al-'Aziz (sultan of Wadai), 75

'Abd al-'Aziz (Ottoman sultan; r. 1861-76), 272

'Abd al-'Aziz (*soming dogala*), 84, 147 (land), 266

'Abd al-Bari (Wazir), 121-2, 130, 184, 269

'Abd al-Fattah (*malik al-korayat*), 75, 245

'Abd al-Karim (Kiliba), 108

'Abd al-Karim b. Salih (founder of Wadai), 30

'Abd al-Majid (Tunjur ruler), 26

'Abd al-Majid (Ottoman sultan; r. 1839-61), 272

'Abd al-Qadir Dalil (Mahdist governor), 284

'Abd al-Qadir Wir (founder of *daadinga* lineage), 48-9

'Abd al-Rahman Kalbas (*aba dii-mang*), 75, 175

'Abd al-Rahman Jokha (*aba dii-mang*), 174

'Abd al-Rahman al-Rashid (sultan; r.1787/8-1803), 46, 56-60, 63-73, 82, 89, 98, 119, 147, 159, 223, 232

'Abd al-Rahman b. 'Abd Allah (Tunjur in Medina), 32

'Abd al-Rahman al-Mahdi, 277

'Abd al-Rahman w. Makki (*faqih*), 289

'Abd al-Rahman b. Muhammad al-Husayn (Keira), 128

'Abd al-Rahman w. al-Nujumi (Mahdist general), 268

'Abd al-Rahman Shattut (Keira), 276

'Abd al-Razzaq (*abbo shaykh daali*), 201-3

'Abd al-Sid (Wazir), 75-6, 82, 130, 249

'Abdullahi b. Muhammad (the Khalifa; 1846-99), 14, 281-2

Abeche (capital of Wadai), 74

Abzayd al-Shaykh 'Abd al-Qadir (missionary), 42, 224

Abu 'Amr 'Uthman b. Idris (ruler of Borno), 16

Abu 'Asal (palace; Jabal Marra), 43

Abu Bakr b. Muhammad al-Fadl (Keira), 90, 96, 123

Abu'l-Bashar b. Muhammad al-Husayn (Keira), 130

Abuja (peace negotiations), 261, 303

Abu'l-Judul (Umm Judul; southeast of al-Fashir), 66

Abu Jummayza (Muhammad Zayn), 282-3

Abu Kawda (pretender), 286, 292

Abu'l-Khayrat b. Ibrahim Qarad ("shadow sultan"), 98, 283

Abu Kundi (Wadai), 43-4

Abu'l-Likaylik (general), 78

Abu Mukhayr (estate; Dar Beira), 157

Abu'l-Qasim (sultan; r. c. 1739-52), 44, 48-9, 50, 54, 58, 91, 134

Abu'l-Sakaring (dynasty; Taqali), 28

Abu Shok (IDP camp), 301

Bahr (*abbo jabbay*), 59, 63
Bahr al-'Arab (river), 82-5
Bahr al-Ghazal (river and region), 2, 18, 24, 38, 81, 83, 169, 262
Bahram b. 'Abd Allah al-Damiri (*'alim*), 224
Bakhit b. Adam Bosh (Wazir), 124, 130-1, 266
Bakhit (the slave & Adam's ear), 215
Bakhita bt. Muhammad al-Husayn (*mayram*), 276
banana, 106
Banda (people), 169, 248
bandaging sagal (title-holder), 121
Bani Halba (Arab nomad group), 17, 30, 82, 205
Bani Hilal (Arab nomads), 26
Bani Husayn (people), 3
Bani Jarrar (people), 37, 67
Baqqara (people and region), 4, 13, 16, 22, 170-1
Bara (town: Kordofan), 4, 56, 76-7 (battle), 105, 127, 180, 200 (battle)
baraka (spiritual charisma), 221
Baraq (*faqih*), 218
Barbour, K.M., 2
Barr al-Sudan Fazara (region of the Fazara), 17
Barriyab (holy lineage), 150-1
Barth, Heinrich (travelling scholar), 5, 29
basmala ("In the name of God, the Compassionate, the Merciful"), 27
Basna; see Musabba'at
Batalesa (Arab tribe), 27
Bayd (estate), 148

al-bayda (drum), 183
bayt al-jibaya ("the house of tribute"; synonym for *fashir*), 105
bayt al-nahas (drum-houyse), 93
bayt al-qadim ("the old palace" in al-Fashir), 101, 115, 187
Bayuda (desert region), 17, 76
Beaton, A.C. (Sudan Political Service), 172, 194
Beigo (people speaking a Daju dialect), 24, 37, 51, 52, 60 (no longer enslaveable), 90, 119-121, 130, 181, 205
Benghazi, 74
Berber (town; the Nile), 224
Beri-a (language), 10
Berti (people), 12, 13, 17, 18, 31, 52, 106, 178-9, 181
Bidayriyya (people), 4
Bidderi (Bagirmi)
Bideyat (people), 3, 13, 17, 37, 230
Bilio (district; Dar Berti), 160
Binga (people), 169-70, 250-1
Bir Natrun (district), 243, 250
Birged (people), 4, 12, 13, 18, 27 (founder), 31, 37, 51-2, 269
Birinjil (Birged district), 118
Blue Nile, 4
Bonaparte, Napoleon, 71-2
books, 68-9, 234
Borno (kingdom); see Kanem-Borno
Bosh b. Muhammad al-Fadl ("shadow sultan", 1874-5), 277
Braukämper, Ulrich, 16, 22
Brehm, A.E. (traveller), 250
Brenner, L., 91

British in Darfur, 299-300
Browne, W.G. (traveller), 67, 69-
  70, 82, 96-7, 116, 216, 257-8
Bruce, James (traveller), 69
al-Bukhari (Traditionist), 233
Bulala (people; Chad), 264
Burckhardt, John Lewis (travel-
  ling scholar), 5, 77
Buuranga (Fur *orre*), 101

Cairo, 126
cannon, 43, 70, 200-1
Central African Republic, 8
Chad (Lake), 10, 25, 169
Chad (Republic), 4, 7,8, 18, 26
chorte (Daju language; "chief/
  drum"), 23, 165
cima kura/cima gana, 140
clarified butter (Ar. *simn*), 205
Comprehensive Peace Agreement
  (CPA), 302
Constantinople, 79
Copper ore, 80
Cuny, Charles (traveller), 234,
  255-6, 272

Daali (Dalil Bahr; Keira ruler), 29,
  34-5, 164
Daalinga (*orre*; Lewing), 170
al-Dabba (town on the Nile), 76
Daju (people), 14, 21-5, 30, 31,
  181, 205
D'Albano, G. (traveller), 37
dam (collective fine), 215
Damascus, 76
D'Anania, G.L., 24, 30-1, 166,
  253
Danaqla (people), 15, 55, 127,
  180 252

dar (tribal homeland), 18
Dara (capital; southern *maqdu-
  m*ate), 84-5, 131, 187, 249,
  285, 291
Dar aba diima (province), 34, 164
Dar abo uumo (province), 34, 164
Dar Daali (province), 34, 66, 164
Dar al-Falah (library; Mecca),
  196
Darfur Peace Agreement (DPA),
  303
Dar al-gharb (province), 34, 164
Dar Hamid (people), 4
Dar al-rih (northern province),
  65-6, 164
Dar al-takanawi; see Dar al-rih
Daranga (mess), 101
Darfour, Félix (Haitian patriot),
  73
Darfur Development Front, 301
date-palms, 3
Da'ud al-Mirayn (Tunjur ruler),
  30
al-Daw b. al-Masri (*faqih*), 270,
  276
Dawra (Zaghawa), 173
demography; see population
denguyeh (slave), 249-50
Deriba (lakes), 2
Desaix, L.C.A. (French general),
  71
Description de l'Égypte, 72
dhurra (common millet), 3
Diima (district), 6, 154 (estates
  in)
Dikayrab Hawwara (traders), 31
dimlij (local chief), 177, 243 (copper bracelet),
Dinka (people), 53

Fulbe (people), 14-5, 227, 228 (holy men), 270, 280
Fulfulde (language of the Fulbe), 15
Funj Sultanate, 4, 5, 55, 76, 166
Fuqara; see *faqih*
Fur (people), 3-4, 10-11, 21, 24, 166-78, 230-1 (Islamisation of)
Fur/Bani Halba frontier, 19, 82
Fur/Zaghawa frontier, 19, 182-3
fursan ("horsemen"), 41, 54, 195-9
furusiyya (knightly ethos), 121
Futa Toro (Senegal), 42
Fuugokwa (Fur, "mountain people"), 4

Gaeta, Giovanni; see Ahmad Agha
Garsila (market; Wadi Debarei), 242
Gelege (people; Fongoro), 171
Gelli (district; Dar Konyir), 158
Gessi, R. (colonial official), 279
Gezira Scheme, 300
ghazwa (raiding party), 81, 243-51
Ghudiyat (people; Kordofan), 53
Ghulam Allah b. 'A'id (missionary), 222
Giggeri (Keira), 42
Gitar (Daju king), 24
goni (*faqih*), 228
Gordon, C.G. (Governor-general), 278-9, 281
Gordon Memorial College, 13
Gros, R., 26, 28, 29
groundnuts, 3

Gula (people), 169-70, 205
Guldo (village), 3
gum arabic, 80, 181, 241, 258
Gura'an (people), 3
Gurli (Gerli; district), 43, 50
Gurri (district, Kerne), 42

Haaland, Gunnar, 19
Hababin (people; central Kordofan), 247-8
Habbaniyya (Arab nomad group), 17, 83-4, 205
habboba (royal women & ritual experts), 93, 95, 116-7
Habib b. Tayrab, 56
Haiti, 73
Hajang Keingwo (Turra district), 98
Hajjam Hasab Allah (Masalit ruler), 282
hajaray/"rock people", 10
al-hajj, title of one who has made the pilgrimage, 14
hakura (sultanate & modern usage), 18, 51-2, 134-61
Hakurat al-sultan, 6, 106, 176
Hamad 'Abd al-Qadir (*qadi*), 290
Hamar (people), 4
Hamdan Abu 'Anja (Mahdist general), 268
Hamid (Wazir), 146 (rights over nomads)
Hamid w. Faris (missionary), 223-4
Hammad b. Umm Maryum (*faqih*), 37
Hamza b. al-Imam (merchant), 128, 253-4, 273, 276
Hanafi (Berti), 108

Hartmann, Robert (traveller), 127
Harun; see Muhammad Harun al-Rashid
Hasab Allah Jiran (soldier), 56-7
Hasab Allah b. Muhammad al-Fadl (Keira), 131, 273, 277
Hasan, Yusuf Fadl 16
Hasan al-Kaw (*faqih*), 230
Hasan Siqiri (*maqdum*), 85, 186-7 (history)
hashasha (unit of exchange), 243
Hashim b. Ahmad al-Futi (Alfa Hashim; Tijani leader), 295
Hashim b. 'Isawi (Musabba'at leader), 53-5, 65-8, 195, 239
Hasim b. 'Umar (Qimr sultan), 182
Hasib b. Kharut (*abbo irlingo*), 50
Hausaland, 244
Hawwa bt. 'Abd al-Rahman al-Rashid (*mayram*), 126
Hawwara (people; Kordofan), 252-3
hijab (amulet), 228-9
Hicks, W. (British general), 281
Hilan b. Isi (sultan of Kobe), 58
hizb (portion of the Qur'an), 228
Horowitz, M., 13
horsemen; see *fursan*
horses, 196-8
Hotiyya (Arabs), 182
Hufrat al-Nahas (district; source of copper ore), 80, 243, 248, 264
human sacrifice, 96

Ibn Abi Zayd (jurisprudent), 229
Ibn Sa'id (geographer), 25
Ibrahim, Hasan Ahmad, 281

Ibrahim b. 'Abd al-Qadir Wir (*abbo daadinga*), 77
Ibrahim b. Bakaw (Darfur sultan), 224-5
Ibrahim Bal b. 'Ali al-Futawi, 156
Ibrahim Qarad b. Muhammad al-Husayn (sultan; r. 1873-4), 98, 131 (succession of), 265-7, 270-4
Ibrahim b. Ramad (*abo konyunga & malik al-nahas*), 56-7, 60, 67-8, 118, 130
IDP (internally displaced peoples), 19
Idris (*imam* of Turra), 39
Idris 'Abd Allah (*qadi*), 290
Idris Alawma (ruler of Borno, 1580-1617), 47
Idris al-Mahasi (merchant), 254
al-Idrisi (geographer; d. 1166), 25
ihya al-mawat (opening-up new land), 135
iiya baasi (sultan's sister), 116
iiya kuuri (sultan's premier wife), 102, 116
'imma (head covering), 94
Inga (district), 117
Iran (rope-dancers from), 105
'Irayqat (Arab nomad group), 17, 30, 81, 82 (campaign against), 108, 289
'Isa Kull Barid (*aba diimang*), 175
'Isawi b. Janqal (Musabba'at leader), 54
Ishaq (*khalifa*), 53, 56, 58-9, 63, 80, 91, 98, 119, 194-5
Islam & Islamisation, 38-9, 63-4, 221-37, 230-32

Kabkabiyya (town & district), 43, 50, 65, 187, 242, 279, 286
Kadama (Wadai), 30
Kaja/Katul (mountains), 54-5
Kajmar (Kordofan), 76
Kalmar (IDP camp), 301
Kalokitting (village), 3
Kaltuma (Zaghawa princess), 50
Kamala Keirei (Turra district), 98
Kamal Keirei (Khiriban district), 141, 152-3 (land disputes)
kamni (title-holder), 98, 112
Kanem-Borno (state), 9, 16, 25, 26, 34, 79, 139-41 164, 173
Kanembu (people), 14, 15
Kanuri (people), 15
Kapteijns, L, 280
Kara (people), 169-70, 174, 248
Karakiriit (division of the Fur people), 10
Karari (battle), 286
karama (miracle), 221, 292-4 ('Ali Dinar's)
Karnoi (wells), 109
Kartakayla (*malik*), 147 (land)
Kas (town; southwest), 224
Katsina (Northern Nigeria), 125
Kawahla (people), 4
Kawra (pass), 64
Keira (Fur royal lineage), 11, 231 ('Abbasid descent of)
Kerio (settlement), 14, 63, 223, 226-7, 229 (mosque)
Kerne (*shartaya*: district), 6, 43, 154, 278
khabir (large-scale merchant), 241, 253-6
khalifa, 46 & see sultan; succession

Khalil b. 'Abd al-Rahman (*aba diimang*), 175
Khalil b. 'Abd al-Sid (*maqdum*), 85
Khalil b. Ishaq (Keira dynast), 56
Khalil b. Ishaq (jurisprudent), 229
khalwa (Qur'an school), 228
Khamis b. Janqal (Musabba'at leader), 48
Khandaq (town), 12
Kharja (oasis), 251
Kharut b. Hilan (sultan of Kobe), 50
khashm al-bayt (clan or descent group), 19
khashm al-kalam (sultan's speaker), 97
Khatmiyya (Sufi order), 220, 292
Khayr Qarib (slave), 131
Khiriban (settlement), 14, 91, 135, 154
Kiliba (ruling lineage of Galla Zaghawa), 108
Kinana (*iiya baasi*), 56, 232-3
Kinana (people), 67
Kitab Daali (sultanic law), 34-5, 212-13
Kitchener, H.H. (British general), 286-7, 296
Kobara (*shartaya*; southwest), 171, 242
Kobe (Zaghawa sultanate), 50, 90, 181, 183
Kobbei (town: trade centre), 4, 65, 70, 105, 121, 156, 233, 242, 251-59
Kofod (district), 156, 252
Kolge (locality; *fashir*), 39
Komora (*fashir*, Terjil district), 46

Shaw Dorshid (Tunjur ruler), 27, 29, 31, 34, 252-3
Shawa (settlement; central Darfur), 227
al-Shawa Kasa (district; al-Fashir), 289
Shawaya (mosque), 291
Shawnga (district in Dar Birged), 52
Shaykan (Kordofan; battle), 77, 281
Shaylfut (Muhammad Kurra's adopted son), 62, 195
Shendi (town), 12, 30, 55
shillukh (facial scars), 33
Shinuda al-Jawhari (Copt; merchant), 255-6
Shoba (fashir), 50-1, 65, 100-1
Shoba (al-Tawila district), 139
Shuqayr, Na'um (Condominium official), 46
Shuwayhat (lineage; Kordofan), 151
sijill (court document), 138
Sila (people speaking a Daju dialect & state), 24, 25, 187, 205, 242, 283
Simiyat (people & district), 106, 205-8, 288, 290
Sinnar (town: capital of the Funj Sultanate), 4, 33, 76, 105, 212, 223, 239
Slatin, R.C., 26, 79, 230 279, 284, 287
slaves & slave raiding, 240, 244-51
Sodiri (Kordofan), 78
som (meetng area), 107

soming dogala (palace pages), 66, 107
Spaulding, Jay, 12, 223
stone-terracing and walls, 3-4, 149
Sudan, 6, 64, 259 (& Darfur), 299-304 (& Darfur)
Sudan Peoples Liberation Army/ Movement (SPLA/M), 302
The Sudan Times, 223
sudasi (slave), 249
Sufism, 221
suicide, 57, 76, 130
Surro (shartaya; southwest), 171
Sulayman (doctor), 71
Sulayman b. Ahmad Jaffal (Kinani Arab & chief of Birged Kajjar), 51-2, 143-4
Sulayman Solongdungo (Keira Sultan, r. c. 1650-80), 29, 34, 36-9, 64, 99
Sulayman al-Zubayr, 278-9
Sulma (village; Wadi Azum), 172
sultan (institution): claims to descent, 89; owns the land, 133-4; ritual cycle, 92-9; succession, 90-2; taboos, 97-8; titles, 88-9
sultan al-haddadin ("the chief of the blacksmiths"), 95
Suwanga (people; Fongoro), 171
Syria, 71-2

Ta b. Kwore (Zaghawa; Kobe sultan), 184
Ta'aisha (Arab nomad group), 17, 80, 171, 205
Tabaldiyya (district; battle), 59, 85